The British Working Class, 1832–1940

STUDIES IN MODERN HISTORY

General editors: John Morrill and David Cannadine

This series, intended primarily for students, tackles significant historical issues in concise volumes which are both stimulating and scholarly. The authors combine a broad approach, explaining the current state of our knowledge in the area, with their own research and judgements. The topics chosen range widely in subject, period and place.

Titles already published

THE TUDOR PARLIAMENTS: Crown, Lords and Commons, 1485–1603
Michael A.R. Graves

FRANCE IN THE AGE OF HENRI IV: The Struggle for Stability (2nd Edn)
Mark Greengrass

THE EAST INDIA COMPANY: A History, 1600–1857
Philip Lawson

POLITICS UNDER THE LATER STUARTS: Party Conflict in a Divided Society, 1600–1715
Tim Harris

IMPERIAL MERIDIAN: The British Empire and the World, 1780–1830
C.A. Bayly

'PAX BRITANNICA'? British Foreign Policy, 1789–1914
Muriel E. Chamberlain

BRITAIN AND LATIN AMERICA IN THE NINETEENTH AND TWENTIETH CENTURIES
Rory Miller

IRELAND SINCE 1880: Conflict and Conformity (2nd Edn)
K. Theodore Hoppen

BRITANNIA OVERRULED: British Policy and World Power in the 20th Century (2nd Edn)
David Reynolds

SWEET LAND OF LIBERTY? The African-American Struggle for Civil Rights in the Twentieth Century
Robert Cook

THE EMERGENCE OF A RULING ORDER: English Landed Society, 1650–1750
James M. Rosenheim

PERSECUTION AND TOLERATION IN PROTESTANT ENGLAND, 1558–1689
John Coffey

THE AMERICAN IRISH
Kevin Kenny

THE RULE OF LAW, 1603–1660: Crowns, Courts and Judges
James S. Hart, Jr.

THE EVOLUTION OF THE MODERN MIDDLE CLASS IN BRITAIN, 1850–1950
R. Trainor

THE EUROPEAN COLONIAL EMPIRES, 1815–1919
H.L. Wesseling

CHILDREN AND CHILDHOOD IN WESTERN SOCIETY SINCE 1500 (2nd Edn)
Hugh Cunningham

BLACK LEADERSHIP IN AMERICA (2nd Edn)
J. White

THE BRITISH IN THE AMERICAS, 1480–1815
A. Mcfarlane

POPULAR RADICALISM: The Working Class Experience, 1780–1880
D.G. Wright

THE BRITISH WORKING CLASS, 1832–1940
Andrew August

The British Working Class, 1832–1940

Andrew August

Harlow, England • London • New York • Boston • San Francisco • Toronto
Sydney • Tokyo • Singapore • Hong Kong • Seoul • Taipei • New Delhi
Cape Town • Madrid • Mexico City • Amsterdam • Munich • Paris • Milan

PEARSON EDUCATION LIMITED

Edinburgh Gate
Harlow CM20 2JE
United Kingdom
Tel: +44(0) 1279 623623
Fax: +44(0) 1279 431059
Website: www.pearsoned.co.uk

First edition published in Great Britain in 2007

© Pearson Education Limited 2007

The right of Andrew August to be identified as author of this work has been
asserted by him in accordance with the Copyright, Designs and Patents Act 1988.

ISBN: 978-0-582-38130-8

British Library Cataloguing in Publication Data
A CIP catalogue record for this book can be obtained from the British Library

Library of Congress Cataloging-in-Publication Data
August, Andrew, 1962–
 The British working class, 1832–1940 / Andrew August. — 1st ed.
  p. cm.
 Includes bibliographical references and index.
 ISBN 978-0-582-38130-8
 1. Working class—Great Britain—History—19th century. 2. Working class—Great
Britain—History—20th century. 3. Social classes—Great Britain—History—19th century. 4.
Social classes—Great Britain—History—20th century. I. Title.

HD8390.A93 2007
331.0941'09034—dc22

2006052173

10 9 8 7 6 5 4 3 2 1
10 09 08 07

Set by 35 in 10/13.5pt Sabon
Printed and bound in Malaysia (CTP-VVP)

The Publishers' policy is to use paper manufactured from sustainable forests.

Contents

Acknowledgements   viii

Introduction   1

Part One 1832–70   7
Introduction: Britain in 1832   9

1 Forming the urban working class   13

   Migration 13
   Urbanization 16
   Housing and sanitation 17
   The family and community 21
   Conclusion 24

2 Labour in the 'factory age'   30

   Hours of labour 31
   Scale and technology 33
   Skill, sex roles and authority 34
   Industrial conflict 39
   Conclusion 43

3 Leisure and the urban worker   51

   Popular leisure in the early nineteenth century 51
   Early and mid-Victorian working-class leisure 52
   Repression and reform 57
   The limits of reform 60
   Conclusion 61

4 Working-class identity and politics   68

   Class and identity 68
   Politics and worker frustration in the 1830s 73
   Chartism 75
   Mid-Victorian radicalism and protest 78

Resisting and manipulating the mid-Victorian state 80   ✓
Conclusion 81

Part Two 1870–1914   89
Introduction: Discontinuity in 1870?   91

5 The 'traditional' working-class community   95

The working-class neighbourhood 96
Housing and sanitation 97
The family economy 100
Conclusion 105

6 Control, conflict and collective bargaining in
   the workplace   110

Employer initiatives and worker responses 111
Gender and age 113
Unionization 116
The state and worker organizations 120
Conclusion 121

7 Expanding leisure opportunities   127

Informal leisure 129
Commercial leisure 132
Philanthropic leisure and self-help 135
Conclusion 139

8 Class identity and everyday politics   146

Complex identities 146
Party politics 153
Informal politics 156
Conclusion 159

Part Three 1914–40   165
Introduction: The working class and the Great War   167

9 Old and new working-class communities   173

Population 173
Migration 176
Housing 178
Health 182
Family economies and communities 183
Conclusion 186

10 Unemployment, dislocation and new industries   191

Growth and unemployment 192
Employer initiatives in the workplace 194
Unions, conflict and the state 198
Conclusion 202

11 Cinema, dance hall and streets   207

Informal leisure 209
Commercialized leisure 212
Associations, clubs and the regulation of leisure 218
Conclusion 221

12 Patriotism, politics and identity   227

Patriotism, nationalism and empire 228
Formal and informal politics 233
Conclusion 237

Conclusion: Change and continuity   243
Epilogue   247
Bibliography   251
Index   281

Acknowledgements

In writing this book, I have had the pleasure of engaging with the work of two generations of historians who have examined the lives of working-class men and women in Britain. Since the development of the 'new' social history nearly half a century ago, scholars have shone light on previously ignored aspects of working men and women's home and community, work, leisure and politics. They have also debated with one another about the proper approaches to their subjects and interpretations of their findings. These arguments and insights formed the bases for my work, and my debt to these historians is immense.

More personally, I have learned a great deal from colleagues who have helped me refine and sometimes reconsider my ideas. Through conversation and/or correspondence, David Cannadine, Andrew Davies, Geoff Eley, David Feldman, Marjorie Levine-Clark, Andrew Plaa, David Ruth and Susan Thorne have taught me much. The members of the Delaware Valley British Studies Reading Group, and especially its conveners Seth Koven and Lynn Hollen Lees, offered many hours of enjoyable intellectual stimulation and pushed me to refine my thinking. Penn State Abington provided a supportive environment and a sabbatical leave to work on the book. Jeannette Ullrich and the library staff filled innumerable interlibrary loan requests without complaint. Two student researchers, Shawn Anderson and Tiffany Sherman, assisted with the early stages of the project. At Pearson/ Longman, a series of editors have overseen the often slow progress of the manuscript. Andrew MacLennan encouraged my ambitions from the start, Heather McCallum weathered delays with only slightly strained patience, and Christina Wipf-Perry has finally seen the project through to completion. The series editors for Studies in Modern History, David Cannadine and John Morrill, offered valuable criticism throughout, from the original proposal to a completed draft. Remaining errors in detail or concept result from my own failings.

Beyond the world of historians, colleagues and editors, my work on this book has benefited from the joys and distractions of life with my family. My wife, Barbara Fink, read and commented on the manuscript, offering a layperson's insights and useful suggestions. More importantly, her presence has enriched my life immensely. I agreed to take on this project shortly before the birth of our elder daughter and began writing around the time of her sister's arrival. Thus, this book's genesis and development have proceeded alongside the extraordinary experience of their early childhood. This book is dedicated to Maddie and Talia.

Introduction

In a review written shortly before his 1993 death, E.P. Thompson, one of the founders of the study of social history in Britain, described class as 'a concept long past its sell-by date'.[1] Though in the rest of the essay Thompson revealed an unwillingness to cast aside class analysis, this statement reveals a striking lack of confidence in the approach he had advocated 30 years before in *The Making of the English Working Class*.[2] At that point Thompson, alongside other pioneering social historians, rejected the predominant focus on political leaders and institutions in historical research to concentrate on social history. In the intervening decades, a generation of scholars inspired by these models uncovered the lives of workers, sought to understand their political activities, and developed the practices and assumptions of social history. They produced a large corpus of rich and varied studies, many of which transcended Thompson's own conception of social history in analysing work and political movements, but also family life, neighbourhoods, sex roles and gender ideologies, education, leisure and many other subjects.[3]

Until the early 1980s, as social historians mined the archives, published their findings and debated with colleagues, they remained confident in the assumptions that supported their project. Though their approaches and interests varied, and they often argued fiercely with one another, most social historians accepted the centrality of material factors, of workers' experiences of social conditions and economic change. Economic change drove social change, which led to the development of classes with distinct interests and consciousness. Political conflict reflected these social structures.[4] In a seminal article, Eric Hobsbawm, another founding father of social history, focused on the social position of the best-paid workers (the 'labour aristocracy') in the mid-nineteenth century 'to explain its political attitudes'. By examining social and class structures, he claimed, a political position 'is easily understood'.[5] While most social historians avoided simple economic determinism and the pitfalls of reading politics or identity too directly from economic conditions, the central importance of social conditions formed the basis and justification for this tradition of social history.[6]

In the 1980s and 1990s historians built on feminist and linguistic theory to challenge the methods of social history and its emphasis on social conditions. They denied the primacy of the social realm, advocating a focus on language and culture instead.[7] Some challenged the utility of class analysis and the existence of class as anything other than an ideological or discursive construct.[8] Though some claims associated with this 'linguistic turn' go too far in rejecting study of the social sphere, cultural approaches have enriched efforts to understand the lives of working people. Historians now recognize that identities are multiple, contingent and constructed.[9] We no longer assume that class consciousness and class politics derive automatically from economic and social conditions.[10] By abandoning established assumptions about social change and class politics, we can consider new chronologies that challenge accepted narratives of continuity and discontinuity.[11]

In its emphasis on class and its social basis, traditional social history underestimated the complexity of identity, fixing it around class consciousness.[12] Working-class men and women did not think about their worlds exclusively in terms of class. They also identified with others on the basis of gender, craft, religion, locality, nation, empire, and other ways as well. This does not mean, however, that class identity was weak or unimportant.[13] As Linda Colley notes, 'Identities are not like hats. Human beings can and do put on several at a time.'[14] Though they adopted other identities at the same time, working people in Britain throughout this period continued to understand their place in the social structure through the lens of class.

This understanding did not automatically appear out of the structural conditions of working-class life; it had to be learned. Identities develop out of the stories we tell (and hear) that help place us in the world. Narratives tell us who we are, and they define boundaries and identify who we are not.[15] We form our identities through the language of these narratives. In the nineteenth and early twentieth centuries, working people had at their disposal 'pluralities of language . . . allowing them to recognize themselves in diverse possible ways'.[16] In order for any particular narrative or narratives to take hold and sustain the growth of identity, however, the stories must find fertile ground in experience, in social conditions, in relationships with others. Class identity thrived among working people because their experiences allowed narratives of class to resonate. The shared experiences of poverty and crowded conditions in working-class neighbourhoods, of poor working conditions and economic insecurity, and of popular leisure activities sustained working-class identity. Class narratives of community, of political exclusion, of conflict in the workplace and of resentment against interventionist authorities made sense in light of these experiences. As historian Joanna Bourke notes, the 'routine activities of everyday life' nurtured class identity as a 'metaphor for defining oneself and other people'.[17] As working men and women took action based on their identities, they also influenced their environment and the identities of their family members, co-workers and neighbours. They told stories that interpreted events or conditions. They associated with others, made leisure choices, and defined other people as like them or not. Thus, social conditions shaped identities, and identities shaped social conditions.

The social history tradition assumed that certain types of political activity would grow naturally out of social conditions. The course of political development in Britain and of working-class participation in politics does not, however, fit easily with deterministic ideas about class. Most British workers did not readily embrace socialism or support movements to overthrow the social and political order. Historians' search for explanations of the 'failure' of British workers' politics eventually gave way to the abandonment of the assumption that such class politics were to be expected.[18] Attempts to read party affiliation or political activism directly from social position were doomed to failure. There is no 'true' form of working-class politics.[19] Thus, working-class support for radical, liberal, conservative or socialist political movements depended on a variety of contingent factors, and many working-class men and women had little interest in formal politics.

While only a minority immersed themselves in formal politics, struggles over power and resources pervaded everyday life.[20] In households, neighbourhoods, workplaces, streets and pubs, working-class men and women negotiated 'aspects of inequality, authority, and the capacity to define the meanings of the world'.[21] At times these struggles reflected and reinforced multiple identities other than class. Gender ideologies and identities were manifest in struggles between spouses over household resources and responsibilities. Street battles between Catholics and Protestants revealed and reproduced sectarian differences. On the other hand, informal politics could also strengthen class identity. On the shopfloor, workers engaged in myriad informal struggles with employers. Class tensions played out in interactions with representatives of the state or with middle-class philanthropists. The dynamic politics of everyday life were far more salient than the formal politics of parties or mass movements in working-class lives.

In a recent address to an organization of historians and other scholars, David Feldman noted the influence of recent historiographic trends: 'following the turn to culture and the now commonplace emphasis on the formative rather than merely reflective capacities of language, histories of class formation are so rare that the NACBS [North American Conference on British Studies] might plausibly declare them an endangered species'.[22] The insights of the 'turn to culture' should not, however, blind us to the importance of class in modern British history. We should abandon simplistic notions of identity and of social determination, but social conditions remain relevant in considering the identities and experiences of historical actors. Working men and women comprehended their lives through languages and narratives, but they embraced those narratives that made sense in light of the conditions of their lives, including narratives of class.

This book examines working-class life during the period 1832–1940. As with any chronological structure imposed by historians, the dates are somewhat arbitrary. The start date falls around the end of the first phase of industrialization, the 'period of the classic Industrial Revolution' in a common view.[23] By the 1830s the writing was on the wall for hand-loom weavers, as power-looms spread and wages declined precipitously.[24] A new political order operated in the 1830s, building on parliamentary reform and the passage of the New Poor Law. Not coincidentally, the start date of this work corresponds to the end point of Thompson's *The Making of the English Working Class*.[25] At the other end, in 1940, the British joined the fight in the Second World War, and the experience of that war created new conditions in British society that justify ending the work here. On the other hand, solid arguments could be made for starting in 1850 or ending in 1945 or even 1975. The scope of this book does not necessarily suggest sharp discontinuities in working-class life in 1832 or 1940, and the question of continuities and discontinuities will be taken up further in the conclusion.

A further chronological structure divides the book into three sections, with breaks in 1870 and 1914. These correspond with major changes in the contexts of working-class life: the end of the mid-Victorian boom around 1870, and the start of the First World War in 1914. Once again, however, somewhat different chronological frontiers might make equal sense. Within each chronological section of the book, four chapters analyse community and family, work, leisure, and politics and identity. These chapters reveal the experiences of working-class men and women in homes and neighbourhoods, work and leisure. They analyse their multiple identities and the everyday politics that nurtured and reflected the importance of class in the lives of British workers.

Notes

1 E.P. Thompson, 'The making of a ruling class', *Dissent* 40 (1993), 380.

2 D. Cannadine, *The Rise and Fall of Class in Britain* (New York: Columbia University Press, 1999), 16–17; E.P. Thompson, *The Making of the English Working Class*, 2nd ed. (New York: Vintage, 1966).

3 G. Eley and K. Nield, *The Future of Class History: What's Left of the Social?* (Ann Arbor: University of Michigan Press, forthcoming 2007), chs 2, 6. I am grateful to Geoff Eley for the opportunity to see the manuscript ahead of publication.

4 Cannadine, *Rise and Fall of Class*, 7; C. Tilly, *Stories, Identities and Political Change* (Lanham: Rowman & Littlefield, 2002), 5.

5 E.J. Hobsbawm, 'The labour aristocracy in nineteenth-century Britain', in *Labouring Men: Studies in the History of Labour* (New York: Basic Books, 1964), 274.

6 G. Eley and K. Nield, 'Starting over: the present, the post-modern and the moment of social history', *Social History* 20 (1995), 362.

7 G. Stedman Jones, *Languages of Class: Studies in English Working Class History* (Cambridge: Cambridge University Press, 1983), 7, 22.

8 P. Joyce, *Democratic Subjects: The Self and the Social in Nineteenth-Century England* (Cambridge: Cambridge University Press, 1994), 1, 12.

9 J.W. Scott, 'The evidence of experience', *Critical Inquiry* 17 (1991), 785, 792; C.K. Steedman, *Landscape for a Good Woman: A Story of Two Lives* (New Brunswick: Rutgers University Press, 1987), 13.

10 Stedman Jones, *Languages of Class*, 20–1.

11 E.F. Biagini, *Liberty, Retrenchment and Reform: Popular Liberalism in the Age of Gladstone, 1860–1880* (Cambridge: Cambridge University Press, 1992), 6, 10; P. Joyce, *Visions of the People: Industrial England and the Question of Class 1848–1914* (Cambridge: Cambridge University Press, 1991), 2, 336.

12 J. Epstein, *In Practice: Studies in the Language and Culture of Popular Politics in Modern Britain* (Stanford: Stanford University Press, 2003), 6–7.

13 D. Mayfield and S. Thorne, 'Reply to "The poverty of protest" and "The imaginary discontents"', *Social History* 18 (1993), 233.

14 L. Colley, *Britons: Forging the Nation 1707–1837* (New Haven: Yale University Press, 1992), 6.

15 M. Somers, 'Narrativity, narrative identity and social action: rethinking English working-class formation', *Social Science History* 16 (1992), 603; Tilly, *Stories, Identities and Political Change*, 11.

16 G. Eley and K. Nield, 'Farewell to the working class?' *International Labor and Working-Class History* 57 (2000), 19.

17 J. Bourke, *Working-Class Cultures in Britain 1890–1960: Gender, Class and Ethnicity* (London: Routledge, 1994), 4, 25.

18 Mayfield and Thorne, 'Reply', 228.

19 T. Griffiths, *The Lancashire Working Classes c.1880–1930* (Oxford: Clarendon Press, 2001), 268–9; N. Kirk, *Labour and Society in Britain and the USA, vol. I: Capitalism, Custom and Protest, 1780–1850* (Aldershot: Scolar Press, 1994), 7.

20 A. August, 'A culture of consolation? Rethinking politics in working-class London, 1870–1914', *Historical Research* 74 (2001), 195–6.

21 Eley and Nield, 'Farewell to the working class', 11.

22 D. Feldman, 'Immigrants in British history: a problem of integration?', Semi-Plenary Address, North American Conference on British Studies, October 2005.

23 M. Berg and P. Hudson, 'Rehabilitating the Industrial Revolution', *Economic History Review* 45 (1992), 37.

24 D. Bythell, 'The hand-loom weavers in the English cotton industry during the Industrial Revolution: some problems', *Economic History Review* 17 (1964), 346; J.S. Lyons, 'Vertical integration in the British cotton industry, 1825–1850: a revision', *Journal of Economic History* 45 (1985), 423.

25 Thomson, *Making of the English Working Class*.

PART ONE

1832–70

Introduction: Britain in 1832

In 1834 a distressed Salford clergyman complained that industrial development had 'drawn together a most heterogeneous population, consisting in no small degree, of the unsettled, the discontented and the depraved; so as to render our trading districts . . . the moral sewers of the community – a confluence of the scum and the offscouring of society'.[1] This man's anxiety reflects the disorienting pace of change in the first decades of the nineteenth century. The British population soared and cities stretched and strained to accommodate new residents. Industrialization brought upheaval in work and its organization. These transformations created new social conditions in cities and towns, a growing and affluent commercial and industrial elite alongside widespread misery and discontent. Decades of war with France helped forge Britain into a nation, but it was a nation divided by religious differences, regional identities and resentments, and fears about social conditions and political power.

During the first three decades of the nineteenth century the British population grew at an astonishing rate. Between 1801 and 1831 the population of England and Wales expanded by 56 per cent, while that in Scotland rose by 50 per cent.[2] According to one estimate, nearly 60 per cent of the English population in the late 1820s were under the age of 24.[3] In 1801 London stood as the lone British city with over 100,000 residents. By 1831 six more had crossed this threshold.[4] Some cities, particularly northern textile centres, experienced spurts of dizzying expansion. In the 1820s Manchester grew at a 3.9 per cent annual rate, while Bradford's growth reached 5.9 per cent per year.[5] From 1810 to 1850 the population of Bradford increased from 16,012 to 103,778.[6] Glasgow housed 77,000 residents in 1801, but reached 275,000 some 40 years later.[7] It is little wonder that observers like the Salford clergyman were shocked by such transformations.

Industrialization provided the motor for much of this change. In 1811 1.7 million workers laboured in industrial occupations, and this rose to 3 million (40 per cent of all workers) in 1841. Cotton manufacture stood out as the leading industrial sector of the first half of the century. In 1830 more than 400,000 workers processed cotton.[8] Cotton mills multiplied rapidly. For example, Manchester housed only three cotton mills in 1794, but there were 66 in the town by 1821.[9] The factory contributed to the sense of rapid change that created anxiety, as in an 1832 complaint about factory discipline in the *Poor Man's Advocate*: 'We have exchanged . . . occasions of innocent enjoyment and recreation for one continued round of gloomy, unceasing, and ill-requited toil'.[10] Across the economy, though, factories remained rare in the early 1830s, and even in cotton, non-factory workers including hand-loom weavers outnumbered those in the mills.[11] Nearly three-quarters of the British population depended on manual labour for their survival, and only a small fraction of these worked in factories in the middle of the nineteenth century.[12]

Popular discontent and political contention added to the sense of anxiety in the first third of the nineteenth century. George Macaulay fretted in 1828 that Britain faced 'another crisis analogous to that which occurred in the seventeenth century . . . It remains to be seen whether two hundred years have made us wiser'.[13] Extraordinary mass movements around the Catholic question and in favour of parliamentary reform caught the attention of the powerful in Westminster, leading to the passage of Catholic emancipation in 1829 and the 1832 Reform Act. The latter eliminated some of the most egregious biases in the electoral system, for example by abolishing representation for dozens of boroughs that had been under the direct control of private individuals. It also established the £10 borough franchise, making all adult men who occupied a house of that annual value eligible to vote. As the limitations of the 1832 Act came into focus, though, they became as significant as its achievements. Four out of five adult men remained unable to vote. As the Whig leader Grey commented in 1831, 'there is no one more decided against annual parliaments, universal suffrage, and the [secret] ballot, than I am. My object is . . . to put an end to such hopes and projects'. In the minds of many, the 1832 property qualification marked out the distinction between the working class and the middle class.[14]

In the popular struggle for political reform in the early nineteenth century, radicals appealed to a growing sense of British patriotism. The massive mobilization and enthusiastic patriotism evident during the wars against France morphed into claims for active citizenship in the following decades. Reformers adopted the mantle of true patriots, striving to rescue the nation from corrupt politicians. At a huge reform gathering in 1819, brass bands accompanied the 60,000 marchers with repeated choruses of 'God Save the King' and 'Rule Britannia'.[15] In 1820 support for the spurned Queen Caroline tapped into popular patriotism and hostility to the new King, George IV. The Queen's detractors were painted as foreigners, while she adopted the mantle of Britannia. In one pamphlet illustration, English, Scottish and Irish men, united in their British identity, supported the Queen's crown.[16] Despite this image, the Irish were not integrated into British identity in the way the English, Welsh and Scottish were. In the three nations a strong sense of Britishness developed alongside regional and local ties.[17] Neither these more narrow affiliations, nor frustration with a particular monarch undermined the pervasive loyalism and British identity among working men and women in England, Scotland and Wales. Similarly, these identities coexisted with the growing sense of class among the manual labouring populations of British cities and towns.

Notes

1 M. Hewitt, *The Emergence of Stability in the Industrial City: Manchester, 1832–67* (Aldershot: Scolar Press, 1996), 26.

2 C. Cook and J. Stevenson, *The Longman Handbook of Modern British History 1714–2001*, 4th ed. (London: Longman, 2001), 151.

3 E.A. Wrigley and R.S. Schofield, *The Population History of England 1541–1871* (London: Edward Arnold, 1981), 217; L. Colley, 'Whose nation? Class and national consciousness in Britain 1750–1830', *Past and Present* 113 (1986), 103.

4 F.M.L. Thompson, *The Rise of Respectable Society: A Social History of Victorian Britain 1830–1900* (Cambridge, MA: Harvard University Press, 1988), 28.

5 J.G. Williamson, *Coping with City Growth during the British Industrial Revolution* (Cambridge: Cambridge University Press, 1990), 223.

6 T. Koditschek, *Class Formation and Urban-Industrial Society: Bradford, 1750–1850* (Cambridge: Cambridge University Press, 1990), 79.

7 W.W. Knox, *Industrial Nation: Work, Culture and Society in Scotland, 1800–Present* (Edinburgh: Edinburgh University Press, 1999), 40.

8 Thompson, *Rise of Respectable Society*, 23, 25.

9 M. Harrison, *Crowds in History: Mass Phenomena in English Towns, 1790–1835* (Cambridge: Cambridge University Press, 1988), 97.

10 J. Belchem, *Industrialization and the Working Class: The English Experience 1750–1900* (Portland: Areopagitica Press, 1990), 45.

11 Thompson, *Rise of Respectable Society*, 25, 31–2.

12 H. Cunningham, *The Challenge of Democracy: Britain 1832–1918* (London: Longman, 2001), 20, 24.

13 K. Robbins, *Great Britain: Identities, Institutions and the Idea of Britishness* (London: Longman, 1998), 147.

14 E.P. Thompson, *The Making of the English Working Class*, 2nd ed. (New York: Vintage, 1966), 811; L. Colley, *Britons: Forging the Nation 1707–1837* (New Haven: Yale University Press, 1992), 346–9, 362; P. Harling, 'Equipoise regained? Recent trends in British political history, 1790–1867', *Journal of Modern History* 75 (2003), 893, 897–8; Thompson, *Rise of Respectable Society*, 16.

15 Colley, *Britons*, 337; T. Koditschek, 'The making of British nationality', *Victorian Studies* 44 (2002), 393–4.

16 R. McWilliam, *Popular Politics in Nineteenth-Century England* (London: Routledge, 1998), 8–11.

17 L. Colley, 'Britishness and otherness: an argument', *Journal of British Studies* 31 (1992), 314.

CHAPTER ONE

Forming the urban working class

In the 1850s a young stonemason, Henry Broadhurst, found himself out of work in his Oxfordshire birthplace and decided, 'to seek my fortune further afield'. Thus began a period of years in which 'I was like Cain, A wanderer on the face of the earth'. After numerous short stops in various towns and a six-year stay in Norwich, he finally settled in London.[1] Broadhurst's experience, leaving his place of birth, moving from town to town, and joining a growing urban population, was characteristic of working-class life in the middle decades of the nineteenth century. Broadhurst recalled, 'the changes and chances of commercial life and the caprices of fashion keep a large army of working men in a state of motion, sometimes over short distances, sometimes from the southern counties to the western, or the eastern to the northern. Few men escape this experience'. Like Broadhurst, though, most eventually settled in a city or town, and these migrants joined those already working in the cities to form the mid-Victorian working class.

Migration

The mid-nineteenth-century British working population was a mobile one. One study found that 52 per cent of urban dwellers in 1851 were not living in their birthplace. But this includes large numbers of young children, and three-quarters of 65–74-year-olds lived some distance from their birthplaces.[2] Some towns had particularly high concentrations of migrants. In Bradford 70 per cent of adults were migrants.[3] Many travelled from a rural area to a nearby town. In Preston 70 per cent of migrants originated within 48 km (30 miles) of the city.[4] Some migrants, however, moved from town to town, and those with valued skills were particularly likely to move long distances.[5] Large numbers of Irish men and women moved to British towns, and the Irish-born comprised as much as a fifth of the populations of towns such as Dundee and Liverpool.[6]

The typical migrant moved as a teenager or young adult. Harriet and Ann Jones moved from their home in Welshpool to nearby Shrewsbury some time between 1861 and 1871 (they were 24 and 25 in 1871). There they lived and worked as servants in the household of Phillip Williams, a cattle dealer.[7] In Preston young women migrants like these swelled the population of 15–19- and 20–4-year-old women to more than 10 per cent higher than the number of 10–14-year-olds.[8] Young married couples also migrated in large numbers. John Davies, who worked as an iron puddler in his Welsh home town of Dowlais, moved with his wife Mary Ann and their young son and daughter to Middlesbrough, over 400 km (250 miles) away. John and Mary Ann were both in their twenties when they moved, and they had at least two more children once settled in Middlesbrough.[9] Overall, nearly two-thirds of migrants to cities in the 1850s were between the ages 15 and 29.[10]

Migrants were 'pushed' and 'pulled' into leaving their homes. When local economic conditions soured, people hit the roads to escape impoverishment. In the 1840s the collapse of rural hand-loom weaving in Yorkshire drove thousands into rapidly growing towns like Bradford.[11] Similarly, the flow of emigrants from Ireland accelerated in the late 1840s and early 1850s, during and immediately following the famine.[12] For those who could make their way to the coast and across the Irish Sea, migration to British towns offered a chance to leave the crisis behind. Famine in the Scottish Highlands drove many to migrate into areas of Fife and East Lothian in the 1840s.[13] Even without the pressure of an economic crisis, though, many young people were expected to leave home. One observer (from the Lune valley) noted, 'Almost all our boys go off to the manufacturing districts when they are 12 years of age or earlier'.[14] The Jones sisters, Harriet and Ann, probably left their Welshpool home because their father's farm did not need their labour and thus could not support them.[15]

Migrants often left home to follow the call of opportunity. Booming industries and towns with healthy labour markets pulled new residents from surrounding districts and sometimes from further afield. In Staffordshire the growing coal mines and iron and pottery trades brought migrants to the Potteries district in the 1840s. Many sought better opportunities in trades they already knew, and came from existing centres of coal mining or iron manufacturing.[16] Potential migrants learned of specific opportunities from kin, former neighbours or even through advertisements. John Davies, the iron puddler from Dowlais, followed a well-worn path to Middlesbrough in the 1860s, where an established Welsh migrant community probably included kin or friends familiar with the iron industry there.[17]

Decisions to leave home most often included a combination of 'push' and 'pull' factors involving work opportunities and family considerations. Even in crises such as the Irish famine, potential migrants learned of opportunities from those who had blazed the trails earlier. But their decisions reflected complex considerations of ties at home as well as opportunities elsewhere. As historian Lynn Lees observes, 'Emigrants were people touched by social and economic changes who had the resources, the will, the information, and the aspirations to move'.[18] In less dire circumstances as well, migration decisions reflected both the appeal of the destination and conditions at home. Amos Kniveton learned his father's trade, boot and shoemaking, and settled in his home village of Astley Green, near Manchester. Shortly after establishing his own workshop, he recognized that there was not enough work for his father and himself in the village. He answered an advertise-ment and moved about 70 km (43 miles) to Morecambe to follow a better opportunity in his trade.[19]

Migration must have been stressful and disorienting, particularly for those without networks of kin or acquaintances in their new homes. A character in a story by Lancashire dialect poet Edwin Waugh describes this lost feeling: 'I keep lookin' up an' down to see if I can leet of onybody fro our side, – but I can find noan. I'm like as I wur born alive an' kin to nobry'.[20] A migrant from Limerick to London found that the friend he was counting on for help died before his arrival. He ended up at the mercy of a sweating employer who demanded that he work seven 15-hour days per week in return for lodging and meagre support. He had little choice but to accept the offer: 'I had no friends and thought I had better take it'.[21]

It appears, however, that most migrants enjoyed the help and companionship provided by relatives or friends already settled at their destination. Irish, Welsh and Scottish migrants formed distinct clusters in growing mid-Victorian cities.[22] In the Staffordshire Potteries, Irish migrants congregated in Burslem, Welsh migrants in Hanley. Nearby Etruria, in contrast, had only three Irish-born residents in 1861.[23] Migrants within England also sought out acquaintances from their home villages. Families from Kirkham occupied four of the eleven houses in Birk Street, Preston in 1861, though migrants from that village made up only about 1 per cent of the city's population. Lodgers also often resided with families from their home towns and villages.[24] The shelter and assistance offered by such acquaintances or relatives could be essential in helping newcomers find their way. John O'Neill, an Irish-born shoemaker, offered his brother, sister-in-law and their children lodging in his home when they arrived in London. O'Neill viewed helping the new arrivals as his obligation.[25]

These communities of migrants also offered crucial assistance in finding employment. Employers relied on migrants to recruit more workers from their home towns and new migrants could obtain essential references from kin or acquaintances.[26] John O'Neill formed one link in a chain of migrant shoemakers from Munster to London. He found a job with the help of previous migrants and offered similar assistance to those who followed him.[27] Thus, migrants relied upon networks of relatives or acquaintances to ease the transition to their new homes. This support helped migrants survive economically, but also offered important cultural and emotional buffers against disorientation, loneliness and alienation.

Urbanization

Migrants like John O'Neill arrived in rapidly changing urban environments. By 1871 nearly two-thirds of the population of England and Wales lived in cities and towns, compared to about a third at the start of the century.[28] Though the dramatic expansion of some towns moderated after mid-century, others took off. Sheffield grew by over 50 per cent from 1861 to 1881. Many mining towns also stood out as centres of rapid expansion in the second half of the century.[29] Migrants into cities in the first half of the century can take credit for much of the remarkable expansion in those decades. In the 1840s, for example, 60 per cent of the growth of London, Liverpool, Birmingham and Manchester is attributable to migrants into these massive cities. As young migrants settled in, married and raised families, their children increased the population further, and this natural increase accounted for 62 per cent of growth in these cities during the 1850s.[30] Halifax grew from 37,014 residents to 65,510 in the 1860s. Yet in 1871 81 per cent of the town's population was born within 48 km (30 miles) of the town's centre, and 54 per cent were born in Halifax itself.[31] Catherine Kelly and Patrick Mannion, both Irish immigrants to Stafford, married in that town in 1859 and had four sons by 1871. Both through their migration and the growth of their family, this couple contributed to the expansion of Victorian Stafford.[32]

As towns grew, important shifts in residential patterns developed. In smaller towns it was common for the wealthy and the workers to live near one another in socially mixed districts. But as many towns expanded beyond the narrow confines of their eighteenth-century boundaries, new housing developments attracted the wealthy away from increasingly crowded central areas, creating a growing segregation of rich and poor. In Bradford this process was well under way by mid-century, with most £10 property holders living in three middle-class areas, physically and socially elevated above the industrial and lower-class districts. In succeeding decades bourgeois districts grew and spread further from the centre of town.[33] In Birmingham enterprising middle-class families like the Southalls and the Cadburies left the central district, settling in the exclusive suburb of Edgbaston.[34] Residential segregation by class was by no means complete in mid-Victorian cities, but working-class migrants and their children increasingly crowded into low-lying central districts.[35] New transport systems, too expensive and inconvenient for workers, linked affluent areas with commercial districts in the centre of town and encouraged class segregation.[36] Skilled and unskilled workers shared the densely populated streets in working-class neighbourhoods.[37]

Housing and sanitation

As migration and natural increase filled increasingly crowded cities, workers struggled to find adequate housing. By maximizing the number of houses on their land and the number of tenants in their houses, landlords could do well even when letting to poor tenants. Landlords divided the former homes of the affluent into tenements for workers, many of whom rented single rooms.[38] New houses built intentionally for working-class tenants filled open spaces. In developing working-class housing, cheapness and the efficient use of space were the highest priorities. Working-class houses varied from the worst lodging houses and cellars to two-up two-down terraces, but nearly all shared two key characteristics. The organization of workers' housing left limited privacy, as most were built around courts and shared facilities were nearly universal. Second, working-class housing was concentrated in particular areas of cities, close to employment opportunities, and increasingly abandoned by the wealthy.

In theory, lodging houses provided temporary accommodation for migrants or transient workers, but many impoverished families lived in them for extended periods. They offered dormitory-style rooms, with shared beds and no privacy. Middle-class observers were scandalized by the unsanitary conditions in these overcrowded lodgings, but even more by the mixing of children and adults of both sexes.[39] One observer of lodging houses in Manchester complained of 'Young men and young women; men, wives and their children – all lying in a noisome atmosphere, swarming with vermin, and often intoxicated . . . villainy, debauchery and licentiousness are here portrayed in their darkest character'.[40] Cellar dwellings offered comparably bad sanitation but also a bit of privacy, and were particularly common in Manchester and Liverpool. Typically the poorest cellar dwellings included a single room about 3 by 3.65 metres (10 by 12 feet), with a ceiling 1.8 metres (6 feet) high and an unpaved floor. Without windows, damp and dark, cellars like this housed entire families like the Flaherty family, parents and five children, who lived in a cellar in John Street, Manchester in 1871.[41]

Both more common and less objectionable than either lodging houses or cellar dwellings were working-class houses built around courts. Some of these resulted from building over the open space behind older houses, with a narrow alley providing access to the court of newer cottages. Others were built from scratch as working-class housing, frequently in the back-to-back pattern that used space most efficiently. Back-to-backs were built in rows of terraces facing on to a court. Abutting the rear of each terrace and facing the opposite direction was another row of houses, so that houses were enclosed on three sides. Access to the court was limited to narrow passages between the houses on the street. The typical back-to-back had one main multi-purpose room on the ground floor, perhaps 3.65 metres (12 feet) square, plus a small scullery and often a cellar. The second storey contained one bedroom or two very small ones. In some places the typical back-to-back had a third storey with an additional bedroom. The narrow courts on to which these houses opened contained privies, pumps and other communal facilities. In many industrial cities, back-to-backs accounted for more than two-thirds of all houses.[42] In Scotland most workers lived in large tenement houses built on courts. These stone blocks, typically four stories high, included 16 or more one and two-roomed tenements, again sharing facilities in the court.[43]

Terraced houses that opened in the back provided the superior form of working-class housing. A two-up two-down house would include two main floor rooms (usually one behind the other) and two upstairs bedrooms. If a family could afford an entire house, this form provided a little more opportunity for differentiated uses of space. Bedrooms could be divided between sexes, for example. But two-up two-down terraces were more expensive than other forms of housing, and families often had to bring in lodgers to help defray the high rent. Even when no lodgers were present, the mid-Victorian working-class terraced house would still commonly share the privy and wash-house with a number of other houses.[44]

While middle-class housing in this period increasingly emphasized privacy and strictly defined functions for various rooms, residents of most working-class housing shared space and facilities. In the typical Sheffield back-to-back house, historian Sidney Pollard notes, 'The daily activities of the family were concentrated in the living room, which served as kitchen, scullery, dining-room, living-room, as wash-room and bathroom, and on wet days the clothes were hung up in it to dry'.[45] Outside the house, residents shared courts and essential facilities.[46] Common privies, wash-houses, water supplies and even sinks drew residents together, but could also lead to conflict.[47] Kathleen Dayus, who grew up in a mid-century Birmingham back-to-back, recalled the dry privies shared by the houses in her court: 'At the end of the yard stood three ashcans and five lavatories, or closets as we called them. These each consisted of a square box with [a] large round hole in the middle. Us children had to hold the sides of the seat otherwise we could have fallen in . . . You can imagine the stench in the summer! . . . There were always rows over whose turn it was to clean the closets'.[48]

Crowded conditions complicated this space sharing, as booming populations squeezed into central districts. Housing provision in settled areas of towns failed to keep up with demand. In Blackfriars parish, Glasgow, for example, the population increased 40 per cent from 1831 to 1841, but the number of houses did not change.[49] In one London district, while the population grew by over 3,000 between 1851 and 1861, only 84 houses were built.[50] Families jammed into existing houses and new working-class housing, often living in a single room. In 1861 nearly two-thirds of all Scots lived in one or two rooms. In Newcastle in the same year (1861) 39 per cent of families (including nearly half the population) occupied single rooms. In some cases, families occupying single rooms took in lodgers as well.[51] In the most crowded working-class areas, population densities reached 120 people per hectare (300 people per acre) or more.[52]

These working-class neighbourhoods grew without significant government oversight. Aside from older, ineffective building regulations in London, government intervention in housing provision began tentatively in the 1840s, after much urban growth had already taken place.[53] Manchester, for example, outlawed the construction of back-to-back houses in 1844. But through most of the century, building regulation existed in only a few cities and was not consistently enforced even in these areas.[54] One historian has described such regulation as 'partial, irregular and often evaded'.[55] Even late in the century when by-laws were more firmly in place, they affected new construction only, while the vast majority of workers lived in housing built during the unrestricted earlier decades.

In this unregulated environment, increasingly crowded working-class neighbourhoods grew unsanitary and unhealthy. Inadequate provision for the waste created by these growing populations was the greatest culprit. In the absence of water closets, cesspools and dungheaps dotted working-class districts, often leaking into their surroundings. Around mid-century, partly in response to cholera epidemics, authorities attempted to improve sanitary facilities. Manchester's attempts to clean out cesspools and privies led to the disposal of about 70,000 tons of human waste per year. Improved methods, spreading gradually from the 1840s, used pails or pans, which could be removed and cleaned.[56] But despite the gradual spread of slightly more healthy sanitary systems, most residents of working-class districts still faced an overwhelming shortage of facilities. Middleton Place, Glasgow, a typical mid-century Scottish tenement, housed about 130 people when it was built around 1850. It included a single privy in the court.[57] Parliament Street in Manchester had some 380 inhabitants sharing a privy.[58] It is no surprise that all this waste created horrible smells; as one Leeds resident told an observer, 'the smell was bad enough to raise the roof off his skull'.[59]

The inadequate sanitation, alongside a lack of clean water and the varied dangers of living in crowded conditions, created problems more serious than the stench. Elevated death rates accompanied the feverish growth of nineteenth-century cities. Crude death rates in London, Liverpool, Manchester and Birmingham were more than a third higher than rural figures in 1841 (27.34 versus 20.39 per thousand).[60] The following three decades did not see consistent improvement, as Manchester's death rates in the period 1863–6 were nearly identical to those in 1838–42.[61] Early death caused by urban conditions was far more common in crowded working-class districts than in the more pleasant environs into which the affluent settled. Some 62 per cent of Liverpool labourers' children died before their fifth birthday.[62] The older central districts of Edinburgh had death rates from 29 to 37 per thousand in 1863, compared with rates of 15 to 17 in the more affluent New Town areas.[63] In Liverpool the average life span of the gentry and professional classes in 1840 was 35, while the child of a labourer could expect to live only an average of 15 years. An 1849 cholera outbreak in London killed 17 per cent of the population in the poorest districts but only 2 per cent in the most affluent.[64] The immediate environment had decisive effects on health. In Scottish tenements death rates in the 'back lands', built on the rear of plots with less light and ventilation than houses built along the street, were often 15 to 30 per cent higher than in front tenements. Crowding into a single room facilitated the spread of diseases, when even those suffering from tuberculosis had to share beds with family members or lodgers.[65]

Government intervention in health and sanitation, as in housing, had limited impact before late century. Despite extensive investigations of the miserable conditions in urban working-class districts, efforts to improve the health of these districts were halting and inconsistent. In the 1840s, the central government instituted a series of laws, culminating in the Public Health Act of 1848. But these and other regulations that followed in the 1850s and 1860s were predominately permissive, allowing local authorities to take action, but not requiring such intervention. Local governments moved slowly, if at all. In Lancashire, for example, ten years after the Public Health Act, only 400,000 out of 2.5 million people came under the authority of any public health board, and most of the boards had extremely limited powers.[66] Only at the end of the 1860s, with the passage of the 1866 Sanitary Act and the beginnings of a new, more activist approach by local governments, did sanitary reform begin to clean up the mess.

The family and community

In these crowded and unhealthy districts families grew, neighbours congregated and communities developed. Nearly everyone lived in family groups, which functioned as the basic economic units in these communities. In the insecure conditions of working-class existence, people relied on their families to help them through tough times. The family, particularly relationships between mothers and children, also provided the emotional core of working-class life. On the other hand, conflict and inequality pervaded working-class family life, as husbands and wives struggled over their distinct roles and unequal access to resources. Despite the upheavals of migration, the challenges of the new urban environment and the pressures created by economic insecurity, the working-class family remained resilient, if not always harmonious.

More than 90 per cent of residents of working-class districts lived with relatives.[67] While pre-industrial families were generally simple, built around the nucleus of parents and children, nineteenth-century working-class families often included kin beyond the nuclear family, which were twice as common in labouring families in the mid-nineteenth century than in a sample of pre-industrial communities.[68] In some towns, such as Preston and York, more than one in five households included extended relatives, though elsewhere the proportion was somewhat lower.[69] Non-relatives were also common in mid-nineteenth-century households, but here important class differences appear. Middle-class households commonly included live-in domestic servants, often migrant girls. Working-class households, on the other hand, took in lodgers to increase the family income.[70] In 1861 almost one third of households in Stockport included lodgers or kin.[71]

Families began with working-class couples meeting in the streets or through mutual acquaintances. Young working-class men and women enjoyed freedom to find their own mates, relatively unencumbered by parental or community restrictions. Nonetheless, conventions established and reinforced by families and neighbours did shape courtship patterns.[72] Romance played an important part in the formation of a working-class couple. William Smith, a shoemaker, recalls meeting the woman who would become his wife: 'I was smitten at once. It was love at first sight'. The tremendous obstacles presented by economic insecurity, poor health and the general conditions of working-class life presented young couples with formidable barriers, and many relationships failed. But couples who stayed the course settled in to face the challenges of working-class life together. The shared experience of the difficulties and burdens of family life gradually replaced the romantic bond as the central feature in working-class marital relationships. The miner Edward Rymer recalled that at his wife's death he felt 'lonely and desolate without her. We had braved the storm and ruthless tempest in all its fury for 40 years'.[73] Despite the depth of feeling apparent here, for most working-class men and women other emotional ties gradually grew more significant than the bond between spouses: men with their mates at work or at the pub, women with their children, kin and neighbours.[74] Relationships between mothers and their children were particularly strong. A factory worker described its importance: 'when under the olive branches of my mother's affections, I often forgot all the ills of my daily life. She too felt so happy when I came home . . . and laid my small wages in her lap, that the tear would sometimes start to her eye'.[75]

As this passage shows, both emotional and economic bonds tied the working-class family together. Many families relied on multiple earners – the husband, wife and children – as well as on the contributions of resident kin and the income contributed by lodgers. Hopefully, when one earner faced unemployment, others could tide the family over the crisis. Families were particularly vulnerable at specific points in their development. When first married, a couple would probably both be employed and they would find themselves in a relatively strong economic position, particularly since a significant portion of couples lived with a parent or parents for the first stage of their marriage.[76] When the couple had children and formed their own independent household, economic conditions became more difficult.

With more mouths to feed, expenses rose, but it became more difficult for the mother to earn. At this stage many women gave up paid work outside the house, though some continued to find ways to bring resources into their strained household economies, for instance by taking in lodgers.[77] As the children grew older, they entered the labour force and contributed to the household economy, easing the crunch. In the Potteries district of Staffordshire, boys generally began working around age nine, while girls could earn wages from about age eleven.[78] One remarkable feature of working-class family economies in this period is that children remained in their parental households for an extended period, even as their wages (and contributions to the household) grew, and often after they married. Many couples lived with parents well into their twenties, at which time they started new households.[79]

Other economic links also tied families together. Relatives could be valuable sources for employment opportunities. Peter Taylor, who grew up in Paisley, got a job working as a bottler in the brewery in which his father worked. His connections did not prevent him from being sacked, but his older brother then got him apprenticed as a mechanic.[80] Firms in the Potteries relied on family connections for recruitment as well. John Finney, who was 15 in 1851, sought work at Wedgwood, where his father worked as a fireman. Of course, when a firm failed, the impact on families with multiple earners losing work could be disastrous.[81]

To some extent, the interdependence of family members extended to kin and neighbours outside the household. An illness, death or period of unemployment could have devastating effects on families, and neighbours and kin stepped in to help. When one Lancashire man became ill, his neighbour, Nancy Beswick, took the initiative, offering the sick man food, visiting his wife and helping out in other ways. High death rates left many children orphaned. Kin and sometimes neighbours took in the needy children and raised them.[82] The elderly who were unable to support themselves also relied on kin and were often taken in by their relations. It appears that kin provided the most significant help and stepped in more frequently in serious crises than did unrelated neighbours.[83] Though working-class families did seek aid from other sources in crises, neighbours and particularly kin provided essential support for unstable family economies. This aid allowed the working-class family to survive under the pressures of migration, poverty and industrialization.

These families were not, however, simply sources of aid and emotional support. They were also arenas in which power and resources were distributed, often unequally. In both times of crisis and relatively stable moments in the family cycle some members of households enjoyed privileged access to scarce resources. For example, the husband or father generally ate the biggest portions and the best food. One observer noted that a typical mid-Victorian London working-class supper would include cheese and bread for the husband, while the wife and children made do with bread and fat.[84] Husbands expected to enjoy these unequal shares and they expected a degree of power in the household as well. These issues, power and resources, often led to conflict in working-class families and violence was not uncommon. Despite wives' efforts to defend themselves, husbands could generally overpower them, enforcing women's subordination with their fists.[85]

Conclusion

Even in the upper reaches of the working class, a scarcity of basic commodities often complicated this unequal distribution of resources. Data on wages and the cost of living reveal improvements in real wages from around 1820. Even unskilled workers saw significant gains, though skilled workers enjoyed greater benefits.[86] On the other hand, tables of wages and costs of living do not reflect the challenges facing working men and women in this period. The upheaval involved in migration and new forms of work, the terrible overcrowding and miserable sanitary conditions, and, most notably, high levels of mortality persisted through the first three-quarters of the century.[87] In addition, wage figures over the long term do not reflect the periodic economic downturns that left many working people facing underemployment and impoverishment. This insecurity confronted relatively well-paid skilled workers as well as the unskilled. Though on a national scale the real income of workers appears to have improved in the mid-Victorian years, it is difficult to measure the extent to which these gains compensated for the insecurity and miserable conditions suffered by workers in their growing urban communities.[88]

Notes

1 H. Broadhurst, *Henry Broadhurst, M.P.* ([1901]; New York: Garland, 1984), 11, 12.

2 M. Anderson, 'Urban migration in Victorian Britain: problems of assimilation?' in E. François, ed., *Immigration et Société Urbaine en Europe Occidentale, XVIe–XXe Siècle* (Paris: Editions Recherche sur le Civilisations, 1985), 81–2.

3 T. Koditschek, *Class Formation and Urban-Industrial Society: Bradford, 1750–1850* (Cambridge: Cambridge University Press, 1990), 100.

4 M. Anderson, *Family Structure in Nineteenth Century Lancashire* (Cambridge: Cambridge University Press, 1971), 38.

5 C.G. Pooley and J. Turnbull, *Migration and Mobility in Britain since the Eighteenth Century* (London: UCL Press, 1998), 13.

6 M. Anderson, 'The social implications of demographic change', in F.M.L. Thompson, ed., *The Cambridge Social History of Britain 1750–1950, vol. II: People and Their Environment* (Cambridge: Cambridge University Press, 1990), 6.

7 C.G. Pooley and J.C. Doherty, 'The longitudinal study of migration: Welsh migration to English towns in the nineteenth century', in C.G. Pooley and I.D. Whyte, eds, *Migrants, Emigrants and Immigrants: A Social History of Migration* (London: Routledge, 1991), 166–7.

8 Anderson, *Family Structure*, 39.

9 Pooley and Doherty, 'Longitudinal study', 167–9.

10 J.G. Williamson, *Coping with City Growth during the British Industrial Revolution* (Cambridge: Cambridge University Press, 1990), 40.

11 Koditschek, *Class Formation*, 101–2.

12 L. Lees, *Exiles of Erin: Irish Migrants in Victorian London* (Ithaca: Cornell University Press, 1979), 39.

13 Pooley and Turnbull, *Migration and Mobility*, 15.

14 Anderson, *Family Structure*, 40.

15 Pooley and Doherty, 'Longitudinal study', 166.

16 M. Dupree, *Family Structure in the Staffordshire Potteries 1840–1880* (Oxford: Clarendon Press, 1995), 91.

17 Pooley and Doherty, 'Longitudinal study', 167.

18 Lees, *Exiles of Erin*, 40–1.

19 Pooley and Turnbull, *Migration and Mobility*, 159.

20 Anderson, *Family Structure*, 156.

21 Lees, *Exiles of Erin*, 92.

22 R. Lawton, 'Mobility in nineteenth century British cities', *Geographical Journal* 145 (1979), 218.

23 Dupree, *Family Structure*, 89–90.

24 Anderson, *Family Structure*, 101, 102.

25 Lees, *Exiles of Erin*, 132.

26 Anderson, *Family Structure*, 155.

27 Lees, *Exiles of Erin*, 91.

28 C.M. Law, 'The growth of urban population in England and Wales, 1801–1911', *Transactions of the Institute of British Geographers* 41 (1967), 130; P.J. Waller, *Town, City, and Nation: England 1850–1914* (Oxford: Oxford University Press, 1983), 7.

29 P. Joyce, *Work, Society and Politics: The Culture of the Factory in Later Victorian England* (New Brunswick: Rutgers University Press, 1980), 104; R. Dennis, *English Industrial Cities of the Nineteenth Century: A Social Geography* (Cambridge: Cambridge University Press, 1984), 44.

30 Williamson, *Coping with City Growth*, 18.

31 S.J.D. Green, *Religion in the Age of Decline: Organisation and Experience in Industrial Yorkshire, 1870–1920* (Cambridge: Cambridge University Press, 1996), 52–3.

32 J. Herson, 'Migration, "community" or integration? Irish families in Victorian Stafford,' in R. Swift and S. Gilley, eds, *The Irish in Victorian Britain: The Local Dimension* (Dublin: Four Courts Press, 1999), 167–8, 185.

33 Koditschek, *Class Formation*, 216–17; see also R. Rodger, *Housing in Urban Britain, 1780–1914* (Cambridge: Cambridge University Press, 1989), 2.

34 L. Davidoff and C. Hall, *Family Fortunes: Men and Women of the English Middle Class, 1780–1850* (Chicago: University of Chicago Press, 1987), 57, 369.

35 D. Cannadine, 'Victorian cities: how different?' *Social History* 4 (1977), 464–5; idem, 'Residential differentiation in nineteenth-century towns: from shapes on the ground to shapes in society', in J.H. Johnson and C.G. Pooley, eds, *The Structure of Nineteenth Century Cities* (London: Croom Helm, 1982), 247; D. Cannadine, *The Rise and Fall of Class in Britain* (New York: Columbia University Press, 1999), 87.

36 Dennis, *English Industrial Cities*, 112.

37 Koditschek, *Class Formation*, 449; M. Hewitt, *The Emergence of Stability in the Industrial City: Manchester, 1832–67* (Aldershot: Scolar Press, 1996), 62–3.

38 Dennis, *English Industrial Cities*, 85; N. McCord and D.J. Rowe, 'Industrialisation and urban growth in north-east England', *International Review of Social History* 22 (1977), 45.

39 C. Chinn, *Poverty amidst Prosperity: The Urban Poor in England, 1834–1914* (Manchester: Manchester University Press, 1995), 79–80.

40 J. Burnett, *A Social History of Housing*, 2nd ed. (London: Methuen, 1986), 62.

41 Ibid., 60.

42 Ibid., 72–5; Chinn, *Poverty amidst Prosperity*, 82–3: Rodger, *Housing in Urban Britain*, 32–4.

43 R. Rodger, 'The Victorian building industry and the housing of the Scottish working class', in M. Doughty, ed., *Building the Industrial City* (Leicester: Leicester University Press, 1986), 153–5; Rodger, *Housing in Urban Britain*, 36–7.

44 Burnett, *Social History of Housing*, 77–8; Chinn, *Poverty amidst Prosperity*, 83–4.

45 S. Pollard, *A History of Labour in Sheffield* (Liverpool: Liverpool University Press, 1959), 18.

46 M. Daunton, *House and Home in the Victorian City: Working-Class Housing 1850–1914* (London: Edward Arnold, 1983), 12.

47 Rodger, 'The Victorian building industry', 162.

48 Chinn, *Poverty amidst Prosperity*, 164–5.

49 E. Gauldie, *Cruel Habitations: A History of Working-Class Housing 1780–1918* (New York: Harper & Row, 1974), 83.

50 F. Sheppard, *London 1808–1870: The Infernal Wen* (Berkeley: University of California Press, 1971), 289.

51 Daunton, *House and Home*, 16.

52 Koditschek, *Class Formation*, 129; A.S. Wohl, *Endangered Lives: Public Health in Victorian Britain* (London: J.M. Dent, 1983), 291.

53 L. Clarke, *Building Capitalism: Historical Change and the Labour Process in the Production of the Built Environment* (London: Routledge, 1992), 108–9.

54 Rodger, *Housing in Urban Britain*, 48–9; Burnett, *Social History of Housing*, 93–4, 157–9.

55 Burnett, *Social History of Housing*, 158.

56 Wohl, *Endangered Lives*, 96–7.

57 Rodger, 'The Victorian building industry', 157.

58 Burnett, *Social History of Housing*, 66.

59 Gauldie, *Cruel Habitations*, 74.

60 Williamson, *Coping with City Growth*, 12.

61 In 1838–42 Manchester death rates were 33.78 per thousand, compared with 33.32 in 1863–6. N. Kirk, *Growth of Working-Class Reformism in Mid-Victorian England* (Urbana: University of Illinois Press, 1985), 113.

62 Gauldie, *Cruel Habitations*, 102.

63 R. Gray, *The Labour Aristocracy in Victorian Edinburgh* (Oxford: Clarendon Press, 1976), 14.

64 W. Seccombe, *Weathering the Storm: Working-Class Families from the Industrial Revolution to the Fertility Decline* (London: Verso, 1995), 76.

65 Rodger, 'The Victorian building industry', 154, 164.

66 Wohl, *Endangered Lives*, 148–50.

67 Dupree, *Family Structure*, 100–1.

68 Seccombe, *Weathering the Storm*, 64–5; S. Ruggles, *Prolonged Connections: The Rise of the Extended Family in Nineteenth-Century England and America* (Madison: University of Wisconsin Press, 1987), 5.

69 Dupree, *Family Structure*, 102.

70 Anderson, *Family Structure*, 46; Seccombe, *Weathering the Storm*, 64.

71 R. Burr-Litchfield, 'The family and the mill: cotton mill work, family work patterns and fertility in mid-Victorian Stockport', in A.S. Wohl, ed., *The Victorian Family: Structure and Stresses* (New York: St Martin's Press, 1978), 189.

72 F. Barret-Ducrocq, *Love in the Time of Victoria: Sexuality and Desire Among Working-Class Men and Women in Nineteenth-Century London*, trans. J. Howe (New York: Penguin, 1992), 85–6.

73 D. Vincent, *Bread, Knowledge and Freedom: A Study of Nineteenth-Century Working Class Autobiography* (London: Europa Publications, 1981), 46, 54; M. Levine-Clark, *Beyond the Reproductive Body: The Politics of Women's Health and Work in Early Victorian England* (Columbus: Ohio State University Press, 2004), 132.

74 J. Gillis, *For Better, For Worse: British Marriages, 1600 to the Present* (Oxford: Oxford University Press, 1985), 251; Anderson, *Family Structure*, 77.

75 Vincent, *Bread, Knowledge and Freedom*, 83.

76 Anderson, *Family Structure*, 53.

77 Seccombe, *Weathering the Storm*, 34; Burr-Litchfield, 'The family and the mill', 191.

78 Dupree, *Family Structure*, 157.

79 Burr-Litchfield, 'The family and the mill', 192; Seccombe, *Weathering the Storm*, 62.

80 Vincent, *Bread, Knowledge and Freedom*, 67.

81 Dupree, *Family Structure*, 166.

82 Anderson, *Family Structure*, 147–9.

83 Dupree, *Family Structure*, 328, 344.

84 L. Oren, 'The welfare of women in laboring families: England, 1860–1950', in M.S. Hartman and L. Banner, eds, *Clio's Consciousness Raised: New Perspectives on the History of Women* (New York: Harper & Row, 1974), 228.

85 A.J. Hammerton, *Cruelty and Companionship: Conflict in Nineteenth-Century Married Life* (London: Routledge, 1992), 45; N. Tomes, 'A "torrent of abuse": crimes of violence between working-class men and women in London, 1840–1875', *Journal of Social History* 11 (1978), 332–3.

86 A.J. Taylor, ed. *The Standard of Living in Britain in the Industrial Revolution* (London: Methuen, 1975). P.H. Lindert and J.G. Williamson, 'English workers' living standards during the Industrial Revolution: a new look', *Economic History Review* 2nd ser. 36:1 (1983), 1–25; J.G. Williamson, 'Debating the British Industrial Revolution', *Explorations in Economic History* 24 (1987), 283.

87 Seccombe, *Weathering the Storm*, 71–80; E. Royle and J.A. Sharpe, *Modern Britain: A Social History 1750–1997*, 2nd ed. (London: Arnold, 1997), 174.

88 Williamson's attempts to quantify these factors as 'urban disamenities' is less than convincing. J.G. Williamson, 'Was the Industrial Revolution worth it? Disamenities and death in 19th century British town', *Explorations in Economic History* 19 (1982), 221–45; see the criticism in Seccombe, *Weathering the Storm*, 72–3.

CHAPTER TWO

Labour in the 'factory age'

In 1842 William Dodd published an account of miserable conditions in textile factories. Describing himself as a 'cripple,'
incapacitated through work in such a factory, Dodd emphasized the physical dangers facing factory workers due to accidents and the strain of
standing at machines through 12-hour shifts. Of those unable to continue
working, he complained, 'the great evil to be blamed is the long hours of
labour, and standing chiefly in one position'. He quoted an employer who
admitted that 'small particles of cotton and dust with which the air in most
rooms of factories is impregnated, not unfrequently lay the foundation of
distressing and fatal diseases'. Dodd also lamented that innovations in
the use of machinery intensified labour, cut wages, and reduced the size of
the workforce: 'this . . . mania at present existing among manufacturers,
to couple their machines, and do with fewer hands'. Due to the spread
of mechanization, according to Dodd, women and children could 'do the
work of men, the men were cast off, or reduced in point of wages to a level
with the women'.[1]

Dodd's account and others like it contributed to a trend in which the
textile factory dominated understandings of modern manufacturing and
work in the 'factory age'.[2] The decline of hand-loom weaving in cotton
appeared to herald a new era, representing the progress of technology
and ingenuity to some, the threat of lost ways of life to others. But the
experience of workers in textile factories should not be seen as 'typical'
of mid-Victorian labour. In fact, there was no typical work environment
in this period, only a vast range of types of employment and experiences
of workers. In the so-called 'factory age' most manufacturers were small
workshops, and shops of all sizes flourished alongside the biggest new mills.
Though power-looms displaced hand-looms in cotton, hand technology

still ruled the day in many trades. For some workers the division of labour and new technologies diluted skills and threatened traditional sources of autonomy at work. However, many older skills survived, new technology often demanded expert hands, and some workers found ways to maintain control over their work. Gender and age roles in the workplace were in flux in this period, and the experiences of men, women and children as workers differed in significant ways.

These diverse conditions in various trades and regions and even within a single trade or district grew out of the dynamic economic conditions in mid-Victorian Britain. The British population maintained double-digit growth rates each decade of the nineteenth century.[3] Pig iron output quadrupled from 1840 to 1870.[4] Expansion across the economy bred an atmosphere of chaotic competition amidst changing market conditions. Increasing capital concentration, new technologies and the collapse of traditional regulation of the labour force through apprenticeship demanded new strategies from workers and employers as they struggled over the organization of work.[5] These pressures affected workers in every town and every trade differently, but manual workers across regions and trades faced long hours, difficult conditions and economic insecurity.

Hours of labour

By present standards, workers in mid-Victorian Britain worked excessively long days. Seven-year-old Charles Shaw began work as a 'mould runner' in the Potteries in 1839: 'I had to work from between five and six o'clock in the morning, and work on till six, seven or eight o'clock at night'.[6] Though longer hours were common, 12 hours appears to have been accepted as the normal work day in many trades.[7] More than 60 hours of work in a week would not have seemed unusual to mid-Victorian working men and women, and many extended their hours during busy seasons.[8]

The work week was, however, in flux during this period. Saint Monday, the custom of not working or working shorter hours on Monday, persisted in many areas in the mid-nineteenth century. In Birmingham for example, Monday was the most popular day for weddings throughout the first half of the century. Thirty-seven per cent of all weddings in St Martin's parish church between 1791 and 1851 took place on Saint Monday.[9] An observer of Dundee power-loom weavers complained of their spending 'Saturday, Sunday and Monday . . . indulging their passion for whisky'.[10] Even when workers showed up on Mondays, they worked less. Charles Shaw recalled of Mondays: 'the place in which I worked bore a holiday aspect'.[11] In the years around mid-century some employers offered a half-holiday on Saturday, closing a couple of hours early in part to entice workers to give up Saint Monday.[12] Whether workers took Saint Monday off or enjoyed a Saturday half-holiday, the working week remained lengthy, however. One particularly egregious example involved the employer Thomas Beckett, a tinplate manufacturer, who shortened the Saturday workday by 2 hours, but added 40 minutes working time Monday to Friday, increasing the overall work week by 20 minutes.[13] In the pottery where Charles Shaw found little work done early in the week, he was forced to compensate with extended hours Wednesday to Friday, often facing 14- or 15-hour days.[14] For women who took Saint Monday off from paid work, domestic chores easily filled the time. Elizabeth Pritchard noted, 'don't work much on Monday, don't play, but do washing and fetch coals'.[15]

Though efforts to preserve Saint Monday persisted in some trades far into the nineteenth century, many workers faced short work weeks against their will. When she had work, a London needlewoman worked from 6.00 in the morning to 10.00 at night making trousers, commenting 'that is what I call my day's work'. But during slack winter months she struggled to find work for one or two days in the week.[16] North Staffordshire coal pits suffered from reduced demand in the summer, contributing to an overall average of only about five days' work per week over the year.[17]

From the coal mines to sweated manufacture in London, and in just about all other manual jobs except domestic service, the threat of slack work caused economic insecurity. In many manufacturing trades earnings dried up predictably due to seasonal slack, but also during downturns in trade cycles. Even skilled workers could not count on uninterrupted regular work to support their families. Robert Knight of the Boilermakers' Society urged skilled workers to enjoy periods when they were fully employed, 'for as certain as night will return, so surely will the clouds of depression again surround us with gloom, loss of work, and consequent suffering'.[18] Printer W.E. Adams recalled conditions in Macclesfield in early 1855: 'steady men, industrious men, have great difficulty in obtaining bread'.[19] Available work did not necessarily ensure economic security either, as families faced increased expenses during periods when they had many young, non-earning children. Historian John Foster notes that in industrial towns such as Oldham, Northampton and South Shields, 'poverty was not so much the special experiences of a particular group within the labour forces as a regular feature of the life of almost *all* working families at certain stages of their development'.[20] Despite the diversity of work experiences, workers across industries and regions experienced long hours and economic insecurity.

Scale and technology

Little else, however, was consistent across the diverse mid-Victorian economy. A common dichotomy sets out two prototypical work environments for the period: the great textile factories of the North (particularly Lancashire and the West Riding) and the small ironworks and engineering work-shops of Birmingham.[21] Factories employing hundreds of workers have attracted the most attention, appearing to be characteristic of the age. In England combined spinning and weaving firms in the cotton trade averaged 310 workers in 1850, growing to an average of 429 by 1890.[22] The average Scottish cotton mill grew in size from 216 to 304 workers between 1850 and 1867.[23] Still larger enterprises concentrated in shipbuilding and engineering on Tyneside, where 3,800 hands found work at Armstrong's engineering and ordnance works in 1863.[24] Even Armstrong's was dwarfed in this period, however, by the Dowlais ironworks in South Wales, the world's largest, employing 5,000 in 1840.

These large enterprises, though, were not typical. In the West Riding of Yorkshire woollen and worsted mills averaged 45 and 76 hands respectively in 1838.[25] By 1870 the average West Riding woollen firm still employed only 70 operatives.[26] In the main Scottish urban areas in 1851 more than four-fifths of all industrial firms employed under 20 hands.[27] In London, subcontracting to small shops proliferated in the mid-nineteenth century in manufacturing trades such as tailoring and cabinetmaking.[28] In Birmingham, small enterprises and workshops drove industrial growth.[29] The 'workshop of the world' remained an apt description of British indus-trial structure.[30]

The new factories also drew attention to technologies with the potential to transform work and the economy. In some industries competition drove intense rivalries in adopting new methods and new machines. For example, carpet manufacturers in the Midlands, Lancashire and Yorkshire struggled to apply new power-weaving technology.[31] In cotton, 80,000 power-looms competed with 300,000 hand-looms in 1829. By 1846 255,000 power-looms overwhelmed the surviving 60,000 hand-looms.[32] Even in Birmingham the number of steam engines in use expanded nearly fivefold between 1835 and 1870.[33] New techniques did not, however, always involve steam power or complex machinery. In boot manufacture, riveting (attaching the sole to the upper with nails) increasingly replaced sewing in cheap, mass-produced footwear.[34]

What is most remarkable about technology in this period, however, is that its progress was uneven and slow, despite pressures of competition and a dynamic market. According to one estimate, power-looms accounted for only 22 per cent of silk-looms in 1870.[35] Even in cotton, perhaps the most mechanized of all industries in this period, hand-mule spinning remained significant into the 1880s, and before the 1860s few employers committed exclusively to the 'self-acting' mule.[36] Advances in technology that speeded production in one part of an industry often spurred demand in parts of the industry that continued to use older methods. In lace and hosiery manufacture, for example, manufacturing machinery that increased capacity drove the expansion of hand-finishing work.[37]

A number of factors slowed the replacement of hand work in the nineteenth century. Employers facing pressure to reduce costs enjoyed alternatives to the search for more efficient machines. In the clothing and furniture industries employers subcontracted work to small masters and hired home workers, creating the 'sweated system'. They saved on production costs by paying low piece rates and shedding overhead costs. Workers faced longer hours and often enlisted family members, whose labour was necessary to make up for the reduced piece rates. Often the spread of out-work corresponded with an intensification of the division of labour. In Sheffield manufacturing a saw became a seven-step process, with different workers concentrating on grinding or toothing, for example.[38]

These strategies became attractive because machine technology brought its own problems. Many machines were unable to deliver on the glittering promises of their inventors. Some did not work effectively for decades after their introduction. For 35 years after their initial introductions, persistent problems beset steam jollies, intended to press moulds in pottery manufacture. Often, machines were adequate only for the most simple and lowest quality branches of trades. Thus, in the Potteries machines could be used to prepare the clay, but until late in the century the actual manufacture was done by hand.[39] A Sheffield file-cutter's poem expressed a hearty scepticism of the efficacy of the steam hammer: 'They say it will cut files as fast as three men and a lad,/ But two out of three, it's a fact, they are bad'.[40] Fluctuating demand also made investment in machinery risky for employers, who faced large expansions of fixed capital costs in mechanizing.[41]

Skill, sex roles and authority

New methods of production, even when they did not involve the introduction of machines, put pressure on skilled workers. Enjoying technical knowledge and authority over access to their trades, this most favoured section of the working class faced the threat of dilution, lower wages and a loss of control over work processes. Despite these pressures, many workers successfully defended their skilled positions or carved out new responsibilities that assured their privileges. Even where new machines transformed manufacturing, they did not always eliminate the need for workers with technical ability. In engineering, mechanized lathes and other machine tools created new categories of skilled workers, fitters and turners.[42] Skilled men made up close to half the workforce in large Tyneside engineering and shipbuilding works.[43] Hugh Stowell Brown marvelled at the abilities of skilled fitters at the railway works in which he was employed: 'I have seen a fitter take two rough pieces of wrought iron of more than one pound weight each . . . chip them to a surface almost perfectly smooth, and then with files so perfect the surface that when placed one upon the other the lower piece would hang to the upper by the force of molecular attraction, as if glued to it'.[44] In cotton spinning the self-acting mule, spreading in the second third of the century, demanded a skilled hand to adjust the quadrant nut and oversee variations in the yarn.[45] The positions of these workers depended on more than technical ability, however. To preserve their status, craftsmen needed to restrict that knowledge and limit access to the trade. Mule spinners hired their own assistants, thereby controlling entry to the trade. Typographers in London limited the numbers of apprentices and defended their status.[46]

Though these workers successfully maintained their positions, some employers reorganized production, implementing more complex divisions of labour and undermining craft workers. In London cabinetmaking, for example, a subcontracting system developed in the 1830s and 1840s in which individual workers specialized in sawing, turning, fretcutting, polishing, upholstery or carving. The organization of skilled cabinetmakers decried this 'sub-division of labour, which diminishes the necessity of skill in certain productions'.[47] Subdivided outwork also spread in tailoring and in shoemaking, in which the process of 'making' the shoe was divided into riveting and finishing, diluting the skill of the shoemaker.[48]

Highly skilled workers, who were overwhelmingly adult men, faced another threat through the substitution of low-paid child or female labour for their own. Carpet manufacturers hired increasing numbers of boys, originally as assistants to the adult men who worked the looms. These 'creelers' worked for the manufacturers, not the weavers themselves, and the employers soon sought to expand their numbers and responsibilities, placing these boys at the looms to do the jobs of weavers.[49] As subcontracting and subdivision increased in London tailoring, so did the presence of women workers. The women who sewed seams or buttonholes earned far lower wages than did the skilled men who could manufacture entire garments.[50]

Skill distinctions were closely linked to age and sex roles. The work of children played a crucial role in early industrialization, in mines, factories and domestic manufacturing. As child labour conditions in mines and factories became widely publicized, government regulation reduced its importance. Legislation in 1833, 1842 and 1844 restricted the hours and conditions of young workers. Though children continued to work in the preparatory phases of many trades, as learners, and in home manufacturing and small workshops, the overall importance of child labour declined.[51] With this decline, gender roles in the workforce grew increasingly important.

With few exceptions, jobs in the Victorian economy were done either by men or women, but not by both. The most common job for women, an overwhelmingly female one, was domestic service. In 1851 about one in ten British women worked as a domestic servant.[52] Even in industries employing both men and women, jobs were generally segregated by sex. In the manufacture of pearl buttons, for example, men cut the material and turned it on a lathe, while women drilled holes and polished the buttons.[53] In the Courtauld silk mill in Essex over half the workers were women weavers. No men worked looms in the mill; the men maintained the machinery, worked as overseers, or did clerical work.[54] Women earned lower wages than did men, and were considered unskilled.

Even in the unusual cases in which men and women held similar jobs, women earned less. In Glasgow both men and women minded self-acting mules, but men worked the finer counts of thread, and this work paid higher wages.[55] Both men and women worked as cotton weavers in Lancashire mills and they earned the same piece rates. Yet men worked more overtime, often wove heavier cloth that paid higher piece rates, ran more looms than women did, and tuned their own machines. Though cotton weaving was more equitable than any other trade, even in these mills men earned more and were seen as more skilled.[56]

To some extent, definitions of skill reflected actual technical ability, and men monopolized this knowledge as boys became apprentices and learners on track to become skilled and relatively well-paid workers. In lace making, boys worked as threaders and could eventually move into the adult men's jobs as twisters. Girls, on the other hand, worked as bobbin winders, which did not lead to advancement into the ranks of skilled workers. Sometimes, though, the distinction between skilled and unskilled work was an imagined one. Women's work, even when it was difficult like many sewing tasks, was simply assumed to be unskilled, and paid accordingly low wages.[57] The creation and perpetuation of this division of labour between men and women reflects the dynamic interaction of interests and ideologies held by workers and employers.

Many male workers believed that it was in their interest to restrict women's access to their trades. When John Brinton added a new form of loom to weave carpets in his works, the union of male weavers struck to prevent women from operating the new machines. Similar strikes occurred in the tailoring, hosiery and silk industries.[58] In 1833 Glasgow spinners struck against the employment of women. The men's union argued against women's employment (at lower pay) and harassed and intimidated women workers. Eventually, the employer agreed to pay women similar piece rates (though women generally worked smaller mules and thus still earned less).[59] When employers sought to substitute women for men, the men often fought back.[60]

On the other hand, it was often in employers' interests to replace male workers with low-paid female labour. In many cases employers developed factory manufacturing on a foundation of women's labour, with few male employees. The Courtauld silk factory employed 1,089 in 1861 and only 189 were male.[61] The factory workforce in Bradford, a centre of worsted fabric manufacturing, illustrates the advantages of employing women. In 1833 adult men in Bradford factories earned an average of 23s. 6d. per week. Women in the same factories averaged only 9s. 2d. in weekly wages. Perhaps not surprisingly only 6 per cent of workers in these factories were men.[62] In addition, fewer women belonged to unions, which made them appear a more amenable workforce in employers' eyes.

However, an increasing stress on women's vulnerability and domestic responsibilities moderated some employers' efforts to feminize their workforces, and many male workers also embraced these ideas.[63] The notion that men should be the primary breadwinners while women were responsible for the home spread in both middle-class and working-class culture.[64] The Scottish Typographical Society warned that allowing women to be printers 'unfit them for the active and paramount duties of female society'. Scottish tailors complained that young women who sought employment before taking 'their proper place as the wife' would depress the wages of those 'that later in life may have to support them'.[65] Male workers professed concern for the morality of women workers as well.[66] Employers accepted some of these arguments, embracing the definition of skill as a masculine preserve, for example.[67] Supervisory roles remained the jobs of men, even when the workers being supervised were women, as in the Courtauld silk factory.[68]

Employers also clung to the assumption that women were incapable of repairing machinery, reserving these jobs for men. One particularly obvious example of ideology trumping employer interests involved the marriage bar. In many trades employers refused to hire married women, even though this strategy was more likely to cost employers than benefit them economically.[69] In Glasgow men continued to dominate spinning on fine counts, which paid the highest wages, even though women workers were plentiful and experienced as spinners.[70] Though it did not prevent the employment of women in many low-paid jobs, ideas about women's unfitness for industrial work and the male breadwinner model tempered the trend towards feminization in industry.

Though restricted to low-paid jobs, women and children contributed significantly to their household budgets. Even skilled men in the Cowans' paper mill near Edinburgh brought in, on average, only 44 per cent of their families' incomes.[71] Overall, about a third of the industrial workforce in mid-century Britain was female, and in textiles the proportion was much higher.[72] Employed women not only faced long hours and low wages, they also remained responsible for domestic work, with minimal help from their husbands.[73] A London tailor in the low-quality 'slop-trade' noticed the burdens facing his wife: 'Now she slaves night and day, as I do: and very often she has less rest than myself, for she has to stop up after I have gone to bed to attend to her domestic duties'.[74] The employment of older children remained important as well: 88 per cent of Preston boys aged 14 were employed.[75]

In the diverse mid-Victorian economy, patterns of authority and autonomy at work varied widely. In some factories, such as Bradford's worsted mills, employers or foremen asserted direct and effective control.[76] In a far more common pattern, even in large-scale works, layers of authority distributed control over work in complex patterns. In the Wedgwood pottery works, overseers exerted responsibility over teams of workers. Within these teams some of the more skilled workers paid and presumably managed the work of their own assistants (who were mostly women and children).[77] Cotton spinners in Lancashire employed and disciplined their piecers.[78] This subcontracting system relieved employers of the burdens of recruitment, discipline and oversight, while giving skilled spinners autonomy and authority. In tailoring and other trades in which sweated outwork spread, increasingly deskilled and impoverished workers worked at their own pace in their own homes, without the oversight of an employer. Despite their autonomy at work, low pay made it necessary for them to work long hours to scratch out a meagre living.[79]

In many mid-Victorian workplaces control over the process and discipline of work became a source of struggle and negotiation.[80] In engineering, fierce conflict accompanied the development of a piece-work system that included investing a 'piece master' with authority to hire and oversee workers. Although the workers were defeated on this and other issues in a lockout in 1852, piece work remained atypical in engineering works.[81] At a Tyneside locomotive factory the employer's efforts to impose discipline on his workers included fines for making excessive noise, smoking, and leaving without informing a foreman. The regulations even prohibited leaving by 'any Door other than that adjoining the Office'. Despite efforts like this, engineering workers maintained a good deal of autonomy. Among the first tasks learned by an apprentice was 'keeping nix', 'keeping a bright look-out for the approach of managers or foremen . . . to give prompt and timely notice to men who may be skulking, or having a sly read or smoke, or who are engaged on "corporation work" – that is, work of their own'.[82] Dyke Wilkinson became an apprentice in Birmingham in the 1840s. He learned to carve out autonomy in the workplace, keeping a book open on his bench while working. He constructed a false tool rack in which to hide the book when 'Mr John' appeared. When his employer entered the workshop in slippers in order to surprise the workers, they pelted him with 'rotten potatoes, stale bread', etc. 'You are no master of mine' Wilkinson told him, 'but only a man who buys my labour for a good deal less than it is worth'.[83] Thus, workers, particularly skilled men, retained some autonomy in the workplace. Unskilled men, women and children often worked under the authority of a male worker, rather than under the direct supervision of an employer or manager.

Industrial conflict

Throughout this period unions organized a small slice of the workforce, primarily skilled men. Out of a total working-class population of just over 20 million, about a quarter of a million workers belonged to unions in 1850, and twice as many were unionists in 1870.[84] Union membership fluctuated, depending on overall economic conditions (growing during booms, shrinking in depressions) and local situations in particular trades.[85] The Masons' Union, for example, doubled its membership during the 1860s, a period in which it enjoyed a number of victories in conflicts with employers. However, membership dropped by 24 per cent from 1868 to 1870 after significant defeats.[86] Skilled workers most commonly possessed the resources, bargaining position and craft traditions that supported unionization. Significant exceptions to the narrow skilled basis of unions existed in cotton weaving and coal mining, in which unions adopted more open and inclusive approaches.[87]

Unions were legal, but the law circumscribed their activities. Despite overturning a strict prohibition on unions 1824, Parliament quickly restricted worker organizations to questions of wages and working hours and outlawed most picketing.[88] The situation improved somewhat in 1859, when a law allowed peaceful pickets in legal trade disputes (those concerning hours or wages).[89] Unions suffered important setbacks in the following dozen years, however. In an 1866 court case, *Hornby* v. *Close*, the judges refused to back a union that sought to recover funds from a dishonest treasurer and raised broader questions about the legality of unions. Though a new Trade Union Act passed in 1871 protected union funds, a Criminal Law Amendment Act broadened the prohibitions on strike behaviour. For example, strikers could be jailed for hooting at strike-breakers. The following year a case found that threatening to strike on behalf of a co-worker dismissed for union activity constituted a criminal conspiracy.[90] Throughout this period workers faced intimidation and prosecution based on master and servant laws that made violations of contract on the part of workers criminal offences. Only in 1875 did unions and their members obtain adequate legal standing, as union activities became illegal only if they included conduct criminal in other contexts, and the inequities of the master and servant laws were undone.[91]

In addition to these legal problems, unions at mid-century confronted fierce middle-class hostility. During the 1859–60 building strike *The Times* defended employers who demanded that workers sign 'the document' assuring that they belonged to no union: a union 'binds a man to one of the most unjust and mischievous codes ever devised, depriving him, for example of the use of his hands for an hour, while the master's document binds him to nothing at all but to be his own master'.[92] Unionization was an anathema to established political economy, which denied that unions could control wages and objected to attempts to restrict economic activity.[93] Employers cooperated in efforts to crush union activity. In the 1859–60 building strike the Central Association of Master Builders organized strike-breakers and drafted 'the document'. Its 'Anti-Strike Committee' sought to 'set the men free from the ruinous tyranny of "society" despots, and the pernicious influence of unions'.[94] In the late 1860s, however, a number of employers grew more willing to accept roles for unions, particularly if union leaders could function as 'managers of discontent', helping to contain conflicts between employers and workers.[95] Some political economists also moderated their categorical opposition to unionization in the 1860s.[96]

Many labour conflicts involved struggle over wages. Through most of this period wage disagreements caused more strikes by masons than any other type of conflict, though in the 1860s struggles over control grew more common.[97] In cotton districts employers imposed wage cuts during downturns and workers sought increases when business was good, sparking numerous strikes and lockouts. For example, during a downturn in 1847 employers cut wages 10 per cent. In 1853, when the cotton trade had revived, workers sought the restoration of their wages. In Stockport and Blackburn strikers won the 10 per cent increase. In Preston, however, employers decided to take on the union, with the organized support of other cotton masters from around the district. The 28-week lockout involved 26,000 workers and ended in defeat for the workers.[98]

The 1853–4 Preston lockout shows that, even when wage issues touched off industrial conflict, control and union recognition often became the central issues between employers and workers. In Preston workers sought a standard list of prices across mills, including a 10 per cent increase. Employers enforced the lockout against the specific wage demand and the notion of a standard union list: 'to this spirit of tyranny and dictation the masters can no longer submit'.[99] The establishment of standard rate lists in cotton weaving and spinning exemplifies the links between wages and union recognition. The Blackburn weaving list, created in 1853, institutionalized the union's role by requiring union representatives to inspect the looms. At Padiham workers struck to win the Blackburn list in 1859. Employers offered a wage increase of 10 per cent, though this still fell short of the Blackburn standard. More importantly, they adamantly refused to allow the union secretary to inspect their machinery. After 29 weeks the workers won and employers had to accept the union role. Though ostensibly about wages, these conflicts quickly became struggles over union recognition and control.[100]

Critics of trade unions in this period have focused on elitism, bureaucratization and moderation, particularly after 1850.[101] Many unions fought to exclude women and unskilled labourers from their trades. They tended to focus on the specific concerns of skilled workers. Attempts to move beyond sectional concerns and form national labour organizations across trades attracted scant support.[102] Yet some unions did move beyond narrow sectionalism, helping other workers organize and strike. The London Compositors, for example, supported the builders' unions in the 1859 conflict, sent funds to striking cork cutters, and even loaned their counterparts in Paris £400 to support their union.[103] Scottish unions organized in local trades councils that supported the organization of unskilled workers.[104]

As organizations of skilled workers grew and a few amalgamated across the country, their leaders made significant alliances with middle-class Liberals and cultivated moderate images. Unions such as the Amalgamated Society of Engineers (ASE) emphasized unemployment, sickness, disability and funeral benefits. Union leaders concerned to protect their organizations' resources and improve public perceptions of unions tried to avoid costly and controversial strikes. William Allan of the ASE testified before a Royal Commission that 'the executive council does all it can to prevent strikes'.[105] Some important union officials moved into Liberal political circles. Union leaders Robert Applegarth and George Potter, at odds over other issues concerning the leadership of the labour movement, both cooperated closely with the Liberal Party.[106]

Despite the apparent moderation of union leaders, however, industrial conflict remained widespread in this period. A list of the most famous and largest conflicts would include the masons' strike in 1841, the widespread strike in Lancashire, Cheshire and parts of the Midlands in 1842 (often called the 'Plug Riots'), the 1852 engineering lockout, the Preston and other cotton strikes of 1853–4, the Midlands glassmakers' strike in 1858–9, the nine-hours movements among builders in 1859–60 and on Clydeside in 1866 and the 1866 strike of Sheffield ironworkers.[107] A focus on these 'highlights' obscures the much greater frequency of local and short-lived conflicts. In engineering, for example, strikes in the 1850s and 1860s tended to focus on particular firms or small informal associations of firms. In 1866 workers at Beyer, Peacock & Co., a Manchester locomotive firm, struck against a foreman whom they considered unqualified. After two months the firm conceded and dismissed the foreman.[108] Despite its leader William Allan's stated opposition to strikes, the ASE supported this and other strikes, including financially supporting 179 strikes by other unions in a 13-year period in the 1850s and 1860s.[109]

Even when union officials remained uninvolved or opposed strikes, local worker initiatives led to conflict with employers. Following the engineers' defeat in the massive lockout of 1852, the ASE left the negotiation of working conditions to specific workshops and district committees.[110] At times, the ASE executive sought to restrain local organizations without success. In 1863 the Manchester District Committee printed placards against piece work. When the union authorities instructed them to remove the placards, the district committee refused.[111] Local initiative also held sway in the building trades. Between 1850 and 1875, for example, the majority of masons' strikes involved 20 or fewer workers. Even the major 1859–60 lockout began when employees of a single employer struck without the approval of the union leadership.[112] Attempts to build district-wide unions in coal mining foundered on the persistent autonomy and militancy of local communities. When a successful organization developed in North-umberland, its leadership's moderation did not prevent 23 strikes in a 22-year period in the village of West Cramlington alone.[113] Though the South Lancashire Weavers' Union sought to control militants, the leader-ship's efforts could not prevent cotton workers in Ashton and Stalybridge from striking in 1861.[114]

Some industrial conflicts did not involve formal union organizations at all. This pattern is particularly apparent in the building trades, where informal work groups formed the basis for widespread actions against employers.[115] Carpenters and joiners in Leeds presented demands for work rules and hours' reductions. The workers' committee represented union and non-union men and made no mention of any union organization. The workers won most of their demands at the end of a two-week lockout.[116] Bricklayers imposed limits on their own productivity, defining a standard of 800 bricks per day, though the union had no official policy on the matter. In shipbuilding and engineering, informal work groups initiated struggles with employers. The massive Clyde conflict of 1865–6 had its origins among semi-skilled workers, whose action eventually dragged the unionized and skilled workers into a strike over the nine-hour day.[117] Non-unionized female textile workers in Scotland staged numerous small strikes, including one in February 1863 involving 260 weavers against Ebenezer Hendry & Sons.[118]

Thus, statements of union leaders such as William Allan must be read carefully, as they represent efforts to put a moderate face on unions in order to neutralize hostility in the public and Parliament.[119] The persistent contention over wages, control and even union recognition drew its energy from rank and file workers and local organizations, at times in defiance of more moderate union bureaucrats. This continued militancy, however, was most often restricted to the skilled male workers who defended their relatively privileged positions against other workers. They fought these battles within the capitalist system, challenging employers' control but not their ownership of the means of production or right to profit.[120]

Conclusion

These workers accepted the legitimacy of the complex and varied mid-Victorian capitalist economy. Despite its complexity, manual workers shared the experience of labour. Work meant long hours in dirty, often hot and unhealthy conditions. Workers considered manual labour a crucial facet of their identities as working class. Thus, in Manchester warehouses, both clerks and packers worked long hours. The clerks worked in a clean environment, used literacy and numeracy at work and did not perform manual labour. They were clear in distinguishing themselves from workers. Packers, on the other hand, worked large machines that pressed bales of cotton goods for shipping. Manual labour, along with the economic insecurity that accompanied it, distinguished the working class in the middle decades of the nineteenth century.[121]

Notes

1   W. Dodd, *The Factory System Illustrated: In a Series of Letters to the Right Hon. Lord Ashley* ([1842]; London: Frank Cass, 1968), 129, 139, 68, 221.

2   R. Gray, *The Factory Question and Industrial England, 1830–1860* (Cambridge: Cambridge University Press, 1996), 23–4, 238–9.

3   P. Mathias, *The First Industrial Nation: An Economic History of Britain 1700–1914*, 2nd ed. (London: Methuen, 1983), 221.

4   B. Murphy, *A History of the British Economy 1740–1970* (London: Longman, 1973), 542.

5   R. Price, 'Structures of subordination in nineteenth-century British industry', in P. Thane, G. Crossick and R. Floud, eds, *The Power of the Past: Essays for Eric Hobsbawm* (Cambridge: Cambridge University Press, 1984), 122.

6   'An old potter', in J. Burnett, ed., *Useful Toil: Autobiographies of Working People from the 1820s to the 1920s* (Harmondsworth: Penguin, 1977), 299.

7   E. Hopkins, 'Working hours and conditions during the Industrial Revolution: a reappraisal', *Economic History Review* 2nd ser., 35 (1982), 55, 58; M. Dupree, *Family Structure in the Staffordshire Potteries 1840–1880* (Oxford: Clarendon Press, 1995), 60, 70; H. Cunningham, 'Leisure and culture', in F.M.L. Thomson, ed., *The Cambridge Social History of Britain, vol. II: People and their Environment* (Cambridge: Cambridge University Press, 1990), 281; E. Roberts, *Women's Work 1840–1940* (Cambridge: Cambridge University Press, 1995), 20.

8   P. Joyce, *Work, Society and Politics: The Culture of the Factory in Victorian England* (New Brunswick: Rutgers University Press, 1980), 74; E.P. Thompson and E. Yeo, eds, *The Unknown Mayhew* (New York: Schocken, 1971), 110–25, 147, 150.

9 D.A. Reid, 'Weddings, weekdays, work and leisure in urban England 1791–1911: the decline of Saint Monday revisited', *Past and Present* 153 (1996), 145ff.

10 W.W. Knox, *Industrial Nation: Work, Culture and Society in Scotland, 1800-Present* (Edinburgh: Edinburgh University Press, 1999), 45.

11 'An old potter', 301. Shaw reports the holiday atmosphere existed on Tuesday as well.

12 D.A. Reid, 'The decline of Saint Monday 1766–1866', *Past and Present* 71 (1976), 86–7.

13 Reid, 'Saint Monday', 89–90.

14 'An old potter', 302.

15 Reid, 'Saint Monday', 92.

16 Thompson and Yeo, *Unknown Mayhew*, 147.

17 Dupree, *Family Structure*, 70.

18 K. McClelland, 'Time to work, time to live: some aspects of work and the re-formation of class in Britain, 1850–1880', in P. Joyce, ed., *The Historical Meanings of Work* (Cambridge: Cambridge University Press, 1987), 186.

19 D. Thompson, *The Chartists: Popular Politics in the Industrial Revolution* (New York: Pantheon Books, 1984), 331.

20 J. Foster, *Class Struggle and the Industrial Revolution: Early Industrial Capitalism in Three English Towns* (New York: St Martin's Press, 1974), 96; see also T. Koditschek, *Class Formation and Urban-Industrial Society: Bradford, 1750–1850* (Cambridge: Cambridge University Press, 1990), 448.

21 A. Briggs, *Victorian Cities* (Harmondsworth: Penguin, 1968), 186.

22 Joyce, *Work, Society and Politics*, 158–9.

23 D.T. Jenkins, 'The cotton industry in Yorkshire, 1780–1900', *Textile History* 10 (1979), 76.

24 McClelland, 'Time to work', 181.

25 P. Hudson, *The Industrial Revolution* (London: Edward Arnold, 1992), 119.

26 Joyce, *Work, Society and Politics*, 160.

27 R. Rodger, 'Concentration and fragmentation: capital, labour, and the structure of mid-Victorian Scottish industry', *Journal of Urban History* 14:2 (1988), 188–9.

28 D. Blankenhorn, ' "Our class of workmen": the cabinet-makers revisited', in R. Harrison and J. Zeitlin, eds, *Divisions of Labour: Skilled Workers and Technological Change in Nineteenth Century England* (Urbana:

University of Illinois Press, 1985), 35; Thompson and Yeo, *Unknown Mayhew*, 181ff.

29 Hopkins, 'Working hours', 55.

30 R. Price, *Labour in British Society: An Interpretative History* (London: Routledge, 1986), 71.

31 S. Rose, *Limited Livelihoods: Gender and Class in Nineteenth-Century England* (Berkeley: University of California Press, 1993), 106.

32 P.A. Pickering, *Chartism and the Chartists in Manchester and Salford* (Basingstoke: Macmillan, 1995), 29.

33 Reid, 'Saint Monday', 85.

34 R. Samuel, 'The workshop of the world: steam power and hand technology in mid-Victorian Britain', *History Workshop Journal* 3 (1977), 50.

35 J. Lown, *Women and Industrialization: Gender at Work in Nineteenth-Century England* (Minneapolis: University of Minnesota Press, 1990), 40 n. 41.

36 Samuel, 'Workshop of the world', 19.

37 Rose, *Limited Livelihoods*, 20.

38 Samuel, 'Workshop of the world', 49–51.

39 Dupree, *Family Structure*, 243.

40 D. Smith, *Conflict and Compromise: Class Formation in English Society 1830–1914* (London: Routledge & Kegan Paul, 1982), 40.

41 Samuel, 'Workshop of the world', 51–5.

42 J. Zeitlin, 'Engineers and compositors: a comparison', in Harrison and Zeitlin, eds, *Divisions of Labour*, 199; K. Burgess, *The Origins of British Industrial Relations: The Nineteenth Century Experience* (London: Croom Helm, 1975), 12.

43 McClelland, 'Time to work', 181.

44 Samuel, 'Workshop of the world', 41.

45 M. Freifeld, 'Technological change and the "self-acting" mule: a study of skill and the sexual division of labour', *Social History* 11:3 (1986), 323–7.

46 Price, *Labour in British Society*, 79, 81; F. Hunt, 'Opportunities lost and gained: mechanization and women's work in the London bookbinding and printing trades', in A.V. John, ed., *Unequal Opportunities: Women's Employment in England 1800–1918* (Oxford: Basil Blackwell, 1986), 77–9; Zeitlin, 'Engineers and compositors', 193–4.

47 Blankenhorn, 'Cabinet-makers', 41.

48 Samuel, 'Workshop of the world', 50.

49 Rose, *Limited Livelihoods*, 107.

50 J. Morris, 'The characteristics of sweating: the late-nineteenth-century London and Leeds tailoring trade', in John, ed., *Unequal Opportunities*, 111; B. Taylor, *Eve and the New Jerusalem: Socialism and Feminism in the Nineteenth Century* (New York: Pantheon Books, 1983), 114–16.

51 S. Horrell and J. Humphries, ' "The exploitation of little children": child labor and the family economy in the Industrial Revolution', *Explorations in Economic History* 32 (1995), 487, 500–1.

52 Roberts, *Women's Work*, 19.

53 Hudson, *Industrial Revolution*, 125.

54 Lown, *Women and Industrialization*, 45–50.

55 E. Gordon, *Women and the Labour Movement in Scotland 1850–1914* (Oxford: Clarendon Press, 1991), 47.

56 Rose, *Limited Livelihoods*, 157–9.

57 Ibid., 25–9.

58 Ibid., 104, 108.

59 A. Clark, *The Struggle for the Breeches: Gender and the Making of the British Working Class* (Berkeley: University of California Press, 1995), 212–13; Gordon, *Women and the Labour Movement*, 49–50.

60 Rose, *Limited Livelihoods*, 5–6.

61 Lown, *Women and Industrialization*, 43.

62 Koditschek, *Class Formation*, 360.

63 M. Levine-Clark, *Beyond the Reproductive Body: The Politics of Women's Health and Work in Early Victorian England* (Columbus: Ohio State University Press, 2004), 22, 48.

64 L. Davidoff and C. Hall, *Family Fortunes: Men and Women of the English Middle Class, 1780–1850* (Chicago: University of Chicago Press, 1987); Clark, *Struggle for the Breeches*; W. Seccombe, 'Patriarchy stabilized: the construction of the male breadwinner wage norm in nineteenth-century Britain', *Social History* 11 (1986), 55.

65 W.H. Fraser, *A History of British Trade Unionism 1700–1998* (New York: St Martin's Press, 1999), 49, 74.

66 Gordon, *Women and the Labour Movement*, 82–5.

67 Rose, *Limited Livelihoods*, 22–3.

68 Lown, *Women and Industrialization*, 49.

69 Rose, *Limited Livelihoods*, 28, 46–7.

70 Gordon, *Women and the Labour Movement*, 46–9, 54.

71 J.C. Holley, 'The two family economies of industrialism: factory workers in Victorian Scotland', *Journal of Family History* 6 (1981), 59, 63–4.

72 W. Seccombe, *Weathering the Storm: Working-Class Families from the Industrial Revolution to the Fertility Decline* (London: Verso, 1995), 32; Mathias, *First Industrial Nation*, 239.

73 Rose, *Limited Livelihoods*, 164–5; Lown, *Women and Industrialization*, 74; Clark, *Struggle for the Breeches*, 256.

74 Thompson and Yeo, *Unknown Mayhew*, 209.

75 M. Anderson, *Family Structure in Nineteenth Century Lancashire* (Cambridge: Cambridge University Press, 1971), 71, 75.

76 Joyce, *Work, Society and Politics*, 61; Koditschek, *Class Formation*, 364.

77 Dupree, *Family Structure*, 194–5.

78 W. Lazonick, 'Industrial relations and technical change: the case of the self-acting mule', *Cambridge Journal of Economics* 3 (1979), 244–5.

79 Thompson and Yeo, *Unknown Mayhew*, 122–3.

80 Price, *Labour in British Society*, 82.

81 Burgess, *Origins of British Industrial Relations*, 20–3, 26.

82 McClelland, 'Time to work', 183, 197.

83 C. Behagg, 'Secrecy, ritual and folk violence: the opacity of the workplace in the first half of the nineteenth century', in R.D. Storch, ed., *Popular Culture and Custom in Nineteenth-Century England* (London: Croom Helm, 1982), 163.

84 N. Kirk, *Change, Continuity and Class: Labour in British Society, 1850–1920* (Manchester: Manchester University Press, 1998), 62.

85 A.E. Musson, *Trade Union and Social History* (London: Frank Cass, 1974), 17.

86 R. Price, *Masters, Unions and Men: Work Control in Building and the Rise of Labour 1830–1914* (Cambridge: Cambridge University Press, 1980), 72, 62.

87 R. Gray, *The Aristocracy of Labour in Nineteenth-Century Britain, c.1850–1900* (London: Macmillan, 1981), 46; N. Kirk, *The Growth of Working-Class Reformism in Mid-Victorian England* (Urbana: University of Illinois Press, 1985), 278.

88 H. Pelling, *A History of British Trade Unionism* (London: Macmillan, 1963), 23; Fraser, *History of British Trade Unionism*, 13; M. Davis, *Comrade or Brother?: A History of the British Labour Movement 1789–1951* (London: Pluto Press, 1993), 37.

89 Pelling, *History of British Trade Unionism*, 48.

90 Fraser, *History of British Trade Unionism*, 42, 47–8.

91 Price, *Labour in British Society*, 41–2.

92 Pelling, *History of British Trade Unionism*, 45.

93 Kirk, *Working-Class Reformism*, 270.

94 Burgess, *Origins of British Industrial Relations*, 109–10.

95 Price, *Masters, Unions and Men*, 16; Joyce, *Work, Society and Politics*, 70–1; Kirk, *Working-Class Reformism*, 287–88.

96 E.F. Biagini, 'British trade unions and popular political economy, 1860–1880', *The Historical Journal* 30:4 (1987), 815.

97 Price, *Masters, Unions and Men*, 86.

98 Kirk, *Working-Class Reformism*, 247–51, 265.

99 H.I. Dutton and J.E. King, *'Ten Per Cent and No Surrender': The Preston Strike, 1853–1854* (Cambridge: Cambridge University Press, 1981), 39–40.

100 Kirk, *Working-Class Reformism*, 255, 267, 278; Fraser, *History of British Trade Unionism*, 63–4.

101 Kirk, *Change, Continuity and Class*, 5–11; Fraser, *History of British Trade Unionism*, 33–6.

102 Price, *Labour in British Society*, 83.

103 M.C. Finn, *After Chartism: Class and Nation in English Radical Politics, 1848–1874* (Cambridge: Cambridge University Press, 1993), 195.

104 Gordon, *Women and the Labour Movement*, 63.

105 Fraser, *History of British Trade Unionism*, 28, 54.

106 Burgess, *Origins of British Industrial Relations*, 102–3; Finn, *After Chartism*, 196.

107 Fraser, *History of British Trade Unionism*, 21–3, 57–61; Smith, *Conflict and Compromise*, 166–7; N. Kirk, *Labour and Society in Britain and the USA, vol. I: Capitalism, Custom and Protest, 1780–1850* (Aldershot: Scolar, 1994), 164.

108 Burgess, *Origins of British Industrial Relations*, 41.

109 Kirk, *Labour and Society, vol. I*, 168.

110 Price, *Labour in British Society*, 80.

111 Burgess, *Origins of British Industrial Relations*, 37.

112 Price, *Masters, Unions and Men*, 86, 48.

113 Burgess, *Origins of British Industrial Relations*, 180–1.

114 Kirk, *Working-Class Reformism*, 282.

115 Price, *Masters, Unions and Men*, 61–3.

116 Burgess, *Origins of British Industrial Relations*, 122–3.

117 Price, *Masters, Unions and Men*, 77, 66.

118 Gordon, *Women and the Labour Movement*, 120–2.

119 Kirk, *Labour and Society*, vol. I, 167–8.

120 Kirk, *Working-Class Reformism*, 301.

121 M. Hewitt, *The Emergence of Stability in the Industrial City: Machester, 1832–67* (Aldershot: Scolar, 1996), 39–40.

CHAPTER THREE

Leisure and the urban worker

In 1868 Thomas Wright published a fictionalized description of a skilled worker's day of leisure. In 'Bill Banks's day out', a railwayman, his wife and friends don their best clothing and meet outside a pub to go 'Saint Mondaying to Hampton Court'. After downing a quick pint they ride to the palace and tour it. They then enjoy an ample dinner with plenty to drink, and Bill gets involved in an argument with another excursionist who insulted him. The party then returns to town and spends the evening at the Alhambra music hall in Leicester Square, arriving home in atypical style by hiring a cab.[1] The pleasures embraced by mid-Victorian workers such as Bill Banks developed out of well-established popular pastimes, often transformed to suit the new urban environment. Despite the gradual regularization of working hours, Saint Monday and traditional festival days died hard. Fairs and wakes thrived by taking advantage of new audiences brought by rail. Excursions were special occasions, but when regular work days ended, men and women continued to slake their thirsts and seek entertainment in pubs. A vibrant and unruly street life developed in crowded urban neighbourhoods. As entrepreneurs sought to take advantage of new opportunities for profit in the provision of leisure, they created new commercialized amusement, most notably the music hall. In the face of efforts of radicals and middle-class reformers, drink, gambling and raucous conviviality remained central to mid-Victorian working-class leisure.

Popular leisure in the early nineteenth century

The vibrant popular leisure culture of the late eighteenth and early nineteenth centuries formed the raw material for mid-nineteenth-century working-class leisure. A calendar of festivals with highlights around Christmas, Easter,

Whitsun and a summer season of fairs and wakes (festivals with their origins in the dedication of churches) offered opportunities for celebration and enjoyment. Popular amusements were generally raucous, sometimes violent, and often competitive. At Derby, Shrove Tuesday and Ash Wednesday were occasions for games of street football. Hundreds of men and boys on each side sought to carry a ball across one of the goals set up on either side of town. Alongside the games, violent brawling, encouraged by heavy drinking, surged 'at random through the streets, down alleyways, across gardens, in and out of the River Derwent'.[2] At wakes, processions of rushcarts grew competitive, and rivalries often bred violent fights.[3] Even silly competitions were popular, as in a Manchester pub where the publican provided a leg of mutton tied to the top of a well-greased pole, 'to amuse his tired customers, and fill his pockets with their hard-earned pennies'.[4] Local landed elites often supported this popular leisure culture. At Revesby, Lincolnshire, Sir Joseph Banks described his responsibility in 1783 for the local fair: 'I am to feed and make drunk everyone who chooses to come, which will cost me in beef and ale near 20 pounds'.[5]

Despite this elite sponsorship, popular leisure's violence, drunkenness and disorder attracted increasing criticism in the early nineteenth century. Legal prohibitions sought to eliminate blood sports. Bull-baiting, in which dogs were set upon an animal tied up in a ring, was banned in 1835.[6] Radicals also developed a critique of popular leisure in the late eighteenth and early nineteenth centuries. William Cobbett railed against the model of class cooperation represented in elite patronage of popular amusements, asking whether Preston workers 'will again suffer yourselves to be cajoled by ten or a dozen of poor fowls being set a fighting, and three or four horses set a galloping, by the family of Stanley'.[7] Radical leader Henry Vincent advocated education, sobriety and improvement, urging early Chartists to 'fill their minds with knowledge' and 'keep away from pothouse contagion'.[8] Popular non-conformity shared this hostility to rowdiness and drunkenness. Methodist leaders complained of wakes, in which people engaged in 'eating and drinking intemperately; talking prophanely, or at least unprofitably; in laughing and jesting, fornication and adultery'.[9]

Early and mid-Victorian working-class leisure

Despite the hostility of radicals and religious activists, drinking places remained centres of popular relaxation outside the home. According to one 1853 estimate, 70 per cent of working men spent their evenings in pubs.[10] Pubs offered comfort, sociability and a range of services from gambling to labour exchanges, making participation in pub culture natural for working-class men.[11] Pub owners began to invest in larger premises with bright lights, mirrors and plate glass, and elaborate decorations.[12] Growing more numerous and increasingly commercialized, the corner pub maintained its established place in popular leisure.

Some pubs offered libraries and newspapers and organized discussions of political topics.[13] These activities tapped into well-established traditions of radical culture that valued literacy and education. A Mechanics' Institute in Cheltenham threw off middle-class patronage and came under the control of radical working-class men. It developed a wide-ranging library collection including literature, books on science, periodicals and cheap popular reading. Radical political works by Cobbett, Paine, Hunt and Cartwright were in demand at the library as well.[14] While Sunday schools provided the basics of literacy to many working-class Victorians, a commitment to self-education in their leisure time supported independent libraries and radical periodicals.[15]

The competition among drinking places led some owners to offer musical entertainment. Growing out of informal 'free and easies', singing saloons began to charge for entertainment and build larger premises, particularly in London and the North of England. In the 1840s The Grapes Inn in South London could hold 1,000 customers.[16] In 1842 The Jolly Hatters in Stockport opened a new extension, welcoming up to 500 customers, who paid 3d. and received a ticket redeemable for refreshments. As one visitor recalled, 'Shortly after I entered the room, the curtain drew up, and a young woman, in a *stylish undress*, came forward and sang "Meet me by the willow glen"; after which she was rapturously applauded, and withdrew'.[17] Performers adapted existing dances, tricks and songs, but the core of the entertainment in singing saloons came from participatory singing. Another visitor to The Jolly Hatters noted: 'At the end of every verse the audience takes up the chorus with a zest and vigour which speaks volumes – they sing, they roar, they yell, they scream, they get on the legs and waving dirty hands and ragged hats bellow again till their voices crack'.[18]

It was a small step from the large-scale singing saloons of the 1840s to the first stand-alone music halls, which spread in the following decade. They offered professional entertainment, and many music hall proprietors abandoned the refreshment ticket, relying on the appeal of the entertainers to bring in paying customers.[19] Huge showpiece halls, most notably the Alhambra in Leicester Square holding 3,500, reflected the wealth generated by this new model. Large halls also opened in the Midlands and the North. Equally important were the smaller neighbourhood music halls; 200–300 existed in London in 1856. In large halls, the entertainment grew more elaborate, with spectacles, tableaux of famous battle scenes and choruses of dancers. In the 1860s proprietors began to develop the star system, in which entertainers no longer visited and drank with the audiences, instead hustling from hall to hall to perform in many venues in a single night. Yet popular participation remained central, as audiences called out to performers, hooted and jeered in response to topical songs and sang along, often altering the words.[20]

While pubs and smaller music halls in their neighbourhoods offered escape from crowded homes, workers also made excursions to fairs, wakes, races and the seaside. Wakes and fairs remained popular throughout the first three-quarters of the century. Lancashire wakes thrived and expanded after mid-century, combining many of the established amusements, food and drink, games and entertainments, with innovations such as steam-powered rides.[21] In Birmingham a wake was revived at Deritend Pool in 1853. It was, as one journalist noted, 'a very big thing, and the whole of the community . . . seemed to turn out'. The wake survived only a few years at this site, though, as the land was leased for development.[22] Around London, new fairs appeared in the nineteenth century, even as others were abolished. The Stepney Fair revived successfully, drawing an estimated 200,000 visitors in 1844.[23] Opponents abolished the popular Greenwich Fair in 1856, but the more raucous Charlton Fair survived until 1871.[24] In Manchester a reformer and free library supporter professed to being staggered by a fair's appeal: 'the success of this boisterous rival to our noble institution in Byrom-st, so much greater than what attends upon the library during these holidays'.[25]

Crowds gathered to enjoy competition as well, particularly when it afforded an opportunity for gambling. In Warwickshire coal districts, 'when there is such a matter of universal interest as a prize-fight all must go to see it, and it is a day's play'.[26] Horse racing boomed. Around London new races were established at Harrow, Kingsbury, Croydon and elsewhere.[27] In and around Teeside increasing numbers of spectators attended large races at Stockton, Darlington, Hartlepool and Redcar, as well as numerous smaller events.[28] On Bradford Moor a crowd of 15,000 attended the races in 1856.[29] Some races grew more formalized; grounds were enclosed and admission charged. At Stockton a permanent grandstand that could hold up to a thousand people helped raise the quality of the races and the amount of prize money.[30] But many races remained less formalized and commercial, maintaining their 'rough and ready' character and potential for disorder.[31]

Gambling helps account for the persistent appeal of horse racing and prize fights, but working people would bet on almost anything, including silly contests like races to eat hot pudding, or an attempt to consume large amounts of treacle in a short time.[32] Working-class boys and men engaged in games of pitch and toss or cards.[33] Around mid-century, off-site gambling on horse racing spread, fed by a growing sports press and the extension of telegraph and rail lines. One estimate suggests that between 100 and 150 betting houses served the working-class market in London in the 1850s, accepting bets as small as 6d. An 1853 Act that banned gambling houses encouraged the proliferation of street bookies, though spotty enforcement allowed gambling houses to thrive in pubs, and also in coffee rooms and even temperance halls.[34]

Horse racing and gambling exemplify the increasing commercialization of working-class leisure in the mid-nineteenth century. Pubs grew more lavish and decorated. Music halls, though, put ordinary pubs to shame in terms of investment. Estimates of the cost of Charles Morton's rebuilt Canterbury Music Hall in Lambeth, opened in 1854, range from £25,000 to over £40,000. The 33 largest London halls in 1866 had an average capitalization of £10,000.[35] Seaside excursions created business opportunities for railways, agents, boarding-house keepers and providers of entertainment. In the 1860s pleasure piers appeared in a number of resorts, costing an estimated £20,000 to construct.[36] Circuses grew bigger, more expensive and more established, and the amusements offered at fairs became more complex and commercial.[37] Better organized and heavily capitalized, the provision of working-class leisure became big business.

Railway companies took advantage of this growing leisure culture, establishing cheap excursions to horse races, wakes, fairs, prize fights, the seaside and even hangings.[38] Railways allowed relatives and friends to travel further to visit during wakes.[39] Fairs could attract larger crowds from greater distances as well. On the first Whit Monday after the rail line opened between London and Greenwich, 35,000 passengers made the trip for the fair. The fairs at Croydon and Barnet boomed when connected to London by rail.[40] Samuel Smiles, self-help advocate and secretary of the South East Railway Company, recognized the demand for these raucous amusements, and his company offered excursions to prize fights. Perhaps the railway's greatest impact on popular leisure was to encourage excursions to the seaside or other interesting destinations. Beginning in the 1840s, Sunday schools, temperance organizations, friendly societies and even employers sponsored trips from industrial cities. Many workers could afford cheap excursions, such as those to wakes' celebrations in Lancashire.[41]

During Whit week of 1850, over 200,000 people left Manchester on cheap excursions. Rail excursions also brought millions to the Crystal Palace Exhibition in 1851.[42]

Participation in this commercialized leisure culture cost money. Because of their higher wages and women's responsibility for household expenses, men had more money to spend on drink, gambling or other amusements. In addition, as men's working hours gradually shortened, they enjoyed more time for leisure. Women still faced domestic work at home in their 'free' time. But despite men's greater access to time and money for leisure, women managed to participate in the new working-class leisure culture. Though some pubs were male preserves and drinking with work mates remained an important form of male bonding, many women also went to pubs, in groups with other women or together with men.[43] In some places a young woman entered a pub with a man as a sign of commitment.[44] Courting couples attended music halls and singing saloons as well.[45] When not courting, young men and women attended music halls in separate groups. Married women enjoyed the music hall with their husbands, though it appears that they were less likely to attend when they had small children, which constrained their earning opportunities and added to household expenses and duties.[46] Working-class women even enjoyed gambling on horses.[47]

Working-class women and men integrated leisure in their daily lives. As commons and greens fell victim to private use, the streets took on increasing importance in working-class leisure. Punch and Judy men, street singers and preachers, and all sorts of hawkers and dealers plied their trades in urban streets. One observer described the scene in Manchester: 'Itinerant bands blow and bang their loudest; organ boys grind monotonously; ballad singers or flying stationers make roaring proclamations of their wares. The street is one swarming buzzing mass of people'.[48] Local men and especially women met to trade gossip, while children played, youths promenaded flirtatiously, and pitch and toss games thrived.[49] Even traditions of the charivari lived on in urban streets. In Birmingham communal opposition to marriages that violated local standards inspired boisterous responses. When a man remarried too quickly after his wife's death, a crowd accosted the new couple and 'pelted them with eggs and slush, threw old boots and rotten fruit at them, and assailed their ears with language gross and vile'.[50] Boisterous street life unsettled outsiders, as when foot races extended into more affluent districts. In 1866 a tea dealer in Bolton was shocked by the sight of such a race, seeing 'a man pass by wearing nothing except a pair of drawers', followed by another 'running along the road in a completely nude state, with the exception of a handkerchief which was wrapped around his loins'.[51]

Repression and reform

An increasingly confident and assertive urban middle class, influenced by evangelicalism, viewed this unruly leisure culture with suspicion and attempted to reform or suppress it. Temperance, sabbatarianism and the protection of animals all militated against popular leisure habits.[52] One scandalized observer complained that 'for a whole week . . . have the streets been crowded, the . . . public houses crammed . . . witnesses of all the disgusting immorality, the ribald jesting, the cursing and profanity . . . and other nameless things, in which these fairs and feasts abound'.[53] Another complained of 'what they call their recreations', which either 'ends in a mere riotous debauch, or is continued in the town for many days, to the neglect of employment, self-degradation and the privation of helpless dependants'.[54] Pressure to abolish raucous and, to middle-class eyes irrational and immoral, leisure pursuits contributed to reformers' efforts 'to ameliorate the condition and elevate the tastes of our working class'.[55]

These campaigns, combined with pressures on space and the new police forces' activities, successfully suppressed some popular amusements. At Stamford, bull-running through the streets came under attack from local authorities and the Royal Society for the Prevention of Cruelty to Animals (RSPCA) and ended in 1840.[56] Derby street football, criticized as 'a disgraceful and inhuman exhibition . . . an annual exhibition of rude and brutal barbarism', fell in 1846, victim of an organized effort by the town's leaders and 'respectable inhabitants'.[57] The Greenwich Fair succumbed to a combination of declining profits of exhibitors and showmen and government action in response to a petition from local property owners.[58] Elsewhere, police action overcame violent resistance in shutting down popular celebrations.[59]

Police forces first appeared in many districts in the 1830s and early 1840s, while some county forces developed only in the late 1850s.[60] Police cracked down on disorderly behaviour at surviving festivals. Beginning in 1857, the new West Riding police enforced decorum at the Middlestown Feast. The West Riding police also enforced restrictions on pubs, particularly Sunday closing hours. In addition, the lively street scenes in working-class neighbourhoods attracted police attention. The Derby police force, created in 1835, received instruction that 'Persons standing or loitering on the footway without sufficient cause, so as to prevent the free passage of such a footway . . . may be apprehended and taken before a magistrate'. This encouraged the police to force those using the streets for 'illegitimate' pastimes to 'move on', in what one historian has described as 'a vigorous police battle for control of the streets'.[61] In Wolverhampton a huge majority of prosecutions in the early 1850s concerned order in the streets. These crimes included drunkenness, disorderly behaviour, vagrancy and public nuisances, as well as assaults and petty thefts.[62]

In addition to these efforts to curb 'irrational amusements', many reformers sought to provide working-class men, women and children with more 'rational' alternatives. Middle-class sponsors hoped that proper activities involving workers alongside their social betters would create harmonious relations between the classes. Benjamin Heywood, a Manchester banker, hoped that Lyceums that he founded would provide opportunities for uplifting social evenings involving employers and workers fostering 'a more kindly intercourse between the different classes of people – more of mutual confidence and regard between the working man and his employer'.[63] The moral and intellectual improvement of workers would contribute to this class reconciliation. Henry Solly, founder of Working Men's Clubs under middle-class patronage, believed that through participation in moderate and rational leisure together, respectable middle-class men 'may lift our hardworked brethren by degrees up to very respectable heights of knowledge and education'.[64]

Middle-class reformers sponsored a wide range of acceptable or 'rational' recreation, including libraries, parks (for strolling, but not playing games such as football), choirs and musical education, and even temperance meeting halls as alternatives to pubs.[65] Tea parties and Whit walks, street processions and marching bands sponsored by temperance societies offered alternatives to wakes, fairs and races. Thomas Cook got his start in the travel business by running a temperance railway excursion to compete with race week in Leicester in 1841.[66] Employers sponsored improving education for their workers. William Nelson, an Edinburgh publisher, sponsored an evening for a large crowd of printing workers and their wives to enjoy a lecture on printing, followed by the singing of Scottish songs.[67]

Reformers faced a number of serious obstacles to their project of class reconciliation and moral improvement.[68] Clubs, institutes and lectures could not overcome social gaps and manufacture cross-class bonhomie. The vast majority of workers spurned temperance activities and serious educational offerings. Members of Working Men's Clubs insisted on drinking beer, and eventually hostility towards middle-class patronage led clubs to break with their patrons and become independent, undermining Solly's model of cross-class cooperation. Lyceums and institutes offered more and more entertainment, diluting the educational purpose of their founders. Many also allowed newspaper reading rooms and open political discussion, which undermined the programme of neutralizing working-class politics.[69] By resisting the didactic and puritanical tone of many offerings, workers forced those interested in providing leisure to adjust their expectations. Lord Brougham, President of the Club and Institute Union, admitted, 'the primary objects are relaxation and amusement'.[70] Reform efforts also ran into difficulties when wealthy patrons disagreed over what defined acceptable or 'rational' recreation. Though racing, with its links to gambling and raucous early industrial culture, attracted criticism from many middle-class reformers influenced by evangelicalism, others advocated racing as a 'rational' alternative to popular amusements such as street football.[71]

Middle-class reformers did not enjoy a monopoly on notions of improvement and education in working-class leisure. Indigenous working-class traditions continued to advocate more uplifting forms of enjoyment. Criticizing elite patronage of raucous amusements, union leaders complained of Derby street football, 'Your "betters" have been foremost in this Fete, halloing you like brute dogs to the strife'.[72] This hostility extended to middle-class reformers and their attempts to reshape working-class culture.[73] In Manchester a breakaway New Mechanics' Institution avoided patronage and the project of class reconciliation. It did, however, seek 'to teach our youth how to spend their leisure time with profit to themselves, and advantage to others'.[74] Sunday schools fostered and reflected a working-class culture of self-help and self-improvement, enrolling over 2.5 million British children in 1851.[75] In 1842 22 Owenite socialist branches held classes, while 20 had their own libraries.[76] Manchester Chartists founded a library and Sunday school and developed a series of lectures 'on the arts and sciences, biography, history &c'. Some radicals even embraced temperance as part of a programme to uplift workers politically and socially. Though some Chartist organizations maintained close links with pubs, one Manchester branch resolved that 'abstaining from intoxicating drinks . . . is well adapted to promote the progression of intelligence, and secure real happiness to man'.[77] In Scotland, unions generally met in coffee houses rather than in pubs.[78] This radical improving tradition shared some values with middle-class reformers, but operated in a distinct working-class milieu.

The desire for working-class elevation was not simply a residual effect of fading Chartist and Owenite movements. The growth of two forms of working-class mutual aid, friendly societies and co-operatives, reveals the strength of the improving tradition. In these institutions values of thrift and respectability took distinctly working-class forms, particularly among skilled and better-paid male workers. Friendly societies offered workers insurance benefits, while co-operative shops promised quality goods at fair prices, and paid a 'divi', returned to members out of the surplus. The Oldham Co-operative Society boasted that even some middle-class reformers recognized 'co-operation as the most promising of all agencies in operation to elevate the working class'.[79] Becoming a member of the Oddfellows, a large friendly society, could be seen as evidence of self-respect and status within the community, of the development into a 'steady, thoughtful man'.[80] Co-operatives offered leisure activities as well as economic benefits and moral improvement. In their heartland of northern England, they funded libraries, excursions and educational activities.[81] In Lancashire and Yorkshire, tea parties with music, dancing and sometimes impressive feasts became so common that the *Co-operative News* noted 'The soirées . . . have been so numerous during the present season that space will compel us to curtail our notices of them'. At one society's first tea party, held in 1865 in Halifax, members consumed 136 kg (300 lb) of ham and 45 kg (100 lb) of beef.[82]

The limits of reform

In some co-operative societies the vision of rational improvement became a source of conflict. In the St Cuthbert's Co-operative in Edinburgh, some leaders opposed the extension of credit to shoppers. The membership, however, repeatedly refused to allow a cash-only policy. In addition, members' habits of adjourning to a pub after meetings drew criticism from some of their brethren.[83] In friendly societies, community and conviviality were as important as insurance functions. Monthly meetings, almost always in a pub, and an annual banquet provided opportunities for sociability.[84] In Kentish London, all but one of the 85 registered friendly societies between 1855 and 1870 met in pubs.[85] Thomas Wright joined the Ancient Order of Good Fellows and found (to his dismay), 'unrestricted drinking not only permitted, but in many cases practically enforced at the meetings'.[86] As regulation encouraged stricter financial accounting, money for beer was hidden in friendly society books under 'room rent'.[87] Friendly societies also sponsored numerous railway excursions.[88] Temperance societies and benefit organizations that did not offer the social opportunities of the friendly societies failed to attract large memberships in the mid-nineteenth century.[89] The survival of credit and conviviality in co-operatives and the importance of drink in friendly societies illustrate the gap between the values of working-class members of these societies and those of middle-class reformers.

More broadly, despite the efforts of temperance activists such as Thomas Cook, drink still pervaded working-class life and leisure. Alcohol consumption reached its peak in Britain in the 1870s. Teetotal versions of Working Men's Clubs failed, leading the Club and Institute Union to abandon its attempt to prohibit beer. Drink maintained its crucial place in music hall entertainment, and temperance music halls failed when they were attempted in the 1880s. When Thomas Trevaskis, a Cornwall temperance reformer, attempted to sponsor an alternative to the local festival by offering a fat bullock to roast, he was driven out of Padstow by a stone-throwing crowd.[90] One miner told Parliament in 1842 that if a teetotal miner tried to work with him, 'we would soon take him to the canal', and anti-temperance rioting did occur.[91]

Though the overall level of riot probably declined around mid-century, working-class leisure culture remained rowdy and violent. Music hall audiences sometimes demonstrated their disapproval of the entertainment violently, as in Glasgow, where a hostile crowd bombarded the Great Vance with rivets.[92] Despite the crackdown on some blood sports, cock fighting, ratting and dog fights continued through much of the century.[93] Prize fighting enjoyed a boom in the 1840s and 1850s, as railways brought large crowds from greater distances. The railways also brought excursionists to public hangings, such as the execution of John Gleeson in Liverpool in 1849, attended by 100,000 spectators.[94] Public executions ceased in 1868, but as late as 1877 the *Oldham Chronicle* reported that 'cock-fighting and prize fighting are no doubt practised to an alarming extent at the present day, but it is done under cover'.[95] Even where police succeeded in suppressing organized violence, spontaneous rowdy and sometimes violent activities defied efforts to impose order on the streets.[96]

Conclusion

The significant differences between the leisure habits of workers and those above them in the social structure also disappointed those who hoped that new leisure patterns would bring the classes together. The pub grew increasingly class-specific, as drinking in these establishments became unrespectable for any man of property.[97] Most music hall visitors were workers, though a segment of the lower-middle class shared in this aspect of working-class culture.[98] Meanwhile, middle-class audiences began to dominate the theatres, which became unwelcoming to working-class visitors.

Exclusivity formed part of the attraction of remodelled theatres with higher ticket prices and stall seating.[99] Even those activities that appealed across class lines remained segregated. Working-class gamblers, for example, used the services of street bookies or specific gambling houses catering to small-scale betting. Wealthier gamblers could bet on credit with more established and legal bookmakers.[100] Seaside resorts appealed to particular classes, and if a resort became the playground of working-class excursionists, more affluent vacationers found new, more exclusive spots.[101] Working-class men and women, and entrepreneurs who catered to them, built a distinct leisure culture separate from middle-class entertainments and resistant to efforts to tame and reform it.

Notes

1 T. Wright, 'Bill Banks's day out', *The Savage Club Papers* 2 (1868), 214–30; P. Bailey, *Leisure and Class in Victorian England: Rational Recreation and the Contest for Control, 1830–1885* (London: Methuen, 1987), 100–1.

2 A. Delves, 'Popular recreation and social conflict in Derby, 1800–1850', in E. Yeo and S. Yeo, eds, *Popular Culture and Class Conflict 1590–1914: Explorations in the History of Labour and Leisure* (Brighton: Harvester Press, 1981), 89–90.

3 R. Poole, 'Oldham wakes', in J.K. Walton and J. Walvin, eds, *Leisure in Britain 1780–1939* (Manchester: Manchester University Press, 1983), 76; J.K. Walton and R. Poole, 'The Lancashire wakes in the nineteenth century', in R.D. Storch, ed., *Popular Culture and Custom in Nineteenth-Century England* (London: Croom Helm, 1982), 107.

4 W. Dodd, *The Factory System Illustrated: In a Series of Letters to the Right Hon. Lord Ashley* ([1842]; London: Frank Cass, 1968), 100.

5 R.W. Malcolmson, *Popular Recreations in English Society 1700–1850* (Cambridge: Cambridge University Press, 1973), 69, 43, 50, 67–8; Poole, 'Oldham wakes', 79.

6 Malcolmson, *Popular Recreations*, 45–7; H. Cunningham, *Leisure in the Industrial Revolution, c.1780–c.1880* (London: Croom Helm, 1980), 22–3.

7 Cunningham, *Leisure in the Industrial Revolution*, 39; J.M. Golby and A.W. Purdue, *The Civilisation of the Crowd: Popular Culture in England 1750–1900* (New York: Shocken Books, 1985), 61–2.

8 O.R. Ashton, 'Chartism and popular culture: an introduction to the radical culture in Cheltenham Spa, 1830–1847', *Journal of Popular Culture* 20 (1987), 63.

9 E.P. Thompson, *The Making of the English Working Class*, 2nd ed. (New York: Vintage, 1966), 408.

10 Delves, 'Popular recreation', 103.

11 B.H. Harrison, *Drink and the Victorians: The Temperance Question in England 1815–1872*, 2nd ed. (Keele: Keele University Press, 1994), 46–8; Bailey, *Leisure and Class*, 22.

12 Bailey, *Leisure and Class*, 29, 40–1.

13 Ibid., 23.

14 Ashton, 'Chartism and popular culture', 69.

15 J. Walvin, *Leisure and Society, 1830–1950* (London: Longman, 1978), 53.

16 Cunningham, *Leisure in the Industrial Revolution*, 166.

17 Dodd, *The Factory System*, 184, italics in original; Bailey, *Leisure and Class*, 42–3.

18 Bailey, *Leisure and Class*, 43–4.

19 D. Kift, *The Victorian Music Hall: Culture, Class and Conflict*, trans. R. Kift (Cambridge: Cambridge University Press, 1996), 32; Bailey, *Leisure and Class*, 154–5.

20 Bailey, *Leisure and Class*, 154–6, 159–61.

21 Poole, 'Oldham wakes', 82–3.

22 D.A. Reid, 'Interpreting the festival calendar: wakes and fairs as carnivals', in Storch, ed., *Popular Culture and Custom*, 135.

23 M. Judd, ' "The oddest combination of town and country": popular culture and the London fairs, 1800–1860', in Walton and Walvin, eds, *Leisure in Britain*, 15; H. Cunningham, 'The metropolitan fairs: a case study in the social control of leisure', in A.P. Donajgrodzki, ed., *Social Control in Nineteenth Century Britain* (London: Croom Helm, 1977), 168.

24 Judd, 'London fairs', 27.

25 M. Hewitt, *The Emergence of Stability in the Industrial City: Manchester, 1832–67* (Aldershot: Scolar Press, 1996), 187.

26 Golby and Purdue, *Civilisation of the Crowd*, 78.

27 D.C. Itzkowitz, 'Victorian bookmakers and their customers', *Victorian Studies* 32 (1988), 9; Cunningham, *Leisure in the Industrial Revolution*, 25.

28 M. Huggins, 'Horse racing on Teeside in the nineteenth century: change and continuity', *Northern History* 23 (1987), 104.

29 R.D. Storch, 'The problem of working-class leisure: some roots of middle-class moral reform in the industrial North: 1825–50', in Donajgrodzki, ed., *Social Control*, 152.

30 Huggins, 'Horse racing', 105.

31 Bailey, *Leisure and Class*, 97–8; Huggins, 'Horse racing', 106.

32 Bailey, *Leisure and Class*, 34.

33 M. Clapson, *A Bit of a Flutter: Popular Gambling and English Society, c.1823–1961* (Manchester: Manchester University Press, 1992), 79–80, 90–1; C. Chinn, *Better Betting with a Decent Feller: Bookmaking, Betting and the British Working Class, 1750–1990* (New York: Harvester Wheatsheaf, 1991), 98–101.

34 Itzkowitz, 'Victorian bookmakers', 8, 16, 25; Huggins, 'Horse-racing', 113; Chinn, *Better Betting*, 72; Hewitt, *Emergence of Stability*, 189–90.

35 Bailey, *Leisure and Class*, 29, 155; Cunningham, *Leisure in the Industrial Revolution*, 170.

36 Cunningham, *Leisure in the Industrial Revolution*, 164.

37 Ibid., 173–4; Reid, 'Interpreting the festival calendar', 139; Walton and Poole, 'Lancashire wakes', 112–13.

38 Cunningham, *Leisure in the Industrial Revolution*, 159.

39 Poole, 'Oldham wakes', 81; Walton and Poole, 'Lancashire wakes', 113.

40 Cunningham, 'Metropolitan fairs', 167; Cunningham, *Leisure in the Industrial Revolution*, 159.

41 Golby and Purdue, *Civilisation of the Crowd*, 137; Walvin, *Leisure and Society*, 19–20, 50–1; D.A. Reid, 'The "iron roads" and the "happiness of the working classes": the early development and social significance of the railway excursion', *Journal of Transport History* 17 (1996), 60–2; Poole, 'Oldham wakes', 80–1.

42 Walvin, *Leisure and Society*, 20–1.

43 A. Clark, *The Struggle for the Breeches: Gender and the Making of the British Working Class* (Berkeley: University of California Press, 1995), 39.

44 Harrison, *Drink and the Victorians*, 43.

45 Bailey, *Leisure and Class*, 43.

46 D. Höher, 'The composition of music hall audiences 1850–1900', in P. Bailey, ed., *Music Hall: The Business of Pleasure* (Milton Keynes: Open University Press, 1986), 81–2.

47 Itzkowitz, 'Victorian bookmakers', 25.

48 Hewitt, *Emergence of Stability*, 186.

49 Bailey, *Leisure and Class*, 28; Walvin, *Leisure and Society*, 3–4; Clapson, *A Bit of a Flutter*, 80.

50 B. Bramwell, 'Public space and local communities: the example of Birmingham, 1840–1880', in G. Kearns and C.W.J. Withers, eds, *Urbanising Britain: Essays on Class and Community in the Nineteenth Century* (Cambridge: Cambridge University Press, 1991), 40.

51 Bailey, *Leisure and Class*, 94–5, 141.

52 Ibid., 31.

53 Storch, 'The problem of working-class leisure', 144.

54 B. Lancaster, *Radicalism, Cooperation and Socialism: Leicester Working-Class Politics 1860–1906* (Leicester: Leicester University Press, 1987), 49.

55 Judd, 'London fairs', 27.

56 Cunningham, *Leisure in the Industrial Revolution*, 77–8.

57 Delves, 'Popular recreation and social conflict', 90–1, 95; Malcolmson, *Popular Recreations*, 140.

58 Cunningham, 'Metropolitan fairs', 170–1.

59 R.D. Storch, 'The policeman as domestic missionary: urban discipline and popular cutlure in northern England, 1850–1880', *Journal of Social History* 9 (1976), 489–92.

60 R.D. Storch, 'The plague of the blue locusts: police reform and popular resistance in northern England, 1840–1857', *International Review of Social History* 20 (1975), 70; C. Steedman, *Policing the Victorian Community: The Formation of English Provincial Police Forces, 1856–80* (London: Routledge & Kegan Paul, 1984), 6.

61 D.J.V. Jones, *Crime, Protest, Community and Police in Nineteenth-Century Britain* (London: Routledge & Kegan Paul, 1982), 21; Storch, 'Plague of the blue locusts', 85–6; Storch, 'Policeman as domestic missionary', 482; Delves, 'Popular recreation', 98.

62 R. Swift, 'Urban policing in early Victorian England, 1835–86: a reappraisal', *History* 73 (1988), 226; Jones, *Crime, Protest, Community and Police*, 150.

63 Cunningham, *Leisure in the Industrial Revolution*, 99; Bailey, *Leisure and Class*, 48, 55–7.

64 Bailey, *Leisure and Class*, 120.

65 Cunningham, *Leisure in the Industrial Revolution*, 154, 94–5, 102–3; Bailey, *Leisure and Class*, 59.

66 Bailey, *Leisure and Class*, 57, 59; Reid, 'Iron roads', 58, 68–9.

67 R.Q. Gray, *The Labour Aristocracy in Victorian Edinburgh* (Oxford: Clarendon Press, 1976), 100; Hewitt, *Emergence of Stability*, 124–5.

68 P. Bailey, 'The politics and poetics of modern British leisure: a late-twentieth-century review', *Rethinking History* 3:2 (1999), 141.

69 Bailey, *Leisure and Class*, 57, 59, 126–8; P. Joyce, *Work, Society and Politics: The Culture of the Factory in Later Victorian England* (New Brunswick: Rutgers University Press, 1980), 171; Storch, 'The problem of working-class leisure', 150; Hewitt, *Emergence of Stability*, 142.

70 Bailey, *Leisure and Class*, 110.

71 Delves, 'Popular recreation and social conflict', 110–11.

72 R.D. Storch, ' "Please to remember the fifth of November": conflict, solidarity and public order in southern England, 1815–1900' in Storch, ed., *Popular Culture and Custom*, 80.

73 Bailey, *Leisure and Class*, 60.

74 Cunningham, *Leisure in the Industrial Revolution*, 98.

75 T. Laqueur, *Religion and Respectability: Sunday Schools and Working Class Culture 1780–1850* (New Haven: Yale University Press, 1976), 158, 246.

76 B. Taylor, *Eve and the New Jerusalem: Socialism and Feminism in the Nineteenth Century* (New York: Pantheon Books, 1983), 231.

77 P.A. Pickering, *Chartism and the Chartists in Manchester and Salford* (London: Macmillan, 1995), 133, 127.

78 W.W. Knox, *Industrial Nation: Work, Culture and Society in Scotland, 1800–Present* (Edinburgh: Edinburgh University Press, 1999), 95.

79 N. Kirk, *The Growth of Working-Class Reformism in Mid-Victorian England* (Urbana: University of Illinois Press, 1985), 157.

80 G. Crossick, *An Artisan Elite in Victorian Society: Kentish London 1840–1880* (London: Croom Helm, 1978), 194.

81 M. Purvis, 'The development of co-operative retailing in England and Wales, 1851–1901: a geographical study', *Journal of Historical Geography* 16:3 (1990), 315; J.K. Walton, 'Co-operation in Lancashire 1844–1914', *North West Labour History* 19 (1994–5), 115.

82 P. Gurney, *Cooperative Culture and the Politics of Consumption in England, 1870–1930* (Manchester: Manchester University Press, 1996), 66.

83 Gray, *Labour Aristocracy*, 125, 128; P. Johnson, *Saving and Spending: The Working-Class Economy in Britain 1870–1939* (Oxford: Clarendon Press, 1985), 131–2.

84 P.H.J.H. Gosden, *Self-Help: Voluntary Associations in the 19th Century* (London: B.T. Batsford, 1973), 22, 48–9.

85 Crossick, *Artisan Elite*, 178.

86 Golby and Purdue, *Civilisation of the Crowd*, 120.

87 Gosden, *Self-Help*, 48–9.

88 Reid, 'Iron roads', 62.

89 Gosden, *Self-Help*, 59; Crossick, *Artisan Elite*, 179–80.

90 Bailey, *Leisure and Class*, 60, 99, 122, 169–70.

91 Storch, 'The problem of working-class leisure', 154.

92 Bailey, *Leisure and Class*, 160.

93 Walton and Poole, 'Lancashire wakes', 106; Walvin, *Leisure and Society*, 36; Hewitt, *Emergence of Stability*, 188–9; Storch, 'Policeman as domestic missionary', 487–8.

94 Walvin, *Leisure and Society*, 26–7.

95 Joyce, *Work, Society and Politics*, 286; Walvin, *Leisure and Society*, 28.

96 Bramwell, 'Public space', 44.

97 Harrison, *Drink and the Victorians*, 46.

98 Höher, 'Composition of music hall audiences', 84–5.

99 Cunningham, *Leisure in the Industrial Revolution*, 135–6.

100 Itzkowitz, 'Victorian bookmakers', 18.

101 Walvin, *Leisure and Society*, 79.

CHAPTER FOUR

Working-class identity and politics

In an autobiography published in 1880 printer Thomas Frost recalled the frustration felt by many workers in the aftermath of the 1832 Reform Act: 'United with the trading classes in the agitation of 1831, the working men were overlooked in the measure of Parliamentary Reform which they had helped necessitate'. Middle-class men 'having gained their object by the aid of the working men, betrayed their allies'. Workers, 'abandoned by their late allies' in the middle class, then 'formed in 1837 a political organization of their own', known as Chartism.[1] This narrative of class exclusion and mobilization contributed to the development of working-class identity in mid-Victorian Britain. The conditions described in previous chapters – intimate neighbourhoods, experiences at work and a distinctive leisure culture – nurtured this sense of class. Alongside class identity, working men and women identified in other ways, around skill, gender, nation and empire, sectarian differences, etc. Despite the complexity of worker identities, Chartism successfully mobilized large numbers around a programme of radical and class politics. Following the collapse of Chartism, activists turned to new strategies that attracted less widespread support. Throughout the period, many workers embraced national identity and its key components – Protestantism, monarchy and empire. Class conflict, though, persisted in the pervasive informal politics of working-class life.

Class and identity

Many workers embraced respectability as a key component of their complex identities. Though subjective and malleable, respectable virtues encompassed self-discipline and improvement, industry and thrift, independence and proper personal behaviour.[2] Working-class respectability grew out of the culture of political radicalism, association and improvement in the first half of the nineteenth century. By defining themselves as 'respectable', working people necessarily identified other workers as 'rough', or lacking in respectability. Yet no consistent distinction between the rough and respectable can be drawn, as respectable standards varied greatly and individuals embraced and discarded respectable norms in different contexts.

For some, respectability meant avoiding a pauper funeral or maintaining a clean grate or pavement in front of the house, even under conditions of impoverishment.[3] For others, respectability demanded membership in a friendly society or participation in a co-operative. Those involved in chapel and temperance activities, however, might view the conviviality of friendly societies or co-operatives to be evidence of 'rough' behaviour. Individuals exhibited respectable behaviour at times, though they also participated in activities that did not meet the demands of respectable values. For example, parading in a Sunday suit emphasized respectability, yet many of these suits were then pawned on Monday morning, revealing an unrespectable lack of thrift.[4] The description of 'Bill Banks's day out' in Chapter 3 reveals the difficulty in sorting out rough and respectable leisure; it is impossible to draw a consistent distinction between rough and respectable. Furthermore, even those workers who aspired to respectability or identified as a skilled elite maintained their identity as workers and their consciousness of class.[5]

For some working-class men and women, participation in church or chapel activities helped define respectability. A significant minority of workers, perhaps between 15 and 40 per cent, attended religious service regularly.[6] In some cases they worshipped in overwhelmingly working-class congregations. Among Oldham's George Street Independent Methodists in the mid-1830s, nearly 95 per cent were manual workers.[7] When a Wigan Church of Christ congregation opened a new meeting site in Wigan Lane, 'the audience was composed of men and women of the lowest class . . . the women were the wives of these men'.[8] On the other hand, nearly 20 per cent of the Congregationalist chapel in Regent Street, Oldham came from the upper and middle classes. Even here, though, a significant majority of attenders were working class.[9] Those who did not attend regularly were seldom completely cut off from religious life. Sunday schools expanded dramatically in the first half of the nineteenth century, and most working-class children attended such schools. In areas where church attendance was low, reverence for the Bible remained pervasive in working-class culture. In one Birmingham slum court, two-thirds of households had Bibles, including some where nobody could read.[10] Those who stayed away from religious services might sing hymns, send their children to Sunday school, and attend community-wide activities with religious content, such as wakes celebrations. Working-class men and women defy categorization into respectable religious and rough secular groups.

Despite the difficulty in drawing boundaries around the respectable, respectability did encourage increasingly fixed gender roles in the mid-nineteenth century. The distinction between 'work' and domestic roles defined respectable masculine and feminine virtues. The masculine ideal dictated that men support themselves and their families through their labour and was reflected in calls for wages adequate to provide for an entire family.[11] Women's employment disrupted proper gender roles and interfered with domestic responsibilities.[12] Engels complained that unemployment forced men to rely on their wives for support (and to do housework): 'It deprives the husband of his manhood and the wife of all womanly qualities'.[13] Skill in household tasks defined respectable working-class women's roles (in contrast to an emphasis on leisure in middle-class domesticity).[14]

The ideal of domestic respectability carried some appeal for working-class men and women. For men, it served as a valuable strategy in labour struggles. By appealing to values similar to those held by their employers, working-class men could argue against the employment of women where feminization threatened their positions. The withdrawal of women and children from the labour market would help protect male workers, but it would also prove 'highly congenial to the feelings and habits of Englishmen, as conducive to domestic comfort and kindly affections, as tending to establish the authority of fathers, and as making each man responsible for the comfort, respectability, and the education of his family', as one worker wrote in the *Trades' Newspaper*.[15] The domestic ideal also promised some women relief from the double burden of long hours in employment along with domestic chores. A woman who spent some 30 years in factory work supported this notion, claiming 'We are – not slaves!'[16]

Actual conditions fell far short of the rhetoric of domesticity. Inadequate and insecure wages made it impossible for most families to survive on men's earnings alone. Alongside their domestic duties, women continued to earn wages.[17] But notions of respectability helped undermine women's wages and work opportunities, supporting male claims to a prior right to employment, marginalizing women workers and enforcing the division of labour by sex.[18] Industrial work was seen as inappropriate for women, even though women remained essential in the workforce.[19] In the home, the new ideal offered a formula for the patriarchal authority of men. William Marcroft, a respectable Oldham worker and co-operative movement leader, noted of the working-class wife: 'The husband is the altar of her worship'.[20]

While gender ideals linked to respectability cultivated a gap between working-class men and women, distinctions in the workplace further divided workers. Skilled workers' identification with their craft marked them off from the unskilled mass. The Boilermakers' Society expressed pride in the skilled worker's 'perfect knowledge of his trade, such acquisition becomes his own personal capital'.[21] In an Edinburgh procession call-ing for electoral reform in 1866, various skilled trades marched around symbols of their crafts. For example, 'The Bookbinders . . . carried some fine specimens of Binding, along with a Flag and several Banners with Mottos appropriate to the Occasion'.[22] Those men who were able to defend skilled positions fought to enforce hierarchies in the workplace.

Workplace distinctions did not, however, define a separate stratum of skilled 'labour aristocrats', divorced from other workers and lacking in class consciousness. Skill did not guarantee workers privileged positions or economic security in the dynamic mid-nineteenth-century economy.[23] For example, despite their skill, hand-loom weavers faced miserable con-ditions and even starvation in the 1840s.[24] In addition, the emphasis on skill distinctions in the workplace misses the role of community outside work in the development of class identity. At mid-century, families of skilled and unskilled workers lived in the same neighbourhoods, clustering on the basis of kinship, proximity to workplaces and ties to their neighbours, rather than skill distinctions.[25] Marriage patterns also raise questions about a simple distinction between skilled and unskilled workers. In Rochdale, while sons of workers revealed a strong tendency to marry daughters of workers, there was no evidence of endogamy among skilled groups in this period.[26] In Edinburgh, on the other hand, some sons of skilled men tended to marry daughters of skilled workers. This pattern did not hold across all skilled groups, however. Only 37.7 per cent of engineers' sons and 30.4 per cent of ironmoulders' sons married daughters of skilled workers between 1865 and 1869.[27]

Though distinctions of skill and respectability blur under careful scrutiny, hostility between Irish and non-Irish workers marked a more persistent division in the working class. Anti-Irish sentiment grew out of a deep-seated anti-Catholicism in Britain, encouraged by anti-Catholic demagogues. In 1851 John Sayles Orr's agitation touched off attacks on the Irish population in the vicinity of Greenock, Clydeside. The same year, Stockport Tory politicians and anti-Catholics helped fan the flames of riots in which one Irish resident was killed, two churches destroyed and 24 Irish families left homeless.[28] Hatred of the Irish on sectarian grounds exacerbated a perceived economic rivalry. In industrial regions the Irish stood accused of undermining wages and serving as strike-breakers. An English cotton worker complained that 'it is the Irish who keep wages down'.[29]

At times, however, shared identity as workers overcame ethnic hostilities between native workers and Irish immigrants. Even in Lancashire, English and Irish workers cooperated during periods of increased industrial conflict. Many Irish immigrants stood with other Preston workers in 1853, and employers had to import blackleg labour from Ireland. Some of these replacement workers were convinced by English and earlier immigrant Irish workers to return home. In 1863, riots in Stalybridge united English and Irish workers, who joined in a large crowd attempting to rescue Irish protesters who had been arrested.[30] Despite the venom of popular anti-Catholicism, popular literature in the Lancashire dialect reveals an affectionate attitude towards Irish characters.[31] A significant Irish presence in Chartism, exemplified by O'Connor and O'Brien among the national leadership, many mid-level leaders and mass support, also reveals class cooperation across the ethnic divide.[32]

Popular Protestantism also formed an essential building block of British national identity in the nineteenth century. The association of Protestantism with traditional liberties and of Catholicism with tyranny developed through the eighteenth century, forged in repeated wars against the Catholic French.[33] National symbols such as the monarchy reinforced this Protestant British identity. The 1831 coronation of William IV inspired large-scale popular celebrations. In Bristol, though the corporation failed to organize the day's events, worker organizations stepped forward, filling the streets with 'the public spirit of the mechanics and artisans of this city', so that, according to the *Bristol Mercury*, 'the ardent feelings of the people more than compensated' for the lack of official observance.[34] Popular enthusiasm for the monarchy waxed and waned in the middle decades of the nineteenth century, and the monarch's perceived sympathy with popular causes drove a good deal of this support. Thus, at the time of these coronation celebrations, William IV was widely expected to support parliamentary reform. Similarly, Queen Victoria benefited from the popular perception that she was responsible for commuting the death sentences of Chartists involved in the Newport rising of 1839. A street ballad lauded Victoria: 'Blessings attend her for the pardon she gave'.[35] At other times, though, Victoria's popularity sagged, particularly after her withdrawal from public life following the death of Prince Albert.[36]

By the end of Victoria's reign, the monarchy would be closely associated with the empire, and images, narratives and celebrations of empire would become ubiquitous in British culture. But even before this, working-class Britons were conscious of empire and racial difference.[37] Workers sought to distinguish themselves from imperial subjects, embracing the notion of the 'free-born Englishman' and rejecting 'wage slavery'. Organizations such as the British and Foreign Anti-Slavery Society mobilized working-class men and women against slave conditions around the world.[38] The missionary exploits of David Livingstone sparked the imagination of workers such as the 500 factory hands in Ashton-under-Lyne who gathered in 1857 to hear of his African exploits.[39] Visitors to the 1851 Great Exhibition saw a display representing Indian trades that portrayed 'a lean, starved-out regiment of squalid beggars', according to an exhibit guidebook.[40] Though evidence of working-class enthusiasm for conquest and domination of foreign territory is rare in this period, consciousness of racial difference and imperial power helped shape the identities of British workers.[41]

While Protestantism, hostility to outsiders, support for the monarchy and awareness of empire all contributed to British identity, this national consciousness coexisted with complex sub-national identities. Lancashire workers expressed English patriotism, as in a message from workers in Ashton asserting that, even if 'our institutions are faulty then they are still praiseworthy. England is still the freest country on Earth'. Yet dialect literature in the North of England also reveals the salience of local identities: 'Tyke' in Yorkshire, 'Geordie' in the North East, or 'Lanky' in Lancashire.[42] Scottish and Welsh identity also coexisted with more fractured regional consciousness.[43] Irish immigrants maintained loyalties to their places of origin, and street battles reflected these local identities.[44] Violent conflict was common in colonies of navvies constructing rail lines in the 1840s. In northern England and Scotland, English workers fought Scots. But at other times Yorkshiremen fought Lancastrians, and varied English and Scottish workers combined against the Irish.[45] These simmering regional antagonisms reveal the shifting and complicated identities of workers.

Politics and worker frustration in the 1830s

To many workers, the state appeared hostile to worker interests, as governments resisted pressure from the Ten Hours movement and passed a Factory Act that did nothing to ease the conditions of adult workers in the mills.[46] The New Poor Law of 1834 gave more evidence of what many began to see as a 'great Whig betrayal' on the part of the party that had passed the 1832 reforms. Chartist leader Bronterre O'Brien recalled the collapse of faith in an alliance of workers and the middle class. The 'delusion has passed away . . . it vanished completely with the enactment of the Starvation Law [New Poor Law]'.[47] Union organizers and striking workers confronted a repressive regime that convicted organizers such as the 'Tolpuddle Martyrs' in 1834 and the Glasgow spinners' leaders in 1838.[48] The 1835 Municipal Corporations Act required the establishment of new borough police forces that would help control working-class districts.[49] In the view of one trade union leader, 'The whigs intended to bring the working classes down to the level of the miserable pauper under the poor law amendment act'.[50]

The Poor Law Amendment Act of 1834 (the New Poor Law), reforming poverty relief in England and Wales, focused workers' attention on the political system. It required the construction of workhouses and discouraged 'outdoor relief' – aid given to the poor who remained outside workhouses. Its punitive tone and hostility towards outdoor relief clashed with workers' established notions of a right to assistance.[51] A shoemaker, Samuel Kydd, recalled the popular response to the law: 'the labourers of England believed that the new poor law was a law to punish poverty; and the effects of that belief were, to sap the loyalty of the working men, to make them . . . brood over their wrongs, to cherish feelings of revenge, and to hate the rich of the land'.[52]

Despite the crusading zeal of Edwin Chadwick, secretary of the Poor Law Commission, implementation of the new system varied from place to place. Some local guardians ignored the central authority's directions, refusing to implement punitive measures. Though most workhouses fell far short of Chadwick's draconian ideal, workers facing economic insecurity still found good reason to despise the New Poor Law. Some guardians took seriously the idea of 'less eligibility' – that conditions in the workhouse should be so unpleasant that only the really desperate would seek indoor relief. In Leicestershire paupers who refused work, offended the matron or master or behaved badly faced solitary confinement and a diet of bread and water. Those who did not enter workhouses enjoyed scant support, which was inadequate to maintain even the most meagre standard of living. Applicants for outdoor relief suffered a variety of humiliations and investigations. Inspectors could demand to examine their cupboards and closets, and possessions had to be sold or pawned. Those who died while in the workhouse or could not afford a proper funeral suffered the humiliation of a pauper burial.[53]

Horrifying and often exaggerated stories of conditions in workhouses spread. Because the law allowed the bodies of those dying in the workhouse to be dissected, stories spread of 'nattomy soup' and the feeding of human flesh in workhouse dinners.[54] Chartist leader Feargus O'Connor wrote of a boy starving in a workhouse who gnawed his fingers to the first joint. A pamphlet calling for the 'painless extinction' of excess poor populations was attributed to a poor law commissioner or supporter.[55] The reality and the myth of conditions in the workhouse served the purpose of deterring relief applications, which was a goal of the new law. They also, however, fuelled hostility toward the state on the part of working people.

Chartism

The governments of the 1830s excluded workers from suffrage, failed to address social grievances, crushed union organizations, instituted the new police to discipline working-class communities, and introduced the punitive Poor Law. In this context, political radicalism, which blamed a corrupt political system for the ills of the nation, developed a wide following. Radicals emphasized that a monopoly on power allowed the wealthy to continue their oppression of the poor. Taxation policies that favoured rich land-owners enforced the propertied classes' hold on power and left the masses in poverty.[56] The exclusion of working men from the franchise allowed the government to act against them in legislation and repression. The tyranny of unrepresentative government was to blame for the grievances of working people. As Chartist leader Bronterre O'Brien wrote in 1837, 'Knaves will tell you, that it is because you have no property you are unrepresented. I tell you, on the contrary, it is because you are unrepresented that you have no property'.[57]

In 1838 the London Working Men's Association drafted the 'People's Charter', and its six demands (manhood suffrage, annual parliaments, the secret ballot, payment of MPs, equal electoral districts and the abolition of property qualifications for MPs) became the focus of working-class political activity. In the summer and autumn of 1838 a series of meetings marshalled mass support for the Charter and elected representatives to a Chartist national convention. A petition bearing 1,280,000 signatures in support of Chartist demands gained only 46 votes in the House of Commons (to 235 against) in July 1839. The convention and other activities collapsed amidst hundreds of arrests, and the first wave of Chartism collapsed.[58] The second peak of Chartist activity included another convention and rejected petition in 1842, followed by widespread strikes in English and Scottish industrial districts. However, workers were unable to enforce their economic demands or win the Charter by striking. The authorities again responded aggressively, and mass arrests contributed to the calming of the situation. Hundreds were tried and more than two dozen transported.[59] Though the main Chartist impetus faded after this, in the spring of 1848 Chartists organized a series of meetings around the country, another national convention and another petition.[60] Though this petition contained nearly 2 million signatures validated by the House of Commons clerks (and many more that they rejected), mass support for Chartism in 1848 was concentrated in a handful of localities. The government moved against the remaining leadership, hundreds were imprisoned, and Chartism after 1848 had a limited following.[61]

Chartists adopted a variety of tactics, and activists saw 'moral force' (peaceful agitation) and 'physical force' as complementary tactics, as in the phrase, 'peaceably if we may, forcibly if we must'.[62] In late 1838 and 1839 Chartists in many northern cotton towns began arming with pikes and even firearms, though the only notable armed confrontation of those years occurred in Newport, where two dozen were killed and 125 arrested in a rout of several thousand colliers and ironworkers by a small contingent of troops. In 1848 Chartists were at the centre of an insurrection that was able to take over one Bradford district for two weeks until military reinforcements defeated it. Chartists justified the resort to arms as a response to government repression, 'We, Sir, have taken up a purely defensive position, and shall only use arms when attacked'.[63] But militants also hoped to intimidate the government, using the threat of insurrection as a strategy.[64] At the other end of the strategic continuum, cooperation with middle-class reformers briefly engaged a number of Chartist leaders. In 1842 the Complete Suffrage Union, promoted by middle-class reformer Joseph Sturge, developed a network of local associations and sought the support of some Chartist leaders. The alliance fractured when Chartists insisted on support for the Charter, and middle-class reformers with more limited goals refused.[65]

The failure of class cooperation highlights the extent to which Chartism, in both its support and its vision, was a distinctly working-class movement.[66] One Manchester observer, John Watts, noted that 'the working class as a mass had been taught to believe . . . that the enactment of the principles of the charter was the great measure that was to produce their salvation'.[67] Chartism appealed to workers across trades, building on grievances of wage earners and working-class communal ties.[68] Alongside the emphasis on political corruption, Chartists spoke a language of class.

According to O'Connor in 1838, 'the working men were pressed down by the capitalists . . . The whole question resolved itself into the battle between labour and capital'.[69] Class understandings were essential in linking support for the Charter to social concerns. Richard Pilling explained his support for O'Connor: 'it was always a wage question and ten hours bill with me'.[70] In factory towns, Chartist agitation became a flashpoint for hostility between mill owners and workers. Employers threatened to dismiss operatives who attended the Kersal Moor demonstration outside Manchester. Thousands of workers on torchlight marches paraded past employers' mills and 'dramatically underscored the isolation of the mill owner and the physical vulnerability of the mill'.[71] In 1842 Staffordshire miners resolved that 'nothing but the People's Charter can give us the power to have a fair day's wage for a fair day's work'.[72] O'Connor recognized the class identity of Chartist supporters, the 'fustian jackets, blistered hands and unshorn chins'. He embraced the symbolism of class in donning a fustian suit himself, symbolically renouncing his own status as a gentleman and embracing the working-class status of his followers.[73]

Despite its ultimate failure, Chartism's class appeal and its message linking political change to social improvement extended across Britain. O'Connor's *The Northern Star* attained an extraordinary popularity. Ben Brierly recalled reading the *Star* each week to his father and five other men who shared a subscription.[74] Chartist leaders engaged in national speaking tours. One of O'Connor's tours included stops in London, Bristol, Manchester, Queen's Head, Bradford, Leeds, Newcastle, Carlisle, Glasgow, Paisley and Edinburgh, all within less than a month.[75] Chartist leaders emphasized political radicalism, blaming the flawed political system for the nation's problems. They also, however, stressed the particular suffering of workers. In the words of one Manchester Chartist, William Butterworth, the 'sole cause of their having to work so hard and so long was because they were not represented in parliament'. R.J. Richardson, whose arguments for reform used well-established radical notions such as the 'birthright of Englishmen', noted that Chartism was a 'bread, beef and ale question' and would provide the people with 'a fair share of the good things in life'.[76] James Leach sought 'an alteration in the institutions of this country as will guarantee to labour that protection which it so imperatively demands'.[77]

The ideology at the centre of Chartism, claiming that the political structure made economic reform impossible, became less viable from the early 1840s when governments changed direction. A series of policies made it clear that even an unreformed Parliament could act in ways that benefited workers. Peel's 1842 budget, cutting consumption taxes and levelling an income tax on the affluent, offers but one example. The Mines Act of 1842, the Factory Act of 1844 and Ten Hours Act of 1847, repeal of the Corn Laws and other reforms undermined the notion that the existing system could only produce 'class legislation'.[78]

Reforms alone do not, however, account for the rapid deterioration of mass support for Chartism after 1842, with only a mild resurgence in 1848. The state defeated Chartism through coercion as well as reforms. Mass arrests, show trials, transportation and imprisonment destroyed the local leadership of the movement.[79] Troops disposed of insurrections in Newport and Bradford. Chartist agitation, petitions, conventions and demonstrations simply did not work in the face of a determined and powerful state. A Chartist leader described the formula for repression: 'Place *Fustian* in the dock, let *Silk Gown* charge the culprit with being a "physical force Chartist" . . . and forthwith *Broad Cloth* in the jury box will bellow out "GUILTY" '.[80] Chartist leader Ernest Jones used the metaphor of a 'goodly ship' to describe Chartism: 'through the force of adverse winds and currents, it ran aground'.[81]

Mid-Victorian radicalism and protest

As mass support for Chartism faded, activists continued to seek reforms. Some sought accommodation with middle-class radical Liberals. This cross-class alliance required some compromise. In Leicester, working-class leader John Markham allied with radical Liberal John Biggs, who supported a number of reforms involved in the Charter, but not manhood suffrage. In 1852 Markham took a seat on the town council as a Liberal.[82] In the wake of the Chartist defeat, Thomas Frost urged his fellow Chartists to join the middle-class dominated Parliamentary Reform Association, 'and endeavour to use its machinery for the furtherance of our own aims'.[83] Opposition to the Crimean War also brought together Chartist leaders and middle-class radicals. Bronterre O'Brien launched a lecture tour in the North of England and Scotland in early 1856 on behalf of the Stop-the-War League, a collaboration of Chartist and middle-class reformers.[84]

Many working-class leaders, however, responded to the loss of Chartist momentum by focusing on social problems and social change. This stress on social reforms alienated them from middle-class reformers in the early 1850s, most of whom maintained commitments to political economy and rejected interventionist policies. Ernest Jones's *People's Paper* continued to call for social and land reform, linking Chartists to socialists, rather than to middle-class radicals.[85] Class remained central to these efforts, as reflected in Clydeside union leader James McNeal's 1857 reminder: 'labour lives in hovels and starves in rags and capital lives in palaces and feasts in robes'.[86] By the 1860s, however, Liberal hostility to social reforms and working-class organization softened, making it easier to build cross-class coalitions.[87] For example, in 1862 John Stuart Mill defended trade union organization in his influential *Principles of Political Economy*.[88] At this point, even those like Ernest Jones, who had rejected earlier collaborations, called for a broadly based movement for reform, including middle-class radicals.[89]

A willingness to work with middle-class reformers did not, however, imply the abandonment of the values and perspectives that had shaped Chartist activism. A tactical decision to compromise and work with reformers who were not committed to the Charter in its entirety made sense in light of the collapse of Chartist strategies. The emphasis on social reform built on a persistent strand within Chartism and reflected the failure of broader political goals. George Cowell, leader of the Preston weavers in the strike of 1853 argued: 'Nothing but the People's Charter, I believe, will elevate the condition of the people, or ever succeed in emancipating them from the yoke of the factory tyrants'. Yet Cowell studiously avoided inserting political demands into the conflict: 'until the ten per cent [wage increase] is secured, I think everything else should be kept out of the question'.[90] However, this pragmatism lacked the mass appeal of Chartism. In 1862 one leader lamented that 'attempts to evoke an agitation on behalf of mere expedients have been a lamentable failure'.[91]

Not all politically engaged workers rallied around the Charter and its radical descendants. In some regions many supported the established political parties. Popular Protestantism moved some workers to embrace the Tories, as a Wigan radical complained: 'They are Tories because they are Churchmen and anti-Papists'. In Lancashire and the West Riding of Yorkshire, over a hundred popular Conservative societies organized working-class support, often around paternalism and the shared interests of elites and workers. Both Tory and Liberal factory owners in Lancashire mobilized their employees behind political banners. As one observer noted with dismay: 'Each individual operative comes to identify with the mill at which he works, and . . . accepts its political shibbolthes [sic]'. In Blackburn an 1852 procession of workers pledged support for their mill owners' Liberal political ambitions. The following year, Tory mill owners' hands marched in a procession of 15,000 dressed in party colours to celebrate the employers.[92]

Resisting and manipulating the mid-Victorian state

The most hated innovations of the early Victorian state, the Poor Law and the police, sparked significant opposition in working-class communities. 'Can you wonder at it, sir,' said a London costermonger to journalist Henry Mayhew, 'that I hate the police? They drive us about, we must move on, we can't stand here, and we can't pitch there'.[93] In 1856 a new law expanded and regulated local police forces, and offered Treasury grants for those forces judged 'efficient' by inspectors.[94] Surveillance of working-class districts became a crucial function of new police forces. The first Metropolitan Police handbook instructed officers to be involved in 'watching the conduct of loose and disorderly persons'.[95] One working-class activist complained in *Poor Man's Guardian*, 'A man could not talk to his neighbour without one of these blue devils listening'.[96] An observer noted in 1863: 'The administration of criminal justice is the commonest, the most striking, and the most interesting shape, in which the sovereign power of the state manifests itself to the great bulk of its subjects'.[97]

Popular hostility to the new police forces led to violence. In Leeds a conflict between off-duty soldiers and police in June 1844 escalated into a widespread popular anti-police riot. Crowds turned out to confront police, though the soldiers disappeared back to their barracks early in the struggle. Local working people cleared the streets of police presence. The following evening a counter-offensive succeeded in re-establishing police authority.[98] Major riots like this were relatively rare, but small-scale resistance to police activities remained common. Frequently, neighbourhood residents whom the police confronted could rally groups of supporters to rescue them and attack the police. In Walsall in 1859, police ordered a small group of Irish residents to move along in the street. One woman 'called on the others to "fetch pokers to split the b——s skulls". Pokers were fetched, and two policemen injured'. The confrontation continued, as police rein-forcements chased the offenders into a house but were then attacked by a larger group, who succeeded in injuring three more policemen.[99] Police forces met resistance when they challenged working-class life in the streets.

Though police often faced attacks, violent protests against the Poor Law administration were far rarer. This does not indicate that working people accepted the Poor Law and its punitive approach to poverty. In Lancashire unemployment linked to the cotton famine intensified worker opposition to the Poor Law. A series of large demonstrations vented this frustration. One speaker complained that those impoverished 'for no cause of their own' faced conditions 'worse than felons in gaol'. A meeting of spinners complained that demanding work from those forced to apply for relief would 'aggravate rather than mitigate their misfortune'.[100] Joseph Barker, who suffered a period of severe poverty as a child, objected to the implications of the Poor Law: 'Poverty is not a crime . . . It is in reality no disgrace'.[101]

Though it is impossible to calculate exact percentages, it is clear that, in the words of historian Lynn Lees, 'a high proportion of workers' families would have applied for poor law aid at least once and probably more often during their adult lives'. Those in need approached Poor Law officials as savvy consumers of relief. They understood how to appeal to guardians and how to get what they could out of the system, accepting relief without accepting the moral condemnation that accompanied it.[102] Women emphasized their infirmity in claiming poor relief. One Brighton woman appealed to the guardians: 'gentlemen I have an apsess broke in my head and it is impossible fore me to ern money by my needle'.[103] Similarly, working-class people who disliked the police, and even attacked them on other occasions, called on the police when it served their needs. Residents of Jennings' Buildings, a slum in London where police faced significant threats and violence, relied on these same officers to make arrests in cases of theft or other crimes.[104] Thus, working-class views of the state were complex. Working-class people were not shy about rejecting state activities they perceived as illegitimate or oppressive, such as the policing of everyday activities in the streets or the moral strictures of the New Poor Law. But they also accepted aid from government representatives when it served their own needs and priorities. There was little revolutionary sentiment, even during the heyday of Chartism. Yet Chartism reveals a working-class population willing to mobilize in the face of what was perceived to be a corrupt and oppressive state. When the government proved itself capable of reform (and of crushing Chartism), workers continued to resist the most offensive state intervention in their lives – the policing of their streets.

Conclusion

Previous chapters discussed other avenues of working-class assertiveness during this period. Advocates of 'rational' recreation could not tame working-class leisure, but workers did take advantage of middle-class patronage and assistance when it came without the trappings of autocratic paternalism and moralistic snobbery. Even when middle-class lecturers provided it, workers enjoyed 'a little intellectual cock-fighting or rat-worrying'.[105] The confrontational side of working-class struggle is also evident in battles over wages, working conditions and union recognition. Even when national union leaders professed moderation and respectability, workers on the ground kept the initiative in industrial conflict. Thus, though the massive mobilization of Chartism faded from the 1840s, workers in their own neighbourhoods, workplaces and leisure activities remained assertive and independent. They resisted oppression, whether by the state, middle-class moral reformers, or employers.

Notes

1 T. Frost, *Forty Years' Recollections: Literary and Political* (London: Sampson Low, Marston, Searle & Rivington, 1880), 98.

2 N. Kirk, *Change, Continuity and Class: Labour in British Society, 1850–1920* (Manchester: Manchester University Press, 1998), 115–16.

3 N. Kirk, *The Growth of Working-Class Reformism in Mid-Victorian England* (Urbana: University of Illinois Press, 1985), 230; Kirk, *Change, Continuity and Class*, 130–1.

4 P. Bailey, 'Will the real Bill Banks please stand up? Towards a role analysis of mid-Victorian working-class respectability', *Journal of Social History* 12 (1979), 342.

5 R.Q. Gray, *The Labour Aristocracy in Victorian Edinburgh* (Oxford: Clarendon Press, 1976), 139, 143; M. Hewitt, *The Emergence of Stability in the Industrial City: Manchester, 1832–67* (Aldershot: Scolar Press, 1996), 204–5.

6 S. Thorne, *Congregational Missions and the Making of an Imperial Culture in Nineteenth-Century England* (Stanford: Stanford University Press, 1999), 59.

7 M. Smith, *Religion in Industrial Society: Oldham and Saddleworth 1740–1865* (Oxford: Clarendon Press, 1994), 199.

8 P. Ackers, 'West end chapel, back street Bethel: labour and capital in the Wigan Churches of Christ, c.1845–1945', *Journal of Ecclesiastical History* 47 (1996), 303.

9 Smith, *Religion in Industrial Society*, 128.

10 H. McLeod, *Religion and Society in England, 1850–1914* (New York: St Martin's Press, 1996), 79, 106.

11 B. Taylor, *Eve and the New Jerusalem: Socialism and Feminism in the Nineteenth Century* (New York: Pantheon Books, 1983), 263; K. McClelland, 'Rational and respectable men: gender, the working class, and citizenship in Britain, 1850–1867', in L. Frader and S. Rose, eds, *Gender and Class in Modern Europe* (Ithaca: Cornell University Press, 1996), 286; S. Rose, *Limited Livelihoods: Gender and Class in Nineteenth-Century England* (Berkeley: University of California Press, 1992), 127.

12 M. Levine-Clark, *Beyond the Reproductive Body: The Politics of Women's Health and Work in Early Victorian England* (Columbus: Ohio State University Press, 2004), 48.

13 Rose, *Limited Livelihoods*, 128.

14 E. Gordon, *Women and the Labour Movement in Scotland 1850–1914* (Oxford: Clarendon Press, 1991), 80.

15 A. Clark, *The Struggle for the Breeches: Gender and the Making of the British Working Class* (Berkeley: University of California Press, 1995), 199.

16 Ibid., 236.

17 Ibid., 253; Taylor, *Eve and the New Jerusalem*, 273–4.

18 Gordon, *Women and the Labour Movement*, 79–80; Rose, *Limited Livelihoods*, 137; McClelland, 'Rational and respectable men', 285.

19 Levine-Clark, *Beyond the Reproductive Body*, 50.

20 Kirk, *Growth of Working-Class Reformism*, 219.

21 K. McClelland, 'Time to work, time to live: some aspects of work and the reformation of class in Britain, 1850–1880', in P. Joyce, ed., *The Historical Meanings of Work* (Cambridge: Cambridge University Press, 1987), 191.

22 Gray, *Labour Aristocracy*, 92.

23 J. Belchem, *Industrialization and the Working Class: The English Experience, 1750–1900* (Portland: Areopagitica, 1990), 157.

24 T. Lummis, *The Labour Aristocracy, 1851–1914* (Aldershot: Scolar Press, 1994), 18.

25 T. Koditschek, *Class Formation and Urban Industrial Society: Bradford, 1750–1850* (Cambridge: Cambridge University Press, 1990), 449; Kirk, *Change, Continuity and Class*, 126; Kirk, *Growth of Working-Class Reformism*, 230.

26 R. Penn, *Skilled Workers in the Class Structure* (Cambridge: Cambridge University Press, 1984), 181–2.

27 Gray, *Labour Aristocracy*, 112.

28 D.M. MacRaild, *Irish Migrants in Modern Britain, 1750–1922* (New York: St Martin's Press, 1999), 173–4.

29 Kirk, *Growth of Working-Class Reformism*, 318; MacRaild, *Irish Migrants*, 167.

30 Kirk, *Growth of Working-Class Reformism*, 330, 319.

31 P. Joyce, *Visions of the People: Industrial England and the Question of Class, 1848–1914* (Cambridge: Cambridge University Press, 1991), 283.

32 D.G. Wright, *Popular Radicalism: The Working-Class Experience 1780–1880* (London: Longman, 1988), 145–6; MacRaild, *Irish Migrants*, 132–5; L.H. Lees, *Exiles of Erin: Irish Migrants in Victorian London* (Ithaca: Cornell University Press, 1979), 225–9; J. Epstein, *The Lion of Freedom: Feargus O'Connor and the Chartist Movement, 1832–1842* (London: Croom Helm, 1982), 270–1; P. Joyce, *Work, Society and Politics: The Culture of the Factory in Later Victorian England* (New Brunswick: Rutgers University Press, 1980), 243.

33 L. Colley, *Britons: Forging the Nation 1707–1837* (New Haven: Yale University Press, 1992), 368.

34 M. Harrison, *Crowds and History: Mass Phenomena in English Towns, 1790–1835* (Cambridge: Cambridge University Press, 1988), 257–8.

35 D. Thompson, *Queen Victoria: The Woman, The Monarchy, and the People* (New York: Pantheon Books, 1990), 35.

36 A. Tyrrell, ' "God bless Her Little Majesty": the popularising of the monarchy in the 1840s', *National Identities* 2 (2000), 121.

37 Colley, *Britons*, 368–9.

38 R. Gregg and M. Kale, 'The Empire and Mr Thompson: making of Indian princes and English working class', *Economic and Political Weekly* 32 (1997), 2283; J. MacKenzie, 'Another little patch of red', *History Today* 55 (2005), 26.

39 Thorne, *Congregational Missions*, 64.

40 L. Kriegel, 'The pudding and the palace: labour, print culture, and imperial Britain in 1851', in A. Burton, ed., *After the Imperial Turn: Thinking With and Through the Nation* (Durham: Duke University Press, 2003), 236.

41 For an argument stressing the limits of working-class consciousness of and support for imperial expansion in this period, see B. Porter, *The Absent-Minded Imperialists: Empire, Society, and Culture in Britain* (Oxford: Oxford University Press, 2004).

42 Joyce, *Visions of the People*, 107, 283.

43 K. Robbins, *Nineteenth-Century Britain: Integration and Diversity* (Oxford: Clarendon Press, 1988), 7.

44 Lees, *Exiles of Erin*, 222.

45 MacRaild, *Irish Migrants*, 168.

46 D. Thompson, *The Chartists: Popular Politics in the Industrial Revolution* (New York: Pantheon Books, 1984), 24–5.

47 E.P. Thompson, *The Making of the English Working Class*, 2nd ed. (New York: Vintage, 1966), 822; E. Royle, *Chartism*, 3rd ed. (London: Longman, 1996), 14.

48 Thompson, *The Chartists*, 20–2.

49 D. Taylor, *The New Police in Nineteenth-Century England: Crime, Conflict and Control* (Manchester: Manchester University Press, 1997), 31–2.

50 R. Sykes, 'Early Chartism and trade unionism in south-east Lancashire', in J. Epstein and D. Thompson, eds, *The Chartist Experience: Studies in Working-Class Radicalism and Culture, 1830–1860* (London: Macmillan, 1982), 157.

51 L.H. Lees, *The Solidarities of Strangers: The English Poor Laws and the People, 1700–1948* (Cambridge: Cambridge University Press, 1998), 77, 115.

52 Thompson, *The Chartists*, 29–30.

53 Lees, *Solidarities of Strangers*, 149, 186–9, 151.

54 Ibid., 150–1.

55 M.E. Rose, 'The anti-Poor Law agitation', in J.T. Ward, ed., *Popular Movements, c.1830–1850* (London: Macmillan, 1970), 85–6.

56 G. Stedman Jones, 'Rethinking Chartism', in *Languages of Class: Studies in English Working Class History 1832–1982* (Cambridge: Cambridge University Press, 1983), 90–179.

57 Royle, *Chartism*, 92–3.

58 Ibid., 23–7.

59 Wright, *Popular Radicalism*, 130; J. Belchem, *Popular Radicalism in Nineteenth-Century Britain* (New York: St Martin's Press, 1996), 79.

60 G. Stedman Jones, 'The mid-century crisis and the 1848 revolutions', *Theory and Society* 12 (1983), 517.

61 Wright, *Popular Radicalism*, 136–8.

62 R. Sykes, 'Physical-force Chartism: the cotton district and the Chartist crisis of 1839', *International Review of Social History* 30:2 (1985) 211.

63 Ibid., 212; Royle, *Chartism*, 26.

64 Thompson, *The Chartists*, 67; Hewitt, *Emergence of Stability*, 237.

65 Thompson, *The Chartists*, 263–4; Wright, *Popular Radicalism*, 134–5; Belchem, *Popular Radicalism*, 83–4; Epstein, *Lion of Freedom*, 288–93.

66 Epstein, *Lion of Freedom*, 313.

67 Hewitt, *Emergence of Stability*, 200.

68 Stedman Jones, 'Rethinking Chartism', 95, 98; Thompson, *The Chartists*, 173.

69 Thompson, *The Chartists*, 251; M. Finn, *After Chartism: Class and Nation in English Radical Politics, 1848–1874* (Cambridge: Cambridge University Press, 1993), 67.

70 R. McWilliam, *Popular Politics in Nineteenth-Century England* (London: Routledge, 1998), 61–2.

71 J. Epstein, 'Rethinking the categories of working-class history', in *In Practice: Studies in the Language and Culture of Popular Politics in Modern Britain* (Stanford: Stanford University Press, 2003), 21.

72 Wright, *Popular Radicalism*, 128; F.C. Mather, 'The general strike of 1842: a study in leadership, organisation and the threat of revolution during the Plug Plot Disturbances', in R. Quinault and J. Stevenson, eds, *Popular Protest and Public Order: Six Studies in British History 1790–1920* (New York: St Martin's Press, 1974).

73 P.A. Pickering, *Chartism and the Chartists in Manchester and Salford* (Basingstoke: Macmillan, 1995), 169–72.

74 Thompson, *The Chartists*, 51.

75 P.A. Pickering, 'Class without words: symbolic communication in the Chartist movement', *Past and Present* 112 (1986), 145.

76 Hewitt, *Emergence of Stability*, 207, 195, 222.

77 N. Kirk, 'In defense of class: a critique of recent revisionist writing upon the nineteenth-century English working class', *International Review of Social History* 32 (1987), 36 n. 105.

78 Stedman Jones, 'Rethinking Chartism', 177; Kirk, *Growth of Working-Class Reformism*, 155.

79 Kirk, 'Defense of class', 46.

80 Belchem, *Popular Radicalism*, 93–4.

81 A. Messner, 'Land, leadership, culture, and emigration: some problems in Chartist historiography', *The Historical Journal* 42 (1999), 1094.

82 B. Lancaster, *Radicalism, Cooperation and Socialism: Leicester Working-Class Politics, 1860–1906* (Leicester: Leicester University Press, 1987), 77, 79–80.

83 Frost, *Forty Years' Recollections*, 204.

84 M. Taylor, *The Decline of British Radicalism, 1847–1860* (Oxford: Clarendon Press, 1995), 255–6.

85 G. Claeys, *Citizens and Saints: Politics and Anti-Politics in Early British Socialism* (Cambridge: Cambridge University Press, 1989), 283–4.

86 Gordon, *Women and the Labour Movement*, 62.

87 Kirk, *Growth of Working-Class Reformism*, 165; Finn, *After Chartism*, 251–60.

88 E.F. Biagini, 'British trade unions and popular political economy, 1860–1880', *The Historical Journal* 30:4 (1987), 815; E.F. Biagini, *Liberty, Retrenchment and Reform: Popular Liberalism in the Age of Gladstone, 1860–1880* (Cambridge: Cambridge University Press, 1992), ch. 3.

89 Wright, *Popular Radicalism*, 172.

90 H.I. Dutton and J.E. King, *'Ten Per Cent and No Surrender': The Preston Strike, 1853–1854* (Cambridge: Cambridge University Press, 1981), 55, 59.

91 Hewitt, *Emergence of Stability*, 229, 303, 283.

92 Joyce, *Work, Society and Politics*, 243, 205, 212; McWilliam, *Popular Politics*, 91, 94.

93 H. Mayhew, *London Labour and the London Poor* ([1861–2]: New York: Dover, 1968), 1:20.

94 D. Philips, *Crime and Authority in Victorian England: The Black Country 1835–1860* (London: Croom Helm, 1977), 54.

95 Taylor, *New Police*, 101; R. Storch, 'The policeman as domestic missionary: urban discipline and popular culture in northerm England, 1850–1880', *Journal of Social History* 9 (1976), 487.

96 R. Storch, 'The plague of the blue locusts: police reform and popular resistance in northern England, 1840–57', *International Review of Social History* 20 (1975), 66.

97 V.A.C. Gatrell, 'Crime, authority and the policeman-state', in F.M.L. Thompson, ed., *The Cambridge Social History of Britain 1750–1950, vol. III: Social Agencies and Institutions* (Cambridge: Cambridge University Press, 1990), 259.

98 Storch, 'Plague of the blue locusts', 74–5.

99 Philips, *Crime and Authority*, 149.

100 Kirk, *Growth of Working-Class Reform*, 259.

101 Lees, *Solidarities of Strangers*, 155–6.

102 Ibid., 182, 168–9, 205–7.

103 Levine-Clark, *Beyond the Reproductive Body*, 65.

104 J. Davis, 'Jennings' buildings and the royal borough: the construction of
     the underclass in mid-Victorian England', in D. Feldman and G. Stedman
     Jones, eds, *Metropolis London: Histories and Representations since 1800*
     (London: Routledge, 1989), 28.

105 Hewitt, *Emergence of Stability*, 149.

PART TWO

1870–1914

Introduction:
Discontinuity in 1870?

As noted in the introduction, any chronological break imposed by historians is arbitrary and open to debate. Given this caveat, however, a number of factors in British society make 1870 a reasonable choice. Though urbanization continued, the development of core working-class districts in major cities slowed in the last decades of the century, more stable working-class communities settled in, and urban growth concentrated in outlying districts. Economic conditions shifted in the early 1870s, as decreasing prices and profits led many observers to complain of a 'great depression'. New leisure patterns developed during this period as well, with the development of professional football, mass newspapers and the growth of syndicates in the music hall business. Images of empire and the monarchy pervaded these new media and contributed to a changed political landscape in the wake of the 1867 Reform Act. This act enfranchised many working-class men, and the parties began competing in earnest for working-class votes.

British men and women continued to settle in urban environments in the late-Victorian and Edwardian period. While nearly a third of the British population lived in cities of 100,000 or over in 1871, 43 per cent lived in such large cities in 1911. Almost 78 per cent of the British population in 1911 lived in urban areas of any size, compared with around two-thirds 40 years earlier.[1] However, the rapidly expanding centres of mid-Victorian urban growth slowed in the late nineteenth century. Preston had increased from 51,000 residents to 70,000 between 1841 and 1851, an increase of over 37 per cent in a decade. But from 1891 to 1901 the city grew by less than 5 per cent (108,000 to 113,000 inhabitants). Similarly, Birmingham and Liverpool's era of rapid growth came to an end. Both cities expanded by less than 10 per cent in the decade before 1901, and central districts of some large cities lost population.[2] On the other hand, some late-Victorian cities did grow rapidly, particularly new industrial cities, resort towns and suburban centres. Middlesbrough, a small port town of 5,463 in 1841, developed into an iron manufacturing city of 39,284 in 1871, and continued to expand rapidly, becoming a centre for large-scale steelworks with a population of 104,767 in 1911.[3] The market town of Croydon, along the London–Brighton road, housed 20,000 residents in 1851. By 1901 the expanding metropolis brought Croydon into a suburban role, and its population swelled to 134,000.[4] Four London suburbs were the fastest growing areas in England and Wales in the 1880s: West Ham, Leyton, Tottenham and Willesden.[5] As the settled districts of large cities spread outwards, they swallowed smaller neighbours, forming 'conurbations'. By 1881, 40 per cent of the population of England and Wales lived in the six largest conurbations (around London, Manchester, Birmingham, Leeds and Bradford, Liverpool and Newcastle).[6]

Beginning in 1873, the British economy entered a period of slowed growth, limited export expansion and declining profits.[7] Though the mid-Victorian boom did end in the early 1870s, notions of a 'great depression' in the late nineteenth century can be misleading. The British economy continued to grow, albeit more slowly than in previous decades. Though British exports expanded only gradually, they remained significant. At the turn of the century, British goods accounted for nearly a third of all exported manufactures in the world (and exports picked up in the first decade of the twentieth century).[8] Pressure on profits caused by declining prices was hardly mourned by wage earners, whose purchasing power increased dramatically with the fall in prices (though profits and prices recovered after 1900). Nonetheless, even if economic performance in Britain does not warrant the gloomy diagnosis of 'great depression', British businesses faced new competitive pressures and new challenges beginning in the early 1870s.

One set of businesses that successfully navigated late nineteenth-century conditions were those entrepreneurs who developed mass commercial leisure opportunities for workers. Many male workers enjoyed shorter working hours beginning in the 1870s, and rising real wages provided increased resources to spend on leisure. Though informal leisure remained important, commercialized mass amusements became a central part of working-class culture. These included professional football and pervasive gambling, the increasingly standardized offerings at music halls, the Sunday newspaper geared to the working-class audience, and seaside holidays. As historian Gareth Stedman Jones notes, starting in the 1870s a new working-class culture developed, 'clearly distinguished from the culture of the middle class' and characterized by 'the pub, the sporting paper, the race-course and the music-hall'.[9]

Alongside these mass amusements grew new forms of mass politics. Political reform in 1867 (1868 in Scotland) and 1885 enfranchised a significant number of workers, ultimately extending the franchise to all rate-paying householders and to lodgers of property worth a minimum of £10 per year, though both qualifications were subject to a year's residency requirement. Working-class men accounted for about 60 per cent of the electorate in the wake of these changes.[10] Many Conservatives feared the impact of the expanded electorate. Viscount Cranborne complained in 1867 that reform would transfer power to 'those who have no other property than the labour of their hands. The omnipotence of Parliament is theirs'.[11] These fears proved without foundation, as Conservatives competed successfully in the new political environment. Both Liberals and Conservatives attracted significant working-class support in the decades following the 1867 reform.

Notes

1 L. Lees, 'Urban networks', in M. Daunton, ed., *The Cambridge Urban History of Britain, vol. III: 1840–1950* (Cambridge: Cambridge University Press, 2000), 70.

2 B.R. Mitchell, *Abstract of British Historical Statistics* (Cambridge: Cambridge University Press, 1962), 24–7; P.J. Waller, *Town, City, and Nation: England 1850–1914* (Oxford: Oxford University Press, 1983), 25; N. McCord and D.J. Rowe, 'Industrialisation and urban growth in north-east England', *International Review of Social History* 22 (1977), 52.

3 A. Briggs, *Victorian Cities* (Harmondsworth: Penguin, 1968), 247; McCord and Rowe, 'Industrialisation and urban growth', 47–9.

4 Waller, *Town, City and Nation*, 165.

5 D. Feldman, 'Migration', in Daunton, ed. *Cambridge Urban History*, 198.

6 Lees, 'Urban networks', 71; E.J. Hobsbawm, *Workers: Worlds of Labour* (New York: Pantheon Books, 1984), 180.

7 S. Pollard, *Britain's Prime and Britain's Decline: The British Economy 1870–1914* (London: Edward Arnold, 1989), 7; K. Burgess, *The Challenge of Labour: Shaping British Society 1850–1930* (London: Croom Helm, 1980), 44.

8 Pollard, *Britain's Prime and Britain's Decline*, 15.

9 G. Stedman Jones, 'Working-class culture and working-class politics in London, 1870–1900: notes on the remaking of a working class', in *Languages of Class: Studies in English Working Class History 1832–1982* (Cambridge: Cambridge University Press, 1983), 207.

10 R. McKibbin, C. Matthew and J. Kay, 'The franchise factor in the rise of the Labour Party,' in R. McKibbin, *The Ideologies of Class: Social Relations in Britain 1880–1950* (Oxford: Clarendon Press, 1994), 79.

11 A. Briggs, *Victorian People: A Reassessment of Persons and Themes 1851–1867*, rev. ed. (Chicago: University of Chicago Press, 1972), 284.

CHAPTER FIVE

The 'traditional' working-class community

Grace Foakes, who grew up in a Wapping tenement in the first years of the twentieth century, recalled her intimate neighbourhood: 'This was a little community which lived almost entirely within itself'. A descendant of Irish immigrants, Foakes noted the well-defined boundaries of her world, in which a bridge marked the edge of the neighbourhood, beyond which 'They were a community on their own and so were we'.[1] Many late-Victorian and Edwardian working-class children grew up in settled districts whose rapid growth earlier in the nineteenth century had slowed. Though reformers took increasing interest in the miserable sanitary state of poor neighbourhoods, housing conditions in central districts continued to deteriorate, streets grew crowded and mortality rates remained high. Some regularly employed and relatively well-paid workers were able to take advantage of new cheap trams and even trains, moving into new working-class suburbs with better housing and sanitation. But most workers could not afford to move far from their places of work and remained in established working-class districts.

In these neighbourhoods they built strong bonds based on kinship and mutual aid. Established residents could count on their neighbours when difficulties struck (and they often did). Their close-knit communities enforced standards of behaviour and respectability and marked off hierarchies of status and authority. Women held together these neighbourhood bonds, and their efforts kept their families afloat as well. Precarious family budgets relied on women's domestic management, contributions from children old enough to earn, and the often irregular wages of the 'breadwinner'. In these communities, what would be recalled later in the twentieth century as 'traditional' working-class ways of life developed.

The working-class neighbourhood

A.S. Jasper grew up in East London early in the twentieth century. His family moved frequently, living in nine different houses between 1910 and 1918, but all were in the same Hoxton district, close to employment opportunities for family members.[2] David Brindley worked as a porter at Canada Dock Goods Station in Liverpool. After marrying in 1887, he and his family rented a number of homes over the years, remaining near his work and generally keeping to a single North Liverpool area.[3] Local contacts and connections kept families like the Jaspers and the Brindleys in the same neighbourhoods, even when they had to move house. According to Beatrice Webb, in poor urban districts people resembled 'the circle of suicides in Dante's Inferno; they go round and round within a certain area'.[4]

New suburbs did, however, attract some working-class families, particularly those with a regularly employed breadwinner. Workmen's trains in London, originally limited to the Great Eastern Railway extending north and east of the East End, served booming working-class suburbs in West Ham, Leyton and Willesden. West Ham grew from 19,000 residents in 1851 to 267,000 in 1891.[5] Elsewhere, trams played a more important role in bringing working-class commuters from new suburbs into central workplaces. Beginning in the 1890s, electrification and the municipal takeover of tram lines reduced costs for riders.[6] In Glasgow tram ridership increased more than fourfold between 1887 and 1913.[7]

Many workers, though, found suburban migration expensive and inconvenient. The lack of employment for women meant that men's wages needed to be both regular and adequate to support the family. Commuting costs and the expense of eating in coffee shops added to the financial burden. Joseph Kirkham, a painter living in Battersea, noted that his wife could provide dinner for the entire family for what his dinner cost in a cook-shop near his work. In the 1870s, even when trams and trains did offer affordable fares, they lacked schedules appropriate for many workers. Thomas Abrey, a North London carpenter, complained that the tram from his area did not begin running until 6.40 a.m., too late for building or engineering workers.[8] Even after trams and trains grew cheaper and more convenient, many workers continued to live in central districts.

Established working-class neighbourhoods offered valuable amenities. Pubs and street performances provided entertainment and diversion. Local shops offered the cheap goods in small quantities and credit essential to many working-class family budgets. Networks of kin and neighbours, cultivated over years of residence in the same district, provided aid, social ties and community feeling.[9] Marriage records reveal that in some working-class districts nearly all newly married couples came from the same parish, and more than two-thirds lived on the same street.[10] Even those in relatively new working-class districts could develop these close ties over the course of a few decades. One observer, Lady Bell, commented that residents of a Middlesbrough neighbourhood 'have as deeply-rooted an attachment to it as though it were a beautiful village. There are people . . . who have been there for many years, and more than one who has left it has actually pined to be back again'.[11]

Housing and sanitation

Lady Bell expressed surprise that working people felt such a connection to 'hard-looking, shabby, ugly streets', and much of the new working-class housing in the last decades of the century was drab and monotonous. New housing in England from the late 1870s did, however, reflect improved regulatory standards. The model by-laws of 1877, which provided guidance to local authorities in developing housing regulations, dictated wider streets, open space at the rear of every house, enhanced windows and drainage, and individual privies that could be emptied without waste being transported through the house. Housing constructed according to new regulations also included more space. Typical mid-century back-to-back housing included around 40 square metres (450 square feet) on two floors. By the end of the century, by-law houses included at least 54 square metres (580 square feet), and often over 70 square metres (750 square feet).[12] Generally, new housing also offered more private space, with less sharing of facilities.[13] Scottish building regulations became compulsory beginning in 1892, though tenements remained typical of Scottish working-class housing.[14]

Despite the gradual spread of new working-class housing built to better standards, middle-class concern with conditions in poor neighbourhoods intensified in the second half of the century. Some reformers sought to provide an improved environment for workers, both morally and physically, by constructing model dwellings. These developments offered better physical conditions but also enforced rules that were meant to reshape tenants morally. Most of the model dwelling companies sought a return on their investment of 4–5 per cent, to prove that decent housing for workers was possible under market conditions. Yet this determination forced rents upward, leaving the dwellings beyond the reach of all but the regularly employed and skilled. In addition, regulations and moral supervision alienated many workers, who preferred less regimented private rental housing. The London Trades Council expressed resentment against model dwellings because of their ugliness and the 'irksome restraint through the conditions and regulations'.[15]

Local authorities also began to provide working-class housing on a limited scale before the First World War. Liverpool blazed the trail in this area, constructing a tenement building, St Martin's Cottages, in 1869. The London County Council (LCC) became the most aggressive and significant provider of council housing after 1890. It built tenements in central districts, such as the Boundary Street development in Bethnal Green. After 1898, however, the LCC decided to focus on building suburban council estates, such as Totterdown Fields in Tooting. A political shift in 1907, when Moderates replaced Progressives as the LCC majority, took the wind from the sails of this experiment, and the First World War would interrupt council housing schemes entirely.[16]

Despite these innovations, older houses constructed before regulation remained typical of working-class neighbourhoods, particularly in central districts. New by-law housing represented only about 1 per cent of the housing stock each year.[17] Model dwelling companies confined their activities almost exclusively to London, where they housed 123,000 people out of a population of over 4.5 million. The overall impact of municipal housing remained small. Liverpool boasted the highest proportion of council house residents in England: 1.3 per cent of the population at the start of the First World War.[18] Overall, Scottish local authorities that provided dwellings housed just 1 per cent of their populations.[19]

Perhaps more significant than by-law, model, or council housing in improving working-class living conditions at the end of the nineteenth century was the spread of the water closet. Older privy types represented a significant health hazard. One Preston resident recalled their emptying: 'the night soil men would go round the back with a barrow, dig the stuff out . . . take it back down the lobby and tip it into the street. Then later . . . a cart would come and they'd scoop it up . . . conditions by modern standards were really awful'.[20] The worst forms were gradually replaced either by more easily emptied pails or by water closets. In Birmingham, for example, nearly three-quarters of all facilities were ash pits in 1871, but by 1894 only 14 per cent were ash pits, 45 per cent were water closets, and 41 per cent used pails. The early twentieth-century saw the triumph of water closets in many cities. In Manchester 98 per cent of all facilities were water closets in 1913, reflecting the local government's willingness to contribute to the conversion of pail toilets and privies.[21]

Though the conversion to water closets improved sanitary conditions even in older working-class districts, overall housing conditions for most working people remained unhealthy, in part due to crowding. Clearances for the construction of railways, new roads, commercial property or simply in the name of destroying slums reduced the housing available to workers who needed to remain close to employment opportunities.[22] Railways alone occupied between 5 and 9 per cent of land in central districts of London, Liverpool, Manchester, Birmingham and Glasgow in 1900, and railway construction had displaced as many as 4 million people in the previous half century.[23] Slum clearances displaced many thousands more. Even where replacement housing was constructed, rents were generally too high for those who had inhabited the crowded and unsanitary houses that were destroyed. In one Limehouse demolition, 286 families lost their homes. Only 12 could afford to live in the new model housing constructed on the site by the Peabody Trust, a model dwelling company.[24] When displaced by various 'improvements', many working people who had strong ties to their neighbourhoods and workplaces crowded into nearby houses, exacerbating conditions in these areas.

Mrs Wilkinson, born in Barrow at the start of the twentieth century, grew up in a five-room house with eight siblings and her parents. She shared a bedroom containing two beds with her four sisters.[25] According to official standards that allowed two adults per room with children under ten counting as half, this family was not 'overcrowded'. But even by this tolerant measure, more than 11 per cent of the population of England and Wales in 1891 lived in overcrowded conditions.[26] Though this figure declined to around 8 per cent in 1911, many cities still had high rates of overcrowding. The problem was significantly worse in Scotland, where in 1911 a shocking 55.7 per cent of Glasgow's population lived more than two per room.[27] Thomas Bell recalled growing up in a Glasgow tenement, in what he described not as a slum but as 'something next door to it'. Bell's family lived in two rooms, and 'there were eight of us in these two rooms'.[28]

Not surprisingly, crowded conditions led to the spread of disease. Though the installation of water closets led directly to a drop in diseases such as enteric fever, other health problems persisted at high levels.[29] In a 1901 lecture, Robert Koch, who isolated the tuberculosis bacillus, complained that the consumptive living under crowded conditions could not help but spread the disease. According to *The Times*, Koch claimed: 'However cautious he might be, the sufferer scattered the morbid matter secreted by his diseased lungs every time he coughed . . . it was the overcrowded dwellings of the poor that we had to regard as the real breeding places of tuberculosis'.[30] Infant mortality reflects the generally unhealthy conditions in crowded working-class districts. While the 1908 rate of infant mortality throughout Birmingham was 145 deaths per thousand, in the crowded working-class areas of St George's and St Stephen's mortality figures reached 213 and 232 per thousand infants.[31] Though better nutrition contributed to a gradual decline in mortality rates, this class differential remained striking.[32]

As conditions in central districts deteriorated, neighbourhoods became more exclusively working class.[33] Earlier in the century, posh developments drew affluent middle-class families out of central districts. In the last decades of the nineteenth century, residential segregation spread, as lower-middle-class suburbs developed, and even some well-paid manual workers moved into distinct suburban areas. In Cardiff, for example, some skilled workers left the central districts and moved to Canton and Cathays to the north and west. Yet they settled in distinct areas, segregated from the lower ranks of the middle class.[34] This social gap between skilled workers and clerks or other non-manual employees grew sharper in Kentish London as well, with manual workers occupying particular sections of these suburban districts.[35] Whether in new by-law housing or deteriorating slums, manual workers were increasingly segregated geographically.

The family economy

The poor conditions in working-class districts were obvious to contemporaries. Helen Dendy (later Bosanquet) emphasized another striking feature of London poor neighbourhoods: 'Swarming up and down the doorsteps or camping out in the roadway, are countless numbers of puny, dirty children'.[36] By the last decades of the nineteenth century, middle-class couples limited their fertility, while most workers still had large families. In Birmingham in 1900 the affluent Edgbaston and Harborne ward had a birth rate of 18.6 per thousand, compared with the poor St Stephen's ward, where births totalled 36.9 per thousand. Late in the nineteenth century, though, some families of skilled workers began to limit their fertility. Thus, Balsall Heath, a district with many relatively well-paid workers, registered 24.3 births per thousand.[37] Mr Riley born in 1900 in Lancaster, had only one sibling. His father, a skilled woodworker, 'didn't want a big family'.[38]

Upper-working-class families like the Rileys began controlling their fertility for a number of reasons. Perhaps the most important relates to the increasing expense of raising children. Before 1870 it was common for children to begin earning wages before age 10 in factories and around age 11 in other trades.[39] Girls also made essential contributions to their families by minding younger siblings and doing domestic work.[40] The institution of compulsory education beginning in the 1870s replaced more flexible and often informal working-class schools with a standard, legally enforced school day and gradually raised the school-leaving age. Compulsory schooling interfered with children's ability to contribute to their family's economy, and created a tremendous burden for poor families.[41] Among better-paid workers, investment in education became a sign of respectability. These families grew less reliant on children's contributions to the household, and husbands and wives began to cooperate in having fewer children.[42]

While only a minority of working-class couples successfully limited their fertility around the turn of the century, the desire to have smaller families appears nearly universal among working-class women in this period. Without effective birth control or their husbands' cooperation, most working-class women had little control over their fertility. Mrs Mitchell, born in Preston early in the twentieth century, was one of eight children and recalled, 'In those days there was no birth control . . . If it happened, it happened'.[43] Many women, however, were less fatalistic than this quote would suggest. They tried a variety of measures to escape repeated pregnancies: avoiding sex with their husbands, using homemade pessaries, or attempting to end their pregnancies through abortion.[44] After having two children in two years, one woman recalled taking the advice of friends who recommended an abortifacient. 'I took their strong concoctions to purge me of the little life that might be mine. They failed, as such things generally do, and the third baby came'.[45] Despite women's recourse to these dangerous and unreliable methods, large working-class families remained typical in the first years of the twentieth century. As one child of the Edwardian working class recalled, 'My mother nursed a bit of bitterness because she had a big family and would have liked to have done different'.[46]

Working-class women's concerns over family size reflect their responsibility for making ends meet. Husbands and wives recognized their distinct responsibilities in working-class marriages. A good husband turned over a reasonable amount of money to his wife each week. Once this was done, it fell to women to make sure that the rent was paid, and food, clothing and all other necessities provided. This division of responsibilities was nearly universal. One East London woman complained that men 'think they're giving you a fortune; 23 shillings mine gives me and four babies to keep . . . I would rather he'd stick to the few ha'pence, and he keep the home, but there, *he couldn't do it*.[47] A man who provided fairly could be excused almost any other behaviour. Though William Harding assaulted his wife with a fire poker, he defended himself in court by noting that he had given her a portion of his earnings. The presiding magistrate in the case, Mr Cooke, commented that 'it was clear that the prisoner took her home the money directly' and ordered his release.[48]

This transaction, in which men provided resources for their families, lay at the heart of marital relationships.[49] In some cases men turned over their entire wages to their wives, and the women then provided small sums for their husbands' leisure. Men who allowed their wives this level of control over the purse were seen as model husbands, and this pattern appears to have been more common in the North than, for example, in London. Some of these men were so proud of being model husbands that they bragged 'that all they have is what the "missus allows them" '.[50] At the opposite end of the spectrum lay those husbands who spent freely on drink after receiving their wages, turning only a meagre remainder over to their wives. Desperate women facing this situation still had to provide for their families despite their husbands' irresponsibility. Though William Hibbard had beaten his wife and treated her cruelly for years, when he offered her only 1s. out of his (already inadequate) 9s. pay, she could take no more. She stabbed him outside the pub.[51]

The most common pattern, however, involved husbands handing over a set amount to their wives and keeping the rest of their wages for their own spending. In East London, George Acorn's father provided 18s. for the family's needs, whenever his earnings allowed it. This amount was fixed early in their marriage, and it did not change with the increasing expenses of a growing family.[52] Maud Pember Reeves described the challenges facing wives of relatively well-paid workers who provided 'round about a pound a week' for their families. While the husband 'expects the same amount of food', the wife confronts new expenses with each baby. 'She has more mouths to fill, and grows impatient because he does not understand that . . . a boy of three, plus a baby, makes the old problem into quite a new one'.[53]

The focus on men's contribution to the household economy reveals the continued embrace of the male breadwinner ideal.[54] Union leader Henry Broadhust advocated 'a condition of things where wives and daughters would be in their proper sphere at home', supported by their husbands.[55] Despite the appeal of the male breadwinner model and the withdrawal of some school-aged children from the workforce, the wage of the husband and father still provided little more than two-thirds of the family income.[56]

Of course, this varied tremendously. Skilled workers with only young children at home might provide the only support for their families. As children grew up, however, they were expected to earn their keep and contribute to the family economy.[57] Many married women also earned money for their households, taking in boarders or earning wages for part or full-time work. Robert and Mary Ann Lyons lived in Bethnal Green with one daughter and two sons. Robert, Mary Ann and their oldest son Albert all worked as boot makers, while their daughter, Frances, was a tailoress.[58]

Good husbands contributed to their wives' household budgets, but women faced a much broader set of familial responsibilities. They had to find ways to provide for their families' needs, and this often took great effort and resourcefulness. As John Blake recalled, 'When he handed over his quota to Mum, and he had kept a small amount for pocket money, he considered his duty had been carried out but Mum only started from then, with all the worry of making ends meet'.[59] Resourceful shopping and bargaining could stretch meagre budgets. For example, women in Birmingham could obtain meat cheaply by waiting until shops were ready to close on Saturday night. Without refrigeration, the shops could not keep the meat until Monday, so they sold it off cheaply. One resident recalled, 'People round the area . . . They'd wait and wait . . . They used to start off with half a crown parcels, you know. Come down to two bob'. Women also used credit from local merchants and the pawnshop to manage their budgets.[60] A Lancaster resident recalled, 'You either owed the milkman, the coalman, the doctor, or you were in arrears with the rent. There were a lot of arrears in them days'.[61] In London, 'like the majority of neighbours', John Blake's mother 'had to augment her income from the weekly wage packet from Dad, by full use of the tallyman and the pawnbroker'.[62]

The most pressing project women faced involved feeding their families. Consumers benefited from a substantial drop in prices in the late nineteenth century. Retail food prices fell 30 per cent between 1877 and 1887. For those enjoying regular work, wages held steady or rose, yielding an increase in real wages of 60 per cent for urban workers between 1860 and 1900.[63] Even so, bread dominated working-class diets, forming the basis for two meals per day. For the main meal, women combined some form of cheap protein with potatoes and vegetables. One boy recalled his mother making 'sheep's head broth', including 'a few bones and half a sheep's head . . . that went in and a few vegetables chopped into it and that was it, a meal'.[64] When resources were short, however, working-class diets grew more monotonous and even more dependent on bread. Women created meals from almost nothing, such as the 'sop' eaten in Birmingham, which consisted of bread mashed in hot water with the drippings from a tea pot on top.[65] One York woman complained, 'I'm dead sick of bread and butter – nothing but bread and butter until I hate the sight of it'.[66]

In the struggle to keep their families afloat, women relied on essential aid from their neighbours. A resident of Barrow recalled frequent borrowing of 'a little bit of tea, a little bit of sugar, a shilling . . . Often they knocked, "Can I borrow a cup of sugar? Have you a bit of margarine?" '. These small debts were repaid carefully, 'otherwise the system would have broken down'.[67] As another woman reported, 'You always got it back'.[68] Neighbours even lent items for pawning.[69] Perhaps more importantly women provided one another with essential services, such as minding children. Maria Francis, who lived in the London neighbourhood of Somers Town, regularly watched her neighbour's three-year-old.[70]

At confinement, neighbourhood women showed their value. Even when a doctor or formally trained midwife attended a birth, neighbourhood women looked after the mother and helped with her domestic tasks. Katherine Roberts, a district nurse in London noted, 'I almost always find a friend has "stepped in" to help, and they do all they can in spite of their own work'. Some of these informal nurses, often widows or older women, earned their livings by helping out their neighbours.[71] A local woman named Martha delivered babies in Lancaster, charging a few shillings, which could be paid off over a number of weeks. A Barrow woman recalled of the neighbourhood midwives who helped her mother, 'they were such good friends a lot of them'.[72] The neighbour and 'unofficial midwife' who helped at Walter Southgate's birth became his godmother.[73]

Neighbours also stepped in at times of sickness and death. In Barrow, 'When they were ill they used to get a sheep's head and a marrow bone and then twopennyworth of pot herbs and make a good pan of soup, and some split peas and barley and take them a good bowl of soup in at night'.[74] When women had to enter the hospital, neighbours took in their children.[75] When someone in the neighbourhood died, local women, often the ones who attended childbirths, came to lay out the dead.[76] Men would collect money for co-workers who lost children.[77] George Acorn recalled the generosity of neighbours when his brother died, 'Relatives and neighbours, all, to be sure, very poor, vied with each other in doing little things for us'.[78]

This mutual aid was essential to survival in working-class neighbourhoods. In his East End neighbourhood, Walter Southgate found that 'mutual aid was the keystone of existence when difficult times came along'.[79] Women helped out their neighbours as part of a web of mutual obligation, rather than in the expectation of a specific favour in return. Though some services such as attendance at a childbirth brought payment from neighbours, women also helped their neighbours in order to maintain the local safety net.[80] 'Neighbours used to stick together and help each other, because they knew they'd be in the same boat anytime'.[81] Women who helped their neighbours also gained respect and standing in the community. Their ability and willingness to help others made them the 'matriarchs' of these close-knit communities.[82]

These formidable women used their standing to enforce codes of behaviour. In crowded neighbourhoods women could keep a close eye on activities. They developed strict standards and used gossip as a powerful tool to maintain them. One observer commented, 'These people have their own code . . . and infractions of it were intensely resented by the people themselves'.[83] Violations caused damage to reputation, as Robert Roberts recalled, 'the health, honesty, conduct, history and connections of everyone in the neighbourhood would be examined . . . and finally allotted by tacit consent a position on the social scale'.[84] Networks of gossip and information helped enforce hierarchies of status and respect in working-class districts. In extreme cases, ostracism by one's neighbours could make life in a working-class community unbearable.[85]

Conclusion

The public and collective nature of these judgements, formulated in the corner shop, at doorsteps, or around shared facilities, helped mark working-class neighbourhoods as distinctive. They reinforced the values of a 'traditional' working-class way of life that grew in the settled and insular neighbourhoods of the late nineteenth-century working class. The dense web of interdependence and intimacy developed out of crowded conditions. Poverty and insecurity encouraged mutual aid, without which many women would have found making ends meet impossible. Though these communities imposed a rigid conformity, many children of the neighbourhoods recalled them fondly. Despite the difficulty of their lives, for many residents of close-knit working-class districts 'There was poverty, disease, dirt and ignorance, and yet to feel one belonged outweighed all else'.[86]

Notes

1 G. Foakes, *Between High Walls: A London Childhood* (London: Shepheard-Walwyn, 1972), 2, 22.

2 R. Dennis, 'Modern London', in M. Daunton, ed., *The Cambridge Urban History of Britain, vol. III: 1840–1950* (Cambridge: Cambridge University Press, 2000), 117.

3 C.G. Pooley and J. Turnbull, *Migration and Mobility in Britain since the Eighteenth Century* (London: UCL Press, 1998), 240.

4 P.J. Waller, *Town, City, and Nation: England 1850–1914* (Oxford: Oxford University Press, 1983), 28.

5 J. Burnett, *A Social History of Housing 1815–1985*, 2nd ed. (London: Methuen, 1986), 164.

6 R.J. Dennis, *English Industrial Cities in the Nineteenth Century: A Social Geography* (Cambridge: Cambridge University Press, 1984), 123; J. Armstrong, 'Transport and the urban environment', in Daunton, ed. *Cambridge Urban History*, 237–8, 241–2.

7 W. Seccombe, *Weathering the Storm: Working-Class Families from the Industrial Revolution to the Fertility Decline* (London: Verso, 1995), 133.

8 G. Stedman Jones, *Outcast London: A Study in the Relationship between Classes in Victorian Society* (New York: Pantheon Books, 1984), 208–9.

9 Stedman Jones, *Outcast London*, 173; A. August, *Poor Women's Lives: Gender, Work and Poverty in Late-Victorian London* (London: Associated University Presses, 1999), 36.

10 E. Ross, 'Survival networks: women's neighbourhood sharing in London before World War One', *History Workshop Journal* 15 (1983), appendix.

11 Waller, *Town, City, and Nation*, 100.

12 Burnett, *Social History of Housing*, 158–9, 161.

13 M. Daunton, *House and Home in the Victorian City: Working-Class Housing 1850–1914* (London: Edward Arnold, 1983), 20ff.

14 R. Rodger, *Housing in Urban Britain, 1780–1914* (Cambridge: Cambridge University Press, 1995), 49.

15 Stedman Jones, *Outcast London*, 182–5, 193–4, 187; Burnett, *Social History of Housing*, 177–8.

16 Burnett, *Social History of Housing*, 185–7.

17 Rodger, *Housing in Urban Britain*, 49.

18 Daunton, *House and Home*, 193–4.

19 R. Rodger, 'The Victorian building industry and the housing of the Scottish working class', in M. Doughty, ed., *Building the Industrial City* (Leicester: Leicester University Press, 1986), 183.

20 E. Roberts, *A Woman's Place: An Oral History of Working-Class Women 1890–1940* (Oxford: Basil Blackwell, 1984), 133–4.

21 Daunton, *House and Home*, 248–55.

22 Stedman Jones, *Outcast London*, 172–4.

23 Waller, *Town, City, and Nation*, 161.

24 Stedman Jones, *Outcast London*, 203.

25 Roberts, *Woman's Place*, 129–30.

26 Burnett, *Social History of Housing*, 144–5.

27 R. Rodger, 'Political economy, ideology and the persistence of working-class housing problems in Britain, 1850–1914', *International Review of Social History* 32 (1987), 113.

28 T. Bell, *Pioneering Days* (London: Lawrence & Wishart, 1941), 18.

29 Daunton, *House and Home*, 253.

30 Rodger, 'Political economy', 113–14.

31 S. Meacham, *A Life Apart: The English Working Class 1890–1914* (Cambridge, MA: Harvard University Press, 1977), 156.

32 J.M. Winter, 'The decline of mortality in Britain 1870–1950', in T. Barker and M. Drake, eds, *Population and Society in Britain 1850–1980* (New York: New York University Press, 1982), 107, 115.

33 Stedman Jones, *Outcast London*, 326.

34 M.J. Daunton, *Coal Metropolis: Cardiff 1870–1914* (Leicester: Leicester University Press, 1977), 138.

35 G. Crossick, *An Artisan Elite in Victorian Society: Kentish London 1840–1880* (London: Croom Helm, 1978), 249.

36 A. Davin, *Growing Up Poor: Home, School and Street in London 1870–1914* (London: Rivers Oram Press, 1996), 64.

37 C. Chinn, *They Worked All Their Lives: Women of the Urban Poor in England, 1880–1939* (Manchester: Manchester University Press, 1988), 134; see also E. Ross, *Love and Toil: Motherhood in Outcast London 1870–1918* (Oxford: Oxford University Press, 1993), 94–5; M. Haines, 'Social class differentials during fertility decline: England and Wales revisited', *Population Studies* 43 (1989), 321.

38 Roberts, *Woman's Place*, 91.

39 S. Horrell and J. Humphries, 'Child labour and British industrialization', in M. Lavalette, ed., *A Thing of the Past? Child Labour in Britain in the Nineteenth and Twentieth Centuries* (Liverpool: Liverpool University Press, 1999), 88.

40 Davin, *Growing Up Poor*, 88.

41 Seccombe, *Weathering the Storm*, 109.

42 D. Levine, *Reproducing Families: The Political Economy of English Population History* (Cambridge: Cambridge University Press, 1987), 191.

43 Roberts, *Woman's Place*, 86.

44 Ross, *Love and Toil*, 102.

45 M.L. Davies, *Maternity: Letters from Working Women* ([1915]; New York: Norton, 1978), 45.

46 P. Thompson, *The Edwardians* (Chicago: Academy Chicago, 1975), 64.

47 Ross, *Love and Toil*, 72.

48 August, *Poor Women's Lives*, 124–5, 133.

49 E. Ross, ' "Fierce questions and taunts": married life in working-class London, 1870–1914', *Feminist Studies* 8 (1982), 582.

50 Ross, *Love and Toil*, 76–7; Roberts, *Woman's Place*, 110–11.

51 Ross, 'Fierce questions and taunts', 582.

52 August, *Poor Women's Lives*, 125.

53 M. Pember Reeves, *Round About a Pound a Week* ([1913]; London: Virago, 1979), 155.

54 W. Seccombe, 'Patriarchy stabilized: the construction of the male breadwinner wage norm in nineteenth-century Britain', *Social History* 11 (1986), 54.

55 Seccombe, *Weathering the Storm*, 114.

56 Levine, *Reproducing Families*, 175.

57 L.H. Lees, 'Getting and spending: the family budgets of English industrial workers in 1890', in J. Merriman, ed., *Consciousness and Class Experience in Nineteenth-Century Europe* (New York: Holmes & Meier, 1979), 173.

58 August, *Poor Women's Lives*, 102–20.

59 J. Blake, *Memories of Old Poplar* (London: Stepney Books, 1977), 8.

60 Chinn, *They Worked All Their Lives*, 66, 73–7.

61 E. Roberts, 'Working-class standards of living in Barrow and Lancaster, 1890–1914', *Economic History Review* 30 (1977), 316.

62 Blake, *Memories of Old Poplar*, 8.

63 J. Burnett, *Plenty and Want: A Social History of Food in England from 1815 to the Present Day*, 3rd ed. (London: Routledge, 1989), 115; J. Belchem, *Industrialization and the Working Class: The English Experience, 1750–1900* (Portland: Areopagitica Press, 1990), 198.

64 Roberts, *Woman's Place*, 157.

65 Chinn, *They Worked All Their Lives*, 62–3.

66 Meacham, *A Life Apart*, 82.

67 Roberts, *Woman's Place*, 191.

68 Ross, 'Survival networks', 11.

69 Chinn, *They Worked All Their Lives*, 35.

70 *Camden and Kentish Towns, Hampstead, Highgate, Holloway and St Pancras Gazette*, 12 October, 1889; Ross, 'Survival networks', 12.

71 Ross, *Love and Toil*, 116, 120.

72 Roberts, *Woman's Place*, 106–7.

73 W. Southgate, *That's the Way It Was: A Working Class Autobiography 1890–1950* (London: New Clarion Press, 1982), 11.

74 Roberts, *Woman's Place*, 191.

75 Ross, 'Survival networks', 13.

76 Roberts, *Woman's Place*, 189.

77 Ross, *Love and Toil*, 193.

78 G. Acorn, *One of the Multitude* (London: William Heinemann, 1911), 40.

79 Southgate, *The Way It Was*, 22.

80 Ross, 'Survival networks', 14; Roberts, *Woman's Place*, 187.

81 Meacham, *A Life Apart*, 59.

82 Chinn, *They Worked All Their Lives*, 37.

83 Davin, *Growing Up Poor*, 37.

84 R. Roberts, *The Classic Slum: Salford Life in the First Quarter of the Century* (Harmondsworth: Penguin, 1973), 42.

85 M. Tebbutt, *Women's Talk? A Social History of Gossip in Working-Class Neighbourhoods, 1880–1960* (Aldershot: Scolar Press, 1995), 77; Chinn, *They Worked All Their Lives*, 107.

86 G. Foakes, *My Part of the River* (London: Shepheard-Walwyn, 1974), 56.

CHAPTER SIX

Control, conflict and collective bargaining in the workplace

Alfred Williams worked for 23 years in the large railway works in Swindon. His recollections, published in 1915, reveal his bitter disenchantment with changes at the works. He complained of the impact of machinery on the pace of work. 'New machinery has revolutionized many branches of the labour and it usually happens that . . . the men are hustled into double activity'. Workers earning piece rates faced cuts that forced increased effort: 'The prices have been cut again and again'. As the power of foremen grew, Williams chafed under their authority, noting that 'Most foremen are excessively autocratic and severe with their men'. His overseers disliked intelligent workers, preferring men who 'creep about, are rough, ragged, and round-shouldered . . . are servile and abject'. Most disconcerting to Williams was the extension of discipline and authority over workers. Early in his career, 'The workman was not watched and timed at every little operation', but lately, 'The supervisory staff has been doubled or trebled' and 'supervision of the sheds is much more strict'.[1]

The pressures Williams faced in his factory reflected broader conditions in the late-Victorian and Edwardian workplace. The mid-Victorian boom, a period in which British manufacturing dominated world markets nearly without rival, gave way to the 'great depression', as new competition put pressure on profits. In this context, employer efforts to maximize productivity and profitability threatened many workers' status, autonomy, pay, and even their jobs. Workers fought what was often a rearguard action against employer offensives. Though many unions gained recognition and collective bargaining rights, employers battled workers over control in the workplace. As the first decade of the twentieth century came to a close, the accumulated frustration of many workers led to militancy and new conflicts with employers.

Employer initiatives and worker responses

In the new economic environment of the 'great depression', employers faced increasing pressure on profits, and they stepped up efforts to get more out of their workers. Employer strategies included new technology, strengthened discipline and control over work, new payment schemes and reduced dependence on skilled male workers. Employers and workers had struggled over many of these issues in the mid-Victorian period, but the new economic conditions created more urgency for employers. Even so, attempts to impose these approaches varied tremendously, by industry, region and employer, and each tactic met significant barriers.

One approach to cutting costs – expanding the scale of manufacturing – remained less common in Britain than elsewhere. Steam power engaged in British industry did soar to 10 million horsepower in 1907, perhaps five times its level in 1870.[2] Factories grew more common in certain trades, such as the Leicestershire hosiery and boot and shoe industries.[3] With the transition from wood to iron ships, the scale of shipyards increased, and 20 of them employed over 2,000 hands at the end of the century.[4] But the typical British employer did not follow the American lead in combining to form huge corporations built on bureaucratized mass production in large factories.[5] Even where large-scale manufacture spread, such as in Clydeside engineering, many small firms persisted. In some growing trades such as ready-made clothing manufacture, decentralized manufacturing expanded, as wholesalers distributed materials to small workshops and factories as well as to workers in their own homes.[6]

Most British employers were also slow to embrace and invest in new technology. In engineering, for example, most employers adopted new machine tools gradually rather than implementing wholesale technological transformation.[7] In the Potteries one worker complained that 'a revolution was taking place in methods of production', yet mechanization in this trade remained partial and irregular into the twentieth century.[8] British businesses were reluctant to bear the huge financial costs of large-scale mechanization, and they faced the prospect of battles with unions over the imposition of new machines. As skilled labour remained plentiful, it made little sense for most industries to mechanize rapidly.[9]

Where employers did embrace new machines, they could transform the division of labour and upset authority structures in the workplace. In engineering, mechanization disrupted skill hierarchies, expanding work opportunities for semi-skilled operatives and reducing demand for skilled men. When combined with more aggressive supervision, machines could undermine worker control of the pace and rhythm of work. Alfred Williams complained, 'New machinery is continually being installed in the sheds. This is driven at a high rate and the workman must keep pace with it'.[10] A boot and shoe employer boasted of the potential profitability of Leicester shoe manufacture this way: 'It is the result of keener supervision, better organization in the factories, the most approved equipment, and good management, generally'.[11]

With or without technological advance, employers sought to improve profitability through 'keener supervision', restructuring the labour process to gain control over workers and work. Taylorism, an American approach to 'scientific management', stressed carefully calculated piece rates, the creation of a distinct stratum of experts to manage production, and employer control over work. British employers did not wholeheartedly embrace the Taylorist approach, but they did put into place some of its principles.[12] Some employers created new supervisory officials, such as the 'feed and speed' men: 'Fixed to each machine was a chart indicating the speeds to be employed, and the feed and speed men, armed with feedmeters, perambulated the shop to ensure both men and machine were working to their utmost capacity'.[13] Overseers could earn bonuses if their workers produced more rapidly. Increased regulation of worker behaviour exacerbated this quickening of the pace of work. Some 500 women in one factory had their time in the lavatory tallied by a male overseer. If they totalled over four minutes in a month, they were fined. This kind of oversight led a Salford worker to lament 'a multitude of petty tyrannies and humiliations in the course of workshop life'.[14]

Employers also adjusted payment schemes to maximize worker productivity. At times, this involved switching from piece rates to day wages. Lasters in the footwear trades, for example, earned piece rates negotiated shop by shop. As Leicester footwear manufacturers introduced machines for lasting, the union sought to maintain the old piece rates to enjoy the fruits of increased productivity on the new machines. However, in the aftermath of an employer victory in the lockout of 1895, most lasters had to accept day wages.[15] Skilled engineering workers, on the other hand, preferred time wages to piece rates, and their union fought employer efforts to introduce piece work. Despite this effort, payment by the piece spread, and over a third of skilled engineering workers in the union received piece rates in 1906, compared with just over 10 per cent in 1861.[16]

These employer initiatives threatened skilled men who had emerged in the mid-Victorian boom as the highest paid and most autonomous wage earners. Skilled footwear workers complained of the increasingly common view that the 'knowledge of leather, its attributes and uses, are becoming day by day apparently less a necessity to the workman than the fact of being competent to direct or control some intricate piece of machinery'. In their view, 'leather produced under such conditions would be void of those symmetrical proportions, the artistic outlines, and the life – so to speak' of work done by skilled craftsmen. Within two decades of this 1881 complaint, however, semi-skilled operatives had replaced skilled lasters in the Leicester footwear industry.[17] Between 1899 and 1914 fewer than two-thirds of sons of skilled workers held skilled jobs at the time of their marriages (compared to more than 80 per cent from 1839 to 1854). The largest portion of the others were in semi-skilled work.[18] A boilermaker, John Hill, complained in 1908: 'With improved machinery our craft is at a discount, and a boy from school now tends a machine which does the work of three men'.[19] Yet despite new machinery and the addition of large numbers of less-skilled workers, most engineering employers failed to displace skilled craftsmen. In 1914 60 per cent of workers in firms associating with the Engineering Employers' Federation were categorized as skilled.[20]

Gender and age

To defend their status, skilled workers continued to struggle against feminization. In 1883 a Kidderminster carpet manufacturer named Henry Dixon modified some of his looms to make draperies and hired women to run them. This sparked a fierce conflict with his male weavers. The ensuing strike and demonstrations led to violence when police and soldiers challenged the crowds.[21] In some cases employers successfully moved lower-paid women into the workforce. One union representative complained in 1908: 'the women are ousting the men in most trades, including the iron trades. Many women are doing the light kind of drilling, etc., which used to be done by men'.[22] The 1909 report of the Royal Commission on the Poor Laws observed that the 'sub-division of labour and specialisation of machinery favours the intrusion of women into many trades hitherto occupied by men'.[23]

Even where women did encroach on the work of skilled men, employers and male workers generally fixed a new sexual division of labour that kept men's and women's jobs distinct. For example, in tailoring, a complex division of labour confined women to poorly paid jobs such as making buttonholes or finishing trousers. In one small East London waistcoat workshop, three women tacked the edges of the cut fabric, made the buttonholes and felled the linings, while two men stitched the seams and edges and pressed the garments. More expensive garments involved more male handiwork, as Charles Booth's social survey noted, 'As price and quality decline, so women take an increasing share in the shop work'.[24]

For most employed women, this finely tuned division of labour was irrelevant, as they worked in overwhelmingly female occupations. The most common form of women's employment remained domestic work, whether done on a live-in basis or as day servants. In London over half of employed women performed domestic service, and more than 40 per cent in Edinburgh did so, though the proportion elsewhere was lower.[25] Women dominated certain manufacturing trades as well, including dressmaking, millinery and box manufacture. Thus, most women's work remained distinct from men's, as the authors of a Birmingham study of women's work in 1907 wrote: 'as a rule men and women do different work and the relation between men and women workers is, on the whole, that of two non-competing groups'.[26]

Employers also attempted to cut costs by employing larger numbers of young workers at low wages. Formal apprenticeship grew rarer, but employers hired large numbers of boys under the pretence of training them. One observer described these youths 'set to some work which only calls for intelligence of the meanest kind . . . he remains week after week, year after year'. The low pay offered to these learners made the system appealing to employers, as another contemporary observer noted: 'As long as boys are cheap, work will be done by them rather than by machines or men'.[27] The proliferation of low-paid young workers was evident in engineering, where despite union efforts to maintain a ratio between 'apprentices' and fully trained men of 1:4, some employers in Scotland went as far as employing 6:1 learners to adult workers. On the other hand, compositors in the printing trades successfully maintained strict limits on apprenticeship.[28]

With the spread of compulsory education, the age at which boys and girls could enter full-time employment rose. A national minimum school-leaving age was set at 10 in 1880 and raised progressively to 12 (14 in Scotland) in the following decades.[29] Many working-class children earned wages in addition to attending school all day. An investigation into 'The child slaves of Britain' described one Glasgow boy who 'working in the morning for a milkman and in the evening for a grocer "put in" . . . an eight hour day' beyond school hours.[30] Edith Hogg's investigation of child labour found many examples of 'little match box makers working habitually from the time that school closes till eleven, or even midnight'.[31] In 1874 new regulations modified 1844 legislation by prohibiting employment of children under 10 in regulated textile factories. They preserved the provision that workers under age 13 in the factories could attend school part of the day. John R. Clines began work in an Oldham cotton mill at the age of 10, attending school for a few hours daily. Looking back at the exhausting work among the spinning frames, he noted: 'School somehow seemed less terrifying and revolting once I had become a half-timer in the mill'.[32]

For many working-class families, including those dependent on low-wage home manufacture like box making, the value of children's work appeared far greater than that of elementary schooling. One matchbox maker discussed keeping her children home to work. 'Of course, we cheat the school board,' she noted. 'It's hard on the little ones, but their fingers is so quick'.[33] Susan Nasmyth, who earned money running errands and performing odd jobs, told a journalist 'I don't stop away from school 'cept it's to do this . . . I never goes "mooching" [truant]'. Some children also stayed out of school to watch younger siblings or help with domestic work at home. A London settlement worker recognized 'how tempting it is to keep Mary Jane at home, at least on washing day'.[34]

Most working-class youths welcomed the moment when they reached the school-leaving age and could enter the workforce full time. One worker recalled how the noise of a workshop 'falling as it did on the ears of a young boy starting his first job, was an exciting sound, for it meant the end of childhood and the beginning of manhood'.[35] The presence of so many school-leavers in some factories and workshops was less thrilling to the skilled male workers who saw them as potential low-wage replacements. A witness before the Royal Commission on Labour complained of boy labour in the boot and shoe trade, calling it 'the greatest evil we have in the trade'. An engineering 'apprentice' recalled the attitude of the man assigned to oversee his training: 'the chief preoccupation of the man over me was to prevent me from learning how to do his work . . . and he hardly spoke to me all day'.[36]

Adult workers like this man fought back against the range of employer initiatives. When lasting machines appeared in footwear factories, some workers did their best to undermine the innovation: 'if they run a machine for five minutes at full speed, they seem to think it necessary to stop it and see that no breakage has occurred . . . [taking] care not to let a machine beat a shop mate working by hand on the same job . . . [to] keep the cost of production as high as possible'.[37] Efforts to impose regulation, discipline and a more scientific division of labour in the Thorneycrofts engineering firm in London met stubborn resistance from skilled workers. Workers defied attempts to separate sharpening and grinding into a separate department by demanding access to the emery wheel to do their own grinding. New supervisory workers faced harassment, and speed-ups resulted in spoiled work. Eventually, 'the harsh repressive features were withdrawn'.[38]

More organized worker efforts to control changes at the workplace had mixed results. Engineering workers at Maxim-Nordenfelt staged a lengthy strike against the imposition of piece work for fitters and turners. In the end, the unionized workers lost and were replaced by non-union labour.[39] On the other hand, an observer of attempts to implement new machinery in engineering shops reported: 'I have seen factories recently erected . . . without automatic feed of any description because "we are obliged to have one man to one machine" '.[40] At the Birmingham brass manufacturing firm Smith & Chamberlain, the union objected to 'the employment of women to turn at the lathe and file', which had been men's work. Enlisting the support of brass workers throughout Birmingham, the union won the continued exclusion of women from this work.[41]

Unionization

In struggles like these, workers increasingly organized in unions. In 1870 about half a million British workers belonged to trade unions, but by 1914 unions enrolled 4 million.[42] This expansion occurred in three bursts, one in the early 1870s, the second beginning in the late 1880s, and the third in the years preceding the First World War. Between these bursts of union growth, which corresponded to upswings of worker militancy and strike activity, weaker unions limped along or faded, while more established unions generally held their own. Despite periods of retrenchment, in each peak of union activity membership reached new heights, as union organization extended from a core of mostly skilled men to include less skilled and even women workers.

In the early 1870s a strong labour market with little unemployment provided the backdrop for an intensification of strike activity. According to one estimate, the number of strikes in Britain jumped from only 30 in 1870 to a peak of 365 in 1873. The *London Illustrated News* complained in 1872 of 'strikes for more pay and fewer hours of work . . . spreading through all industrial occupations'.[43] Strikes spread beyond well-established organizations of skilled men, as dockers, gas-stokers and unskilled workers in building trades and shipbuilding all joined the wave of organization and confrontation.[44] Miners organized in huge numbers, and in South Wales 70,000 miners walked out in 1873.[45] When the economy turned downwards, organizations of the low-paid and unskilled workers suffered. The Amalgamated Association of Miners, which had organized the 1873 strike, collapsed in 1875. Other new organizations of workers outside skilled sectors struggled to survive until the next surge of union growth.[46]

Dock workers in many port cities organized unions in the early 1870s, and these organizations faced typical difficulties holding together in the lean years that followed.[47] In August of 1889, however, a massive strike on the London docks augmented the surge in unionization gathering steam across Britain. Once again, a favourable economic climate, low unemployment and high demand for unskilled labour encouraged workers to organize and gave them bargaining power.[48] *The Times* expressed surprise at the extent of union growth and militancy, exaggerating the numbers involved in a successful miners' strike: 'even ten years ago it would have been out of the question for 300,000 work-men to combine so perfectly as to stop work at one moment and to resume it at another'.[49] Union rolls grew from perhaps 750,000 in the late 1880s to nearly a million and a half in 1892. While 119,000 workers across all trades went out on strike in 1888, in 1890 nearly 400,000 struck and most gained at least some of their demands.[50]

Many of the unions formed in this period enrolled unskilled labourers, but they faltered in the economic downturn that began in the early 1890s. A counter-attack by employers undermined many of the gains won just a few years before. In Cardiff the Dockers' Union suffered a crippling defeat in an 1891 strike. On the London docks employers wrested control over hiring decisions away from the union, and membership in the Dockers' Union fell from 56,000 in 1890 to 22,913 in 1892, and below 14,000 by 1900.[51] In the face of employer hostility and difficult economic conditions, 'general' unions survived by focusing on semi-skilled workers whom employers could not afford to lose. Gas-stokers, platers' assistants in shipyards and machinists in engineering trades remained in unions, while the truly unskilled and casual workforce fell away.[52]

Even during the counter-offensive from the early 1890s, many employers recognized unions and accepted them as representatives of workers. Despite a thorough victory in the 1897–8 lockout, the Engineering Employers' Federation acknowledged the union's legitimacy and enshrined its role in channelling disputes between workers and their employers. Employers in mining and cotton spinning had established similar structures following lockouts in the early 1890s.[53] Accepting unions and collective bargaining agreements offered advantages to employers. Wage agreements generally calculated increases or decreases based on the 'state of the trade' or 'selling price sliding scales'.[54] Employers also hoped to use arbitration procedures and the influence of union leadership to control workers and prevent local stoppages. As one employer claimed, 'the members of a well-governed Union are more easily controlled than a body who are all non-Unionists'.[55]

Despite these advantages, not all employers embraced collective bargaining and union recognition at the turn of the century. Railway companies, in particular, fought hard to avoid recognizing unions. Ammon Beasely, manager of the Taff Vale Railway, refused to negotiate with union leader Richard Bell, claiming, 'I cannot permit the workmen themselves to take the management of the concern out of my hands'.[56] In 1907, when Bell's union voted overwhelmingly in favour of a strike, Lloyd George, President of the Board of Trade, sought to mediate and invited employers and union leaders to meet with him at Whitehall. The employers, determined to manage their employees 'without intervention by the unions', refused to sit in the same room with union leaders. Only by shuttling between two rooms was Lloyd George able to hammer out an agreement and avoid the strike.[57]

Such intransigence was rare by the start of the twentieth century, and in most large trades employers sought accommodation with the unions. Collective bargaining agreements strengthened union administration. At times, this curtailed local initiatives by workers. Complex grievance procedures could neutralize disputes without solving underlying issues. Restrictions on strike activity discouraged direct action against employers.[58] On the other hand, some collective bargaining structures effectively defended workers' interests. In cotton spinning, agreements between employers and the union culminating in the Brooklands Agreement of 1893 helped protect skilled workers' control over spinning machines.[59]

Whether or not collective bargaining tied the hands of workers on the shopfloor, the years from the mid-1890s to the early years of the twentieth century were inauspicious for worker advances. Unemployment remained high, outside a brief economic upturn in 1898–1900.[60] Employer associations, formed in growing numbers beginning in the 1890s, strengthened employers in trade disputes. Anti-union groups supported labour replacement and victimization of activist workers and offered financial backing

for firms involved in disputes.[61] Courts also backed employers and reinforced the unfavourable conditions for strike activity. While union efforts
to blacklist and boycott employers who refused to pay fair wages were
declared to be illegal conspiracies, employer blacklists of union activists
passed muster in the courts.[62] Thus, collective bargaining structures that
tempered industrial conflict spread during a period in which economic
conditions, employer organization and legal judgments all made strikes
less likely to succeed.

When conditions grew more favourable, particularly from 1910 on,
workers vented their frustration over a decade of falling real wages and
accumulating grievances in a new surge of militancy and union expansion.
Shipyard workers staged numerous local strikes, despite a pact with employers prohibiting them. One Boilermakers' Union official observed, 'The
men are tired of the agreement', and in 1912 the union voted to withdraw
from it.[63] Unions in building, cotton spinning and engineering also pulled
out of accords with employers.[64] Strikes grew larger and more frequent
across the economy. In 1908 just under 400 strikes had involved a total of
224,000 workers. The number of strikes jumped to 857 in 1912 and peaked
at 1,497 in 1913. The numbers of workers involved grew rapidly as well.
The 1912 strikes involved 1,233,000 workers, including participants in a
national coal strike. Union membership, which had grown haltingly since
the slump in the early 1890s, reached 2.5 million in 1910 and soared to
4 million three years later.[65]

Initiative in these conflicts came from workers themselves, rather than
from union officials. The national railway strike of 1911 began with an
unauthorized walkout of workers in Liverpool and spread rapidly before
union leadership agreed to call for a nationwide strike.[66] Local disputes
in engineering as early as 1908 helped force out the conciliatory national
union general secretary, and escalating conflict on the ground eventually led
to the withdrawal from agreements with employers.[67] One union official,
commenting on the organization of previously unaffiliated workers, observed,
'The Workers' Union is not so much directing the strikes as following
them, and is making members by the thousand'. This union, formed in
1898, grew from 4,500 members in 1910 to 143,000 in 1914.[68]

The Workers' Union enrolled primarily engineering machine workers
whom the Amalgamated Society of Engineers had ignored. Other semi-
skilled or unskilled workers, who had remained outside the labour movement since the brief flourish of general unionization in 1889–90, organized
and staged strikes and joined unions after 1910. Dock strikes in London,
Liverpool and the Humber led to extraordinarily high levels of unionization

among dockers and seamen.[69] Women joined unions as well, and the Workers' Union employed Julia Varley in Birmingham to build membership among women. As was the case with men, however, women often went out on strike first and then joined unions. Another women's union activist, Mary Macarthur, urged, 'A strike of unorganised workers should always be utilised to form a trade union amongst them'.[70] Though the Workers' Union encouraged women to join, many male trade union leaders remained sceptical. Will Thorne, the gasworkers' leader, commented in 1914: 'Women do not make good trade unionists and for this reason we believe that our energies are better used towards the organization of male workers'.[71]

The state and worker organizations

The state took an increasingly active role in industrial relations late in the nineteenth century. Government intervention sometimes took its traditional form of restricting unions, cracking down on strikes and protecting strike-breaking labour. However, officials increasingly sought to play a more balanced role, encouraging union recognition by employers and moderation on the part of both unions and business. Thus, the Royal Commission on Labour's report of 1894 encouraged the Labour Department of the Board of Trade to mediate labour disputes, seeking to develop 'common interests, by employers and workmen'.[72]

The legal status of trade unions reflects the contradictory impact of the state's role in industrial relations. Laws passed in 1871 and 1875 protected the legal status and funds of unions, freed workers from the draconian restrictions of the old master and servant legislation, and legalized picketing.[73] In the 1890s, however, employers found sympathetic allies in the courts. Judicial decisions against activist workers and unions culminated in the Taff Vale decision of 1901, which forced the Amalgamated Society of Railway Servants to pay damages incurred by the railway during a strike.[74] Court rulings against the labour movement severely constrained union activities and motivated unions to organize politically, leading to the creation of the Labour Party. In 1906 Parliament restored union immunities and reasserted the freedom to picket.

Governments reacted to growing unionization and waves of strike activity with a great deal of ambivalence. Generally, the government advocated collective bargaining and conciliation between employers and unions. For example, in 1901 the Labour Commissioner at the Board of Trade urged the government to support quarry workers in their fierce battle against their employer, Lord Penrhyn, suggesting that the Board of Trade 'lend official support to the quarrymen's claim that their grievances be negotiated by trade union representatives in accordance with the accepted practice of collective bargaining in other industries'.[75] On the other hand, government officials remained sceptical of pickets and supported employer efforts to break strikes. In 1903 a Board of Trade official criticized a bill protecting peaceful picketing, arguing that picketing 'never is and never can be peaceful, but always is and always must be a form of terrorizing'.[76] During strike waves the government intervened on behalf of employers, enforcing law and order by defending strike-breaking workers and cracking down on militant workers. The most notable example of government repression of strikers in this period occurred at Featherstone, Yorkshire in 1893, where troops killed three striking miners.[77] The wave of large strikes in the years before the First World War brought these contradictory approaches into relief. The government sent troops to Wales in 1910 and to a number of ports in 1911. Yet government mediators, particularly George Askwith, intervened aggressively in strike after strike, mediating disputes and seeking to bring employers and workers together. While these efforts did not always benefit workers, they do make clear the government's commitment to play an active role in industrial relations.[78]

Conclusion

As mid-Victorian prosperity gave way to the more troubled economic climate of the late-Victorian and Edwardian period, employers felt the pressure of declining profits. Their attempts to make labour more productive through technology, stricter discipline, piece rates, and expanded use of youth and female labour disrupted the workplace and sparked conflict with workers. Increasing numbers of workers joined unions and struck against employers, particularly when low unemployment strengthened their bargaining positions. Employers themselves organized to take on unions, but many came to accept worker organizations as legitimate and signed collective bargaining agreements with the unions. These agreements, often on employer terms, did not prevent renewed militancy in the years before the First World War, when unionization reached far beyond a core of skilled workers and large strikes disrupted trade. Conflict between employers and workers increasingly drew the attention of governments, which tried to mediate between the two parties, while still enforcing law and order against striking workers.

The shared experiences of manual labour that linked workers in mid-Victorian Britain grew more powerful in the late-Victorian period. Working conditions remained difficult, as noted by a skilled worker on Clydeside: 'The conditions under which the moulder worked were vile, filthy and insanitary . . . smoke would make the eyes water. The nose and throat would clog with dust'.[79] Economic insecurity persisted, endemic in the lives of the working class. The growth of the semi-skilled workforce helped bridge the gap between skilled men and others in the workforce. Employer initiatives subjected even skilled workers to new forms of discipline and subordination in the workplace. Unions, no longer restricted to a skilled elite, united millions of workers in the labour movement. Experiences in the workplace and conflict with employers reinforced class ties that developed in the working-class neighbourhoods of late-Victorian and Edwardian Britain.

Notes

1 A. Williams, *Life in a Railway Factory* ([1915]; New York: Garland, 1980), 302, 78, 56, 240, 304, 267.

2 P.J. Waller, *Town, City and Nation: England 1850–1914* (Oxford: Oxford University Press, 1983), 69.

3 B. Lancaster, *Radicalism, Cooperation and Socialism: Leicester Working-Class Politics 1860–1906* (Leicester: Leicester University Press, 1987), 22–3, 100–1.

4 K. McClelland and A. Reid, 'Wood, iron and steel: technology, labour and trade union organisation in the shipbuilding industry, 1840–1914', in R. Harrison and J. Zeitlin, eds, *Divisions of Labour: Skilled Workers and Technological Change in Nineteenth Century England* (Urbana: University of Illinois Press, 1985), 153–4.

5 N. Kirk, *Change, Continuity and Class: Labour in British Society 1850–1920* (Manchester: Manchester University Press, 1998), 164–5.

6 J. Morris, 'The characteristics of sweating: the late nineteenth-century London and Leeds tailoring trade', in A.V. John, ed., *Unequal Opportunities* (Oxford: Basil Blackwell, 1986).

7 J. Zeitlin, 'Engineers and compositors: a comparison', in Harrison and Zeitlin, eds, *Divisions of Labour*, 222; K. Burgess, 'New unionism for old? The Amalgamated Society of Engineers in Britain', in W. Mommsen and H. Husung, eds, *The Development of Trade Unionism in Great Britain and Germany, 1880–1914* (London: George Allen & Unwin, 1985), 171.

8 R. Whipp, *Patterns of Labour: Work and Social Change in the Pottery Industry* (London: Routledge, 1990), 114, 21.

9 A. Reid, 'The division of labour and politics in Britain, 1880–1920', in Mommsen and Husung, eds, *Development of Trade Unionism*, 152.

10 Williams, *Life in a Railway Factory*, 5.

11 Lancaster, *Radicalism, Cooperation and Socialism*, 165.

12 K. Whitston, 'The reception of scientific management by British engineers, 1890–1914', *Business History Review* 71 (1997), 211–12, 223–6.

13 W.W. Knox, *Industrial Nation: Work, Culture and Society in Scotland, 1800–Present* (Edinburgh: Edinburgh University Press, 1999), 149–50; Zeitlin, 'Engineers and compositors', 203–4.

14 S. Meacham, *A Life Apart: The English Working Class 1890–1914* (Cambridge, MA: Harvard University Press, 1977), 109–10, 138.

15 Lancaster, *Radicalism, Cooperation and Socialism*, 43, 106, 108–9.

16 Burgess, 'New unionism for old', 173.

17 Lancaster, *Radicalism, Cooperation and Socialism*, 44, 109.

18 A. Miles, *Social Mobility in Nineteenth- and Early Twentieth-Century England* (New York: St Martin's Press, 1999), 30.

19 R.J. Morris, 'Skilled workers and the politics of the "Red" Clyde', *Journal of the Scottish Labour History Society* 18 (1983), 9; A.J. McIvor, *A History of Work in Britain, 1880–1950* (Basingstoke: Palgrave, 2001), 54.

20 Zeitlin, 'Engineers and compositors', 228.

21 S. Rose, *Limited Livelihoods: Gender and Class in Nineteenth-Century England* (Berkeley: University of California Press, 1992), 112–15.

22 Meacham, *A Life Apart*, 103.

23 A. August, *Poor Women's Lives: Gender, Work and Poverty in Late-Victorian London* (London: Associated University Presses, 1999), 93.

24 Ibid., 79.

25 Ibid., 156; E. Gordon, *Women and the Labour Movement in Scotland 1850–1914* (Oxford: Clarendon Press, 1991), 28. The London figures represent 1881, while the Scottish numbers are for 1901.

26 E. Cadbury, M.C. Matheson and G. Shann, *Women's Work and Wages: A Phase of Life in an Industrial City* (Chicago: University of Chicago Press, 1907), 39.

27 Meacham, *A Life Apart*, 180.

28 Zeitlin, 'Engineers and compositors', 203, 220.

29 D. Rubinstein, 'Socialization and the London School Board 1870–1904: aims, methods and public opinion', in P. McCann, ed., *Popular Education*

and Socialization in the Nineteenth Century (London: Methuen, 1977), 232; J.S. Hurt, *Elementary Schooling and the Working Classes 1860–1918* (London: Routledge & Kegan Paul, 1979), 189, 191.

30 M. Lavalette, 'The changing form of child labour *circa* 1880–1918: the growth of "out of school work" ', in M. Lavalette, ed., *A Thing of the Past? Child Labour in Britain in the Nineteenth and Twentieth Centuries* (Liverpool: Liverpool University Press, 1999), 134.

31 A. Davin, *Growing Up Poor: Home, School and Street in London 1870–1914* (London: Rivers Oram Press, 1996), 193.

32 P. Horn, *The Victorian and Edwardian Schoolchild* (Stroud: Sutton, 1989), 108–13.

33 D. Rubinstein, *School Attendance in London, 1870–1904: A Social History* (New York: A.M. Kelley, 1969), 61.

34 Davin, *Growing Up Poor*, 171, 102.

35 Meacham, *A Life Apart*, 176.

36 M. Childs, *Labour's Apprentices: Working-Class Lads in Late Victorian and Edwardian England* (Montreal: McGill-Queen's University Press, 1992), 55, 54.

37 Lancaster, *Radicalism, Cooperation and Socialism*, 104.

38 R. Price, *Labour in British Society: An Interpretive History* (London: Routledge, 1986), 100.

39 Burgess, 'New unionism for old', 173.

40 Price, *Labour in British Society*, 111.

41 Rose, *Limited Livelihoods*, 104.

42 Kirk, *Change, Continuity and Class*, 177.

43 M.A. Bienefeld, *Working Hours in British Industry: An Economic History* (London: Weidenfeld & Nicolson, 1972), 106.

44 J.E. Cronin, 'Strikes and struggle for union organization: Britain and Europe', in Mommsen and Husung, *Development of Trade Unionism*, 64.

45 H.A. Clegg, A. Fox and A.F. Thompson, *British Trade Unions since 1889, vol. I: 1889–1910* (Oxford: Clarendon Press, 1964), 18.

46 J. Lovell, *British Trade Unions 1875–1933* (London: Macmillan, 1977), 12, 15–16.

47 J. Lovell, 'Sail, steam and emergent dockers' unionism in Britain, 1850–1914', *International Review of Social History* 32 (1987), 232–3.

48 D. Matthews, '1889 and all that: new views on the new unionism', *International Review of Social History* 36 (1991), 49.

49 E. Hobsbawm, 'The "new unionism" in perspective', in *Workers: Worlds of Labour* (New York: Pantheon Books, 1984), 161. The strike actually involved 'only' 100,000 workers.

50 W.H. Fraser, *A History of British Trade Unionism 1700–1998* (New York: St Martin's Press, 1999), 73; Cronin, 'Strikes and union organization', 56, 64.

51 M.J. Daunton, *Coal Metropolis: Cardiff 1870–1914* (Leicester: Leicester University Press, 1977), 186–7; G. Stedman Jones, *Outcast London: A Study in the Relationship between Classes in Victorian Society* (New York: Pantheon Books, 1984), 318; K. Burgess, *The Challenge of Labour: Shaping British Society 1850–1930* (London: Croom Helm, 1980), 85.

52 E. Hobsbawm, 'The "new unionism" reconsidered', in Mommsen and Husung, eds, *Development of Trade Unionism*, 20; J. Zeitlin 'Industrial structure, employer strategy and the diffusion of job control in Britain, 1880–1920', in Mommsen and Husung, eds, *Development of Trade Unionism*, 332; Fraser, *History of British Trade Unionism*, 81, 89.

53 Burgess, *Challenge of Labour*, 91–5.

54 A. McIvor, *Organised Capital: Employers' Associations and Industrial Relations in Northern England, 1880–1939* (Cambridge: Cambridge University Press, 1996), 120; K. Burgess, *The Origins of British Industrial Relations: The Nineteenth Century Experience* (London: Croom Helm, 1975), 311; J.H. Porter, 'Wage bargaining under conciliation agreements', *Economic History Review* 23:3 (1970), 463.

55 J. Melling, 'Non-commissioned officers: British employers and their supervisory workers, 1880–1920', *Social History* 5 (1980), 204.

56 Price, *Labour in British Society*, 126.

57 P.S. Bagwell, 'The new unionism in Britain: the railway industry', in Mommsen and Husung, eds, *Development of Trade Unionism*, 196.

58 Price, *Labour in British Society*, 143, 144.

59 W. Lazonick, 'Production relations, labor productivity, and choice of technique: British and U.S. cotton spinning', *The Journal of Economic History* 41 (1981), 495–6; J. Zeitlin, 'From labour history to the history of industrial relations', *Economic History Review* 40 (1987), 171–2.

60 Clegg, Fox and Thompson, *British Trade Unions*, 489.

61 McIvor, *Organised Capital*, ch. 4.

62 Ibid., 105.

63 J. Lovell, 'Collective bargaining and the emergence of national employer organisation in the British shipbuilding industry', *International Review of Social History* 36 (1991), 85–7.

64 H.A. Clegg, *A History of British Trade Unions since 1889, vol. II: 1911–1933* (Oxford: Clarendon Press, 1985), 81.

65 J. Cronin, 'Strikes 1870–1914', in C. Wrigley, ed., *A History of British Industrial Relations 1875–1914* (Amherst: University of Massachusetts Press, 1982), 76, 90.

66 Price, *Labour in British Society*, 144.

67 Zeitlin, 'Engineers and compositors', 233–4.

68 Lovell, *British Trade Unions*, 45–6.

69 Fraser, *British Trade Unionism*, 119, 116.

70 D. Thom, 'The bundle of sticks: women, trade unionists and collective organization before 1918', in John, ed., *Unequal Opportunities*, 277, 268.

71 J. Hinton, 'The rise of a mass labour movement: growth and limits', in Wrigley, ed., *British Industrial Relations*, 30.

72 Fraser, *British Trade Unionism*, 97.

73 Kirk, *Change, Continuity and Class*, 50–1.

74 McIvor, *Organised Capital*, 105–6; Fraser, *British Trade Unions*, 99.

75 R. Davidson, 'The Board of Trade and industrial relations 1896–1914', *Historical Journal* 21 (1978), 574.

76 Davidson, 'Board of Trade', 582.

77 C. Wrigley, 'The government and industrial relations', in Wrigley, ed., *British Industrial Relations*, 137–8.

78 Cronin, 'Strikes 1870–1914', 91; Wrigley, 'Government and industrial relations', 147–9, 154.

79 Morris, 'Skilled workers', 8.

CHAPTER SEVEN

Expanding leisure opportunities

In a study of Birmingham youths shortly before the First World War, Arnold Freeman discovered: 'Football is the greatest single interest in the life of the ordinary working-boy'. The rise of professional football in the last decades of the nineteenth century exemplifies the dramatic growth of commercialized leisure in the period. Yet the boys' football obsession also reveals the importance of informal leisure. One boy gave Freeman an account of a weekend on which he attended a professional match on Saturday and played football with friends from his street for two hours on Saturday and twice on Sunday. Others reported squeezing a bit of football into the last few minutes of their dinner break from work. 'I go home to dinner and start back at 1.40 then we have a game at foot ball for 10 minutes with the other lads'. This boy shed light on the informal leisure that persisted during work time as well: 'Don't do much work of a Sat morning always talking about football'.[1] The expansion of new commercialized entertainments alongside vibrant informal leisure helps define the 'traditional' working-class culture that developed in late-Victorian and Edwardian Britain.[2]

Many workers could take advantage of this leisure culture due to reduced working hours. During the strike wave of 1872–4, unions sought shorter hours, and an 1876 government commission observed that in 'some of the most important . . . trades, the so-called nine hours movement has been carried to a successful issue'. This typically meant nine and a half hours of work for five days, 7.00 a.m. to 5.30 p.m., including an hour dinner break, and a half day on Saturday.[3] Workers in the late nineteenth century valued time for leisure, even at the expense of higher wages. In an 1866 Newcastle building strike workers held a vote on two competing proposals, one for a $55\frac{1}{2}$-hour week for 30s., the other for a $50\frac{1}{2}$-hour week and 27s. Workers approved the shorter week by 401 to 21.[4] When engineering workers failed to secure the eight-hour day and a cap on overtime in 1897–8, their leader George Barnes complained that the 'margin of leisure has been diminished'. He demanded that workers' share of increased productivity come in the form of 'shortening hours of labour'.[5]

Not all workers shared in this expanded leisure time. Long hours persisted in seasonal trades, sweated manufacturing, domestic service and other non-unionized occupations.[6] Overtime also lengthened workdays. The railway union complained in 1890 that some Scottish rail workers exceeded the ten-hour day by an average of nearly five hours per day. This accounts for the common saying that 'in the winter months a guard never gets the chance of speaking to his children'.[7] Women's domestic work in the home was not bound by reduced hours. Richard Church recalled his mother, who faced the dual burden of paid and domestic work in London, 'having to live two lives in one'.[8] Maud Pember Reeves's study of women in Lambeth revealed women caring for husbands, children and homes from early in the morning, '6.0. – Get up and light fire', until well into the evening, 'sew till time to nurse baby at nine o'clock'.[9]

Married women also had less money to spend on leisure than did men. Married men generally reserved a portion of their pay for their leisure, before handing over the rest for their wives to devote to the household. According to the *Glasgow Herald*, 'no matter how slender the finances of many households, the male must have his sixpence to witness the football'. Most married women, on the other hand, only spent on their own leisure when a surplus remained in the household budget.[10] Despite these constraints on their time and resources, married women did carve out some time and even money for leisure, particularly if their household did not include numerous young children. Some attended music halls and went with friends or husbands to pubs. A boy who grew up in Edwardian Birmingham recalled his mother's preparations for trips to the pub: 'Sunday night it used to tek her about an hour, hour and a half to get spruced up, go up to the corner to have a pint'.[11] Often, though, women integrated leisure with their domestic duties. Thus, boisterous Saturday evening markets served practical needs and provided entertainment. The slow pace of ordering items in the corner shop also created space for gossip with neighbours and the shopkeeper.[12] Overall, as Robert Dolling observed in his years as a parish priest in Portsmouth, 'Women are far more stay-at-home, and get far fewer treats than men'.[13] On the other hand, many single women fared somewhat better, depending on their occupations. The years between school-leaving and marriage offered many working-class women chances to take advantage of leisure opportunities.

Informal leisure

Women of all ages enjoyed the entertainment in the lively street markets in working-class districts. Trips to these markets were more than simply entertainment, of course. Especially on Saturday nights, savvy shoppers could find bargains. Beyond the practical, Alice Cordelia Davis recalled, Peckham's Rye Lane market boasted plenty of activity, including a fortune teller, and a pianist and singer atop a cart performing the latest songs.[14] Vendors at these markets had to compete for attention, and they became entertainers: 'They call them the spielers . . . they'd say, "Right, so-many pounds of tomatoes there, am I asking sixpence?" And the women'd shout, "No!" "Am I asking fivepence even?" "No!" . . . all the women used to love to shout "No!" '.[15]

Amidst the crowds, entertainers and vendors, Saturday night street markets presented a key opportunity for young men and women to see one another and be seen. In Manchester, Shudehill market attracted young working-class men who 'in their own expressive language, "toff themselves up", for Saturday night, and . . . take a tour round "the market" . . . the lads are quite content to promenade up and down the long central avenue'.[16] On Saturdays and Sundays, youths gathered in large numbers in specific streets for the local 'monkey parade'. Young women could be seen 'walking arm in arm . . . singing and shouting and pushing other wayfarers off the curbstone'.[17] John Blake recounted the importance of the promenade during his Poplar childhood: 'All the teenagers walked up and down here, and it was known as "Monkey's Parade". More romance went on here than in any other part of Poplar'.[18] Another Londoner recalled: 'the wide pavements were thronged with groups of lads and girls . . . Scuffles, nudges and shrieks of laughter came from every group'. Many working-class marriages grew out of such flirtations.[19]

Neighbourhood streets provided the most important settings for working-class leisure. Edna Bold, who grew up in Manchester, recalled, 'The "Road" was a social centre where everyone met, shopped, talked, walked . . . We loved the smooth, grey flags where we walked, ran, skipped or danced to a barrel organ'.[20] Robert Roberts recalled his Salford neighbourhood, where people gathered in 'the street – that great recreation room'.[21] Young men, women of all ages, and especially children made the most of the shared space of neighbourhood streets.

Helen Dendy noted of working-class children, 'They live in the roadway . . . wet or dry, hot or cold, the children swarm up and down, eat and drink, play and even sleep, from each morning to late at night'.[22] Children developed countless games in the friendly confines of neighbourhood streets, improvising equipment from objects collected from the road. In 'cherry holes' players threw cherry stones through holes cut in a card.[23] Other youths used cherry stones in games of skittles, targeting a long screw stood on its end so that the 'first contestant to knock down the screw would take all the stones on the ground'. Crowded conditions meant competition for play space in the streets: 'a football descends, like a bombshell, on a group of girls intent on the thrilling amusement of hopscotch'.[24] Pranks amused children in the streets: 'the old parcel under the lamp post tied with a bit of black thread. Persons coming to pick it up and it would be pulled away from them'.[25] Another common prank involved tying two knockers opposite one another together and knocking on one of the doors: 'as it opens inwards it raps the door over the other side of the road. Well, this goes on, with doors opening and closing'.[26]

Children were not alone in enjoying neighbourhood streets. The appearance of organ grinders brought out young couples and neighbourhood women. In Lancashire towns around the turn of the century, observers noted: 'Dancing may often be seen in the alleys and courts . . . A crowd, not only of children, but of young men and women will gather round a barrel organ, and in a few moments many couples will have begun to dance'. One woman recalled the organ grinder's appearance in her Manchester neighbourhood, 'The mothers, come out and dance . . . my mother was one of 'em'.[27] In Joe Toole's Salford neighbourhood, singing 'was a very popular street pastime. Women with children clinging to their skirts would sit upon the stone doorstep of their houses on sultry summer evenings and sing in harmony'.[28]

Through years of gathering in the streets to talk and relax, neighbours in working-class districts forged powerful bonds. A researcher for philanthropist and social investigator B. Seebohm Rowntree described a summer Sunday in a poor York neighbourhood: 'Weather being very warm, men, women, and children are sitting on the pavement most of the evening'.[29] A Preston resident described the informal nature of these interactions: 'Some person would be passing, and someone would be at the door and stop to have a chat, then somebody else would come along and then perhaps three or four would accumulate'.[30] Informal groups of young men or women 'larking about' filled essential functions, building communities and sharing information. Groups of young men exchanged information about jobs, wages and working conditions, as Robert Roberts explains, 'All this was bread and butter talk . . . that had an economic scope and variety to be heard nowhere else'.[31]

The social environment of the streets was not, however, all helpful information and mutual aid. Close confines bred conflict as well as community, and fights counted among the spectacles enjoyed by neighbourhood children.[32] In the York neighbourhood visited by Rowntree's investigator, 'there were several wordy battles between women neighbours, the language being very bad'.[33] In Preston, there were 'fights galore . . . fighting in the streets, fights anywhere, drunken fights'. Groups of young men gathered on neighbourhood streets might easily be set off by some slight, sparking a battle with youths from another street. 'There'd be different streets . . . at war with one another'.[34]

The police continued their efforts to control public space, often trying to curtail the street play of working-class youths. Youngsters suffered blows with sticks, rolled capes and gloves.[35] When youths spotted an approaching policeman they fled, but not always successfully: 'there used to be a policeman, we used to call him Flash Harry . . . And he used to throw that cape as you ran away and he'd fetch you down with it – he'd turn it right between your legs . . . used to cuff you round the ears'.[36] In an ongoing battle between a group of Stepney boys determined to play football in the streets and a policeman they referred to as 'Old Bloodnut', the policeman destroyed the boys' ball. In recounting the incident, David Smith complained, 'I don't know why, 'cos we wasn't hurting anything'. In retaliation, the boys stole his cape from outside a pub. Smith recalled, 'He done our football, we done his cape'.[37]

Police did not bother those who passed their leisure time at home, and many workers relaxed indoors. A Bethnal Green churchman described a typical Sunday for working men: 'they will have lain in bed till about eleven or twelve', followed by a visit to a pub. Around 3.00 p.m. they returned home for 'the great dinner of the week', which leads to 'a lie down on the bed in shirt sleeves until five, with a pot of beer and *Lloyd's Weekly*'. After tea, a walk and visit with friends complete the day's activities.[38] In some families, reading dominated domestic leisure. Harry Burton's London family all used the public library and read together at home, often sharing particular passages by reading them aloud.[39] Home-based hobbies such as pigeon-breeding spread, though they developed associations and competitions that extended their practice beyond the domestic realm.[40] Yet the crowded conditions of working-class housing continued to drive most working people out of their houses, into organized forms of amusement or out into the streets to enjoy the informal leisure of the working-class community. This communal, public leisure culture reinforced the intimacy of working-class districts and distinguished them from the privatized worlds of middle-class neighbourhoods.

Commercial leisure

The entertainment available in the streets of working-class neighbourhoods possessed one great advantage over the expanding commercial leisure options: it was free. Though rising real wages in the last quarter of the nineteenth century increased spending overall, not all working people could afford to pay for amusement. According to one estimate, a third of workers could not afford to spend money on leisure (except for drink).[41] Despite this uneven access to commercial leisure, pubs, music halls, gambling, excursion opportunities, and new phenomena including professional football, helped create the distinctive leisure culture at the heart of the 'traditional' working-class way of life.[42]

Aside from the streets, pubs remained the most important venues for working-class leisure. Though the number of licensed pubs declined between 1875 and 1915 (from one per 223 persons to one per 416 in England and Wales), they remained thick on the ground in established working-class neighbourhoods.[43] Robert Robert's Salford neighbourhood boasted 15 public houses and one licensed hotel, which together served a population of about 3,000. Roberts reports: 'To the great mass of manual workers the local public house spelled paradise . . . there dwelt within a tavern all one could crave for'.[44] In many areas, young women attended pubs openly. Rowntree described typical crowds in York pubs that offered informal musical entertainment: 'The company is almost entirely composed of young persons, youths and girls, sitting round the room and at small tables'.[45] In some areas, though, respectability inhibited single women's public-house drinking.[46]

Though in Roberts' view, 'above all, men went for the ale', pubs provided a variety of other attractions.[47] Pubs continued to offer space to friendly societies, political parties and other associations. All sorts of competitive activities enlivened the atmosphere, including 'darts, draughts, bowls, card-playing and gambling of all kinds'.[48] Publicans organized boxing matches and football clubs.[49] Though few pubs had licences allowing musical performance, as Rowntree observed in York, 'there is music and singing in a great many others'. Audiences joined in the singing, enjoying 'an air of jollity and an absence of irksome restraint which must prove very attractive after a day's confinement in a factory or shop'.[50]

The appeal of music, comedy, spectacle and drink also explains the continuing vitality of music halls, which reached their peak in terms of audience size around the turn of the century. A man at the Pavilion in Leicester told an observer, 'I never miss a Friday night at a 'all, and haven't done these 15 years, I gets paid on a Friday'.[51] Thirty-five London halls attracted crowds totalling 14 million annually in the early 1890s.[52] In the 1880s and 1890s a number of innovations allowed some music halls to transcend their local ties and narrow working-class audiences, making them big business and mass entertainment. The management of these halls worked hard to segregate audiences by class. In the 1890s the Alexandra in Manchester reopened as the Tivoli with box seats costing up to two guineas, maintaining separate entrances and exits for different classes of patrons. Most halls, though, catered to specific social groups.[53] An observer in 1891 drew distinctions between West End establishments, 'bourgeois' music halls elsewhere in London and its suburbs, and the 'minor' halls in poorer districts: 'The audiences, as might be expected, correspond to the social scale of the particular place'.[54]

In many halls, management replaced tables with fixed rows of seats, confining the audience in their seats until the show's conclusion and promoting their orderly exit at that time. This allowed hall owners to plan two shows in an evening. To maintain schedules, they needed to rein in the informal give-and-take between audiences and performers. Syndicates opened halls in numerous cities, presenting uniform programmes of performers, and expanding the star system that nurtured George Leybourne, Alfred Vance, Marie Lloyd and Dan Leno. Yet these innovations did not completely tame working-class audiences.[55] As one Londoner born in 1892 recalled, 'you used to take oranges with you because the orange peel came in handy if you didn't like the artistes'.[56]

Though music halls attracted men and women, professional sport, another key example of commercialized mass leisure at the end of the nineteenth century, appealed overwhelmingly to men. Professional football, which exploded into popularity in the 1880s, had no rival among working-class boys and men, though horse racing, rugby and even cricket attracted some attention. From modest beginnings, attendance at football matches soared rapidly. The first Football Association (FA) Cup in 1872 drew about 2,000 fans. In 1895 42,500 saw the match, and six years later 111,000 filled the stadium.[57] More than 100,000 saw the Hampden International in Scotland in 1902, and football spectators as a proportion of the population were about twice as high in Scotland as they were in England on the eve of the First World War.[58] Entrance fees ranged from 3d. for lesser teams, to 6d. for a regular season match featuring top teams and 1s. to see a championship or international. The cost meant that skilled workers were most likely to attend matches in person, though young workers without families to support also made up a large portion of the crowds.[59] Those who could not afford to see soccer matches in person could read about them in newspapers and talk about them in pubs, on street corners and at work.

Despite elite origins, association football soon became a working-class game, much to the dismay of a journalist in *Scottish Sport*, who described a Glasgow football crowd as, 'the very scum of the city, drunken and brutal in their behaviour and language'.[60] Working-class football followers rejected middle-class amateur pretensions about fair play. They were partisans who wanted their team to win. One observer in Glasgow complained of the working-class fans, who 'greet with a roar of delight some ungoverned brutality or clever, underhand trick' when achieved by their side. Another observer complained of the 'curious' football morality 'under which it is regarded as legitimate to play against the rules and the referee as well as against the opposing team'. Thus, middle-class audiences drifted away, reduced to 'the odd bowler amidst the rows of flat caps' in the stadiums.[61]

While most middle-class men abandoned football, middle-class crowds were less willing to give up holidays at the seaside as working-class visitors to such resorts multiplied. In many parts of Britain, the typical working-class trip to the sea involved one day on a cheap return train ticket. For the poor, charities offered excursions. By 1911 more than half of the English population took a day trip and 20 per cent spent a longer holiday at the seaside. Blackpool led the way in attracting working-class revellers with three entertainment piers, the first electric tramway in the country, and, from the early 1890s, a 150-metre (500-foot) imitation Eiffel Tower. Punch and Judy shows, musicians, Pierrots and various stalls of shooting galleries and vendors all competed for attention.[62] Lancashire cotton employers conceded unusually long breaks in the second half of the nineteenth century, and in many towns better-off workers enjoyed a full week (without pay) in July or August. Workers enrolled in savings clubs to fund these week-long holidays by the sea.[63] Thousands of East Londoners descended on the fields of Kent in the first week of September for a hop-picking working holiday.[64]

The boisterous scenes at destinations popular with working-class crowds disturbed more affluent tourists, and seaside resorts developed strategies to segregate the classes. The town of Bridlington enclosed a section of its promenade and charged admission. It was crucial to the town, explained the local board, that 'the better class of visitors should have a secluded place where they can go away from the rough excursionists who come there in swarms during the season'.[65] Though some towns successfully maintained more respectable fortresses alongside attractions for the urban masses, most targeted specific audiences. In New Brighton those interested in maintaining a high-class clientele struggled with entrepreneurs who, they complained, wanted to attract 'hordes of savages from the backwoods of Lancashire'. These divided agendas undermined one another, as another local observer put it: 'What are we going to try to make New Brighton? Is it to be a Blackpool or a Bournemouth? It cannot be both'.[66]

Philanthropic leisure and self-help

Not everyone could afford a trip to the seaside, but philanthropists stepped in to provide 'rational' and 'improving' leisure for the poor. Adults could attend lectures, mothers' meetings, concerts and even outings. An even broader range of organized activities targeted young men and women, to keep them occupied and out of trouble.[67] In Lambeth alone, historian Jeffrey Cox counted '58 thrift, slate, and friendly societies, 57 mothers' meetings, 36 temperance societies for children, 36 literary or debating societies for young men, 27 Bible classes, 27 girls' or young women's clubs, 25 cricket, tennis, or other sports clubs, 25 savings banks or penny banks, 24 Christian Endeavour societies, 21 boot, coal, blanket, or clothing clubs, 19 adult temperance societies, 17 branches of the Boys' Brigade or Church Lads' Brigade, 13 vocational or adult classes, 13 men's clubs, 10 gymnasiums (usually devoted to recreational classes of some sort), and 10 maternity societies'.[68] The Boys' Brigade, founded in 1883 in Glasgow, set the stage for a number of uniformed youth movements. Such efforts soon found the need to appeal to young people's interests, and for many boys this meant sports. P.E. Halstead recalled a club that he helped organize: 'Every Saturday night, the dining-room became a gymnasium, with a boxing ring established in the middle . . . we were able to profit from the enormous reverence such boys had for athletes like ourselves'.[69] About a quarter of football clubs in Birmingham between 1870 and 1885 had explicit links to religious organizations.[70] Many girls' clubs found it necessary to allow dancing, and even admit men to club dances, as those 'in which girls could only dance with girls were as dull as sandwiches made of bread and bread'.[71]

In some cases these efforts bore fruit, as young workers developed interests in religion, temperance and middle-class moral standards. More commonly, however, participants enjoyed the opportunity to read, play games and escape their crowded urban neighbourhood on an excursion, without necessarily embracing the goals of their sponsors. Arnold Freeman's study of Birmingham youths noted the paradox facing a Boys' Club: 'in so far as it fails to provide amusement it will not attract boys; while in so far as it provides amusement, it is not assisting, except incidentally, the moral and mental unfoldment of the boy'.[72] Leslie Paul recalled that Boy Scouts' influence on working-class boys did not follow the intentions of founder Baden-Powell: 'they leapt at Scouting . . . divining that this was a movement which took the side of the natural, inquisitive, adventuring boy against the repressive schoolmaster, the moralizing parson and the coddling parent'.[73]

Thus philanthropic efforts to use leisure to transform the working class enjoyed limited success. The numbers involved remained far smaller than those participating in commercial leisure. Glasgow ministers estimated in 1875 that some 7,000 boys and girls under age 18 attended music halls regularly, while the rest were at least familiar with music halls and their songs. On the other hand, fewer than 600 joined evening institutes.[74] While middle-class reformers hoped to appeal to rough youths from the poorer segments of the working class, according to Freeman, 'the boys who come are precisely those who need the Club least'.[75] Even though few of the poorest youths participated, some of those who did remained intractable and refused the moral lessons offered by their betters. C.E.B. Russell complained that the boys on sponsored football clubs rejected middle-class notions of fair play and manipulated football leagues: 'it is a common practice for those of a higher age to lie and cheat in order to join, and . . . make certain of winning whatever trophies may be offered. The play is frequently unfair . . . foul and violent tactics take the place of strenuous play'.[76] A local newspaper complained that those who came to Ramsgate on temperance excursions, '*reputed* advocates of total abstinence from intoxicating liquors', did not always live up to expectations.[77]

Religious leaders struggled with working-class attitudes toward Christianity. At Hull an 1896 appearance by the Excelsior Minstrels brought some 600 people, four times the membership of its sponsor, a Primitive Methodist chapel.[78] Much of the audience for this religious music probably adopted 'diffusive Christianity', a combination of occasional church attendance, Sunday school for the children, and a general belief in Christian values. Many who did not attend regularly found their way to church and chapel on Christmas, Easter, the Sunday school anniversary or for the New Year's Eve watchnight service or the autumn harvest festival service.[79] Others attended only for major life-cycle events, as one clergyman bemoaned: 'some I see in the chapel for the last time when I shake hands with them when the marriage service is at an end'.[80]

Even those who did not attend services themselves usually sent their children to Sunday schools. C.F.G. Masterman found that 'streets containing not a single adult worshipper will contribute their swarms of clean and intelligent infants' to Sunday schools.[81] These parents probably wanted their children to receive a basic religious education, though Sunday school attendance offered other benefits, granting the adults peace and quiet for a few hours. The children received 'treats' in return for their attendance, ranging from free food to popular outings.[82] An Anglican clergyman complained of competition in providing rewards for children: 'We are obliged to have treats because of our Dissenting brethren'.[83] Most working-class parents and young people enjoyed the treats, but also believed in the core values of Christianity. One East Londoner recalled his parents as 'a hundred per cent Christians, but not church-goers'.[84]

A significant minority of workers, however, participated more fully. They attended services, joined religious clubs and associations, and structured their lives around the precepts of their church or chapel. A woman who grew up in Edwardian Glasgow recalled: 'Sundays we were at church a lot . . . Monday was the Band of Hope . . . Tuesday was the Girl Guides. You know it seemed to be all church things'.[85] A Barrow man recalled his involvement in a Primitive Methodist chapel: 'We used to live there nearly'. Regular church attendance was most common among workers in Wales, Scotland, Lancashire and Yorkshire.[86]

Even where large numbers of workers attended church regularly, the religious commitment they shared with wealthier co-religionists seldom broke down class divisions. Socially segregated congregations kept middle-class worshippers from contact with their social inferiors. Within socially diverse churches, separate services attracted working-class congregants. As a London minister noted: 'if these people were to come to the ordinary Sunday services, the respectable congregation would be frightened away'.[87] Most middle-class worshippers attended 11.00 Sunday morning services. But most working-class women, generally more involved religiously than their husbands, could not attend this service as it interfered with the preparation of Sunday dinner. Thus, a London study found that 87 per cent of women attending mission services went in the evening.[88] Sunday schools also remained predominately working class, as middle-class congregants refused to enrol their children, or even, in many cases, to allow their daughters to teach in the schools.[89] Some workers contributed to this social segregation by forming their own chapels. In Oakworth, Yorkshire, mill owners dominated the Anglican and Methodist congregations, but a Congregational chapel existed as a 'working man's institution', independent of the town's elite.[90] Others formed Labour Churches, which joined religious sensibilities and socialist politics.[91]

The appeal of independent associations remained strong in working-class culture, as exemplified by friendly societies and co-operatives. Though the convivial activities of friendly societies may have grown less important as the nineteenth century closed, co-operatives provided more extensive educational and leisure opportunities.[92] An American observer commented on British co-operatives' investment in libraries and reading rooms: 'co-operation set before itself the task of becoming mentally independent as being quite as important as that of becoming independent in its groceries'. Societies also sponsored tea parties, excursions, choir groups and large exhibitions, including the National Co-operative Festival, which attracted 41,755 visitors on one day in 1896.[93]

Working-men's clubs, originally the product of philanthropic leadership, increasingly threw off elite patronage and became self-governing and sustaining. The United Radical Club, for example, seceded in 1883 from a club sponsored by Lady Clifden, as 'the patronage of the worthy lady grew irksome at last'.[94] Though many retained a formal political purpose, most members sought sociability and leisure, a place for 'talking, drinking, smoking and association'. Many clubs took on larger premises and began staging shows, eventually hiring professional entertainment and even competing with music halls. As one letter writer to *Club Life* observed: 'From places where men met for a quiet game of cards, or a friendly chat with an occasional song, they had grown into theatres and music halls'. Even though the focus on entertainment increasingly dominated clubs, the majority had libraries and some continued political discussions or educational activities.[95]

Though these clubs illustrate that music-hall style entertainment and 'improving' activities were not mutually exclusive, many radical and socialist working-class leaders criticized the leisure preferences of the majority of the working class. Owen Balmforth, a Huddersfield co-operative leader, complained, 'too much leisure time is nowadays spent in a manner which is extremely questionable'.[96] Salford socialist H.W. Hobart was less generous: 'In the great majority of cases the British workman makes very bad use of his leisure'. Like mid-Victorian radicals half a century earlier, these socialists and co-operators disdained both elite patronage and popular taste.[97]

Socialists could not wean most workers from their preferred leisure activities. Opposition to gambling, for example, made little difference, as working people continued to find opportunities to wager. The sheer ubiquity of gambling reveals its broad acceptance in working-class communities. Small groups of men turned street corners or other spots in their neighbourhoods into arenas for coin or card games. Increasingly, working-class punters bet on events beyond the neighbourhood. Gambling on horses increased dramatically in the last decades of the nineteenth century. The sporting press, particularly *Sporting Life*, *Sportsman*, and *Sporting Chronicle*, each exceeding 300,000 circulation in the late 1880s, provided information crucial to the thriving trade.[98] In some areas gambling on football also spread before the First World War, though the heyday of football coupon betting remained a few years off. Observers recognized that working peopled viewed gambling 'to be entirely legitimate if a man risks no more than he can afford to lose'.[99] Much to his dismay, Rowntree noted the spread of gambling to the point that 'those who know the facts name gambling and drinking as national evils of almost equal magnitude'.[100]

Working-class betters shared their enthusiasm for gambling with those higher on the social scale. Yet even when wagering on the same races, different classes gambled separately. The law distinguished between on-site or credit betting typical of affluent players and cash bets off track. The latter came under increasing legal condemnation directed at working-class gamblers who wagered small amounts, in cash, with one another or with local bookies. London magistrate Horace Smith defended a proposed ban on street betting that left gambling by the affluent unmolested. He claimed the law aimed at 'the protection of the poor; as for the rich, they do not need any protection in such matters'.[101]

Conclusion

The distinctive leisure culture at the heart of the 'traditional' British working-class way of life developed in the late nineteenth century. Close-knit communities in stable working-class neighbourhoods fostered the vibrant street culture at the heart of young people's and women's leisure. Entrepreneurs expanded mid-Victorian excursions and music halls into big business, and professional football took its place as a major preoccupation of working-class men and boys. As commercial leisure grew, so did philanthropists' determination to offer more uplifting alternatives, though most workers remained sceptical of the middle-class values that accompanied improving leisure. Working-class associations also contributed to the range of leisure options available to those workers who enjoyed shorter hours and rising real wages.

Notes

1   A. Freeman, *Boy Life and Labour: The Manufacture of Inefficiency*
    ([1914]; New York: Garland, 1980), 151, 115, 110, 111.

2   E.J. Hobsbawm, *Workers: Worlds of Labour* (New York: Pantheon Books,
    1984), 206–7.

3   M.A. Bienefeld, *Working Hours in British Industry: An Economic
    History* (London: Weidenfeld & Nicolson, 1972), 116, 255 n. 67;
    H. Cunningham, 'Leisure and culture', in F.M.L. Thompson, ed.,
    *The Cambridge Social History of Britain 1750–1950, vol. II: People and
    Their Environment* (Cambridge: Cambridge University Press, 1990), 284;
    J.M. Golby and A.W. Purdue, *The Civilisation of the Crowd: Popular
    Culture in England 1750–1900* (New York: Schocken, 1985), 169;
    G. Cross, *A Quest for Time: The Reduction of Work in Britain and
    France, 1840–1940* (Berkeley: University of California Press, 1989),
    233.

4   Bienefeld, *Working Hours*, 104.

5   Cross, *Quest for Time*, 76, 66.

6   H. Cunningham, 'Leisure', in J. Benson, ed., *The Working Class in
    England 1875–1914* (London: Croom Helm, 1985), 135; C.M. Parratt,
    *More than Mere Amusement: Working-Class Women's Leisure in England,
    1750–1914* (Boston: Northeastern University Press, 2001), 86–8.

7   W.W. Knox, *Industrial Nation: Work, Culture and Society in Scotland
    1800–Present* (Edinburgh: Edinburgh University Press, 1999), 149.

8   R. Church, *Over the Bridge: An Essay in Autobiography* (London: William
    Heinemann, 1955), 75; A. August, *Poor Women's Lives: Gender, Work and
    Poverty in Late-Victorian London* (London: Associated University Presses,
    1999), 126–7.

9   M. Pember Reeves, *Round about a Pound a Week* ([1913]; London: Virago,
    1979), 161; W. Seccombe, *Weathering the Storm: Working-Class Families
    from the Industrial Revolution to the Fertility Decline* (London: Verso,
    1995), 132.

10 T. Mason, *Association Football and English Society 1863–1915*
    (Brighton: Harvester Press, 1980), 148; A. Davies, 'The police and
    the people: gambling in Salford, 1900–1939', *The Historical Journal*
    34 (1991), 111; August, *Poor Women's Lives*, 124–6; Parratt, *More than
    Mere Amusement*, 97.

11 C. Chinn, *They Worked All Their Lives: Women of the Urban Poor in
    England, 1880–1939* (Manchester: Manchester University Press, 1988),
    119.

12 M. Tebbutt, *Women's Talk? A Social History of Gossip in Working-Class Neighbourhoods, 1880–1960* (Aldershot: Scolar, 1995), 61.

13 Parratt, *More than Mere Amusement*, 101.

14 C. Chinn, *Poverty amidst Prosperity: The Urban Poor in England, 1834–1914* (Manchester: Manchester University Press, 1995), 133.

15 A. Davies, *Leisure, Gender and Poverty: Working-Class Culture in Salford and Manchester, 1900–1939* (Buckingham: Open University Press, 1992), 135.

16 Ibid., 136.

17 Parratt, *More than Mere Amusement*, 110.

18 August, *Poor Women's Lives*, 128.

19 M. Childs, *Labour's Apprentices: Working-Class Lads in Late Victorian and Edwardian England* (Montreal: McGill-Queen's University Press, 1992), 101.

20 J. Burnett, ed., *Destiny Obscure: Autobiographies of Childhood, Education and Family from the 1820s to the 1920s* (Harmondsworth: Penguin, 1982), 114, 117.

21 R. Roberts, *The Classic Slum: Salford Life in the First Quarter of the Century* (Harmondsworth: Penguin, 1973), 124.

22 A. Davin, *Growing Up Poor: Home, School and Street in London 1870–1914* (London: Rivers Oram Press, 1996), 64.

23 S. Meacham, *A Life Apart: The English Working Class 1890–1914* (Cambridge, MA: Harvard University Press, 1977), 162.

24 Davin, *Growing Up Poor*, 65–6, 64.

25 Childs, *Labour's Apprentices*, 95.

26 S. Humphries, *Hooligans or Rebels? An Oral History of Working-Class Childhood and Youth 1889–1939* (Oxford: Blackwell, 1981), 121.

27 Davies, *Leisure, Gender and Poverty*, 118–19.

28 A. Davies, 'Leisure in the "classic slum" 1900–1939', in A. Davies and S. Fielding, eds, *Workers' Worlds: Cultures and Communities in Manchester and Salford, 1880–1939* (Manchester: Manchester University Press, 1992), 122.

29 Davies, *Leisure, Gender and Poverty*, 115.

30 Tebbutt, *Women's Talk*, 62.

31 Roberts, *Classic Slum*, 157; Childs, *Labour's Apprentices*, 98, 99.

32 Davin, *Growing Up Poor*, 65.

33 Davies, *Leisure, Gender and Poverty*, 115.

34 Childs, *Labour's Apprentices*, 107, 108.

35 Ibid., 113–14.

36 Meacham, *A Life Apart*, 163.

37 Humphries, *Hooligans or Rebels*, 203–4.

38 D.M. MacRaild and D.E. Martin, *Labour in British Society 1830–1914* (New York: St Martin's Press, 2000), 112.

39 J. Rose, *The Intellectual Life of the British Working Classes* (New Haven: Yale University Press, 2001), 87–8.

40 J. Belchem, *Industrialization and the Working Class: The English Experience, 1750–1900* (Portland: Areopagitica, 1990), 225.

41 Cunningham, 'Leisure', 137.

42 Hobsbawm, *Worlds of Labour*, 185–7, 200, 202–3, 206.

43 Cunningham, 'Leisure', 139.

44 Roberts, *Classic Slum*, 16, 120.

45 B.S. Rowntree, *Poverty: A Study of Town Life* ([1922]; New York: Howart Fertig, 1971), 368.

46 Chinn, *They Worked All Their Lives*, 120; W.H. Fraser, 'Developments in leisure', in W.H. Fraser and R.J. Morris, eds, *People and Society in Scotland, vol. II: 1830–1914* (Edinburgh: John Donald, 1990), 243.

47 Roberts, *Classic Slum*, 120.

48 W. Fishman, *East End 1888: Life in a London Borough among the Laboring Poor* (Philadelphia: Temple University Press, 1988), 305; Cunningham, 'Leisure and culture', 316.

49 R. Holt, *Sport and the British: A Modern History* (Oxford: Clarendon Press, 1989), 149–50.

50 Rowntree, *Poverty*, 366–7, 368–9.

51 J. Crump, 'Provincial music hall: promoters and public in Leicester, 1863–1929', in P. Bailey, ed., *Music Hall: The Business of Pleasure* (Milton Keynes: Open University Press, 1986), 65.

52 S. Pennybacker, ' "It was not what she said but the way in which she said it": the London County Council and the music halls', in Bailey, ed., *Music Hall*, 118.

53 D. Kift, *The Victorian Music Hall: Culture, Class and Conflict*, trans. R. Kift (Cambridge: Cambridge University Press, 1996), 67–8, 72–3.

54 S. Attridge, *Nationalism, Imperialism and Identity in Late-Victorian Culture* (Basingstoke: Palgrave, 2003), 20.

55 P. Bailey, 'Introduction: making sense of the music hall', in Bailey, ed., *Music Hall*, xv, xvii.

56 Childs, *Labour's Apprentices*, 130.

57 W.J. Baker, 'The making of a working-class football culture in Victorian England', *Journal of Social History* 13 (1979), 248.

58 Fraser, 'Developments in leisure', 255; Cunningham, 'Leisure and culture', 314.

59 Mason, *Association Football and English Society*, 155–7; Childs, *Labour's Apprentices*, 135.

60 B. Murray, *The Old Firm: Sectarianism, Sport and Society in Scotland* (Edinburgh: John Donald, 1984), 111.

61 Holt, *Sport and the British*, 174, 161; Mason, *Association Football*, 233; Fraser, 'Developments in leisure', 256.

62 J.K. Walton, *The British Seaside: Holidays and Resorts in the Twentieth Century* (Manchester: Manchester University Press, 2000), 51–3, 94–6; P.J. Waller, *Town, City and Nation: England 1850–1914* (Oxford: Oxford University Press, 1983), 131.

63 J.K. Walton, 'The world's first working-class seaside resort? Blackpool revisited, 1840–1974', *Transactions of the Lancashire and Cheshire Antiquarian Society* 88 (1992), 11; J.K. Walton, 'The demand for working-class seaside holidays in Victorian England', *Economic History Review* 34 (1981), 253–6.

64 C. Ward and D. Hardy, *Goodnight Campers! The History of the British Holiday Camp* (London: Mansell, 1986), 8–12.

65 J.K. Walton, 'Municipal government and the holiday industry in Blackpool, 1876–1914', in J.K. Walton and J. Walvin, eds, *Leisure in Britain 1780–1939* (Manchester: Manchester University Press, 1983), 163.

66 H.J. Perkin, 'The "social tone" of Victorian seaside resorts in the North-West', *Northern History* 11 (1976), 193–4.

67 Cunningham, 'Leisure', 140–1.

68 J. Cox, *The English Churches in a Secular Society: Lambeth, 1870–1930* (Oxford: Oxford University Press, 1982), 58.

69 Fishman, *East End 1888*, 307.

70 Holt, *Sport and the British*, 138.

71 Parratt, *More than Mere Amusement*, 182.

72 Freeman, *Boy Life and Labour*, 128–9.

73 Rose, *Intellectual Life*, 453–4.

74 Kift, *Victorian Music Hall*, 65.

75 Freeman, *Boy Life and Labour*, 129.

76 Meacham, *A Life Apart*, 167.

77 Walton, 'Demand for working-class seaside holidays', 249.

78 Belchem, *Industrialization and the Working Class*, 227.

79 Cox, *English Churches*, 93, 103.

80 S.J.D. Green, *Religion in the Age of Decline: Organisation and Experience in Industrial Yorkshire, 1870–1920* (Cambridge: Cambridge University Press, 1996), 342.

81 Cox, *English Churches*, 80.

82 H. McLeod, *Religion and Society in England, 1850–1914* (New York: St Martin's Press, 1996), 80–1.

83 Cox, *English Churches*, 81.

84 H. McLeod, 'New perspectives on Victorian class religion: the oral evidence', *Oral History* 14 (1986), 32.

85 C.G. Brown, *Religion and Society in Scotland since 1707*, rev. ed. (Edinburgh: Edinburgh University Press, 1997), 149.

86 McLeod, 'New perspectives on Victorian class religion', 40, 33.

87 S. Thorne, *Congregational Missions and the Making of an Imperial Culture in Nineteenth-Century England* (Stanford: Stanford University Press, 1999), 145, 140–1.

88 C.G. Brown, *The Death of Christian Britain: Understanding Secularisation 1800–2000* (London: Routledge, 2001), 160–1.

89 Green, *Religion in the Age of Decline*, 229.

90 McLeod, 'New perspectives on Victorian class religion', 39.

91 M. Bevir, 'The labour church movement, 1891–1902', *Journal of British Studies* 38 (1999), 217–45.

92 E. Hopkins, *Working-Class Self-Help in Nineteenth-Century England* (New York: St Martin's Press, 1995), 55.

93 P. Gurney, *Cooperative Culture and the Politics of Consumption in England 1870–1930* (Manchester: Manchester University Press, 1996), 33–4, 38, 66–74.

94 T.G. Ashplant, 'London working men's clubs, 1875–1914', in E. Yeo and S. Yeo, eds, *Popular Culture and Class Conflict* (Brighton: Harvester Press, 1981), 251.

95 Meacham, *A Life Apart*, 122; Ashplant, 'London working men's clubs', 252, 263; Rose, *Intellectual Life*, 78–9.

96 Gurney, *Cooperative Culture*, 76.

97 C. Waters, *British Socialists and the Politics of Popular Culture, 1884–1914* (Manchester: Manchester University Press, 1990), 7, 188–9; Holt, *Sport and the British*, 146–8.

98 R. McKibbin, 'Working-class gambling in Britain, 1880–1939', in *Ideologies of Class: Social Relations in Britain 1880–1950* (Oxford: Clarendon Press, 1994), 120; D. Itzkowitz, 'Victorian bookmakers and their customers', *Victorian Studies* 32 (1988), 21.

99 Davies, 'Police and the people', 115.

100 McKibbin, 'Working-class gambling', 103–4.

101 Itzkowitz, 'Victorian bookmakers', 19.

CHAPTER EIGHT

Class identity and everyday politics

In describing his Salford neighbourhood, Robert Roberts observed the general lack of interest in party politics or socialism. The Social Democratic Federation Hall 'had, in fact, about as much political impact on the neighbourhood as the near-by gasworks'. The Conservative Club, on the other hand, 'didn't appear to meddle with politics at all', aside from a few days around election time. Though not engaged with high politics, the residents of Roberts's 'classic slum' recognized a complicated hierarchy of streets and families, ranked by status and respectability. Skilled work conferred status, but rough behaviour led to a loss of standing. Irish immigrants 'formed the lowest socio-economic stratum'. Despite these distinctions and the disinterest in the preaching of local socialists, Roberts observed one key link that tied all its residents together: 'The real social divide existed between those who, in earning daily bread, dirtied hands and face and those who did not'.[1] The experience of intimate, class-distinct neighbourhoods, manual labour and economic insecurity, and working-class leisure contributed to this class identity.

Complex identities

Working-class consciousness continued to coexist with other forms of identification. Respectability remained entrenched in late-Victorian and Edwardian working-class culture, though there were not distinct 'rough' and 'respectable' sections of the working class. A range of criteria marked individuals and families as respectable in their own eyes and those of their neighbours. Such distinctions did not consistently reflect economic differences, as the son of a skilled worker in Bolton recalled of the unskilled: 'There were respectable labourers who would mix in various church activities'. For this man, respectability did not reflect possession of a skill and high wages. Rather, religious involvement and temperance conferred respectable status.[2] For others, drinking at home was consistent with respectability, especially for working-class women. A Salford man explained: 'a lot of people, especially women, did their drinking at home, 'cause women in pubs was very, very rare'.[3] On the other hand, settlement worker Anna Martin found London neighbourhoods in which respectable married women visited pubs regularly without sacrificing their reputations.[4]

Family reputations depended a great deal on mothers' perceived housekeeping skill and the children's behaviour. Women devoted energy and resources sweeping hearths, blackening stoves and whitening doorsteps. Adequate Sunday clothes and decent school outfits for children distinguished families from one another, even if these were pawned during the week. Those with pretences to respectability in comparison with their neighbours restricted their children's associations and habits. Mrs Bartle recalled her Poplar childhood in which neighbourhood children 'used to tumble in and out of the passage all day long, and their pals used to run in and out with all their dirty boots'. Her mother, on the other hand, 'kept us well away from the lot of the children, as far as she could'.[5] Gender differences played an important role in respectability, and some parents restricted girls' play, forbidding games like 'overback' (leapfrog), 'that wasn't a thing for girls to do'.[6]

While neighbours kept watch on each other's behaviour, they also stepped in to help preserve reputations. Maud Pember Reeves noted the threat to a whole community's self-respect if one of its members suffered a pauper burial. Neighbours 'will contribute rather than suffer the degradation to pauperism of one of themselves'. She observed the importance of mutual aid in preserving these families: 'respectable but very poor people live over a morass of such intolerable poverty that they unite instinctively to save those known to them from falling into it'.[7] The too-respectable family that kept to itself to avoid contact with rougher neighbours imperilled relationships that might provide essential aid. Excessive privacy or maintaining standards above those of one's neighbours appeared as 'putting on airs'. Expensive and fragile brown boots drew scorn in Grace Foakes's Wapping neighbourhood: 'brown boots were a cut above the station in life to which we all belonged, and no one was tolerated who tried to rise above it'. Thus, many women walked a fine line, trying to maintain standards of respectability, yet cultivating essential links with neighbours.[8]

By staking claims to respectable status, working-class families both distinguished themselves from those they defined as 'rough' and embraced others whom they classed as similarly 'respectable'. Thus a lighterman's wife 'felt that she was with her equals when she went out shopping with the wife of a stevedore or the wife of a shipwright, but never with the wife of a docker or an unskilled labourer'.[9] Even dockers established a hierarchy, with one of the more regular London dockworkers complaining: 'All the scum of London come to the Docks, and an honest man has no chance'.[10] Many people viewed a pauper funeral as the ultimate sign of disrepute.[11] Yet even families that resorted to the parish burial did whatever they could to appear respectably dressed. At pauper funerals in Liverpool, 'a brave effort would be made to wear something black, jackets or skirts being got from pawnbrokers'.[12]

Workers also cultivated ethnic and sectarian differences. Catholics, mainly of Irish birth or descent, embraced an ethnic and religious identity distinct from the Protestant Britishness that surrounded them. Though born in Manchester, Bart Kennedy's mother determined to preserve his sense of Irishness, 'He was born in England, but that would never make him an Englishman!' The Catholic Church helped reinforce this identity, particularly through its schools. Residential concentration could strengthen sectarian identity. In 1900 more than three-quarters of household heads in Back Simpson Street in the heavily Catholic Angel Meadow district of Manchester were Irish immigrants. On the other hand, many Irish Catholics lived amidst mostly Protestant neighbours, and two-thirds of Manchester's Irish population lived outside Angel Meadow.[13]

Though large-scale sectarian violence grew less common in the late nineteenth-century, hostility between sectarian groups continued to divide the working class. Fear of competition for jobs exacerbated long-standing prejudices and contributed to anti-Irish and anti-Jewish sentiment. James Keir Hardie, coal miner and first president of the Independent Labour Party, complained of the Irish collier with 'a big shovel, a strong back and a weak brain'.[14] Police on horseback restrained a crowd of unemployed workers angry about the hiring of Jewish immigrants at a Tottenham factory. Though the police prevented a full-scale riot, the crowd hurled bricks and broke the factory's windows.[15] Religious riots plagued Liverpool, where a battle between the children and mothers of St Anthony's Catholic school and Protestants of St Polycarp's led to the closure of 47 schools for a week in 1908.[16] Some street battles, though, could become shared rituals, shorn of the visceral hatred that once drove them. St Patrick's Day saw school children battle across sectarian lines, but one participant recalled 'it was just something our dads had done before us . . . [we did it] more in fun than in anger'.[17] Similarly, a Liverpool man who later married a Catholic woman recalled heading to the nearby Catholic school to 'attack the kids . . . it was a – a tradition'.[18]

These sectarian differences persisted alongside integration into a common working-class culture. Though Robert Roberts claims that 'deeply ingrained' prejudice divided Protestant and Catholic youths, loyalty to the group of boys from the same street overcame the sectarian divide in his mixed neighbourhood, and he counted an Irish boy among his friends.[19] In some areas, intermarriage grew more common. In Edwardian Stafford about half of all Irish and Irish-descended Catholics married non-Catholics. Among the descendants of Patrick Mannion, who arrived in Stafford on the heels of the Irish famine, four of the six marriages traced between 1859 and 1913 involved non-Catholic spouses. Martin Mannion, one of Patrick's grandsons, reveals both his Catholic identity and integration into broader working-class life in two court appearances in 1883. In the spring, Martin appeared before a magistrate accused of assault in what was probably a sectarian conflict surrounding Salvationist processions. Later that year, though, he and two non-Irish co-workers from the Elley & Co. shoe factory stole some tools and fled, unsuccessfully, on their way to Leicester.[20] J.R. Clynes, Labour Party MP for Manchester who was born in Oldham of Irish parents, expressed this sort of blended identity, claiming to be 'half Irish and wholly Lancastrian'.[21]

Local, regional or national identities often coexisted with class and other forms of identification. As in Robert Roberts's Salford neighbourhood, streets and neighbourhoods held distinct meanings. Birmingham residents recalled, 'Summer Lane was the hardest and toughest in Birmingham but Garrison Lane was rough as well'.[22] Youths and sometimes adults would fight to defend their territory, as a Canning Town youth reported, 'We'd barricade across the street and start aiming stones at one another'.[23] Yet after these ritualized battles children from nearby streets might also cooperate and play together. 'We weren't enemies the rest of the time because we'd go to the same school'.[24]

Despite the development of a common British leisure culture, regional identities remained strong. The embrace of rugby as the typical Welsh game reinforced a sense of national pride in Wales. In the press, Welsh success in rugby became a reflection of the national character, steeped in history: 'the great quality of defence and attack in the Welsh race is to be traced to the training of the early period when powerful enemies drove them to their mountain fortresses'.[25] Yet Welsh rugby pride easily merged with British imperial pride, as in celebrations of the Welsh victory over New Zealand in 1905, in which 'the honour of Great Britain' had been salvaged.[26] In Lancashire cotton unions reinforced the combination of regional and class identification. Their journals, such as the *Cotton Factory Times*, included columns in Lancashire dialect and celebrated the regional distinctiveness of 'factory foaks'. Yet they also covered other districts and unions outside Lancashire cotton.[27] For Welsh rugby fans and Lancashire dialect speakers, working-class identity overlapped and coexisted with local and regional pride.

Celebrations of monarchy and empire reinforced British identity. As the monarchy lost its formal political power, it developed a new ceremonial function. New media, developed in the late nineteenth and early twentieth centuries, helped promote the monarchy, empire and British national identity.[28] Mass newspapers offered vivid descriptions of royal ceremonies. Working-class children encountered patriotic and loyalist messages in school. A 1901 reader designed for elementary school children urged: 'We must be loyal to the Crown, for the Crown is loyal to us, and is the personification of our constitution and of our law'.[29] In her last decades, Victoria gained renewed popularity, reinforced by celebrations such as her jubilee in 1897, during which 'Her photograph adorned the walls of the humblest homes'.[30] Following the coronation of George V, a socialist reflected on popular enthusiasm for the event, observing 'the nation has abandoned itself with so much gusto and good humour to the quite harmless debauch of flag waving and fireworks ordained in the monarch's name'.[31]

In times of war or international tension, enthusiasm for the nation (and for raucous celebration) drove expressions of popular patriotism. An 1877–8 wave of anti-Russian sentiment brought jingoistic crowds into the streets with 'a liberal allowance of torch-light processions, brass bands, bonfires, beer, and "Rule Britannia" '.[32] During the Boer War, crowds moved by the relief of Mafeking joined enthusiastic processions. Working-class organizations participated, as in Southwark, where a radical club's band marched 'round the neighbourhood playing patriotic airs and got a glorious reception from the multitude'. Even in Battersea, a centre of anti-war activity, Mafeking Night saw 'thousands of people outside . . . singing "God save the Queen" . . . til 3.30 a.m.'.[33] Enthusiastic crowds saluted volunteers on their way to fight in South Africa. In Chester residents 'packed the Town Hall Square, and lined the route to the General Railway Station, in order to get a last glimpse of, and give a parting cheer to' the men.[34]

The surge in Victoria's popularity and in patriotic enthusiasm during the Boer War contributed to and reflected the pervasiveness of empire in late-Victorian and Edwardian British culture. Constant reminders of the superiority of the British and their important role in the world appeared in popular literature, music hall songs, advertising and packaging, and in schools.[35] Stories of imperial heroes such as General Gordon, who died in Khartoum in 1885, filled popular books, pamphlets and school readers. Their likenesses adorned jugs and bookmarks, statues and busts.[36] A school reader celebrated: 'probably no other man ever won the love of his countrymen so entirely as did the great hero, General Gordon'. Examples like this encouraged working-class children to 'make the British Empire the first among nations in all that is right and just . . . and to love the flag which, by the bravery and the wisdom of our forefathers, has become so famous'.[37]

Working-class men, women and children celebrated monarchy and empire. Yet the extent of their patriotism and enthusiasm for empire remains unclear. The jingoistic outburst in the late 1870s was short-lived and patchy, exerting little lasting influence on British politics or working-class attitudes.[38] During the Boer War, working-class opinions were mixed, and the most blatant and violent pro-war activities were carried out by young middle-class men.[39] Participation in celebrations of empire did not necessarily indicate commitment to the imperial enterprise; as one observer complained, 'it was difficult to translate ephemeral enthusiasms into a day-to-day acceptance of imperial burdens and obligations'.[40] Even participation in the Volunteer Force, which did require a significant time commitment, reflected more than simple patriotism. As an officer noted of his volunteers, mostly cotton workers from Salford: 'my men join because they like the show, the dress, and they like the camp. I do not think they join from very high patriotic motives'.[41]

One attraction of the volunteers was its reinforcement of a specifically masculine form of working-class respectability. Gender divisions within the British working class are also apparent in sport and union organization, as well as in neighbourhoods and homes. Men and women staked out distinct spaces and gendered subcultures, filling complementary (though unequal) roles in the London neighbourhoods studied by historian Ellen Ross: 'London husbands and wives lived in quite separate worlds, organized around their responsibilities in a fairly rigid sexual division of labour'.[42] The hearth, parlour and scrubbed step were female spaces. Housing reformer Octavia Hill met a young Marylebone girl 'so proud of her first cleaning that she stood two hours watching her passage lest the boys, whom she considered as the natural enemies of order and cleanliness, should spoil it'. The best chair, however, belonged to father. In Alice Linton's Hoxton home, 'dad's old wooden armchair held the place of honour in front of the fireplace. No one would ever dare to sit in that chair, sacred to father alone'.[43]

In working-class marriages, men and women often battled over authority and the fulfilment of responsibilities. If men judged their wives' house-keeping to be inadequate, they made their dissatisfaction clear with their fists. Women challenged husbands who spent too much on drink and supported one another when they turned to the courts against abusive or non-supporting husbands, calling out encouragement such as 'You stick to it', 'Go on wiv'it', 'Get your separation'.[44] On the other hand, marriage also built strong ties between spouses, recognized in Lambeth women's understated reports, "E's all right', or "E's a good 'usbin'.[45]

In the workplace, the gendered division of labour fostered distinct male and female work cultures. As a young apprentice in an Aberdeen bakery, John Paton recalled that when his male co-workers tired of discussing 'the gossip of the bakehouse', one topic 'seemed inexhaustible – women and sex'.[46] Some leisure activities also reinforced distinct gender subcultures. Football belonged to men and boys, and press reports described crowds comprised of 'youths and young men', or 'mostly of young men – with more than a sprinkling of boys'. Saturday afternoon matches put pressure on the domestic routine, as men sought to return home after work and eat before heading to the ground. A Preston observer noted that the men in the crowd had smooth chins 'proving that "the hot water" had been waiting for them when they got from the mill. How the wives must have grumbled and dratted all football matches'.[47] Football became a working-class game, but the collective experience built both masculine and working-class identity.

Despite these complex identities, the sense of difference across class lines remained strong in workers' understandings of their world. As children, working-class boys and girls learned the necessity of hard work, in the first instance by watching their mothers' domestic labours.[48] They also learned to value manual labour through their parents' disdain for white-collar workers, commonly viewed as weak and unproductive.[49] The socially segregated educational system reinforced children's sense of their place in the working class.[50] Mobility out of the working class was rare. Thus between 1839 and 1914 93 per cent of sons of skilled workers remained working class.[51] As Robert Roberts noted, 'skilled workers generally did not strive to join a higher rank'.[52] The stories they heard and their own experiences taught youths that they were working class. Ramsay MacDonald's rather confused plea against class divisions highlighted both the role of culture in building class identity and its reinforcement in experience: 'the separation between the professional classes and labour has made the line of division a purely psychological one which is not with-out its reason in the different modes of life of the two classes'.[53]

Party politics

Class identity did not, however, translate directly into any particular party affiliation or political mobilization. Much to the dismay of activists, most workers did not embrace socialism, and many of those privileged with a vote supported Liberal or Tory candidates. The Labour Party, founded as the Labour Representation Committee in 1900, cooperated with the Liberals to avoid competing for parliamentary seats in England and Wales. While all three parties sought the votes of working-class electors, none dominated this section of the electorate.

Parliamentary reform in 1867 and 1885 enfranchised most working-class men, and Liberal candidates successfully appealed to many of these new voters. They had a better record of supporting suffrage expansion and electoral reform. The Liberals also advocated conciliation between employers and moderate unions, and some two dozen union activists, known as Lib-Labs, won election to Parliament as Liberals between 1874 and 1906. In South Wales, William Abraham, a coal miner and union leader known as Mabon, won his first election in 1885 and dominated his constituency for decades.[54] Gladstone's fiscal policies, including cuts in taxes on commodities such as paper, sugar and malt, drew working-class support to the Liberals.[55] Enthusiasm for Gladstone himself soared, as the *Daily News* noted in its coverage of the 'Grand Old Man's' 1880 speaking tour: 'It is physically impossible that any greater crowds can meet than have hitherto gathered wherever Mr. Gladstone has been announced to speak. Nor can [there] be any louder cheering or more frantic waving of hats and handkerchiefs'.[56] Though later Liberals struggled to reproduce the enthusiasm of Gladstone's heyday, free trade and the promise of the 'big loaf' in the face of the Conservative flirtation with tariffs drove working-class voters to the polls on behalf of Liberal candidates in 1906.[57] Lloyd George's 'People's Budget' and the National Insurance Act of 1911 helped the Liberals represent themselves as advocates for workers. The Boilermakers' Union called the National Insurance Act 'a very distinct advance along the path of progress', endorsing it as 'certainly the greatest measure of social reform ever placed on the Statute Book'.[58]

Yet many working-class voters did not embrace Liberalism, in part because the party fell short on a number of issues. Though it defended the existence of unions and advocated union recognition, the party did not consistently support labour in struggles with employers. In 1871 Gladstone's government passed legislation granting legal protection to unions and their finances, but also included the Criminal Law Amendment Act essentially outlawing picketing.[59] In 1906 Liberal Prime Minister Campbell-Bannerman sought to place 'the two rival powers of capital and labour on an equality so that the fight between them, so far as fight is necessary, should be at least a fair one'.[60] Even this claim of even-handedness contrasted sharply with Liberal governments' bloody military crackdowns on striking workers at Featherstone in 1893 and at Liverpool and Llanelli in 1911. Following the latter incidents, a handful of activists, including Tom Mann, called on troops to refuse orders to fire on strikers, and the Liberal government prosecuted them.[61]

These governments' decidedly mixed record during labour struggles contributed to calls for working-class representation in Parliament. Though Lib-Lab members such as Mabon Abraham represented some constituencies, many local Liberal Party organizations refused to adopt working-class candidates. When Liberals rejected a Stoke mining union leader as a potential candidate in 1875, *The Bee-Hive* newspaper threatened, 'if these blind and brutal prejudices against working men and trade unions cannot be overcome in the Liberal Party, it will be the duty of the working men of the country to separate from that party'.[62] Unions backed the creation of the Labour Representation Committee, precursor to the Labour Party, and Ramsay MacDonald negotiated an alliance with the Liberals designed to foster cooperation in defeating Tory candidates for Parliament.

Nonetheless, many working-class men supported the Tories, particularly in Liverpool and western Lancashire, Glasgow and western Scotland, Birmingham and the West Midlands, and some East London constituencies. In the 1880s and 1890s, for example, Conservatives thoroughly dominated working-class districts in Preston. As the *Preston Herald* observed, 'there were more Conservative trade unionists than Liberal'.[63] The Tories reached out to working-class voters and their families, forming clubs for working men and providing a calendar of events and entertainments through the Primrose League.[64] Conservatives attracted working-class voters by defending popular recreations from the onslaught of puritanical Liberal interference. In 1891 the Tories ran John Griffiths and Joseph Lawrence, two Wolverhampton publicans, in municipal elections against Liberal incumbents. The two emphasized their opponents' support for temperance, and Lawrence's campaign song asserted, 'When I drink that cold water I get creepy an' pale/ So I'll vote for Joe Lawrence and sparkling warm ale'. Both Conservatives won. The town's Tories also benefited from close links to the Wolverhampton Wanderers Football Club. Players from the team campaigned with Tory candidates and appeared at Primrose League events.[65]

Many working-class voters also responded to the Conservative embrace of the monarchy, empire and Protestantism. Disraeli reassured Tory supporters, 'the working classes of England, are proud of belonging to an imperial country, and are resolved to maintain if they can, their Empire'.[66] At times this approach played on workers' hostility to Irish and Jewish immigrants. A pamphlet published in 1892 complained that Irish Home Rule threatened to attract 'thousands of ruined and desperate Irishmen over to England to compete in our markets'.[67] Arthur Forwood, long-time Liverpool councillor and local Conservative Party leader and MP from 1885 to 1898, complained to an enthusiastic crowd, 'The influx of the Irish into Liverpool brought poverty, disease, dirt and misery, drunkenness and crime, in addition to a disturbance in the labour market'.[68] In Lancashire districts with significant Catholic populations, Conservatives appealed to Protestants on sectarian grounds.[69]

Though the party maintained working-class support in certain districts, a number of Conservative positions alienated other working-class voters in the early years of the twentieth century. The Conservative government's association with the Taff Vale decision drove unions that had cooperated with Tories to seek independent labour representation. For example, in Preston the strongest unions supported Conservatives throughout the 1890s but supported the fledgling Preston Labour Party by 1903.[70] Though Tory candidates benefited from nationalist enthusiasm for the Boer War in 1900, the conflict's appeal faded quickly, and the *Primrose League Gazette* in 1901 acknowledged that among working-class voters 'the idea is there, that the war ought to have been over before now'.[71] The Conservative embrace of tariffs, though popular in a few constituencies, drove many working-class voters away from Tory candidates, especially in Lancashire and London in 1906.[72]

The Labour Party took advantage of these issues and made inroads in areas of working-class Tory support. Most Labour candidates held positions that resembled those of the radical wing of the Liberals, but they benefited from class pride and the desire for working-class representation. As early as 1867 *The Bee-Hive* had called for working-class voters to choose representatives 'wherever practicable *from the ranks of labour*'.[73] An observer of the distinction between Labour and Liberal candidates explained that it rested 'upon the independence of Labour, not upon any economic or political doctrine in any ordinary sense at all'.[74] Yet Labour attempts to win mass support fell foul of the distance between union and party activists and the broader working-class population. The long-standing radical and socialist critique of popular culture exacerbated this gap.

James Kier Hardie, the first independent working-class MP, exemplifies this. A committed teetotaller, Kier Hardie once blamed poverty on workers pouring their money down 'their throats in intoxicating drink'.[75] The new Labour Party had difficulty dislodging the well-established parties, but the decade before the First World War did see its establishment as a viable party with a strong claim to compete for working-class votes.

Informal politics

Despite franchise reform, most residents of working-class neighbourhoods could not vote in the early twentieth century. Their major concerns involved daily life in their neighbourhoods, not parliamentary manoeuvring. In working-class communities, men and women battled over the distribution of resources, authority and status. Many of these conflicts were internal to working-class communities, involving spouses competing for house-hold resources or neighbours struggling with one another for authority and status. However, outsiders also intervened in their neighbourhoods, and working-class men and women negotiated complicated interactions with charity workers and representatives of the state. These interactions, both within communities and with outside authorities, reveal a dynamic everyday politics in working-class districts.

Within these communities, elaborate hierarchies of authority and re-putation marked individuals and families. The neighbourhood matriarchs who enforced behavioural standards kept track of indiscretions and pub-licized losses of standing through gossip networks. They wielded power in their streets, making sure that everyone upheld community standards. A man who grew up in Edwardian Birmingham recalled these women: 'They didn't stand no nonsense, which was only right and proper'. If someone stepped out of line, 'They'd soon be straightened out'.[76] After public quarrels in which participants asserted competing claims to respectability and status in the community, other women would judge the result of the struggle: 'heads together and with evidence submitted, they made grim readjust-ments on the social ladder'.[77]

Women battling for respect generally used words, either through gossip or public shouts and accusations. Men more commonly resorted to violence to assert their status and authority. Within their households, men insisted on pre-eminence and often enforced their claims violently, though wives fought back as well. Men also sought status among their peers. Generosity in treating at the pub and expertise in sport or gambling won men esteem. Fighting among individuals or groups helped cement reputations in the masculine culture of these neighbourhoods.[78] In the face of perceived slights or insults, men defended their prestige. In a London pub in 1886, Edmund Lyons knocked off George Hiscock's hat while walking past. Hiscock would not accept this apparent insult, and the two men began to fight.[79] These fights could lead to broader battles in which neighbours defended their reputation collectively. A London resident recalled an incident in which a man from his street took offence at the actions of someone from a different street, and he 'set about the chap'. The other man's neighbours later 'came on' and 'set about all the men in this turning where I lived, and it . . . ended up as a proper battle'.[80]

Outsiders with more peaceful intentions descended upon working-class districts in great numbers. The late-Victorian state adopted increasingly interventionist approaches in confronting working-class communities. The police continued their efforts to control working-class behaviour. With the establishment of compulsory education, school board visitors tried to enforce attendance on parents and children who were not always enthusiastic about school. A variety of new regulations sought to boost the physical health of working-class children and encourage morality in public places. In an effort to improve the health of infants, a sanitary inspector recalled, visitors acted quickly: 'Directly a baby was heard of they pounced down upon it'.[81] Thus, depending on the zeal of local government, working-class communities became the targets of a myriad of new officials, inspectors and authorities.

This state intervention augmented established efforts by middle-class philanthropists to reshape working-class life. Charity workers swarmed working-class neighbourhoods in the late nineteenth century. According to one estimate, half a million unpaid reform workers were active in this period.[82] They offered a broad range of services to the needy, some essential to the survival of working-class families. One mother reflected on the appeal of meals provided in school by volunteers: 'If you spend a bit less on food there's a bit more for coals and boots'.[83] Though philanthropy provided welcome benefits, it also brought regulation and attempts to interfere in working-class life in ways that were far less welcome. In dealing with state authorities and middle-class philanthropists, working-class men and particularly women took advantage of the benefits, but seldom accepted claims to authority and moral superiority.

Poor families learned to manipulate offers of charity. According to historian George Behlmer, they 'were willing to perform rituals of deference as the price for material aid'.[84] They attended meetings or participated in programmes in order to receive benefits. Some, of course, embraced the guidance of their social betters. More commonly, however, those in need learned to adopt the proper pose to get what they needed. Thomas Morgan recalled that his mother 'used to go to a Mothers' meeting . . . all the year round and they used to get a turkey on Christmas. That's all they used to go there for'.[85] Clementina Black's study of women workers discovered that 'many families were receiving assistance from three or four sources at once'. Religious bribery reflects this instrumental approach to charity. Missions were forced to compete with one another in offering clothes and food to boost attendance. One mission worker complained, 'the poor have actually expected to be paid for their religion'.[86]

At times, though, this willingness to play the expected role broke down. Children were the most likely to defy the dictates of well-meaning philanthropists. When Constance Maynard tried to offer Bible readings to factory girls, she found an intractable audience. One girl 'called out loudly "Cock a doodle doo!" and the whole long room went off into shrieks of laughter'. Another attempt by missionaries to organize London youth in a church hall ended similarly. The boys marched around the church hall singing ribald music hall songs and parodies of patriotic anthems. 'This was hardly what the missionaries had in mind and the lady at the small organ did her best to render *Onward Christian Soldiers* fortissimo, without success'.[87] At times adults challenged the authority of charity workers as well. When a care committee refused to serve his children meals because he was employed, a Fulham man replied pointedly, 'You people don't do the work properly'.[88]

State intervention sparked more frequent resistance in working-class neighbourhoods. Police attempts to crack down on widely accepted practices provoked confrontations and violence. School board visitors also faced defiance. One visitor in London's East End recalled, 'parents would stand at the street door and threaten and abuse me in the most dreadful language, and nearly all the people in the street would come out and see what was the matter and sympathise in their view'. Teachers who relied excessively on physical punishment faced the ire of parents. When a head teacher caned an eight-year-old boy who screamed loudly enough to be heard, 'his mother rushed in, and cursed and swore and threatened to a fearful degree. With much difficulty I got her out of the school, but a mob assembled in the yard and street, which was only dispersed by the arrival of the police'.[89] Health measures, when they involved compulsion, triggered opposition as well. Thomas Burt, an early Lib-Lab MP, complained of compulsory vaccination, asserting that he 'did not intend to have my children treated as if they were cattle'.[90]

Examples of hostility to state intervention tell only half the story, however. Working-class men and women also used the state to further their own interests. Women turned to the municipal courts in conflicts with their husbands. They sought protection orders (which did not exist) or even separation orders from the magistrates.[91] Parents appealed to magistrates and school boards against unpopular teachers, and in Camberwell parents blocked the transfer of a well-liked assistant teacher by seeking the aid of the school management committee.[92] Despite their hostility to police efforts to control widely accepted behaviours in their neighbourhoods, working-class men and women were willing to call in the constables when it suited them. Thus governmental and philanthropic authorities met complex combinations of resentment, resistance and welcome in working-class neighbourhoods.

Conclusion

Social change in late-Victorian and Edwardian Britain strengthened the class ties already evident in earlier decades. Stable neighbourhoods nurtured close-knit communities of working-class men, women and children. Despite rising real wages, persistent economic insecurity amidst employer efforts to maximize profits linked workers across skill divides. A distinct working-class leisure culture based in streets, associations and commercial venues reinforced a strong sense of class identity. This consciousness of class coexisted with numerous other forms of identity based on locality, ethnicity, gender and other factors without losing its force. Despite this strong identity, working-class men did not automatically support any particular political party, and all three major parties attracted significant working-class votes. Party politics proved less important in working-class districts than did the pervasive politics of everyday life.

Notes

1 R. Roberts, *The Classic Slum: Salford Life in the First Quarter of the Century* (Harmondsworth: Penguin, 1973), 16–17, 22–3, 19.

2 H. McLeod, 'New perspectives on Victorian class religion: the oral evidence', *Oral History* 14 (1986), 44.

3 A. Davies, 'Leisure in the "classic slum" 1900–1939', in A. Davies and S. Fielding, eds, *Workers' Worlds: Cultures and Communities in Manchester and Salford, 1880–1939* (Manchester: Manchester University Press, 1992), 117–18.

4 E. Ross, ' "Not the sort that would sit on the doorstep": respectability in pre-World War I London neighborhoods', *International Labor and Working-Class History* 27 (1985), 46.

5 A. Davin, *Growing Up Poor: Home, School and Street in London 1870–1914* (London: Rivers Oram Press, 1996), 73.

6 Ross, 'Respectability', 50.

7 M. Pember Reeves, *Round about a Pound a Week* ([1913]; London: Virago, 1979), 68, 39–40; Ross, 'Respectability', 46.

8 Ross, 'Respectability', 44–5, 52; E. Roberts, *A Woman's Place: An Oral History of Working-Class Women 1890–1940* (Oxford: Basil Blackwell, 1984), 196–7.

9 F.M.L. Thompson, *The Rise of Respectable Society: A Social History of Victorian Britain 1830–1900* (Cambridge, MA: Harvard University Press, 1988), 97.

10 M. Brodie, *The Politics of the Poor: The East End of London 1885–1914* (Oxford: Clarendon Press, 2004), 139.

11 Thompson, *Rise of Respectable Society*, 200.

12 J.M. Strange, *Death, Grief and Poverty in Britain, 1870–1914* (Cambridge: Cambridge University Press, 2005), 119.

13 S. Fielding, *Class and Ethnicity: Irish Catholics in England, 1880–1939* (Buckingham: Open University Press, 1993), 15, 64.

14 T. Gallagher, 'A tale of two cities: communal strife in Glasgow and Liverpool before 1914', in R. Swift and S. Gilley, eds, *The Irish in the Victorian City* (London: Croom Helm, 1985), 110.

15 S. Humphries, *Hooligans or Rebels? An Oral History of Working-Class Childhood and Youth 1889–1939* (Oxford: Blackwell, 1981), 196.

16 D. Fitzpatrick, 'A curious middle place: the Irish in Britain, 1871–1921', in R. Swift and S. Gilley, eds, *The Irish in Britain: 1815–1939* (London: Pinter, 1989), 25.

17 Fielding, *Class and Ethnicity*, 34.

18 M. Childs, *Labour's Apprentices: Working-Class Lads in Late Victorian and Edwardian England* (Montreal: McGill-Queen's University Press, 1992), 107–8.

19 Roberts, *Classic Slum*, 170; Fielding, *Class and Ethnicity*, 67.

20 J. Herson, 'Migration, "community" or integration? Irish families in Victorian Stafford', in R. Swift and S. Gilley, eds, *The Irish in Victorian Britain: The Local Dimension* (Dublin: Four Courts Press, 1999), 168–9, 172–4.

21 Fielding, *Class and Ethnicity*, 15.

22 C. Chinn, *They Worked All Their Lives: Women of the Urban Poor in England, 1880–1939* (Manchester: Manchester University Press, 1988), 24.

23 Childs, *Labour's Apprentices*, 108.

24 Humphries, *Hooligans or Rebels*, 189.

25 R. Holt, *Sport and the British: A Modern History* (Oxford: Clarendon Press, 1989), 250.

26 D. Andrew, 'Sport and the masculine hegemony of the modern nation: Welsh rugby, culture and society, 1890–1914', in J. Nauright and T.J.L. Chandler, eds, *Making Men: Rugby and Masculine Identity* (London: Frank Cass, 1996), 64–5.

27 P. Joyce, *Visions of the People: Industrial England and the Question of Classs 1848–1914* (Cambridge: Cambridge University Press, 1991), 135, 139, 315.

28 D. Cannadine, 'The context, performance and meaning of ritual: the British monarchy and the "invention of tradition", c.1820–1977', in E. Hobsbawm and T. Ranger, eds, *The Invention of Tradition* (Cambridge: Cambridge University Press, 1983), 140, 151.

29 S. Heathorn, ' "Let us remember that we, too, are English": constructions of citizenship and national identity in English elementary school reading books, 1880–1914', *Victorian Studies* 38 (1995), 420.

30 P. Readman, 'The Conservative Party, patriotism, and British politics: the case of the general election of 1900', *Journal of British Studies* 40 (2001), 135 n. 114.

31 N. Kirk, 'The conditions of royal rule: Australian and British socialist and labour attitudes to the monarchy, 1901–1911', *Social History* 30 (2005), 83.

32 H. Cunningham, 'Jingoism in 1877–78', *Victorian Studies* 14 (1971), 449.

33 R. Price, *An Imperial War and the British Working Class: Working-Class Attitudes and Reactions to the Boer War 1899–1902* (London: Routledge & Kegan Paul, 1972), 80, 170.

34 S.M. Miller, 'In support of the "Imperial mission"? Volunteering for the South African War, 1899–1902', *Journal of Military History* 69 (2005), 707.

35 J.M. MacKenzie, *Propaganda and Empire: The Manipulation of British Public Opinion, 1880–1960* (Manchester: Manchester University Press, 1984), 4, 254; Miller, 'Imperial mission', 701–3.

36 E.M. Spiers, *The Late-Victorian Army 1868–1902* (Manchester: Manchester University Press, 1992), 183–4.

37 Heathorn, 'Constructions of citizenship', 416, 418.

38 Cunningham, 'Jingoism', 451–3.

39 Price, *Imperial War*, 78–9, 176.

40 B. Porter, *The Absent-Minded Imperialists: Empire, Society and Culture in Britain* (Oxford: Oxford University Press, 2004), 210.

41 H. Cunningham, *The Volunteer Force: A Social and Political History 1859–1908* (Hamden, CT: Archon Books, 1975), 108–9.

42 E. Ross, 'Survival networks: women's neighbourhood sharing in London before World War One', *History Workshop Journal* 15 (1983), 7.

43 E. Ross, *Love and Toil: Motherhood in Outcast London 1870–1918* (Oxford: Oxford University Press, 1993), 80.

44 Ross, *Love and Toil*, 75, 59.

45 Pember Reeves, *Round About a Pound a Week*, 16.

46 W.W. Knox, *Industrial Nation: Work, Culture and Society in Scotland, 1800–Present* (Edinburgh: Edinburgh University Press, 1999), 140.

47 T. Mason, *Association Football and English Society 1863–1915* (Brighton: Harvester Press, 1980), 157–8, 153.

48 Roberts, *A Woman's Place*, 22.

49 J. Belchem, *Industrialization and the Working Class: The English Experience, 1750–1900* (Portland: Areopagitica, 1990), 221.

50 M. Childs, 'Labour grows up: the electoral system, political generations, and British politics 1890–1929', *Twentieth Century British History* 6 (1995), 140.

51 A. Miles, *Social Mobility in Nineteenth- and Early Twentieth-Century England* (New York: St Martin's Press, 1999), 23.

52 Roberts, *Classic Slum*, 13.

53 G. Stedman Jones, 'Why is the Labour Party in a mess?' in *Languages of Class: Studies in English Working Class History 1832–1982* (Cambridge: Cambridge University Press, 1983), 244.

54 E.F. Biagini, *Liberty, Retrenchment and Reform: Popular Liberalism in the Age of Gladstone, 1860–1880* (Cambridge: Cambridge University Press, 1992), 351–2, 383; J. Belchem, *Popular Radicalism in Nineteenth-Century Britain* (New York: St Martin's Press, 1996), 130.

55 E.F. Biagini, 'Popular Liberals, Gladstonian finance, and the debate on taxation, 1860–1874', in E.F. Biagini and A.J. Reid, eds, *Currents of Radicalism: Popular Radicalism, Organised Labour and Party Politics in Britain, 1850–1914* (Cambridge: Cambridge University Press, 1991), 134–62.

56 Biagini, *Liberty, Retrenchment and Reform*, 410.

57 J. Lawrence, *Speaking for the People: Party, Language and Popular Politics in England, 1867–1914* (Cambridge: Cambridge University Press, 1998), 224.

58 D. Tanner, *Political Change and the Labour Party 1900–1918* (Cambridge: Cambridge University Press, 1990), 75.

59 Four years later, in opposition, the Liberals did push to overturn the most objectionable aspects of this law.

60 D. Powell, 'The new Liberalism and the rise of Labour, 1886–1906', *The Historical Journal* 29 (1986), 384, 376.

61 I.C. Fletcher, ' "Prosecutions . . . are always risky business": Labour, Liberals, and the 1912 "don't shoot" prosecutions', *Albion* 28 (1996), 251–78.

62 Lawrence, *Speaking for the People*, 173.

63 M. Pugh, *The Making of Modern British Politics 1867–1939*, 2nd ed. (Oxford: Blackwell, 1993), 88–9; M. Savage, *The Dynamics of Working-Class Politics: The Labour Movement in Preston, 1880–1940* (Cambridge: Cambridge University Press, 1987), 134–5.

64 M. Pugh, *The Tories and the People 1880–1935* (Oxford: Basil Blackwell, 1985), 28–35.

65 J. Lawrence, 'Class and gender in the making of urban Toryism, 1880–1914', *English Historical Review* 108 (1993), 639–40.

66 R. McWilliam, *Popular Politics in Nineteenth-Century England* (London: Routledge, 1998), 95–6, 92; S. Thorne, *Congregational Missions and the Making of an Imperial Culture in Nineteenth-Century England* (Stanford: Stanford University Press, 1999), 3–4.

67 Pugh, *Making of Modern British Politics*, 86.

68 P.J. Waller, *Democracy and Sectarianism: A Political and Social History of Liverpool 1868–1939* (Liverpool: Liverpool University Press, 1981), 141.

69 R. McKibbin, C. Matthew and J. Kay, 'The franchise factor in the rise of the Labour Party', in R. McKibbin, *The Ideologies of Class: Social Relations in Britain 1880–1950* (Oxford: Clarendon Press, 1994), 98–100.

70 Savage, *Dynamics of Working-Class Politics*, 144–6.

71 Pugh, *Tories and the People*, 161.

72 Pugh, *Making of Modern British Politics*, 138, 150.

73 Lawrence, *Speaking for the People*, 171 (italics in original).

74 Belchem, *Popular Radicalism*, 179.

75 Knox, *Industrial Nation*, 169, 170.

76 Chinn, *They Worked All Their Lives*, 42.

77 R. Roberts, *Classic Slum*, 24.

78 P. Walker, ' "I live but not yet I for Christ liveth in me": men and masculinity in the Salvation Army, 1865–90', in M. Roper and J. Tosh, eds, *Manful Assertions: Masculinities in Britain since 1800* (London: Routledge, 1991), 102.

79 A. August, 'A culture of consolation? Rethinking politics in working-class London, 1870–1914', *Historical Research* 74 (2001), 200.

80 Childs, *Labour's Apprentices*, 107.

81 Ross, *Love and Toil*, 207.

82 M. Vicinus, *Independent Women: Work and Community for Single Women, 1850–1920* (Chicago: University of Chicago Press, 1985), 211–12.

83 E. Ross, 'Good and bad mothers: lady philanthropists and London housewives before the First World War', in K.D. McCarthy, ed., *Lady Bountiful Revisited: Women, Philanthropy, and Power* (New Brunswick: Rutgers University Press, 1990), 179.

84 G. Behlmer, *Friends of the Family: The English Home and Its Guardians, 1850–1940* (Stanford: Stanford University Press, 1998), 40.

85 T. Thompson, ed., *Edwardian Childhoods* (London: Routledge & Kegan Paul, 1981), 21.

86 August, 'A culture of consolation', 203.

87 Ibid., 202–3.

88 E. Ross, 'Hungry children: housewives and London charity, 1870–1918', in P. Mandler, ed., *The Uses of Charity: The Poor on Relief in the Nineteenth-Century Metropolis* (Philadelphia: University of Pennsylvania Press, 1990), 184.

89 D. Rubinstein, *School Attendance in London, 1870–1904: A Social History* (New York: A.M. Kelley, 1969), 50, 40–1.

90 Pugh, *Making of Modern British Politics*, 78.

91 J. Davis, 'A poor man's system of justice: the London police courts in the second half of the nineteenth century', *The Historical Journal* 27 (1984), 322.

92 D.M. Copelman, *London's Women Teachers: Gender, Class and Feminism, 1870–1930* (London: Routledge, 1996), 91, 160.

PART THREE

1914–40

Introduction: The working class and the Great War

On the heels of the German violation of Belgian neutrality, the British declaration of war in August of 1914 sparked an enthusiastic response. Three-quarters of a million men enlisted in the first two months of war, and the total reached nearly 2.5 million volunteers by the end of 1915.[1] Though some working-class volunteers signed up to escape a surge of unemployment that corresponded with the outbreak of war, most rushed to the colours out of patriotism. A frustrated union leader described the enthusiasm of many workers for the war effort as 'the chloroforming pill of patriotism'. A Croydon volunteer recalls that he 'began to be interested in the Territorials tramping the streets in their big strong boots . . . News placards screamed out at every corner, and military bands blared out their martial music . . . This was too much for me to resist'.[2] Along with patriotic sentiment and the appeal of martial symbols and music, loyalty to peer groups drove volunteers. 'Pals' battalions, raised on the promise that men who 'joined together should serve together', raised a quarter of a million men in groups based in towns, workplaces or associations.[3]

Despite the impressive response to the call for volunteers, demand for soldiers outran this supply, and the government instituted conscription early in 1916. All told, just short of 6 million British men served in the war. While some of these came home physically unscathed, more than 40 per cent became casualties, and over 720,000 were killed. Working-class men were somewhat underrepresented in these figures, as they volunteered less frequently than did middle-class men. Just over 28 per cent of those employed in industry signed up by February 1916, while some 40 per cent of those in finance and commerce joined the forces. More manual than non-manual workers also enjoyed exemption from conscription because their jobs qualified as war-related work. Officers, overwhelmingly of middle-class origin, suffered higher casualties than did other ranks. Nonetheless, 96 per cent of infantrymen killed in the war were not officers, and the vast majority of these were working class.[4] For millions of working-class men, the war meant horror, misery and a very great chance of suffering injury or death.

Paradoxically, many of those they left behind in Britain enjoyed better living standards than before the war, as Robert Roberts recalled: 'By late 1916, abject poverty began to disappear from the neighbourhood. Children looked better fed'.[5] On Clydeside, according to a post-war observer, 'the population of the area was, during the actual war years, more capable of maintaining a fair standard of comfort than in the pre-war period'.[6] This reflected higher wages, overtime pay, expanded provision of meals for children and munitions workers, and separation allowances.[7] As one soldier's wife receiving this allowance exclaimed, 'It seems too good to be true, a pound a week and my husband away'.[8] One exception to this picture of improving conditions was housing. Housing construction slowed drastically during the war, as building costs skyrocketed and workers shifted to munitions industries or military service. Crowded and unsanitary housing conditions grew more common during the war. One consolation, however, was rent control, which fixed rents at 1914 levels.[9]

The tremendous demand for men and materials strained the British economy. By the end of 1914 16 per cent of workers in small-arms factories and 23 per cent of those in chemical and explosive works had joined the forces. Employers had to use remaining workers more efficiently, and the government encouraged more flexible work rules, including 'dilution' – the employment of unskilled men and women on jobs that had been the preserve of skilled men.[10] The Munitions Act of 1915 suspended restrictive practices crucial to skilled workers' influence over production, demanded union compliance with dilution, and outlawed strikes. The 1915 Act also introduced the leaving certificate system, in which workers in key industries could not take a new job for six weeks without a document from their previous employer certifying that they were no longer needed (this provision was later modified under union pressure). The leaving certificate tied workers to specific jobs, and employers used the threat of dismissal without a certificate to discipline workers.[11] The shop steward at the Beardmore Works on Clydeside, David Kirkwood, complained of this Munitions Act: 'it appeared little short of slavery . . . I resented being in Beardmore's as a slave'.[12]

In the Clyde region, over 10,000 dilutees were in place by August of 1916, mostly in general engineering and marine engineering, and 90 per cent of them women.[13] Some tasks were subdivided, with portions assigned to women. However, the impact of wartime dilution on skilled workers should not be exaggerated. Employers feared losing such workers to competitors and perceived women as unsuitable for many skilled tasks, so they did not embrace substitution of unskilled women in skilled jobs. One surprised observer of employers' unwillingness to put women on skilled work noted simply, 'several firms report that women are not allowed to set their own tools'. An employer told a government committee: 'owing to certain differences in mentality it is perfectly certain that, save in the most exceptional circumstances, women cannot become skilled mechanics'.[14] Thus, despite the concerns of unions, women were often little threat to skilled men. Alf Senior worked in a shipyard during the war: 'I had about twenty women working with me on the launching ways. All they did was just labour. They went across and got the wood . . . we would just have to pick it up and do the job, which saved us from going there. It was all right for us'.[15] Where they did replace men, most women moved out of the jobs at the war's end.[16]

Senior's uncomplaining attitude toward his new co-workers exemplifies the generally high morale of British workers during the war. They embraced the war's goals, driven by patriotism and the sense that the British cause was just. At the front, strong bonds among soldiers kept them fighting even after massive casualties and hardship overwhelmed idealism and patriotism.[17] This willingness to fight on or work on did not imply a blind acceptance of policies and leadership. At the front, the hierarchical military structure and extreme conditions required a certain amount of obedience and cooperation, but men quickly learned to minimize their efforts and, hopefully, the danger they faced. One soldier recalled, 'veterans, myself included, decided to do no more than was really necessary, following orders but if possible keeping out of harms way'.[18] Subversive songs ridiculed those in authority: 'We've got a sergeant-major/ Who's never seen a gun; . . . And when he sees old Jerry/ You should see the bugger run'.[19] Though such humour may seem harmless, many conscripts never adopted the military ethos, and often the negotiated authority of the shopfloor was replicated at the front. One private recalled lying in No Man's Land and hearing an officer in a 'finicking accent' say 'Do you think you might crawl through there'? The soldier's smiling response came: 'I'm afraid not, Sir'.[20]

Embrace of the war was not universal among civilians. The *Contemporary Review* reported the sentiments of a working-class woman that 'She did not see what difference it would make if the Germans did come and rule England. She had always been poor, and she didn't suppose she would be worse off with them than without them'. A minority of union and Labour Party leaders spoke against the war, though Ramsay Macdonald's anti-war stance led to his resignation as party leader. As the war went on, the rising death toll, shortages, and the sense that sacrifice fell unevenly increased working-class scepticism of the war effort. According to a government report, returning soldiers brought a 'much more vivid realization of the actual horrors of war' to their neighbours and co-workers. Suspicion of war profiteering also dented patriotic zeal. One observer complained: 'A shipowner who states that he had made profits, was going to make profits, and had a right to make profits, did more harm [to popular patriotism] than a great naval defeat would have done'. During the strike wave of 1917 a government report observed workers' ambivalence. They sought to protect their trade privileges, but did not want to 'hold up the war to the detriment of their relatives in the trenches . . . One has the impression, in short, of unrest paralysed by patriotism – or, it may be, of patriotism paralysed by unrest'.[21] Despite these examples of scepticism about the war and its conduct, the vast majority of British workers remained willing to do their part to win.

This victory would have been impossible without tremendous sacrifice by millions of men at the front and unprecedented resources marshalled at home in support of the war effort. Yet most of the changes wrought by the war were either temporary or continued prewar processes.[22] Declining fertility, which would transform the working-class family, began before the war. Post-war council houses spread dramatically in response to the housing crisis exacerbated by war, but local governments had begun addressing working-class housing at the turn of the twentieth century. The war accelerated the challenge to skilled men, though most women who replaced male industrial workers during the war left these jobs when it ended. Even the new leisure pursuits that exploded on the heels of the war – jazz and dance halls – were merely the latest manifestation of a distinct commercialized working-class leisure culture. Finally, working-class patriotism, well established before the war, persisted beyond it alongside a scepticism of authority reinforced by the day-to-day experiences of working-class men and women in Britain.

Notes

1 J.M. Winter, 'Britain's "lost generation" of the First World War', *Population Studies* 31 (1977), 452; G.J. DeGroot, *Blighty: British Society in the Era of the Great War* (London: Longman, 1996), 43.

2 DeGroot, *Blighty*, 125, 53.

3 J. Stevenson, *British Society 1914–45* (London: Allen Lane, 1984), 50–1.

4 J.M. Winter, *The Great War and the British People* (Cambridge, MA: Harvard University Press, 1986), 27, 34, 46, 71–3, 84, 86.

5 R. Roberts, *The Classic Slum: Salford Life in the First Quarter of the Century* (Harmondsworth: Penguin, 1973), 203.

6 Winter, *Great War*, 245.

7 J.M. Winter, 'The impact of the First World War on civilian health in Britain', *Economic History Review* 30 (1977), 499–500; C. Wrigley, 'The impact of the First World War', in C. Wrigley, ed., *A Companion to Early Twentieth-Century Britain* (Oxford: Blackwell, 2003), 510.

8 S. Pedersen, 'Gender, welfare and citizenship in Britain during the Great War', *American Historical Review* 95 (1990), 1003.

9 Winter, *Great War*, 242–3.

10 J. Bourne, *Britain and the Great War* (London: Edward Arnold, 1989), 183.

11 A.J. McIvor, *A History of Work in Britain, 1880–1950* (Basingstoke: Palgrave, 2001), 158–9; A. Reid, 'Dilution, trade unionism and the state in Britain during the First World War', in S. Tolliday and J. Zeitlin, eds, *Shop Floor Bargaining and the State: Historical and Comparative Perspectives* (Cambridge: Cambridge University Press, 1985), 54–5.

12 W.W. Knox, *Industrial Nation: Work, Culture and Society in Scotland 1800–Present* (Edinburgh: Edinburgh University Press, 1999), 218.

13 J. Hinton, *The First Shop Stewards' Movement* (London: George Allen & Unwin, 1973), 145–6.

14 L.L. Downs, 'Industrial decline, rationalization and equal pay: the Bedaux strike at Rover Automobile Company', *Social History* 15 (1990), 53; L.L. Downs, *Manufacturing Inequality: Gender Division in the French and British Metalworking Industries, 1914–1939* (Ithaca: Cornell University Press, 1995), 43; Reid, 'Dilution, trade unionism and the state', 51–2.

15 P. Pagnamenta and R. Overy, *All Our Working Lives* (London: BBC, 1984), 130.

16 G. Braybon and P. Summerfield, *Out of the Cage: Women's Experiences in Two World Wars* (London: Pandora, 1987), 121.

17 Bourne, *Britain and the Great War*, 210, 220.

18 D. Englander and J. Osborne, 'Jack, Tommy and Henry Dubb: the armed forces and the working class', *Historical Journal* 21 (1978), 598.

19 G. Robb, *British Culture and the First World War* (Basingstoke: Palgrave, 2002), 179.

20 J. Bourne, 'The British working man in arms', in H. Cecil and P. Liddle, eds, *Facing Armageddon: The First World War Experienced* (London: Cooper, 1996), 344.

21 B. Waites, *A Class Society at War: England 1914–18* (Leamington Spa: Berg, 1987), 203, 69, 232.

22 DeGroot, *Blighty*, 291.

CHAPTER NINE

Old and new working-class communities

John Blake, born in 1899, grew up in a well-established Poplar neighbourhood. His mother raised seven children, managing a family budget built around her husband's wages as a plumber's mate in a Blackwall shipyard. Blake married in 1920 and remained in the neighbourhood 'at the wife's mother's place, in very limited accommodation'. After his wife gave birth to their first and only child, Blake sought to move out of Poplar into the Becontree estate in Dagenham. They secured a cottage on the estate, complete with 'a front and back garden, two bedrooms, living room, scullery and bathroom, and indoor toilet'. Despite the 'comfort of the new cottage', they disliked their new situation. John rose early to reach his work in Poplar and remained away all day. Moving to the estate ruptured 'all our ties, with both our families, and the neighbours of many years'. His wife 'was miserable, not being used to the new surroundings and strange people'. After a few months, the family moved back to Poplar and remained there until bomb damage in the Second World War forced them to move out to Dagenham once again.[1] The Blakes had only one child, and their small family exemplifies working-class fertility decline in this period. Though most families made the transition to new estates more successfully, the dilemmas of exchanging familiar communities for improved housing faced many working-class men and women.

Population

In every decade from 1801 to 1911 the British population grew at an annual rate exceeding 1 per cent. Figures for the following three decades reveal much slower growth rates: about 0.5 per cent annually between 1911 and 1939, due primarily to declining fertility.[2] While British couples married in the 1890s produced an average of 4.34 children, those married in the early 1920s averaged only 2.42 births. Only a portion of working-class couples had successfully limited their fertility before the First World War, but the decline in birth rates after the war extended across the entire population. This cross-class trend reduced the overall fertility rate, but a class differential remained. Professional couples who married in the early 1920s had 1.75 children, while those dependent on wages from manual work averaged 2.70 children. Despite the persistent class difference, working-class fertility declined dramatically.[3]

A woman who grew up in a Burnley weaving family exemplifies this generational shift. Her mother had a large family, and 'mother used to say, "Don't be as daft as me, don't be as daft as me, true"'. Apparently, she took this advice to heart, noting, 'I haven't had a big family of me own'.[4] Another woman, born in Preston in 1899, successfully participated in this fertility decline, discussing the appropriate family size with her husband, 'We thought that two was sufficient'. Not all families were so small. This woman's sister and sister-in-law each had six children. Another Preston woman, born early in the century, became a mother of six and lamented her failure to prevent the expansion of her family. She recalled such efforts as ubiquitous: 'Everybody tried'.[5] The overall figures confirm that most working-class families had some success in controlling their fertility.

Economic factors relating to the costs of raising children help explain the widespread desire to limit fertility. School attendance became mandatory in the 1870s, but the impact of compulsory education on family economies increased at the turn of the century. As school leaving ages rose to 12 in England and Wales and 14 in Scotland, working-class families increasingly accepted compulsory schooling, and truancy rates dropped. Average attendance at London board schools increased early in the century, from 82 per cent in 1900 to 88 per cent in 1904. A school board committee noted this shift: 'The people of London have at least been aroused to a fuller appreciation of the value of sending their children regularly to school'.[6] As children stayed in school longer and attended more regularly, the length of their dependence on parental support increased. Conversely, the establishment of old age pensions reduced parental dependence on grown children. Together these factors created economic incentives to reduce family sizes.

In addition to raising the cost of children by keeping them out of employment for longer periods, school attendance imposed higher standards of health through medical examinations and care committees. By the inter-war period, working-class mothers began to embrace the provision of medical care and emphasis on child and maternal health evident in the Infant Welfare movement.[7] This concern for children's well-being and women's health contributed to fertility decline. One working-class woman reported 'using a preventative', and noted, 'I have better health to serve my husband and children, and more advantages to give them'. Another mother who stopped at her third child recalled that another child would have meant that, 'I could not possibly have reared my eldest girl. I was able to have good medical advice and give her plenty of attention day and night'.[8] A father trying to limit the size of his family by abstaining from intercourse reminded himself: 'I must not forget what the Doctor says. My considerations are for my wife and my four children'.[9]

Women whose husbands showed less sensitivity could control their fertility only with difficulty. A woman who had seven children and two miscarriages complained that her husband 'had not a bit of control over his passions', and lamented, 'a man has such a lot of ways of punishing a woman if she does not give in to him'.[10] A British Medical Association estimate in 1939 suggested that between 16 and 20 per cent of all pregnancies ended in abortion, though nearly all abortions remained illegal. Many women sought to end their own pregnancies by taking abortifacients or trying various strategies rumoured to be effective, such as hot baths, jumping off the table, or running up and down stairs. Unfortunately, others took dangerous drugs or attempted to cause abortions using sharp implements. A woman recalled the injury suffered by another: 'she'd had three an' she'd been pushing a knitting needle or something up her to try to get rid'.[11] A 1930 Ministry of Health report warned that 'intentional abortion is greatly on the increase', causing increased mortality among these women.[12] Safer approaches to birth control that did not require male cooperation, such as the diaphragm, spread slowly among working-class women. According to one study, about a fifth of skilled workers' wives married between 1925 and 1929 used a birth-control appliance (such as the diaphragm, cap or condom), and about half of all appliance-using women used female birth-control devices.[13]

As these statistics show, even when husbands shared wives' determination to limit fertility, most working-class couples did not embrace birth-control technology. Instead, they abstained from sexual relations or relied on withdrawal. Thus, one man reflected, 'After this child is born I feel I will have to leave her alone as we are both frightened that we may have another'.[14] A woman praised her husband as 'an Ideal daddy since little Reggie came he has had no connections with me at all he is afraid of my becoming pregnant again'. Shyness about such matters led women to discuss withdrawal euphemistically: 'My husband is very good and for three years has not had a real "pleasure" in order to keep me right'.[15] A miner's wife commented, 'He was careful, say what you call careful – there was no precautions those days, nothing that we knew anything about – there was just careful'.[16] A couple who had only one child reported the following advice from a bus conductor friend upon their marriage: 'Don't forget, always get off the bus at South Shore, don't go all the way to Blackpool'.[17]

Withdrawal and abstinence, adopted by couples who cooperated in limiting fertility, were not foolproof. A woman writing to Marie Stopes for advice on birth control reported, 'My husband had been withdrawing all that time and the only time I had any suspicion he was not so careful was on his birthday'. This slip led to another pregnancy. Another complained about abstinence: 'our married life is spoiled and we are gradually drifting apart'.[18] Despite these difficulties, couples did have smaller families. A Lancashire woman noted in 1945: 'It is customary – and has been so during the last twenty-five years or so – to have two children and no more if you can avoid it'.[19] The decline in birth rates nationally reflected the determination of working-class men and women to control their fertility.

Migration

National figures highlight the importance of reduced fertility in slowed population growth, but they obscure the second key demographic change in the first half of the twentieth century: the shift of population away from many of the leading industrial centers of the previous century. At the end of the First World War, the loss of export markets caused a severe slump in staple industries, including cotton, coal, iron and steel, and shipbuilding. The regions in which these trades concentrated, particularly Wales, Scotland and the North of England, fell into economic crisis throughout the 1920s and 1930s. Persistent unemployment plagued what had only decades before been booming industrial districts. The miserable economic conditions in these regions led to stagnation or even declines in population. Regional population figures for Wales and the North East reveal population declines in the inter-war period. Scotland's population grew only slightly, by about 2 per cent between 1921 and 1938.[20] When established industries foundered, the towns and cities they nourished sank into stagnation.

In contrast to declining industries that undermined communities dependent upon them, expanding industries drove population growth in the South East and Midlands. The motor trade, which had produced

34,000 vehicles in 1913, turned out 241,000 in 1929. Despite the international economic slump, production doubled over the next seven years,
reaching 481,000 vehicles in 1936.[21] Electrical engineering also grew rapidly,
with manufacturing output surging by 80 per cent between 1929 and 1937.[22]
Demand for labour in these and other growing trades brought migrants
into the South East and Midlands from centres of declining industries. The
New Survey of London Life and Labour, conducted in 1929–31, observed
'the type of migrant whom London now attracts is not so much the low
paid agricultural labourer . . . as the unemployed townsman of the depressed
areas who hopes to find a job'.[23]

Though overall migration figures for the inter-war period did not
exceed nineteenth-century rates, migrants travelled longer distances than
in earlier decades.[24] Many Scottish migrants avoided the nearby but slump-
ing counties of northern England and headed for the South East. London
and its surrounding counties housed 26 per cent more Scots in 1931
than they had a decade earlier.[25] At times, employers in growing trades
recruited workers from declining regions. The new steelworks in Corby,
Northamptonshire brought workers from Scotland in large numbers, while
at the Morris Motors works at Cowley as many as half the workers came
from depressed regions.[26]

These migrants travelled long distances because their homes offered
little but unemployment and poverty. As a South Shields man recalled,
some young workers facing prolonged unemployment fled for more promising pastures. 'I decided to get out. . . . This was the great dream; getting
out of the rut'.[27] One Glaswegian whose search for work led to New York
recalled, 'There was nothing, there was no work, so they were gasping
for a job'.[28] Within Britain, the government encouraged migration from
depressed regions (some of which qualified as 'Special Areas'), by providing financial aid and training to potential migrants.[29] Many more relied on
informal networks and contacts to ease their move. One man who migrated
from Haywood, Lancashire to Birmingham encouraged over 80 more
from his home town to Birmingham and work in his factory.[30] Coming
from South Wales in 1936, one man was surprised to find Slough filled
with Welshmen: 'Thousands lined the streets . . . the accents were so thick
I though we were in Rhondda, with this difference, instead of silent pits,
massive factories all lit up were in full go'.[31]

Connections with previous migrants helped ease difficult transitions.
Without such contacts it could be difficult to find work, as one Durham
man feared: 'I know all the people in Crook and if there was a job here
I might get it; in London I'd have no chance'.[32] Another Durham man

considering migration to southern England to seek work was, according to his wife, 'in a sweat about going, for he's heard that the people are not friendly'.[33] Skilled work grew more difficult to find in the early 1930s, when unemployment rose throughout the country. For older skilled men, the loss of status and community made migration an ordeal. One Welshman who followed his children to Oxford stayed only two months, as the 'insignificance of his position proved too much for him'.[34] Many migrants could find no work and had to return home to live on the dole.[35] When jobs were scarce, hostility to migrants intensified. In Watford a feud developed in 1930 between young residents of the town and Welsh migrants. A newspaper report of a street battle reported one young man's complaint: 'When the Welshmen go we shall get work'. A shortage of housing also drove conflict between migrants and locals. In Luton one resident complained, 'if some of these people would go back to the North, locals might have a hope of getting a house at a reasonable rent'.[36]

Despite this hostility, migrants continued to pour into the growing regions. Amidst a national picture of very slow population expansion, the London area added a million residents between 1921 and 1939 to reach 8.5 million. The South East grew by 18.1 per cent between 1921 and 1938, and the Midlands grew by 11.6 per cent in the same period.[37] The greatest growth rates occurred in suburban zones of the great conurbations, including Greater London and the West Midlands. The suburbs of the seven largest English conurbations accounted for nearly two-thirds of the overall national population growth in the inter-war period. While their urban cores lost population, the outer districts grew by 32 per cent.[38] This centrifugal exodus included tenants of new council houses on the outskirts of large cities. More than 1.5 million people settled on new municipal estates between 1919 and 1937. The largest of these, the London County Council's Becontree estate begun in 1921, housed 89,365 a decade later.[39]

Housing

The unprecedented construction of local authority housing like the Becontree estate in the inter-war period could not overcome a persistent shortage of decent and affordable accommodation. During the First World War house building essentially froze and rent strikes, most notably in Glasgow, drove the government to control rents at 1914 levels.[40] The 1921 census revealed the existence of 8.8 million homes, but it counted 9.7 million families filling them.[41] A resident of Liverpool recalled: 'after the war there wasn't any houses for anybody, everybody had to squeeze in with their parents if they weren't lucky enough to get a couple of rooms . . . I had been living with his parents . . . it was so overcrowded with his parents, brothers and sisters and us with the baby'.[42] Nearly one in eight Liverpool families lived more than two to a room in 1921, well above the figure for England and Wales (5.7 per cent).[43]

Realizing that market forces alone could not rectify this housing crisis, the government stepped in, promising 'homes fit for heroes'. Beginning in 1919, the government offered subsidies to local authorities and guaranteed them against potential losses suffered in providing council houses. High costs and skilled labour shortages limited construction to about 200,000 homes under the programme during the next few years, until the Labour government of 1924 introduced a new scheme of subsidies to local authorities and forged an agreement with the unions to expand the pool of skilled building labour. Local councils built more than 550,000 houses over the following decade. In the 1930s the government shifted its attention and resources to slum clearance, offering funding based on the number of people rehoused from slums. This programme led to the replacement of almost 340,000 of the worst houses in British slums. Though many working-class families remained in deteriorating older housing, these programmes enshrined the government's role in providing decent accommodation where the market would not.[44]

The typical inter-war council house had three bedrooms, a living room, a scullery, and some included parlours. By building well outside the central districts, authorities could afford lower densities, typically 5 houses per hectare (12 houses per acre) compared with 16 (40) for new English housing before the war.[45] The best of these houses were built first, under the 1919 Act. In Liverpool, the first generation of inter-war council houses were at least 80 square metres (854 square feet), though some were as large as 100 square metres (1,060 square feet). Tenants enjoyed electricity, hot water systems, water closets, and upstairs bathrooms. By the late 1920s Liverpool built council houses as small as 58 square metres (620 square feet) and eliminated the separate bathroom. As one resident recalled, 'Our mother loved our new little house but there was one fault, there was no proper bathroom. We only had the bath in the back kitchen'.[46] Though respectable working-class families wanted parlours, they grew less common. While more than half of the first generation of inter-war council houses in Leeds included parlours, only 12 per cent of those built between 1924 and 1933 included them.[47] Despite these declining amenities, council houses offered significant upgrades from deteriorating and crowded private rental housing.

Tenants in council houses appreciated the improved conditions. An original tenant of a Glasgow estate begun in 1935 recalled: 'the place was bran new, toilets an everything; there wis nuhin more that ah wantit'.[48] A Liverpool council tenant agreed: 'Compared with the old houses they were a dream to keep clean and then having running hot water, well, that was wonderful . . . till we came here I had had to go down a yard to the toilet . . . having a toilet next to your bedroom, especially in winter, you felt like the Queen'.[49] A Londoner recalled: 'The things that pleased us most when we first moved here was to have a house of our own, with electric light and a bathroom and a scullery with running water. We'd been in two rooms in Bethnal Green, with a tap and WC three flights down . . . I thought [the new house] was just like a palace'.[50] As the hyberbolic royal comparisons reveal, the contrast with their former lodgings made quite an impression.

These improved conditions came at some cost to those who moved into the new estates. Rents far exceeded those in old central districts. In Manchester average council rents ranged from 13s. to 15s. per week, compared with 7s. to 9s. rent in central slums. In Glasgow rehoused families from the slums 'hud tae pay almost three times what we were payin previous'.[51] Because they now lived outside the central districts, estate residents had to commute to work. On the Becontree estate nearly a quarter of tenants paid over 6s. per week in fares in 1932 and two-thirds worked more than 8 km (5 miles) from their homes.[52] Despite their pleasant houses, council estates lacked amenities. When first built they often had no schools, shops, churches, libraries, doctors, etc. At Liverpool's Norris Green estate, 'The children around here had to go without schooling for a time. Mind you it didn't bother them'. Even when fully constructed, many estates had inadequate shopping and leisure facilities. Residents opened illegal shops in their houses, and pubs sprouted along the fringes of the estates, but the lack of choices created problems for shoppers and drinkers used to the competition of many local shops and pubs.[53] The additional costs, along with difficulty adjusting to new surroundings, led many tenants to leave their council houses, even if it meant a return to poor quality housing in the central districts. During the first ten years of the Watling estate, 47 per cent of residents stayed less than five years. Annual statistics show that in 7 of the first 12 years of the Becontree estate more than 10 per cent of tenants moved out.[54]

Well aware of the extra costs incurred by residents of the new estates, authorities selected tenants whom they considered able to bear the extra costs. The first cohort of residents included skilled workers along with a significant number of clerks, teachers and other middle-class residents. As estates expanded, however, they became overwhelmingly working class. A sample of Liverpool municipal housing between the wars found that 85.2 per cent of tenants were manual workers. A 1934 study of Dagenham (including the Becontree estate) claimed: 'It would have been extremely difficult, if not impossible to have found another area in England with a population of 100,000 containing such an overwhelming proportion of working-people'.[55] With the slum clearance programme of the 1930s, poorer families could enjoy the improved conditions of new estates, but they also faced the increased costs. One former slum dweller complained: 'The corporation thought that they were giving the likes of us the world, getting us out of the slums, but they didn't care that none of us could afford the bloody houses'.[56] Poverty meant that families like these faced only problematic housing alternatives.

Remaining in older housing often meant suffering increasingly poor conditions, especially in houses built before the age of by-laws. Though clearances in the 1930s eliminated some of the worst areas, many working-class families remained in overcrowded and dilapidated housing throughout the period. Recollections of Liverpool families highlight many of the problems in these homes. 'There were holes in the walls, the roof leaked . . . There was no water, you had to get it from a tap in the yard and the toilet was there too. You couldn't describe the filth of the toilet'. Another recalled, 'our old house was in a terrible state, alive with bloody bugs, horrible it was. There were rats too, they were everywhere'.[57] Working-class families that clung to their homes despite these conditions enjoyed the protection of rent controls, originally adopted in 1915. Laws permitted some increases, but controlled rents did not keep up with post-war inflation, and beginning in 1923 landlords could escape the controls only when tenants moved out.[58] Thus many Liverpool families rented one or two dilapidated rooms for as little as 4s. per week (compared with 11s. 9d. for a typical suburban council house without a parlour).[59]

On the eve of the Second World War, working-class housing conditions varied tremendously. Historian John Burnett has estimated that a third of workers lived under very poor conditions. Despite clearances, official figures acknowledged over 200,000 slum houses deserving of demolition in 1939. Another third of working-class families lived in prewar by-law housing, meeting basic standards of sanitation, but falling short of the conditions in the new council housing, where the final third of workers resided.[60] For many, low wages exacerbated by unemployment remained significant barriers to better housing. The high rents and inconveniences of suburban council estates kept even workers with relatively stable wages in older houses and neighbourhoods. Those who moved into the new estates found nicer homes but confronted dramatically increased expenses and sacrificed many amenities of life in established working-class districts. Even on the new estates, some families faced unpleasant conditions. A survey done in the mid-1930s found that 20 per cent of working-class houses in central districts qualified as overcrowded, but over 10 per cent of homes on council estates also exceeded the standard.[61] Thus, housing conditions improved for some working-class families, but many still lived in crowded and poor accommodation.

Health

The significant but uneven improvements in working-class housing contributed to general advances in health in the inter-war period. In 1939 a retired health official claimed the 'English people, on the whole, are today better fed, better clothed, better housed and better educated than at any time of which we have record'.[62] Infant mortality, often seen as an indicator of overall health conditions, declined in England and Wales from 80 per thousand in 1920 to 56 per thousand in 1940. Though Scottish rates were higher, they too improved in the inter-war years. Life expectancies rose throughout Britain. Baby girls born on the eve of the First World War had an expected average life span of nearly 62 years in England and Wales and 53 years in Scotland. In the early 1930s baby girls' expected life spans had increased to 70 in England and Wales and 60 in Scotland.[63]

Along with improvements in housing, better nutrition contributed to these gains. Working-class diets improved during the First World War, and in the following decades per capita consumption of fruit, vegetables, butter, eggs and many other types of foods increased. In 1934, for example, butter consumption exceeded prewar levels by more than 50 per cent. Social surveys in the 1930s found lower levels of poverty than had been common before the war. Yet the positive comparisons with prewar levels of poverty and nutrition mask the persistence of hunger in many working-class families. The British Medical Association developed a minimum dietary standard, adequate for existence, but too low to sustain moderately heavy work for men or proper development for children. In the mid-1930s nearly a third of the population fell short of this standard. As John Burnett notes, 'Despite the general improvement in standards the nutritional inadequacy of the poorest in the 1930s was still vast and alarming'.[64]

Stubbornly high levels of maternal mortality reflect these gaps in nutritional gains. Maternal death rates increased by over 20 per cent from 1923 to 1933, though they did decline in the late 1930s.[65] Despite the expanded provision of antenatal care under the Maternal and Child Welfare Act of 1918, death rates in childbirth reached shocking levels in some areas. In the Rhondda a maternal death rate of 7.20 per thousand in 1933 led to an intensive effort to boost medical services. When the local rate of women dying in childbirth increased in 1934, the scheme was altered to include a distribution of food at the clinics. A dramatic drop in mortality followed, and food distributions in neighbouring districts had the same effect the following year.[66] This experience shows that inadequate nutrition remained a serious health problem for many working-class women.

In addition, class and regional disparities qualify optimistic views of improving health. Infant mortality rates for children of unskilled workers dropped from 152.5 in 1911 to 60.1 in 1939, a 61 per cent decrease. But rates for wealthy babies declined even faster, by 65 per cent.[67] The Birmingham Medical Officer of Health divided the city into three rings that corresponded to class differences. The poorest central districts had a mortality rate for babies aged one month to one year of 50.3 in every thousand babies in 1933. In the outer ring of middle-class residents, only 27.6 out of every thousand babies in these ages died.[68] Thus, though working-class health improved, the class difference in health and mortality remained significant. In addition, the severity of the economic crisis in Wales, Scotland and the North of England compromised working-class health in these areas. Overall mortality in Merthyr Tydfil exceeded the national rate by over 50 per cent.[69] Infant mortality in England and Wales declined to 56 on the eve of the Second World War, but in Scotland, the comparable rate was 74.[70] Thus, though general statistics point to health gains across the British population, working-class families, particularly those in depressed regions, continued to experience elevated mortality levels and poor health.

Family economies and communities

The nutritional gains that contributed to better health reflect an improved standard of living for many in this period. Following the gains during the First World War and a brief spike in prices in its immediate aftermath, real wages rose over the following two decades. Before the war, working-class families spent about three-quarters of their income on food and rent combined. By the late 1930s these necessities demanded less than 45 per cent of the average working-class family budget.[71] Yet poverty persisted. Rowntree found that in York, '*52.5 per cent of the* [working class] *children under one year of age*, [and] *49.7 per cent of those over one and under five . . . are living below the minimum*'.[72] The Pilgrim Trust's investigation of unemployment found that in families of unemployed workers with three or four children, 'almost invariably there was definite want'.[73]

Poverty plagued unemployed families despite government support. The extent of unemployment at the end of the First World War moved governments to expand benefits beyond the unemployment provisions of the 1911 National Insurance Act. Between 1920 and 1934 unemployment relief evolved through some 40 Insurance Acts. Eventually, the system combined insurance payments for 26 weeks and means-tested benefits for those unemployed for longer periods and others not entitled to insurance payments. This dole helped unemployed men and their dependants, though it did not suffice for many families with children. The wife of a Liverpool dockworker recalled, 'When he was laid off, and that happened a lot . . . we just did without'. As historian David Vincent observes, the impact of this system 'was at once substantial and inadequate'.[74]

Working-class women in charge of tight family budgets continued to use a range of strategies in confronting this poverty. Casual jobs selling odd items, cleaning, taking in washing, or making and selling food items could bring in valuable resources. Pawnshops remained important sources of credit, as a Lancaster factory worker noted: 'Queues a mile long on a Monday morning pledging. Queues a mile long on a Friday evening redeeming them out again'. On the Becontree estate outside London there was no pawnshop before 1931, and the 9.30 bus to Barking on Monday mornings was known as the 'pawnshop bus'.[75] Women made the most of scant resources to feed their families. A Newcastle study found that unemployed families derived 23 per cent more calories per penny spent on food than did families with employed men.[76] Despite this efficiency, women still fed their families by denying themselves. The Pilgrim Trust investigation found 'obvious signs of malnutrition in the appearance of the wives of unemployed men with families. They obviously did without things for the sake of their husbands and children'. Another survey agreed: 'where denial is called for it is usually the woman who denies herself for the sake of husband and children'.[77]

In established working-class districts, kin and neighbours remained essential resources in the battle against poverty and adversity. In East London, 'There were so many ways in which a community would stick together. Neighbours would lend things to take down to the pawn shop so that a family could get some dinner'. When a man died suddenly, his son recalled, 'the neighbours, as usual, rallied round and helped the family to get back to normality as soon as possible'.[78] The distinction between neighhours and kin frequently dissolved in new marital ties. A study of two East London parishes in the 1920s found that nearly half of marriages united people living in the same street, and another quarter of new spouses had lived in the same parish.[79] In some cases slum clearances moved neighhours to new estates in blocks, allowing communities to survive in the new environment. Over a hundred families moved from Glasgow's Muse Lane into the Hamiltonhill rehousing scheme, where one resident described what 'would probably be like a very close community. Neighbours helped each other in every respect'.[80] In Liverpool rehousing kept old neighhours together: 'God, how could you be lonely? The whole street was moved out together to here. They were all your old mates. I even had my mother-in-law living opposite to me'.[81] One woman who moved to the Becontree estate in 1929 recalled, 'I didn't like leaving my sisters, but two of my sisters and one of my brothers followed me here'.[82]

On other estates, new neighhours came from different areas and lacked these strong ties. The London County Council deliberately separated former neighhours on the Watling estate, and new residents complained of being lonely.[83] In Liverpool those moving to council estates found 'it was like being in a foreign country with new friends to make and difficulties to overcome'. Some took advantage of the opportunity to set out clearer boundaries with their neighhours: 'People were friendly and you got to know them slowly, but just to say hello to, nothing more. I liked to keep myself to myself'. On Manchester's Wythenshawe estate 'The sort of neighbourly business where you go in and say, are you there Mrs So and So, here's a bowl of soup. Well that didn't kind of happen quite'.[84] Yet many families did settle, establish kin nearby, and develop new relations with neighhours. The survey of Watling found 'particular circumstances compelled the women to establish relationships with each other'. Children also led the way in creating bonds that brought adults into closer contact. 'But it didn't take the children long to get together and soon they were playing football in the road. In the summer they would play cricket and the men would join in'.[85]

The close quarters in working-class neighbourhoods spawned rivalries and conflict as well as mutual aid and neighbourliness. Shared resources bred conflict in established neighbourhoods and on new estates. Two women who shared a porch at Becontree fell into a quarrel when one scrubbed both halves: 'she came out and said, "Why do you have to scrub my half?" . . . I didn't say anything . . . she banged me on the top of the head with a broom. Well . . . I'm not going to put up with that, so I paid her. I hit her back'.[86] A resident of a central district of St Helens in the 1920s pointed out the fragility of good relations in the neighbourhood: 'You'd have eight or ten families in a street . . . There's a lot of feuding going on. You'd have friendly neighbours so long as you were in with the family. Otherwise things could be pretty rough'.[87] Some of those who moved to the new estates were anxious to move into new cottages to escape their old neighhours, but they did not necessarily escape the rivalries and conflicts typical of working-class neighbourhoods.

Conclusion

In the quarter century beginning with the start of the First World War, working-class life in Britain changed in important ways, yet established patterns of family and neighbourhood relations persisted. Smaller families, rising real wages and more extensive relief eased the burdens on many mothers who continued to face the challenges of making ends meet on insufficient and irregular incomes. Improved nutrition and health standards reduced mortality rates. Widespread unemployment, however, left many mired in poverty. New council estates offered an option for working-class families outside the established and often dilapidated central districts. Some found the inconveniences and lack of community on the estates unbearable. Others put down roots and created new working-class neighbourhoods.

Notes

1 J. Blake, *Memories of Old Poplar* (London: Stepney Books, 1977), 8, 45–6.

2 There was no census in 1941, so population calculations are based on estimates for 1939. N. Tranter, *British Population in the Twentieth Century* (New York: St Martin's Press, 1996), 4; D. Baines, 'Population, migration and regional development, 1870–1939', in R. Floud and D. McCloskey, eds, *The Economic History of Britain since 1700*, 2nd ed. (Cambridge: Cambridge University Press, 1994), 30.

3 D. Coleman and J. Salt, *The British Population: Patterns, Trends, and Processes* (Oxford: Oxford University Press, 1992), 68.

4 D. Gittins, *Fair Sex: Family Size and Structure, 1900–1939* (London: Hutchinson, 1982), 91.

5 E. Roberts, *A Woman's Place: An Oral History of Working-Class Women 1890–1940* (Oxford: Basil Blackwell, 1984), 91, 100.

6 D. Rubinstein, 'Socialization and the London School Board 1870–1904: aims, methods and public opinion', in P. McCann, ed., *Popular Education and Socialization in the Nineteenth Century* (London: Methuen, 1977), 257–8; J.S. Hurt, *Elementary Schooling and the Working Classes 1860–1918* (London: Routledge & Kegan Paul, 1979), 188–9; W.W. Knox, *Industrial Nation: Work, Culture and Society in Scotland 1800–Present* (Edinburgh: Edinburgh University Press, 1999), 100, 139.

7 E. Ross, *Love and Toil: Motherhood in Outcast London, 1870–1918* (Oxford: Oxford University Press, 1993), 219.

8 M.L. Davies, ed., *Maternity: Letters from Working Women* ([1915]; New York: W.W. Norton, 1978), 94, 115.

9 W. Seccombe, 'Starting to stop: working-class fertility decline in Britain', *Past and Present* 126 (1990), 182.

10 Davies, *Maternity*, 48–9.

11 Gittins, *Fair Sex*, 90–1, 150, 164; J. Stevenson, *British Society 1914–1945* (London: Allen Lane, 1984), 152; J. Bourke, *Working-Class Cultures in Britain 1890–1960: Gender, Class and Ethnicity* (London: Routledge, 1994), 57; S. Brooke, ' "A new world for women"? Abortion law reform in Britain during the 1930s', *American Historical Review* 106 (2001), 432.

12 J. Lewis, *The Politics of Motherhood: Child and Maternal Welfare in England, 1900–1939* (London: Croom Helm, 1980), 209.

13 Seccombe, 'Starting to stop', 163, 169.

14 W. Seccombe, *Weathering the Storm: Working-Class Families from the Industrial Revolution to the Fertility Decline* (London: Verso, 1995), 175.

15 Seccombe, 'Starting to stop', 177.

16 Gittins, *Fair Sex*, 149.

17 Roberts, *A Woman's Place*, 95.

18 Seccombe, 'Starting to stop', 160–1.

19 D. Levine, *Reproducing Families: The Political Economy of English Population History* (Cambridge: Cambridge University Press, 1987), 212.

20 K. Laybourn, *Britain on the Breadline: A Social and Political History of Britain 1918–1939* (Stroud: Sutton, 1990), 96.

21 J. Foreman-Peck, S. Bowden and A. McKinlay, *The British Motor Industry* (Manchester: Manchester University Press, 1995), 27, 38.

22 P. Dewey, *War and Progress: Britain 1914–1945* (London: Longman, 1997), 99, 234–5.

23 T.J. Hatton and R.E. Bailey, 'Natives and migrants in the London labour market, 1929–1931', *Journal of Population Economics* 15 (2002), 63.

24 P. Scott, 'The state, internal migration, and the growth of new industrial communities in inter-war Britain', *English Historical Review* 115 (2000), 330.

25 M. Harper, *Emigration from Scotland between the Wars: Opportunity or Exile?* (Manchester: Manchester University Pres, 1998), 38 n. 22.

26 Stevenson, *British Society*, 145.

27 'South Shields', in N. Gray, ed., *The Worst of Times: An Oral History of the Great Depression in Britain* (Totowa, NJ: Barnes & Noble, 1985), 104.

28 Harper, *Emigration*, 144.

29 J. Stevenson and C. Cook, *Britain in the Depression: Society and Politics, 1929–1939*, 2nd ed. (London: Longman, 1994), 78.

30 Scott, 'The state', 332–3.

31 Stevenson, *British Society*, 115.

32 Hatton and Bailey, 'Natives and migrants', 77.

33 Stevenson and Cook, *Britain in the Depression*, 104.

34 R. McKibbin, *Classes and Cultures: England 1918–1951* (Oxford: Oxford University Press, 1998), 125.

35 Scott, 'The state', 339; C.E. Heim, 'Structural transformation and the demand for new labor in advanced economies: interwar Britain', *Journal of Economic History* 44 (1984), 589–90.

36 Scott, 'The state', 348.

37 Laybourn, *Britain on the Breadline*, 96; Stevenson, *British Society*, 144.

38 Dewey, *War and Progress*, 158.

39 A. Olechnowicz, *Working-Class Housing in England between the Wars: The Becontree Estate* (Oxford: Clarendon Press, 1997), 5, 7, 30.

40 G. DeGroot, *Blighty: British Society in the Era of the Great War* (London: Longman, 1996), 199.

41 N. Branson, *Britain in the Nineteen Twenties* (Minneapolis: University of Minnesota Press, 1976), 103.

42 M. McKenna, 'The suburbanization of the working-class population of Liverpool between the wars', *Social History* 16 (1991), 177.

43 C.G. Pooley and S. Irish, 'Access to housing on Merseyside, 1919–39', *Transactions of the Institute of British Geographers* 12 (1987), 179.

44 J. Burnett, *A Social History of Housing 1815–1985*, 2nd ed. (London: Methuen, 1986), 226, 233, 243–4; S. Damer, *From Moorepark to*

'*Wine Alley*': *The Rise and Fall of a Glasgow Housing Scheme* (Edinburgh: Edinburgh University Press, 1989), 41–4; Dewey, *War and Progress*, 162–6.

45 Burnett, *Social History*, 236; Dewey, *War and Progress*, 164; S. Glynn and J. Oxborrow, *Interwar Britain: A Social and Economic History* (London: George Allen & Unwin, 1976), 238.

46 McKenna, 'Suburbanization of the working-class population', 178–9.

47 Burnett, *Social History*, 236; M.J. Daunton, 'Introduction', in M.J. Daunton, ed., *Councillors and Tenants: Local Authority Housing in English Cities, 1919–1939* (Leicester: Leicester University Press, 1984), 27–8.

48 Damer, *Moorepark to Wine Alley*, 98.

49 McKenna, 'Suburbanization of the working-class population', 177.

50 Burnett, *Social History*, 236–7.

51 Ibid., 239; Damer, *From Moorepark to Wine Alley*, 119.

52 Olechnowicz, *Working-Class Housing*, 50–1.

53 McKenna, 'Suburbanization of the working-class population', 186.

54 R. Durant, *Watling: A Survey of Social Life on a New Housing Estate* (London: P.S. King & Son, 1939), 16; Olechnowicz, *Working-Class Housing*, 47.

55 B. Waites, *A Class Society at War: England 1914–1918* (Leamington Spa: Berg, 1987), 174–5. Pooley and Irish, 'Access to housing', 184; Olechnowicz, *Working-Class Housing*, 33, 51; Damer, *From Moorepark to Wine Alley*, 42.

56 McKenna, 'Suburbanization of the working-class population', 185.

57 Ibid., 180–1.

58 Dewey, *War and Progress*, 161, 163–4.

59 Pooley and Irish, 'Access to housing', 181.

60 Burnett, *Social History*, 244, 249.

61 Pooley and Irish, 'Access to housing', 181, 187.

62 Sir George Newman, see C. Webster, 'Healthy or hungry thirties?' *History Workshop Journal* 13 (1982), 111.

63 M. Mitchell, 'The effects of unemployment on the social condition of women and children in the 1930s', *History Workshop Journal* 19 (1985), 107; Tranter, *British Population*, 65–6.

64 J. Burnett, *Plenty and Want: A Social History of Food in England from 1815 to the Present Day*, 3rd ed. (London: Routledge, 1989), 267–84.

65 Webster, 'Healthy or hungry thirties', 117; E. Fox, 'Powers of life and death: aspects of maternal welfare in England and Wales between the wars', *Medical History* 35 (1991), 332.

66 Mitchell, 'Effects of unemployment', 115.

67 J.M. Winter, 'The decline of mortality in Britain 1870–1950', in T.C. Barker and M. Drake, eds, *Population and Society in Britain 1850–1980* (New York: New York University Press, 1982), 107.

68 Stevenson and Cook, *Britain in the Depression*, 51.

69 Glynn and Oxborrow, *Interwar Britain*, 201.

70 Webster, 'Healthy or hungry thirties', 116.

71 Stevenson, *British Society*, 117, 126, 134.

72 B.S. Rowntree, *Poverty and Progress: A Second Social Survey of York* (London: Longmans, Green, 1941), 156, italics in original.

73 Pilgrim Trust, *Men without Work* ([1938]; New York: Greenwood Press, 1968), 105.

74 D. Vincent, *Poor Citizens: The State and the Poor in Twentieth-Century Britain* (London: Longman, 1991), 69–70, 72.

75 Ibid., 90, 92; Olechnowicz, *Working-Class Housing*, 60.

76 Burnett, *Plenty and Want*, 273.

77 Pilgrim Trust, *Men without Work*, 139; C. Webster, 'Health, welfare and unemployment during the Depression', *Past and Present* 109 (1985), 220.

78 Vincent, *Poor Citizens*, 84.

79 Bourke, *Working-Class Cultures*, 154.

80 S. Damer, ' "Engineers of the human machine": the social practice of council housing management in Glasgow, 1895–1939', *Urban Studies* 37 (2000), 2016, 2021.

81 M. McKenna, 'Municipal suburbia in Liverpool, 1919–1939', *Town Planning Review* 60 (1989), 300.

82 Bourke, *Working-Class Cultures*, 156.

83 Durant, *Watling*, 26, 60.

84 McKenna, 'Municipal suburbia', 299; A. Hughes and K. Hunt, 'A culture transformed? Women's lives in Wythenshawe in the 1930s', in A. Davies and S. Fielding, eds, *Workers' Worlds: Cultures and Communities in Manchester and Salford, 1880–1939* (Manchester: Manchester University Press, 1992), 90–1.

85 Vincent, *Poor Citizens*, 88; Durant, *Watling*, 15, 26; McKenna, 'Municipal suburbia', 300.

86 Bourke, *Working-Class Cultures*, 160.

87 McKibbin, *Classes and Cultures*, 203.

CHAPTER TEN

Unemployment, dislocation and new industries

Ethel Tillotson was raised in Blackburn, in the heart of Lanca-shire cotton country. As a youth in the 1930s she entered a spinning mill that had survived the worst of the slump. She found the work unpleasant, and continuing problems in the cotton industry left her and other workers working shortened hours. When Philips opened a new factory in Blackburn to build radio components, she went to work there. She described her job: 'You had trays at either side of you, and you had to pick a grid up, and cathodes, heaters and all these and put them on top of each other'. The work was not easy, though Tillotson later downplayed the skill required: 'They were so fragile that it was really surprising how we didn't damage them, but it was a skill that came naturally to you, being in the mill'.[1]

Philips paid Ethel Tillotson and its other assembly workers by the piece. Though the industry was booming, it was also competitive, and employers pushed their workers to maximize productivity. Tillotson recalled being hurried: 'They used to ask you, "Can't you do a little more?"' Many couldn't take the pace: 'When I started work at first there were 20 to 30 starting the same morning as me. By the Friday there was only 10, because they weeded you out'. Tillotson experienced many of the central developments in the working lives of British manual labourers in this period. She moved from a core export industry, cotton, to a 'new industry' dedicated to the consumer market. Her employer used piece rates and aggressive oversight of the pace of work to maximize output. As a female assembly worker, she formed part of a growing cadre of semi-skilled workers in consumer industries that grew in the decades following the First World War.

Growth and unemployment

With the mobilization of nearly 6 million men and the reorientation of economic resources to the war effort, the Great War disrupted the British economy both during the fighting and after. Far-reaching effects such as the loss of export markets and the fiscal impact of war spending continued to shape the inter-war economy.[2] Yet following the dislocation of war and the downturn in 1920–1, the British economy grew at a solid pace in the inter-war period. From 1924 to 1937 GDP per capita rose at an average annual rate of 1.8 per cent, which compares favourably to the second half of the nineteenth century. Industrial production expanded even more impressively, at a 3.3 per cent annual rate between 1927 and 1937, despite the slump that hit in 1929. In 1928 an optimistic assessment by the Liberal Party noted the 'remarkable expansion' of the economy. It admitted some 'adversity' in established export industries, but emphasized 'considerable expansion and prosperity elsewhere'.[3]

Healthy sectors increased their importance in the British labour market. Automobile manufacture employed 227,000 in 1920 and more than double that – 516,000 – in 1938. Building workers accounted for slightly over one-tenth of the workforce in 1920, but these trades employed 1.3 million, over 15 per cent of all workers, in 1938. On the other hand, cotton employment plummetted from 621,500 in 1912 to 393,000 in 1938 and coal mining declined from 1.2 million in 1920 to 702,000 18 years later.[4] Women's employment expanded during this period and also shifted, from textiles and private domestic service to service in shops and public establishments, low-level clerical work and manufacturing in growing industries. Women's employment in the rapidly expanding electrical engineering industry grew by 124 per cent in the 1920s and continued to expand in the following decade.[5] Alongside their growing roles in new industries, women remained responsible for unpaid domestic work.

Despite the growth of new industries, persistent widespread unemployment throughout the period devastated many working-class families. Unemployment shot up in 1921 and counted over a million British workers through the remainder of the inter-war period. Among those covered by the national insurance scheme, 11 per cent on average were unemployed between 1923 and 1929. In August of 1932, at the low point of the slump, 23 per cent of insured workers were unemployed. Because individuals moved on and off the unemployment rolls, perhaps as many as half of insured workers were unemployed at some point during 1932. Even once the recovery reached full force in 1937, a 10.8 per cent unemployment rate persisted among insured workers, and more faced short-time work of only a few days per week.[6] An observer of coal mining noted in 1928, 'short time working is almost universal, spells of employment are irregular and the mass of wage earners is on the verge of destitution'.[7]

Shortages of work hit some trades and regions harder than others. Workers in established staple industries, particularly those dependent on exports such as cotton, coal, iron and steel, and shipbuilding suffered the most. The slump decimated employment in shipbuilding and repair, causing an extraordinary 62 per cent unemployment rate in 1932.[8] In Wales, Scotland and the North of England, areas dependent on depressed industries, unemployment remained high throughout the period and spread beyond core industries. In the Tyneside town of Jarrow nearly 68 per cent of insured workers were out of employment in 1934. Ellen Wilkinson recalled Jarrow during the slump: 'There was no work. No one had a job, except a few railwaymen, officials, the workers in the co-operative stores, and a few workmen who went out of the town to their jobs'.[9] Welsh unemployment averaged 17.5 per cent of insured workers from 1924 to 1929, surged to 36.5 per cent in 1932, and declined only to 23.3 per cent by 1937. In contrast, in the depths of the slump, unemployment in the South East reached 14.3 per cent, and the rate dropped to 6.7 per cent in 1937.[10]

In addition to regional disparities in unemployment, gender, skill and age affected workers' likelihood of facing extended periods without work. Women, less represented in the decimated core export industries, faced lower unemployment rates and shorter spans without jobs than did men. On the other hand, unskilled and low-wage male workers suffered high rates of job loss. In 1931 21.5 per cent of all unskilled male workers were jobless, compared to 11.9 per cent of skilled or semi-skilled men. Men in their twenties and those over 50 had significantly higher rates of unemployment than men between 30 and 49.[11] Young men suffered in competition with boys who earned lower wages. One observer explained: 'the excess representation of males in the age group twenty to twenty-four among [unemployed] claimants . . . is probably due to the preference of employers to pay boys' wages for work that does not require skill and training'.[12] Those over 50 suffered longer periods of unemployment than did younger men. As social reformer William Beveridge noted, 'the older man, once he has lost a job, finds it harder than a younger man to get a new job'.[13]

Prolonged periods out of work, lasting a year or more, were relatively rare before 1929, despite high levels of unemployment throughout the 1920s. During the slump, however, lengthy stretches without employment grew distressingly common. In 1929 7.2 per cent of those unemployed had faced a year or more without work. In 1934 29 per cent of the unemployed were out of work for a year or longer, and even amidst recovery in 1937 28.1 per cent of the unemployed were out of work for a year or more. In 1937 the average long-term unemployed worker remained on the rolls for 144 weeks. The Ministry of Labour noted the specific barriers confronting the long-term unemployed: 'prolonged unemployment has robbed many men of both the physical fitness and the attitudes of mind which would enable them to undertake heavy work under ordinary industrial conditions'. A long-unemployed shipyard worker recalled the demoralization: 'I'd lost my confidence. It was an insidious feeling that you didn't think you could manage again after being away from it for a year or more'. Yet the concentration of long-term unemployment in the depressed industries and regions shows that structural economic problems, not personal failings, accounted for persistent unemployment. In 1936 more than 57 per cent of those unemployed for more than a year had worked in depressed staple export industries including coal, iron and steel, engineering, shipbuilding, cotton and woollens.[14]

Employer initiatives in the workplace

High unemployment left British workers with little bargaining strength in the face of employer efforts to maximize profits in the unpromising inter-war environment. Though during and immediately following the First World War workers enjoyed the advantage in labour relations and won wage increases and shorter hours, conditions after 1920 undermined this position and gave the initiative to employers. Some businesses confronted shrinking international demand and volatile economic conditions by hunkering down, collaborating to avoid competition and squeezing increased productivity out of workers without investing in new approaches or technology. Others adopted new techniques, moving towards mass production and employing the latest technology. Despite unfavourable labour market conditions through most of the period, workers sought to disrupt these changes when they threatened their livelihood or imposed new and obnoxious authority in the workplace.

Before the First World War small and medium-sized firms, often controlled by single families, dominated British manufacturing. In succeeding decades firms grew larger, primarily through mergers. High-profile mergers created huge companies such as ICI and Unilever, which each employed over 50,000 workers in the 1930s.[15] Even beyond the famous goliaths, though, increasing numbers of British workers found employment in big companies with large manufacturing facilities. A 1935 survey found 49 per cent of production workers were employed in firms of at least 500 people. In the rapidly growing sectors of electrical machinery, motor and cycle, sugar and confectionery, and rayon manufacture, more than 40 per cent of the workers toiled in factories larger than 1,000 employees.[16]

Mergers and cartels encouraged 'rationalization', more efficient production, greater intensity of work, lower wages, and shedding excess capacity by closing factories. In the late 1920s advocates of consolidation suggested that large, organized firms could create efficient factories, generate steady profits and strengthen British industry.[17] With the economic collapse of 1929, however, rationalization led to widespread closures and unemployment. The newly merged Unilever proceeded to shut half its margarine factories between 1929 and 1937.[18] Competitive pressures led many inter-war employers to reduce wages. Mineowners imposed deep wage cuts in 1921 on the heels of a four-month lockout, and the fallout from the 1926 lockout and failed general strike included further wage reductions. During the slump of 1929–33 employers again decreased miners' pay.[19] A cotton spinner recalled repeated wage cuts: '33 per cent, $7^1/_2$ per cent, 5 per cent, and it was reduction after reduction after reduction over a period of about six years from 1931 to 1937'. Widespread unemployment made wage cuts possible. Matt Hardy, who worked as a house painter during the slump, recalled his employer's demand that he take a pay cut of '4d. or 5d. an hour', noting that another man had agreed to work for the lower rate. Hardy refused and lost the job. Later he sympathetically remembered the other worker, 'He was so desperate for a job. He did apologise . . . He knew what he was doing was wrong. He just had no option'.[20]

Employers continued efforts to intensify work. A weaver recalled the influence of machines in setting the pace of work, 'Work inside the factory is much harder than it used to be owing to the great speeding up of machinery. The toil is now almost ceaseless'. In the most advanced assembly-line processes, conveyors set the pace, as worker William Ferrie told the BBC in 1934: 'If the management in the factory decide to increase speed by 10 per cent, a thousand hands work 10 per cent faster'. Some employers applied new, more 'scientific' methods to increase productivity. In the Bedaux system, consultants studied each task and developed production norms that became the basis for piece-work rates demanding faster work. Chrissie Minett worked in the creaming department at Peek Frean's biscuit works. The Bedaux system brought a speed-up there: 'Say you had 20 minutes for a tray, they'd alter it so you got to do that tray in 15 minutes. You just had to work faster'. An engineering worker complained that this system represented 'intensive scientific slavery . . . an inhuman system of speed-up that sought to turn people into machines'.[21]

Intensification formed one part of a broader programme of reorganization associated with 'scientific management'. As was the case before the First World War, few British employers embraced Fordist or Taylorite models of factory organization in full, but many sought to increase control over production. One approach involved placing responsibility for the planning and organization of work in the hands of managers rather than craftsmen or foremen. As one observer noted, 'in the past the subtleties of production were to be found in actual manufacture; nowadays they are to be found in the layout or plan of manufacture'.[22] While many employers relied on piece rates to ensure worker discipline, others took advantage of weakened unions to break worker control over production processes. An observer noted in 1935, 'Restrictive practices imposed by trade unions are actually fewer than they were, and of less importance'.[23]

Some employers, particularly in rapidly growing 'new' industries, adopted other facets of the latest production methods. The moving assembly line appeared in Ford's Manchester plant in 1914, less than a year after making its debut in Detroit. In the following decades innovating employers in several industries adopted moving assembly lines. A tailor recalled mechanization and the adoption of the moving line in clothing manufacture by the late 1930s: 'I have lived long enough to see almost every process usurped by the machine . . . with the conveyor belt to carry subdivided portions of the work from one operative to another'. New techniques did not always involve mechanization. At Peek Frean they introduced 'music while you work', based on research to determine which forms encouraged faster work: 'different kinds of music were tried . . . with light music the results were the lowest . . . and fox-trots and one-steps were easy winners'.[24]

Firms on the cutting-edge of new techniques were exceptional, however. A small fraction of British workers toiled on assembly lines in this period.[25] William Morris adopted new technology only incrementally in his motor plant at Cowley in Oxford. Management manipulated piece rates and bonus systems to boost productivity, and selectively used new approaches. Morris finally installed a moving assembly line in 1933.[26] In the shipyards skilled men continued to coordinate work. As Boilermakers' Union leader John Hill described it, the process involved, 'the foreman saying to Mr. So-and-so, "Here you are; these are the plans of that job: get along with it" and there is no need to look after them and watch them and see if they are doing it right'.[27] In the Daimler motor works in Coventry, workers retained some control over the production process, even when they earned piece rates under bonus systems that sought to speed production. George Malin recalled, 'There was scope for your skill then . . . Knowing how to plan the job was the secret of it, especially if you were on payment by results'.[28]

Yet the position of skilled workers grew increasingly tenuous throughout this period. New production methods during the war, followed by the inter-war combination of unemployment, new techniques and the expansion of new industries in the less-unionized South East and Midlands undermined some skilled men. For example, after skilled shipyard workers survived the dilution threat during the war, the collapse of this industry threw many into unemployment.[29] In engineering the proportion of skilled workers declined from 60 per cent in 1914 to 32 per cent in 1933, according to the Engineering Employers' Federation's (probably somewhat inflated) figures.[30] Some engineering employers introduced new machines and redefined work away from skilled craftsmen, as the Engineering Employers' Federation recommended: 'introduce these semi-skilled men on suitable work provided through deskilling the operations and by the supply of jigs and tools'. New facilities in engineering, electrical, motor, cycle and aircraft work located primarily in regions without strong craft traditions. They relied heavily on semi-skilled workers and restricted skilled craftsmen to the margins, as the Amalgamated Engineering Union observed in 1937: 'the only people near the work who may accurately be classified as skilled being the foreman, chargehands, markers out, machine setters and tool makers'.[31]

Though the traditional skilled craftsmen suffered from these trends, skill did not disappear from British industry. As the proportion of skilled engineering workers declined, so did the proportion of unskilled in the trade, both giving way to a predominance of semi-skilled workers. Traditional apprenticeships yielded to more informal learning processes, but workers still developed knowledge and skill on the job.[32] Though women's skills were consistently undervalued, many women possessed significant ability. One observer noted that 'the work in the Rover Company's Female Trimming Department was very highly skilled – much more skilled than Machine Shop work'.[33]

A significant portion of what appears to be deskilling, then, was the decline of traditional craftwork (though not its disappearance) and the spread of semi-skilled work for men or women. In many of the fastest-growing industries in the inter-war period semi-skilled women operating assembly machines provided the bulk of the workforce. As one critic of the preference for girls in manufacturing complained, employers believed that female workers were more suited to some assembly jobs, as their 'suppleness of fingers makes them more suitable than boys'. More dexterous or not, it remained significantly cheaper to employ women than men. Ordinarily, the highest-paid women assemblers earned less than the lowest-paid men who worked as labourers.[34] An employer explained: 'There are certain classes of work which are essentially women's work and should be paid . . . at a rate suitable to it being women's work . . . If there is any attempt to put them on to men's rates, you are simply going to destroy a rising industry'.[35]

Though they preferred girls and women on some assembly jobs, employers still used boys as a source of cheap labour. Apprenticeship continued to deteriorate as youths worked for low wages without developing craft skills. Clydeside engineers complained of employers' use of boy labour, in good times and bad: 'During periods of industrial expansion the tendency is to build up the labour force from below, to engage the maximum amount of juvenile labour . . . In times of depression the general practice is to . . . lay off higher paid operatives and retain the services of juveniles'.[36] Employers benefited from paying boys and girls low rates, but this required constant turnover. An observer of electrical engineering noted that 'the practice of sacking at 18 when higher rates of wages require to be paid, with the taking on of a new younger and cheaper set of youth labour, is widespread'.[37]

Unions, conflict and the state

Workers' ability to organize and oppose employer strategies varied with economic and labour market conditions. Union membership soared during the First World War and its immediate aftermath, reaching a peak of over 8.3 million in 1920, more than double the 1914 figure. From that point, membership slumped below 4.4 million in 1933, partially recovering to nearly 6.3 million in 1939.[38] Government policies during the war spurred union growth. On the docks, union members could gain reserved status as essential workers and avoid enlistment. As union leader James Sexton recalled, 'Many who had been bitterly antagonistic to our union clamoured for admission to it when all the men registered at the clearing house were ruled to be ineligible for military or naval service'.[39] Though union expansion continued during the immediate aftermath of the war, worsening economic conditions undermined many organizations from 1920. The Workers' Union organized semi-skilled engineering workers, growing to 90,000 members in Coventry and Birmingham by 1920. With the downturn, however, membership plummeted to only 15,000 in 1923.[40] Across Britain, though unions struggled throughout the 1920s and early

1930s, overall union membership never dropped below prewar levels, and expansion resumed after 1933.

To ensure stability and facilitate planning, the government backed the extension of collective bargaining during the war. The Whitley Committee, created in 1916, recommended the strengthening of employer associations and unions in collective bargaining agreements: 'an essential condition of securing a permanent improvement in the relations between employers and employed is that there should be adequate organization on the part of both employers and workpeople'.[41] Despite strains on the system during the 1920s and 1930s, collective bargaining survived and even spread. Following a complete employer victory in the engineering lockout in 1922, companies did not attempt to destroy unionization or collective bargaining. They did, however, insist on rolling back worker influence on shopfloor conditions and strengthening procedures for handling grievances through collective bargaining.[42] In cotton, employers seeking wage cuts voted to abolish their collective bargaining agreements in 1931 and 1932. The government intervened to restore the agreements and eventually passed the Cotton Manufacturing (Temporary Provisions) Act in 1934 to give legal sanction to agreed upon wage rates.[43]

Despite state support for collective bargaining during and after the war, not all employers accepted unions. Though car manufacture grew rapidly in the inter-war period, unions struggled to organize its mostly semi-skilled workforce. Employers combined high wages with stiff discipline and supervision to deter labour organization.[44] Hayden Evans, who moved to Oxford from union-rich South Wales, found no union at the Pressed Steel plant: 'there was no trade union and you didn't have any representation. They could pull any punches they liked and threaten you with the sack'. After the 1926 general strike collapsed, employers refused to take activists back, as Dick Martin recalled in Nottinghamshire, 'To those who had been militant, "You're not to come, get off, nothing for you" . . . I knew families that never did get back after the '26 strike'. Frank Dodd's boss in a small chemical company threatened potential organizers, but Dodd started a union anyway: the employer 'threatened to sack the first man that started [a union] . . . but he didn't sack me because I got the union too strong beforehand'.[45]

In well-organized trades, large strikes were common in the last stages of the war and immediate post-war period. As pressure on the pace of work increased, inflation eroded purchasing power, and dilution and conscription threatened, skilled workers in essential industries organized widespread strikes. While only 276,000 workers participated in strikes

in 1916, about three times as many were involved in disputes the following year, and the numbers continued to rise after the armistice, surpassing
2.5 million in 1919.[46] Strikes among engineers became the flashpoint for
industrial conflict during the war. As early as February 1915, Clydeside
engineers struck for higher wages, despite the opposition of the union's
district committee. This 'best organized strike in the annals of Clyde History',
set the stage for a militant organization built around shop stewards rather
than established union leadership.[47] A Manchester shop steward linked
wartime dilution and conscription to the broader question of worker organization: 'If we are beat on these two matters, then the shutters may as well
be put up so far as the working-class movement is concerned'.[48]

Labour struggles continued in the immediate aftermath of the war,
focusing on higher wages, shorter hours and better conditions. Some of
these efforts were successful. For example, after a national railway strike
the union executive boasted of winning 'the eight-hour day, a guaranteed
week . . . extra remuneration for night duty . . . time-and-a-quarter for overtime and time-and-a-half for Sunday duty'. Yet these victories were short-
lived, and unions suffered significant defeats in major confrontations
in the 1920s. Massive wage cuts led to a miners' strike in 1921, but the
railwaymen and transport workers refused to support the miners, and it
collapsed after three months. Engineering employers went on the offensive
in 1922 to establish control over overtime and changing work processes.
The three-month lockout ended in union capitulation and a weakening of
shop steward influence. J.T. Murphy, a Sheffield shop steward movement
leader, noted the impact of the economic downturn on the engineers'
organization: 'You cannot build factory organizations in empty and depleted
workshops while you have a great reservoir of unemployed workers'.[49]
In 1926 miners facing further cuts and reorganization again struck, this
time supported by the broader union movement in the brief general strike.
After nine days the Trades Union Congress called off the general strike,
and the miners strike collapsed in defeat seven months later.[50] With the
important exception of 1926, however, large-scale strikes grew rare once
the economic downturn in 1920–1 put workers on the defensive.

Both during the war, when union leaders sought cooperation with
the government, and after the war, when economic conditions made large-
scale strikes unpromising, conflict between workers and employers often
originated without official union organization. Strikes such as the 1915
Clydeside engineering walkout involved unionized workers without the
endorsement of the executive. At the Rover works in Coventry, women
trimmers resisted a proposal to apply Bedaux rationalization to their

work in 1930. They joined the Workers' Union, which won concessions in negotiations with Rover. The trimmers, however, refused to work under the revised system. The union backed the strike and a group of male workers came out in support as well. Eventually, Rover abandoned the plan.[51] Small-scale resistance also remained an essential characteristic of the shopfloor. Complex bonus schemes did not faze workers who could identify the point at which their efforts received less reward: 'they take care not to reach this point. They figure it all out to a half penny'.[52] On an automobile assembly line the foreman increased the pace of work. When the workers realized this, 'everybody stopped until the track . . . speed was put back again'. Then workers marked the floor with chalk to measure the line's speed.[53]

Though the state did not intervene in small-scale conflicts such as these, government policies in this period disadvantaged workers. Despite promoting collective bargaining, governments acted aggressively against militant leaders and were prepared to use troops against large-scale strikes. In 1919 tanks surrounded Glasgow and striking workers battled police in George Square.[54] In expectation of the general strike of 1926, the government prepared volunteer labour forces and control over the BBC and planned military deployments to key urban centres.[55] In the wake of the strike, the 1927 Trade Disputes and Trade Unions Act outlawed sympathetic or general strikes designed to pressure the government, restricted picketing, banned union organization among civil servants, and made it more difficult for unions to raise political funds. This law fell far short of the draconian demands of some employers and Conservative politicians, but it did restrict union activities.[56]

While new legislation constrained unions, governments did little to address unhealthy and dangerous working conditions until the late 1930s. The most important improvements in working conditions occurred independent of government regulation. In the immediate aftermath of the war, unions pushed successfully for a reduction in working hours, and the 8-hour day or 48-hour week became standard in many industries. A London survey compared conditions in 1928 with those 30 years prior and noted, 'the average London worker now has an extra hour a day to himself compared with then. The bulk of the total reduction took place in the years immediately following the war'.[57] As new industries expanded, particularly in the South and Midlands, factory conditions improved. Electricity allowed for better lighting, quieter conditions and easier shutdowns in cases of emergency. Modern factories provided better ventilation. Factory inspector D.R. Wilson observed the benefits of the shift to new industries, 'light and airy modern, single-storey factories . . . situated in open and healthy surroundings, take the place of the old, many storeyed buildings with their restricted supply of fresh air and daylight. Work is consequently carried on under far more advantageous conditions'.[58] Fatality rates in industrial accidents dropped dramatically between 1915 and 1939.[59]

Despite these improvements, conditions for manual workers remained difficult and often unhealthy. In older staple industries, economic constraints made improvements rare. In cotton mills, for example, workers in cardrooms who prepared material for spinning suffered respiratory illness three times more frequently than those in other departments. On the spinning mules themselves, a carcinogenic oil splashed spinners and piecers, leading to hundreds of fatalities.[60] Newer industries brought their own problems. In a chemical plant opened in 1933, Walter Parkinson recalled the carbon tetrachloride section: 'It was a very bad plant to work on . . . The fumes were very pungent and on top of that there was the danger of chlorine . . . it was a deadly gas to use'.[61] An employee of Pressed Steel at Cowley noted: 'Loss of fingers, thumbs and hands was commonplace in the factory'.[62] In the view of a factory inspector, new manufacturing processes, 'undoubtedly create . . . a desire by the worker for temporary relief from the enforced boredom of occupation . . . more days are lost from vague, ill-defined, but no doubt very real, disability due to *ennui* than from all the recognized industrial diseases put together'.[63]

Conclusion

Thus, manual labour often remained dangerous and unpleasant. Economic and legal conditions made it difficult for workers to do much about these conditions. During the First World War laws gave employers great leeway in shaping the work process and made strikes difficult. In the 1920s and 1930s widespread unemployment, particularly in established staple industries, decimated established working-class communities and weakened organizations of employed workers. As new industries grew, employers sought to limit the influence of unions and maintain control over production. Labour market conditions and weakened unions allowed employers to cut wages, intensify work and adopt new techniques. Facing widespread and prolonged unemployment or new forms of discipline in growing industries, workers in this period experienced poor labour market conditions and intensified subordination to employers.

Despite these conditions, manual workers found enjoyment in their work. A brickmaker who despised his employers stayed at his job 47 years, noting that he 'loved his work'. A woman who worked in a foundry recalled: 'I loved it . . . all them years I worked there it was like going from home to home'. Workers built strong attachments to one another and their jobs through talk and horseplay. The woman recalled, 'we all worked behind each other. And we used to, you know, chat and that'. Another woman recalled the biscuit factory: 'It was like a little club'. Among the men at a Huddersfield textile mill, 'all was friendly and intensely physical in an uninhibited way . . . all over there were mock fights and practical jokes'.[64] This workplace culture was often oppositional. For example, workers in large firms accepted the legitimacy of pilfering. An observer noted of respectable working men: 'They seem to think that because the men have grievances they are justified in such conduct'. The workplace culture also disdained clerical workers, who remained beyond the boundaries of the working class and 'did nothing', in the common view.[65]

Notes

1 P. Pagnamenta and R. Overy, *All Our Working Lives* (London: BBC, 1984), 245.

2 J. Stevenson, *British Society 1914–45* (London: Allen Lane, 1984), 105.

3 S. Glynn and J. Oxborrow, *Interwar Britain: A Social and Economic History* (London: George Allen & Unwin, 1976), 18–19, 89–91.

4 Ibid., 106–8, 96–7.

5 M. Glucksmann, *Women Assemble: Women Workers and the New Industries in Inter-War Britain* (London: Routledge, 1990), 46, 52, 58.

6 Figures for the entire workforce were probably a few percentage points below the insured figures. A. Thorpe, *Britain in the 1930s: The Deceptive Decade* (Oxford: Blackwell, 1992), 61, 63; P. Dewey, *War and Progress: Britain 1914–1945* (London: Longman, 1997), 122, 228–9, 255.

7 N. Whiteside and J. Gillespie, 'Deconstructing unemployment: developments in Britain in the interwar years', *Economic History Review* 44 (1991), 669.

8 T.J. Hatton, 'Unemployment and the labour market, 1870–1939', in R. Floud and P. Johnson, eds, *The Cambridge Economic History of Modern Britain, vol. II: Economic Maturity, 1860–1939* (Cambridge: Cambridge University Press, 2004), 349; Dewey, *War and Progress*, 202.

9 K. Laybourn, *Britain on the Breadline: A Social and Political History of Britain 1918–1939* (Stroud: Sutton, 1990), 10.

10 Dewey, *War and Progress*, 258; Pilgrim Trust, *Men without Work: A Report Made to the Pilgrim Trust* ([1938]; New York: Greenwood, 1968), 19.

11 M. Thomas, 'Labour market structure and the nature of unemployment in interwar Britain', in B. Eichengreen and T.J. Hatton, eds, *Interwar Unemployment in International Perspective* (Dordrecht: Kluwer, 1987), 115–16, 123; Dewey, *War and Progress*, 257; B. Eichengreen, 'Unemployment in interwar Britain: new evidence from London', *Journal of Interdisciplinary History* 17 (1986), 348, 354.

12 Eichengreen, 'Unemployment in interwar Britain', 351.

13 Thomas, 'Labour market structure', 118.

14 Eichengreen, 'Unemployment in interwar Britain', 355; Pagnamenta and Overy, *All Our Working Lives*, 135; Thomas, 'Labour market structure', 114, 133, 134–5.

15 A.D. Chandler, 'The growth of the transnational industrial firm in the US and the UK: a comparative analysis', *Economic History Review* 33 (1980), 405–6; S.N. Broadberry and N.F.R. Crafts, 'Britain's productivity gap in the 1930s: some neglected factors', *Journal of Economic History* 52 (1992), 553.

16 H.F. Gospel, *Markets, Firms and the Management of Labour in Modern Britain* (Cambridge: Cambridge University Press, 1992), 44; H.F. Gospel, 'Employers and managers: organisation and strategy 1914–1939', in C. Wrigley, ed., *A History of British Industrial Relations, vol. II: 1914–1939* (Brighton: Harvester Press, 1987), 160; Glucksmann, *Women Assemble*, 74.

17 L.L. Downs, 'Industrial decline, rationalization and equal pay: the Bedaux strike at Rover Automobile Company', *Social History* 15 (1990), 46–7.

18 N.K. Buxton, 'Economic growth in Scotland between the wars', *Economic History Review* 33 (1980), 553; Broadberry and Crafts, 'Productivity gap', 553.

19 Gospel, *Markets, Firms and Management*, 86–7, 213; W. Lewchuk, *American Technology and the British Vehicle Industry* (Cambridge: Cambridge University Press, 1987), 94.

20 Pagnamenta and Overy, *All Our Working Lives*, 36; C. Wrigley, 'The trade unions between the wars', in Wrigley, ed., *History of British Industrial Relations, vol. II*, 111.

21 Gospel, *Markets, Firms and Management*, 71–2; Lewchuk, *American Technology*, 176; A.J. McIvor, *A History of Work in Britain, 1880–1950* (Basingstoke: Palgrave, 2001), 71; Pagnamenta and Overy, *All Our Working Lives*, 216; Glucksman, *Women Assemble*, 101; Downs, 'Bedaux strike', 59.

22 K. Whitston, 'Scientific management and production management practice in Britain between the wars', *Historical Studies in Industrial Relations* 1 (1996), 54–5.

23 Gospel, *Markets, Firms and Management*, 53.

24 Lewchuk, *American Technology*, 156, 179; McIvor, *History of Work*, 57–8; Glucksman, *Women Assemble*, 97.

25 M. Savage and A. Miles, *The Remaking of the British Working Class 1840–1940* (London: Routledge, 1994), 50.

26 S. Tolliday, 'The failure of mass production unionism in the motor industry, 1914–1939', in Wrigley, ed., *History of British Industrial Relations, vol. II*, 305–6; S. Tolliday, 'Management and labour in Britain 1896–1939', in S. Tolliday and J. Zeitlin, eds, *The Automobile Industry and its Workers: Between Fordism and Flexibility* (New York: St Martin's Press, 1987), 37–8.

27 A. Reid, 'Employers' strategies and craft production: the British shipbuilding industry 1870–1950', in S. Tolliday and J. Zeitlin, eds, *The Power to Manage? Employers and Industrial Relations in Comparative Historical Perspective* (London: Routledge, 1991), 42–3.

28 P. Thompson, 'Playing at being skilled men: factory culture and pride in work skills among Coventry car workers', *Social History* 13 (1988), 51–2.

29 K. Nicholas, *The Social Effects of Unemployment in Teeside* (Manchester: Manchester University Press, 1986), 16, 35–7.

30 McIvor, *History of Work*, 55–6.

31 K. Whitston, 'Worker resistance and Taylorism in Britain', *International Review of Social History* 42 (1997), 12–14; B. Waites, *A Class Society at War: England 1914–1918* (Leamington Spa: Berg, 1987), 153.

32 McIvor, *History of Work*, 55, 60.

33 Downs, 'Bedaux strike', 53.

34 Glucksmann, *Women Assemble*, 61; A.J. McIvor, 'Women's work in twentieth century Scotland', in T. Dickson and J.H. Treble, eds, *People and Society in Scotland, vol. III: 1914–1990* (Edinburgh, John Donald, 1992), 152.

35 L.L. Downs, *Manufacturing Inequality: Gender Division in the French and British Metalworking Industries, 1914–1939* (Ithaca: Cornell University Press, 1995), 117.

36 A. McKinlay, 'From industrial serf to wage-labourer: the 1937 apprentice revolt in Britain', *International Review of Social History* 31 (1986), 4–6.

37 Glucksmann, *Women Assemble*, 62.

38 Wrigley, 'Trade unions', 72.

39 C. Wrigley, 'The First World War and state intervention in industrial relations, 1914–1918', in Wrigley, ed., *History of British Industrial Relations, vol. II*, 40, 59.

40 Tolliday, 'Failure of mass production unionism', 312–13.

41 Gospel, 'Employers and managers', 160.

42 Gospel, *Markets, Firms and Management*, 85–6.

43 Wrigley, 'Trade unions', 106–8; Gospel, *Markets, Firms and Management*, 88–9.

44 S. Tolliday, 'Militancy and organisation: women workers and trade unions in the motor trades in the 1930s', *Oral History* 11 (1983), 42; Tolliday, 'Failure of mass production unionism', 305, 308.

45 Pagnamenta and Overy, *All Our Working Lives*, 270, 176, 17.

46 C. Wrigley, 'Introduction', in Wrigley, ed., *History of British Industrial Relations, vol. II*, 14.

47 J. Hinton, *The First Shop Stewards' Movement* (London: George Allen & Unwin, 1973), 105–6.

48 Waites, *Class Society at War*, 208.

49 Wrigley, 'Trade unions between the wars', 78, 94, 96–7.

50 K. Burgess, *The Challenge of Labour: Shaping British Society 1850–1930* (London: Croom Helm, 1980), 222–5.

51 Downs, 'Bedaux strike', 62, 64–5, 69; Tolliday, 'Militancy and organisation', 46–7.

52 Whitston, 'Worker resistance and Taylorism', 17.

53 Lewchuk, *American Technology*, 156.

54 W.W. Knox, *Industrial Nation: Work, Culture and Society in Scotland, 1800–Present* (Edinburgh: Edinburgh University Press, 1999), 219.

55 Burgess, *Challenge of Labour*, 220.

56 R. Lowe, 'The government and industrial relations, 1919–1939', in Wrigley, ed., *History of British Industrial Relations, vol. II*, 195.

57 Glynn and Oxborrow, *Interwar Britain*, 27.

58 A.J. McIvor, 'Manual work, technology, and industrial health, 1918–39', *Medical History* 31 (1987), 178–9.

59 McIvor, *History of Work*, 133.

60 McIvor, 'Manual work', 169, 181–182.

61 Pagnamenta and Overy, *All Our Working Lives*, 159.

62 Wrigley, 'Introduction', 7.

63 McIvor, *History of Work*, 147.

64 R. McKibbin, *Classes and Cultures: England 1918–1951* (Oxford: Oxford University Press, 1998), 128, 129; C. Langhamer, *Women's Leisure in England, 1920–1960* (Manchester: Manchester University Press, 2000), 25, 92.

65 McKibbin, *Classes and Cultures*, 139.

CHAPTER ELEVEN

Cinema, dance hall and streets

When interviewed for an oral history project, Mrs Fletcher recalled her youthful enjoyment of leisure in inter-war Manchester: 'it was good while it lasted'. From the age of 15 or 16 she sneaked off to the dance halls in Salford. Telling her disapproving father, 'we'd gone out shoppin, or we'd gone looking at the shops', she visited the Empress or the less respectable Dyson's, which she recalled as 'a right dive'. Saturday afternoons at the dance hall were a special treat for this young woman, however, since at the Empress 'it used to be a shilling to go in'. After turning over her weekly contribution to the family budget, this shilling represented her entire weekly leisure money, her 'spends'. Thus, most weeks 'we couldn't afford to go dancing, because if we went dancing on a Saturday afternoon, that was the limit and we'd no money left'.

The highlight of the week, at least when she did not spend Saturday afternoon at the dance hall, came on Saturday and Sunday nights, when area youth would gather for the 'monkey run' in the Eccles New Road. Young men and women, dressed in their finest clothes, would 'Just parade with our eyes all over, "Oh, there's so-and-so. Look who they're talking to"'. The crowds were so thick with promenading youths, 'nobody could walk along it, because of the lads and girls that were there'. The young woman and her friends would catch the eyes of young men, then wait by the shop windows, 'Well invariably they'd come up to the shop window to us'. She boasted, 'Nobody had more lads than Nellie and me'. She recalled fondly: 'I think the monkey run was the happiest days of my life'.[1]

This young woman carefully balanced her resources and her time, blending new commercialized forms of leisure with long-established informal activities. In order to participate in various forms of leisure, working-class men and women needed free time and, when possible, spending money.

The reduction of working hours, won for some in the immediate post-war period and enshrined in legislation in 1934 and 1937, set the normal working week at 48 hours. By the end of the period 4 million manual workers also enjoyed paid holidays, mostly gained through collective bargaining agreements. Despite shortened hours, many workers had little energy left for active leisure during the week, as a miner noted in 1934: 'At the conclusion of my day's work I do not feel like indulging in much exercise, either physical or mental'. At the end of the week, though, many felt free to enjoy Saturday night's activities, as gas worker Herbert Mannion noted: 'Saturday night is the time to let themselves go: no work on Sunday to get up for . . . when the long Sunday-lie-in is their due after a week of attending to the factory buzzer'.[2]

Married working-class women, on the other hand, could not expect a Sunday 'lie-in', and they had less time for pleasure. While men viewed the enjoyment of their free time and money to spend on it as sacred, adult women's domestic responsibilities curtailed their access to leisure. A factory inspector's report of 1933 observed: 'women's work often begins when it nominally ends. The house and dependants make their claims . . . She has, with the possible exception of the unmarried girl, fewer recreations or relaxations than her contemporary male'.[3]

These women also generally spent money on their own leisure only when there was a surplus in the household economy. Thus, a 1939 survey reported a Leeds woman's testimony: 'never get out except to shop; have never been to the talkies'. Their husbands, though, continued to reserve money for their own leisure before contributing a portion of their wages for household expenses. According to the son of a Salford labourer, married men who lacked control over their spending money lost standing among peers: 'if a man handed his wages over in them days [without reserving money for himself], he wasn't a man . . . if he took his whole packet home not opened. It leaked out'. Young single men and women living with their parents often turned over their wages but received 'spends' from their mothers. At age 14, one man remembered, he earned 7s. 6d. per week at his first job and, 'I'd give it my mother'. She gave him back a third of this to spend on himself.[4] As they got older, most youths followed their fathers in dividing their earnings themselves.[5]

Not all men could afford to spend money on their own leisure. In poor households some men devoted their limited resources to the family. Robert Roberts described working men 'without a few coppers to go into a tavern' after work, suffering from boredom and 'waiting for bedtime'.[6] Widespread unemployment left men with lots of time but little money.

The search for work occupied most weekday mornings, but long days of enforced leisure could be demoralizing. If an unemployed man could scrape together a few pennies, he could attend a matinee at the cinema. 'The picture helps you live in another world for a little while', one man told an investigator, and another added 'they make you think for a little while that life is all right'.[7] But without money to spend, many unemployed men passed hours on the streets, 'aimlessly on the market square or the street corners' as one observer commented, 'with the hour-long observation of passers-by, varied by an occasional whiff at a cigarette'.[8]

Informal leisure

Though new commercialized leisure pursuits such as the cinema and dance hall impressed contemporaries, informal leisure in the streets or at home remained central to working-class culture. As was the case before the First World War, the streets of working-class neighbourhoods provided the setting for children's play, community singing and dancing, chats among neighbours, lively markets, courting for young men and women, and con-flict with the police and one another. Though young men and women embraced the cinema and dance hall enthusiastically, a 1939 survey in Manchester found that youths aged 17 to 21 spent half their weekday leisure hours talking in groups on the streets. Perhaps these young people were drawn to the streets by courting opportunities, as a woman who grew up in Salford recalled: 'I used to go and sit on the St John's wall up on Liverpool Street. I used to go there because the boys that I knew went and sat on this wall . . . if some (other lad) was attracted to you . . . They'd say, "Get her to talk to him"'. On the weekends, they might be more likely to attend dance halls and cinema, but they also would not want to miss the chance to promenade in the 'monkey run'.[9]

Those constrained by unemployment, inadequate 'spends' out of the household budget, or just general poverty found free entertainment where they could. In Lancashire, Jack Shaw remembered the limited options for leisure 'if you hadn't got any money. It was a matter of going for a walk. We used to go for a walk on the moors'.[10] For women with little money to spend on leisure, free activities were essential. Glasgow women would window shop: 'The men were at football matches of course, and you would walk up Springburn Road on one side widow-shopping or shopping, and cross over at the terminus and walk down the other side. You could put in your whole Saturday afternoon doing that'.[11] A trip to one of the large street markets common in working-class districts provided entertainment even for those with empty pockets. As one woman noted, 'You could spend a night [out] and not spend a penny'. A Manchester man concurred: 'The open market was a free attraction, and extremely welcome when you were broke'.[12]

On special occasions, working people filled the streets for celebrations, processions and dancing. Communities marked King George V's jubilee in 1935 and the coronation of George VI in 1937 with games, music, dancing and decorations. Every year in Manchester thousands turned out to watch the children dressed in their best clothes marching in Whit walks. The Protestant procession on Whit Monday was followed by the Catholics on Friday. One Ordsall woman's family did not miss a chance to enjoy a procession: 'we always used to watch both Church of England and Roman Catholic, and on Trinity Sunday, the Italians walked around New Cross'.[13] On 5 November residents of London working-class neighbourhoods celebrated enthusiastically. In one poor district of Islington residents spent days building huge bonfires and then added more fuel on Bonfire Night itself.[14] In Glasgow, New Year's celebrations centred around 'first-footing', a round of visits to neighbours culminating in parties. James Kinnear explained the exchange of whisky at the centre of first-footing: 'The principal thing ye had tae get was a bottle of whisky . . . So before ye went tae your eventual party, ye went tae friends . . . the first thing they did was offer you a drink . . . then immediately after, you gave them a shot of your bottle'. Then at the parties people danced and played games until the wee hours: 'Oh you would have thirty or forty people in a wee room playing a reel . . . You danced in the room, and then they would have a singing game'.[15]

As this example shows, not all informal leisure happened in the public space of neighbourhood streets. Despite crowded conditions, the home grew increasingly important as a site for working-class leisure. An observer described one Sheffield woman who played games when she needed to rest from her household duties: 'she sometimes plays cards or ludo "as that is cheaper than the pictures – I have no money for pictures"'.[16] New housing estates generally provided gardens and more space for private leisure. One applicant to the Bolton City Council explained his interest in living on an estate. His family members, 'desire to live in a quieter place and occupy our spare hours gardening'.[17] The architecture of new estates emphasized the private, and the lack of amenities like the old corner shop made it difficult for women to replicate the intense informal social networks of established working-class neighbourhoods, increasing the trend of 'keeping themselves to themselves'.[18] Young men and women purchased new specialty magazines related to hobbies, from *The Motor Cycle Book for Boys* (fortnightly) to *Handcraft Series* (monthly), presumably devoting time to the hobbies as well as the reading.[19] Margaret Burnside's mother mixed private leisure with enjoyment of the street scene outside her Glasgow tenement: 'one of the things my mother liked to do was sit at the room window and do her knitting. And she was very good at knitting or reading. She'd look up and watch all the folk'.[20]

A number of domestic leisure activities shaded into the commercial sector. A Merseyside survey found that about two-thirds of a sample of working-class men and women read a newspaper, magazine or work of fiction in a given week, in part reflecting the legacy of decades of compulsory education.[21] Publishers responded to working-class demand for 'books' by offering cheap magazines and paperback short stories for separate male and female audiences. In contrast to the men's pirates and highwaymen, the publisher of *My Weekly* solicited 'strong love stories of the novelette type, and all subjects of feminine interest . . . All contributions should make their appeal to the working classes'.[22] Despite the gender-specific reading material, some families shared an interest in books. On winter evenings in Mary Gourish's family, 'if we weren't goin' out anywhere the whole family was round the fire, everybody's nose stuck in the book'.[23] Not everyone was a reader, however. In one Manchester household a passion for reading attracted criticism: 'I was always in trouble for reading. "Get your nose out of that book! Put some coal on the fire" '.[24]

Reading was not the only option for those who preferred to stay at home. By the 1930s radio provided an alternative to public leisure for many working men and women: 'We don't bother to go out on a Saturday night when the winter programmes begin. We just settle down by the fire'.[25] The cost of radio sets dropped dramatically in the 1930s, and purchases on credit enabled most working-class households to afford a wireless set and to tune in to the BBC or, where available, foreign services such as Radio Luxembourg.[26] By 1939 over 70 per cent of UK households had radio licences. However, this left about a third of working-class households without radios, as a Merseyside survey noted: 'A clergyman working in one of the poorest parishes in the city declares that there is hardly a set in his district'.[27] Regional differences reflected both the lack of programming in some rural areas and relative affluence of growing areas. In the Midlands 80 per cent of households had radio, while only 61 per cent of Scottish households held wireless licences.[28] Even those without their own sets, though, could listen in pubs or gather in groups around a single radio.[29]

Working-class listeners had strong preferences for entertainment programmes. In one survey 82.5 per cent of working-class respondents listed variety programmes as their favourite type (somewhat higher than the almost two-thirds of the wealthiest respondents who also preferred variety).[30] Dance and light music found enthusiastic audiences as well. A labourer reported inviting another couple to play cards or dominoes in his home: 'If there is a variety or dance band on the wireless we turn it on'.[31] Rowntree's survey of York found that one group of mostly working-class listeners spent 72 per cent of their listening time tuned in to variety, light or dance music and the children's hour.[32] Talks and religious programmes were less universally popular, but sport gained a strong following. On Sundays working-class audiences embraced the light programming on Radio Luxembourg, in contrast to the dour fare presented by the BBC. The labourer who listened to dance music with friends during the week tuned in to foreign stations on Sunday: 'After tea we roll up the carpet, find a foreign station on the wireless giving a dance band, and we dance most of the evening'. The 1.30 p.m. Sunday broadcast on the 'Lux' of *Littlewood's Pools Programme* was the most popular weekly broadcast in one study of York listeners.[33]

Commercialized leisure

While reading often meant buying books, magazines or newspapers, and most radio listeners purchased a wireless set, it was leisure activities such as cinema, dance halls and sport that became big business in this period. The cinema grew rapidly. By the start of the First World War British cinema goers purchased about 7 million tickets per week. The war saw a huge spike in attendance, which exceeded 20 million per week in 1917. Though a tax on tickets and the economic downturn of the early 1920s helped dampen this runaway demand, average weekly ticket sales reached the 20-million mark again in 1925 and remained between 17 and 20 million until the eve of the Second World War.[34] One survey found that 90 per cent of wage-earning Manchester girls attended the cinema at least once a week, and a third went twice a week or more.[35] As one woman recalled of her leisure: 'It was always the cinema'.[36]

In the early years cinema appealed primarily to working-class audiences, particularly to adult women and youths of both sexes. In 1917 an enquiry into cinema found: 'it is most popular in the poorest districts, and is attended by a very large number of children and young people'. Even after the advent of the talkies at the end of the 1920s and the expansion of cinemas in affluent suburbs, a 1934 study found that 80 per cent of cinema goers sat in cheap seats (costing under 1s.).[37] Young working-class men and women attended more regularly than did middle-class youths. A comparison of apprentices with secondary school students revealed 64 per cent of boy apprentices attended weekly, compared to 38 per cent of secondary school boys.[38] While working youths flocked to evening shows, working-class women attended whenever they could squeeze out the time. A London study found that 'Women mainly attend the afternoon performances. It is no uncommon sight to see women slipping into the cinema for an hour, after they have finished their shopping and before the children come home from school'.[39] Many adult men stayed away from the cinemas, as Rowntree's York research found: 'of the adults about 75 per cent are women'.[40] Sid Cove recalled the attitude of his South London parents to going to the pictures between the wars: 'My mum loved it but my dad'd sooner have a drink. My dad'd sooner have a pint'.[41]

Though the film industry more successfully wooed middle-class audiences in the 1930s, the experience and preferences of audiences remained segregated by class. One study of a small southern city in 1936 found: 'The middle and working-classes in a small town go to different cinemas as a rule'.[42] Ticket prices and amenities distinguished different venues. Working-class people either sat in the cheaper seats at newer, fancier cinemas, or they attended the local cheap cinemas, known as 'fleapits' or 'bughutches', for obvious reasons. A Manchester woman recalled the Coliseum in Ardwick, which sold tickets for as little as 2d. Usherettes would spray disinfectant in the air, and 'if it was foggy the fog'd come seeping in and you couldn't see . . . You could hardly see the screen for cigarette smoke sometimes'.[43] Taste also differed by class. The manager of a local 'fleapit' noted: 'Action, horror, low-brow comedy, and musicals, if not too elaborate are what we go for here'. Middle-class audiences embraced dramas and romance more than workers did, and they flocked to both American and British films, while working-class viewers had little patience for the latter. A survey of exhibitors in working-class cinemas noted in 1937: 'exhibitors of this category complain of "old school tie" standards inherent in so many British films. They describe "the horse-laughs" with which the Oxford accents of supposed crooks are greeted . . . English films are either too high-brow (in the Bloomsbury sense) or else too stupid for their audiences'.[44]

The films themselves were only part of the attraction for working-class audiences. Those living in cramped housing sought the warmth, space and elaborate architecture of the newer cinemas: 'you'd be taken out of your . . .

miserable environment for two or three hours, go to this lovely palace and sit in a comfortable seat'.[45] Going to the pictures was often a group activity for young working-class men and women. Sid Cove frequented the Gaumont Palace in Peckham: 'in the winter, when it's cold, you're in a warm building and it's a place for meeting your friends'.[46] In the local Lambeth fleapit, 'all the lads would meet and they could have a laugh or a lark, where they could shout out' during the film. Even at the nicer Trocadero, Elephant and Castle, 'The kids on the top were dreadful. Still shouting, still calling out'. On the other hand, courting couples sought out the darkness and relative privacy of the cinema. 'When you went in the evening time with your young man, you all wanted a seat at the back. You didn't want to be at the front where they were all shouting'.[47] Some theatres offered courting couples double seats in the back row: 'We used to walk, when we were courting, all the way to the Grand and sit in the double seats'.[48]

Working-class youth also filled the new dance halls. A Manchester woman born in 1909 recalled: 'my sister met her future husband at the dance hall in Chorlton. Oh! it was the picking-up place'.[49] The popularity of American jazz and dance styles, beginning during the First World War and exploding in the war's aftermath, drove the construction of commercial dance halls to meet the demand for large, affordable venues. By six years after the armistice, some 11,000 dance halls and night clubs had opened, and in 1925 large dance 'palaises' appeared in the major towns.[50] Young working-class men and women dominated the dance halls, as Robert Roberts recalled: 'In the explosive dancing boom after the war, the young from sixteen to twenty-five flocked into the dance halls by the hundred thousand . . . youth at every level of the manual working class, from the bound apprentice to the "scum of the slum", fox-trotted through the new bliss in each other's arms'.[51] While some halls enforced decorum and maintained order carefully, in others fights often broke out among rival groups of young men. In one Salford district, 'There was a big dance-hall near by called "The Jig", but the fights there were incredible'.[52] For many working-class couples, engagement or marriage put a stop to visits to the dance hall, leaving the halls to courting couples and those hoping to find a companion.[53]

Young working-class men often went to the cinema and dance hall, but as they got older their participation in these activities tended to wane. Their interest in sport generally did not falter, however, and commercialized sport grew in the inter-war period by appealing to men of all ages. Football gates grew substantially. Average crowds at First Division matches increased from 23,000 in 1913–14 to 30,000 in 1938–9, and men who could not afford the 1s. or 1s. 6d. tickets to attend a first-class match watched local clubs. A North Manchester resident recalls the popularity of the Miles Platting Swifts and Manchester North End clubs. His father 'never went to the City, or Manchester (United). Quite honestly I don't think a lot of people could afford it'.[54] In Wales the phenomenal popularity of Rugby Union weathered the economic slump, as crowds remained large throughout the 1930s.[55] Working-class followers of Rugby League clung stubbornly to the code, supporting dozens of clubs, despite its failure to catch on beyond a narrow band of northern England. Professional boxing also grew in the inter-war period, and young working-class spectators filled small, overcrowded halls in London and other large towns nearly every night. Working-class men and boys even followed cricket, despite the sharp class distinctions of the first-class game.[56]

Two new commercialized forms of sport, dog racing and speedway, developed large working-class followings in the inter-war period. The 1926 construction of the first greyhound track designed for mechanical hare-coursing heralded a dizzying expansion. The 'poor man's racecourse' offered on-course betting, cheap admission, evening races, and arenas in or near working-class districts (unlike the horses, which ran in the countryside during working hours).[57] In 1932 over 20 million attended racing at 187 tracks. In the late 1930s one observer commented: 'Uncounted numbers attend the score of London dog tracks which provide 2,000 nights' greyhound racing a year'.[58] The greyhounds often shared facilities with speedway – dirt-track motorbike racing. Speedway arrived in Britain from Austrailia in 1927 and also rapidly attracted a large following. The largest matches may have drawn as many as 80,000 spectators, though attendance figures for speedway are unreliable. Unusual among working-class spectator sports, speedway attracted women as well as men.[59]

Paying spectators drove the growth of these commercial sports, but many who did not pay to attend matches still participated in the culture of sport. Newspapers catered to mass interest in sport. The football specials, appearing by 6.00 on Saturday evening and often printed on coloured paper, offered followers first news of results and full coverage of matches.[60] The BBC broadcast a wide variety of sporting events, offering live coverage of rugby, cricket, the FA Cup Final, the Derby and even tennis from Wimbledon in 1927.[61] In addition to informal games in streets and open spaces, sports clubs under a variety of sponsors organized participation. Pubs sponsored football clubs, and matches drew crowds of spectators: 'it was quite a Sunday afternoon entertainment. The teams had followers, gangs, and chaps that went in the pub that didn't play football . . . they used to shout the team on'.[62] In Bolton, elementary schools, Sunday schools and mills organized leagues of girls and women for rounders. One Bolton woman recalled being 'one of those children who trailed about week after week to rounders' as her mother played on a mill team.[63] Cycling clubs attracted working-class men and women in large numbers. The daughter of a Manchester brass finisher, 'did a lot of cycling in those days [the 1930s], cos, it was safe you see'.[64] The club organized by the socialist *Clarion* boasted over 8,000 members in 1936.[65] Pubs, working-men's clubs and employers also organized angling clubs, but unlike cycling, fishing remained the preserve of men. Competitions drew thousands of fishermen, as in 1926 in Birmingham, when 3,800 anglers competed, stretching 35 km (22 miles) along the river.[66]

Participants in fishing competitions spiced up the proceedings by wagering on the outcome, and gambling remained central to the appeal of sport in working-class communities. In Manchester, 'The daily bet was a way of life, and appealed to women as well as men'.[67] A government committee suggested in 1923 that in most companies with 20 or more employees, at least one took bets for a bookmaker.[68] The football pools began in 1923 and rapidly exploded in popularity. As one gambler noted, 'I think there's a chance of winning a good sum for a small investment. It is better than bookies' coupons'.[69] By the end of the period, some 10 million gamblers played the pools and often working-class families filled out the coupons together, making Wednesday evenings 'family night'.[70] The pools and other wagers offered both the chance 'to win a decent sum' and a diversion for those who studied the forms and discussed their prospects. Even unemployed men scraped together 6d. or 1s. to play, and the Pilgrim Trust found evidence of their interest in 'the dirty and torn sports columns of the papers in Public Libraries, with the rest of the paper untouched (apart from advertisements of vacant jobs)'.[71]

While gambling ranked 'first as an all-round working-class leisure interest', outside the working class gambling was far different.[72] As historian Ross McKibbin notes, 'street betting did not take place in leafy avenues'.[73] More generally, the experience of sport differed across class boundaries. Middle-class sportsmen and women played Rugby Union, tennis, squash or golf. Middle-class followers attended matches less frequently than working-class men, but they did watch golf, tennis and Rugby Union. These sports were distinctly middle class, as dog racing, speedway and Rugby League remained working class.[74] Cricket attracted interest across class lines more than other sports, yet class differences remained powerfully entrenched in 'the national game'. Working-class spectators flocked to league cricket matches in the North and Midlands, where drinking, gambling and noisy local patriotism fitted well with working-class culture, and the one-day matches began at 2.00 p.m. and lasted only five hours.[75] County cricket, on the other hand, held matches during working hours, maintained its traditional exclusivity, and enforced strict boundaries between middle-class 'amateurs' and working-class professionals.[76] Though many working men followed cricket, football remained the quintessential working-class sport, for boys and young men as players, for young and older men as spectators, and for all who participated in the pools. Though *The Times* coverage of the King's attendance at the Cup Final in 1914 declared 'professional football of the best kind is no longer regarded as a spectacle suitable only for the proletariat', football crowds and followers remained overwhelmingly working class.[77]

New commercialized leisure opportunities diverted money and attention away from the long-established local pub, but drinking remained central to many working people's leisure. A Mass Observation study of pubs in the 1930s lamented the declining role of the pub in working-class life at the expense of 'football pools, the cinema, the radio and the *Daily Mirror*'. Yet the survey noted, 'The pub is a centre of social activities . . . for the ordinary pub goer the main scene of social life'.[78] For many adult working-class men, the cinema or dance hall held little appeal compared to a glass at the 'local'. A Manchester woman who grew up in the 1930s recalled of her father: 'He liked going to the pub . . . and have a drink. And that was his life really'.[79] Regulars gathered in the vault or tap room, which was off-limits to women: 'The vault is working class, masculine'.[80] Women were more welcome in the lounge or parlour, the nicest room in the pub. Attitudes toward women's drinking in pubs varied widely, but many women accompanied their husbands to the pub on Saturday night, as one woman recalled of her parents: 'They might go for a drink, you know, Saturday night, cos there was a pub on every corner'.[81] Other times, women went to pubs without their husbands, as a Salford woman reported of an outing with two other women: 'we called in the Nodding Donkey for a gill'.[82] The continued importance of pubs in working-class leisure compounded the inconvenience of new housing estates where drinking spots were rare. A resident of a Bolton estate reported that on the weekends many men 'make tracks to their old localities'.[83]

Though leisure choices abounded in established working-class neighbourhoods, the habit of a week's holiday at the seaside spread from Lancashire and the West Riding into other regions, particularly London and the Midlands. One survey estimated that half the London working class took a holiday in the mid-1930s. Resorts invested in larger and more elaborate facilities in the inter-war period. For example, the New Palace Pier at St Leonards boasted a wide range of amusements including a dance floor for more than a thousand revellers, and 'the most extensive and modern range of Automatic Machines on the South Coast'.[84] Many workers though, particularly in depressed regions, could not afford a week's holiday. In Oldham, where the tradition of saving through a holiday club was well established, such clubs dispersed £138,571 in 1933, a far cry from the 1925 total of £247,804. An Ashton newspaper reported in 1930: 'the number of people spending the Wakes at home was considerably greater than in previous years . . . in the present unsettled state of trade they dare not spend their Wakes savings on seaside pleasures'.[85] Many who could not afford a holiday still made it to the seaside or at least the nearby countryside for day trips, often organized through pubs, friendly societies or other organizations. On the August bank holiday, 'charabancs arrive in Southend crammed to overflowing with East Londoners'.[86] Even day excursions were beyond the reach of some families, particularly those suffering from unemployment. A Salford man, the son of an unemployed labourer, recalled that his family never went on these trips: 'The first time I saw the seaside was after I left school. It was Blackpool'.

Associations, clubs and the regulation of leisure

Alongside the new commercial leisure opportunities, a well-established tradition of working-class leisure organization persisted throughout this period. Working men's clubs attracted drinkers, but most of the 2,626 clubs associated with the Working Men's Club and Institute Union in 1929 offered a broader range of activities. The secretary of the Union, Robert Chapman, described opportunities including 'indoor and outdoor games, concerts, lectures, participation and rivalry in flower and vegetable shows, glee parties, choral societies . . .'. Unions and socialist organizations sponsored leisure activities including youth groups, as one Labour newspaper reported: 'Football, cycling and rambling clubs have been formed, theatrical entertainments, debates and visits to places of interest have been quite numerous'.[87] Co-operative societies grew, with membership soaring to 8.5 million in 1939, and many supported leisure and sport clubs. The Leicester Co-operative Society had its own sports ground with cricket squares, tennis courts, bowling greens and football pitches.[88] Summer holiday camps sponsored by co-operatives also proved popular. When the Coventry society founded such a camp in 1930, it quickly filled to capacity in the summer. Organizers reported, 'bookings for these periods have passed our expectations'.[89] Though it was difficult for many working-class women to find time for structured leisure activities, those who managed to join the Women's Co-operative Guild could enjoy a variety of leisure pursuits. At one Glasgow guild, 'we had a dance and we had hot pie and peas and a wee dance. And we had speakers or somebody comin' demonstrating to us'.[90]

Established union, co-operative or club organizations tell only part of the story of working-class mutualism during this period. Countless small, often temporary, associations grew in working-class communities. For example, in Bolton a pub regular organized a club to raise funds for an outing. Members contributed to the pool, and the men sought donations from the publican and his suppliers. Eventually, the group chose as a destination a pub in the nearby countryside and enjoyed 'an afternoon at bowls, tea afterwards, and then . . . the real business of soaking'. They returned in time for a closing drink at their own pub.[91] More lasting clubs organized sports competitions. In Manchester 400 football and hockey teams and 150 cricket teams used the city parks in 1936–7.[92] In many cases workers started their own sports clubs to avoid participation in established groups dominated by middle-class enthusiasts. When Benny Rothman formed a working-class rambling club in Manchester, 'the rambling clubs that already existed in the North . . . were mainly middle class in origin and outlook . . . The ordinary working class ramblers were shunned, they were looked upon as dirt', in part because of their lack of fancy gear.[93]

These local clubs formed easily in established working-class neighbourhoods where ties among residents and a strong tradition of mutualism fostered cooperation. On new estates efforts to develop such associations met with mixed results.[94] In both types of neighbourhood, organizations sponsored by philanthropic and religious bodies supplemented mutual associations. In this period government took over many of the social and philanthropic activities that Victorian churches had undertaken, but sponsorship of youth movements remained a vibrant arena for religious philanthropy. The Becontree estate boasted 'seven Cub packs, seven Scout troops, one Rover crew, seven Brownie companies, eight Guide companies and one Ranger company', most linked to Sunday schools and religious organizations.[95] Employers also continued to provide facilities and often sponsorship for leisure activities. The Pilkington Brothers glassmaking company sponsored a dozen rugby teams, one of which, the St Helens Recs, finished as Rugby League runners up in 1927.[96]

Though sponsors had their own goals in offering leisure opportunities, working-class participants helped shape the activities. In some cases employers sponsored sports clubs that were 'run by the members for the members; the company does not interfere or dictate'.[97] A relatively successful club for boys in Ancoats allowed the more senior boys to hold dances without the presence of club officials, who noted 'the Club may gain an exaggerated reputation of frivolity but, after all, dancing is . . . more or less . . . a necessity with modern youth'. Sponsors that failed to provide dances, sport or outdoor activity found diminishing audiences. One Manchester club abandoned the Boys' Brigade company and its required drill and Bible class attendance, noting 'its methods had ceased to appeal to the lads of this district'. Instead, they offered billiards, table tennis, draughts and films.[98] The draw of outdoor activities helped drive the growth of the Boy Scouts and Girl Guides, which reached a combined membership of nearly a million in 1937. Though these groups drew primarily middle-class youths, some distinctly working-class troops survived. In many cases the Scout or Guides uniform formed a badge of non-conformity in working-class neighbourhoods, where 'Courage was needed to face the ridicule . . . to wear a Scout kit in the rougher streets'.[99] Even in these movements, leaders abandoned proposed prohibitions on Scouts and Guides marching together and on Guides camping outside, and toned down imperial ideology to appeal to the sensibilities of potential members.[100]

Despite the willingness of some sponsors of philanthropic leisure to compromise with the desires of working-class participants, criticism of popular leisure remained common among religious leaders, middle-class reformers and some socialists. Joan Harley, a social investigator who studied Manchester wage-earning girls' leisure in the 1930s, lamented that her subjects devoted so much time to the cinema and dance hall: 'in so far as young girl wage-earners cannot discriminate between excess and moderation, these activities are to say the least of it not beneficial to them'.[101] An Edinburgh religious leader argued, 'to love betting is to admit a poison into the heart which will inevitably destroy all that makes life fine and fair'.[102] In *The Co-operative News* of 1936, a commentator urged that leisure, 'should not be "dead" time, wasted in empty amusements and listless loafing'.[103]

For the most part, these complaints had little impact on working-class leisure. Even when laws proscribed popular activities, the police had difficulty limiting them. Working-class youths used the streets as places to stand in groups, play games and promenade in the 'monkey runs'. Police efforts to constrain these activities sometimes led to arrests, but could not take control of the streets. In Salford, when young people on parade in Eccles New Road spotted plainclothes police, they would temporarily disappear down side streets: 'We could spot them a mile off and we'd be off down the back, down Winford Street. We'd come back when they'd gone'.[104] Legal prohibitions on working-class gambling proved impossible to enforce. Bookmakers and gambling 'schools' posted lookouts to warn of police. Police raids took these lookouts into custody rather than the bookmakers themselves, as one police detective-sergeant recalled: 'The bookie was very, very rarely caught . . . the feller that was put out, put outside, planted out-side for the police to come . . . would be caught and taken down to the headquarters'. Bribery also helped protect gambling operations from police crackdowns, but the scale of working-class gambling and its legitimacy in the eyes of the community made it impossible to enforce legal prohibitions.[105]

Conclusion

Between 1914 and 1939 many working-class Britons enjoyed expanded leisure with the spread of paid vacations and further reductions in working hours. New ways of taking advantage of this time appeared, as millions attended cinemas and dance halls, listened to the wireless and read new magazines. The home grew more important as a leisure environment, par-ticularly for those working people who moved to new estates. Yet many significant patterns of working-class leisure developed in the Victorian period persisted well into the twentieth century. The streets remained essential leisure spaces, for walking, talking and playing. For many working-class men, the pub held its appeal, and new opportunities could not replace a drink at the local. Men and women enjoyed 'a bit of a flutter' as football coupons supplemented established gambling patterns in working-class communities. Victorian innovations such as the working-class holiday and professional sport reached new audiences. Women still struggled to carve out time and resources for leisure, while men's enjoyment remained privileged in household economies. Vibrant street life, dance halls, 'fleapit' cinemas, small-scale betting on horses or football, and the corner pub all characterized the particular leisure culture of the early twentieth-century British working class.

Notes

1 A. Davies, *Leisure, Gender and Poverty: Working-Class Culture in Salford and Manchester, 1900–1939* (Buckingham: Open University Press, 1992), 107, 90, 106, 103.

2 S.G. Jones, *Workers at Play: A Social and Economic History of Leisure 1918–1939* (London: Routledge & Kegan Paul, 1986), 16–20, 111–12.

3 A.J. McIvor, 'Manual work, technology, and industrial health, 1918–39', *Medical History* 31 (1987), 180.

4 Davies, *Leisure, Gender and Poverty*, 50, 75, 85.

5 D. Fowler, 'Teenage consumers? Young wage-earners and leisure in Manchester, 1919–1939', in A. Davies and S. Fielding, eds, *Workers' Worlds: Cultures and Communities in Manchester and Salford, 1880–1939* (Manchester: Manchester University Press, 1992), 134–7.

6 R. Roberts, *The Classic Slum: Salford Life in the First Quarter of the Century* (Harmondsworth: Penguin, 1973), 49–50.

7 Jones, *Workers at Play*, 119.

8 R. McKibbin, *Classes and Cultures: England 1918–1951* (Oxford: Oxford University Press, 1998), 152.

9 Davies, *Leisure, Gender and Poverty*, 99; Fowler, 'Teenage consumers', 147.

10 N. Gray, *The Worst of Times: An Oral History of the Great Depression in Britain* (Totowa, NJ: Barnes & Noble, 1985), 87.

11 J. Faley, *Up Oor Close: Memories of Domestic Life in Glasgow Tenements, 1910–1945* (Wendlebury: White Cockade, 1990), 118.

12 Davies, *Leisure, Gender and Poverty*, 135–6.

13 Ibid., 124–5.

14 J. White, *The Worst Street in North London: Campbell Bunk, Islington, between the Wars* (London: Routledge & Kegan Paul, 1986), 89.

15 Faley, *Up Oor Close*, 90–1.

16 C. Langhamer, *Women's Leisure in England 1920–1960* (Manchester: Manchester University Press, 2000), 175.

17 J. Bourke, *Working-Class Cultures in Britain 1890–1960: Gender, Class and Ethnicity* (London: Routledge, 1994), 87–8; A. Olechnowicz, *Working-Class Housing in England between the Wars: The Becontree Estate* (Oxford: Clarendon Press, 1997), 9.

18 McKibbin, *Classes and Cultures*, 197–8; A. Hughes and K. Hunt, 'A culture transformed? Women's lives in Wythenshawe in the 1930s', in Davies and Fielding, eds, *Workers' Worlds*, 92–3; M. Tebbutt, *Women's Talk? A Social History of 'Gossip' in Working-Class Neighbourhoods, 1880–1960* (Aldershot: Scolar Press, 1995), 153–4.

19 Fowler, 'Teenage consumers', 145.

20 Faley, *Up Oor Close*, 114.

21 J. McAleer, *Popular Reading and Publishing in Britain 1914–50* (Oxford: Clarendon Press, 1992), 78.

22 McKibbin, *Classes and Cultures*, 495–6, 527.

23 Faley, *Up Oor Close*, 76.

24 Langhamer, *Women's Leisure*, 86.

25 P. Scannell and D. Cardiff, *A Social History of British Broadcasting, vol. I: 1922–1939: Serving the Nation* (Oxford: Basil Blackwell, 1991), 364.

26 Ibid., 359, 361; A. Briggs, *The History of Broadcasting in the United Kingdom, vol. II: The Golden Age of Wireless* (Oxford: Oxford University Press, 1995), 235–6.

27 Davies, *Leisure, Gender and Poverty*, 40; McKibbin, *Classes and Cultures*, 457.

28 M. Pegg, *Broadcasting and Society* (London: Croom Helm, 1983), 7, 12–13.

29 Jones, *Workers at Play*, 107–8.

30 Briggs, *Golden Age of Wireless*, 253.

31 Scannell and Cardiff, *Social History of British Broadcasting*, 364.

32 B.S. Rowntree, *Poverty and Progress: A Second Social Survey of York* (London: Longmans, Green, 1941), 408.

33 McKibbin, *Classes and Cultures*, 462–5; Scannell and Cardiff, *Social History of British Broadcasting*, 364; Rowntree, *Poverty and Progress*, 409.

34 N. Hiley, ' "Let's go to the pictures": the British cinema audience in the 1920s and 1930s', *Journal of Popular British Cinema* 2 (1999), 40–5.

35 D. Fowler, *The First Teenagers: The Lifestyle of Young Wage-Earners in Interwar Britain* (London: Woburn Press, 1995), 116–17.

36 Langhamer, *Women's Leisure*, 166.

37 J. Richards, *The Age of the Dream Palace: Cinema and Society in Britain 1930–1939* (London: Routledge, 1984), 12; S. Rowson, 'A statistical survey of the cinema industry in Great Britain in 1934', *Journal of the Royal Statistical Society* 99 (1936), 115.

38 Fowler, *First Teenagers*, 116.

39 Langhamer, *Women's Leisure*, 165.

40 Rowntree, *Poverty and Progress*, 413.

41 M. O'Brien and A. Eyles, eds, *Enter the Dream House: Memories of Cinemas in South London from the Twenties to the Sixties* (London: Museum of the Moving Image, 1993), 31.

42　Richards, *Age of the Dream Palace*, 28.

43　Langhamer, *Women's Leisure*, 60–1; Richards, *Age of the Dream Palace*, 19.

44　Richards, *Age of the Dream Palace*, 29, 24–5.

45　Langhamer, *Women's Leisure*, 62.

46　O'Brien and Eyles, *Enter the Dream House*, 30–1.

47　Ibid., 27.

48　Fowler, *First Teenagers*, 118.

49　Langhamer, *Women's Leisure*, 117.

50　McKibbin, *Classes and Cultures*, 390–5; Jones, *Workers at Play*, 44–5.

51　Roberts, *The Classic Slum*, 232.

52　E. MacColl, 'Theatre of action, Manchester', in R. Samuel, E. McColl and S. Cosgrove, eds, *Theatres of the Left 1880–1935* (London: Routledge & Kegan Paul, 1985), 233; Davies, *Leisure, Gender and Poverty*, 93.

53　Langhamer, *Women's Leisure*, 167.

54　S.G. Jones, *Sport, Politics and the Working Class* (Manchester: Manchester University Press, 1988), 45; Davies, *Leisure, Gender and Poverty*, 38.

55　R. Holt, *Sport and the British: A Modern History* (Oxford: Clarendon Press, 1989), 252.

56　McKibbin, *Classes and Cultures*, 332–5, 352–3, 366.

57　M. Clapson, *A Bit of a Flutter: Popular Gambling and English Society, c.1823–1961* (Manchester: Manchester University Press, 1992), 144.

58　Jones, *Sport, Politics and the Working Class*, 47; McKibbin, *Classes and Cultures*, 363.

59　J. Williams, ' "A wild orgy of speed": responses to speedway in Britain before the Second World War', *The Sports Historian* 19 (1999), 6, 8–9.

60　J. Hill, *Sport, Leisure and Culture in Twentieth-Century Britain* (Basingstoke: Palgrave, 2002), 45–6.

61　Scannell and Cardiff, *Social History of British Broadcasting*, 282.

62　Davies, *Leisure, Gender and Poverty*, 39.

63　L. Oliver, ' "No hard-brimmed hats or hat-pins please": Bolton women cotton-workers and the game of rounders, 1911–1939', *Oral History* 25 (1997), 44.

64　Langhamer, *Women's Leisure*, 78.

65　Jones, *Sport, Politics and the Working Class*, 108.

66 McKibbin, *Classes and Cultures*, 357–8.

67 C. Chinn, *Better Betting with a Decent Feller: Bookmaking, Betting and the British Working Class, 1750–1990* (New York: Harvester Wheatsheaf, 1991), 144.

68 Jones, *Workers at Play*, 39.

69 Clapson, *A Bit of a Flutter*, 166.

70 McKibbin, *Classes and Cultures*, 374.

71 Davies, *Leisure, Gender and Poverty*, 161; Pilgrim Trust, *Men Without Work: A Report Made to the Pilgrim Trust* ([1938]; New York, Greenwood Press, 1968), 98.

72 Mass Observation, *The Pub and the People: A Worktown Study* ([1943]; Welwyn: Seven Dials Press, 1970), 269.

73 McKibbin, *Classes and Cultures*, 374.

74 J. Benson, *The Rise of Consumer Society in Britain, 1880–1980* (London: Longman, 1994), 130–3.

75 J. Hill, 'League cricket in the North and Midlands, 1900–1940', in R. Holt, ed., *Sport and the Working Class in Modern Britain* (Manchester: Manchester University Press, 1990), 121, 130–4.

76 Holt, *Sport and the British*, 178–9; McKibbin, *Classes and Cultures*, 333–7.

77 Hill, *Sport, Leisure and Culture*, 47; Benson, *Rise of Consumer Society*, 134.

78 Mass Observation, *Pub and the People*, 76, 311.

79 Langhamer, *Women's Leisure*, 154.

80 Mass Observation, *Pub and the People*, 155.

81 Langhamer, *Women's Leisure*, 154.

82 Davies, *Leisure, Gender and Poverty*, 64.

83 Mass Observation, *Pub and the People*, 331.

84 J.K. Walton, *The British Seaside: Holidays and Resorts in the Twentieth Century* (Manchester: Manchester University Press, 2000), 58, 108.

85 Jones, *Workers at Play*, 28.

86 Hill, *Sport, Leisure and Culture*, 79.

87 Jones, *Workers at Play*, 72, 144.

88 Jones, *Sport, Politics and the Working Class*, 75, 112.

89 C. Ward and D. Hardy, *Goodnight Campers! The History of the British Holiday Camp* (London: Mansell, 1986), 37.

90 Faley, *Up Oor Close*, 126; Langhamer, *Women's Leisure*, 170.

91 Mass Observation, *Pub and the People*, 270–1.

92 S.G. Jones, 'Working-class sport in Manchester between the wars', in R. Holt, ed., *Sport and the Working Class in Modern Britain* (Manchester: Manchester University Press, 1990), 75.

93 Jones, *Workers at Play*, 65.

94 Hill, *Sport, Leisure and Culture*, 136.

95 J. Cox, *The English Churches in a Secular Society: Lambeth, 1870–1930* (Oxford: Oxford University Press, 1982), 201; McKibbin, *Classes and Cultures*, 192.

96 Jones, *Sport, Politics and the Working Class*, 85, 133.

97 Ibid., 63.

98 Fowler, *First Teenagers*, 141.

99 T.M. Proctor, '(Uni)forming youth: Girl Guides and Boy Scouts in Britain, 1908–1939', *History Workshop Journal* 45 (1998), 118.

100 A. Warren, ' "Mothers for the Empire"? The Girl Guides Association in Britain, 1909–1939', in J.A. Mangan, ed., *Making Imperial Mentalities: Socialisation and British Imperialism* (Manchester: Manchester University Press, 1990), 102.

101 Fowler, 'Teenage consumers', 137.

102 Jones, *Workers at Play*, 172.

103 Ibid., 167.

104 Davies, *Leisure, Gender and Poverty*, 106.

105 A. Davies, 'The Police and the people: gambling in Salford, 1900–1939', *The Historical Journal* 34 (1991), 91.

CHAPTER TWELVE

Patriotism, politics and identity

Richard Hoggart, in an analysis of working-class culture based primarily on his childhood in inter-war Leeds, noted: 'an inherited assumption of national superiority', as seen, for example, in the phrase 'England is the most important country in the world'. Hoggart reported a widespread fondness for the monarchy that caused 'a great many women in the working-classes to feel well-disposed towards Royalty'. Despite these observations, Hoggart insisted (unconvincingly) that 'Working-class people are not, we know, particularly patriotic', emphasizing the strength of local identities over national or imperial pride. Residents knew the topography of neighbourhoods and communities 'in intimate detail . . . as a group of tribal areas. Pitt Street is certainly one of ours; just as certainly as Prince Consort Street next to it is not, is over the boundary in another parish'.[1]

These strong local identities merged into a wider sense of belonging to the working class. A 'recognizably working-class life' bound together those who knew, 'from the ever-present evidence in the close, huddled, intimate conditions of life, that we are, in fact, all in the same position'. This identity found its corollary in suspicion of 'them', of 'anyone from the classes outside' or 'the world of the bosses'. These 'aren't really to be trusted'. Instead, one should 'only "trust yer own sort" '. Yet this class identity still did not translate into interest in party politics: 'As to politics . . . as far as they can see . . . "Politics never did anybody any good" '. Despite this disinterest, working-class men and women developed strategies for dealing with power and authority: 'their debunking-art, their putting-a-finger-to-the-nose at authority by deflating it, by guying it'.[2] Hoggart's reflections on the working-class culture of his youth point to the complexity of working-class identity and politics in this period.

Patriotism, nationalism and empire

In 1914 patriotic enthusiasm for the war effort bred violence against those seen as outside the patriotic nation. In some cases eager volunteers coerced reluctant co-workers into signing up. In the West Midlands workers staged a charivari, taking the shoes and stockings of those who had not yet volunteered, placing the victims in wheelbarrows, and rolling them in a procession to the recruiting station.[3] Around the country, riots targeted German-owned shops.[4] In Salford a crowd of several thousand surrounded a butcher's shop owned by Herman Pratt, and 'surging forward, broke down the shop door or scrambled through the window . . . some smashed the kitchen windows and hurled the crockery and furniture into the street, others mounted the stairs and began to throw ornaments from the first floor into the street . . . the premises were completely wrecked'.[5]

Working-class patriotism survived the war. A 1929 school trip to the North East Coast Exhibition in Newcastle that included an 'African village' led young Mary Wade to feel lucky, 'Despite all the poverty around us, perhaps this was our first injection of a superiority complex . . . surely we were very fortunate!' Potent symbols reinforced this national pride. A boy who grew up in Shadwell in the 1920s recalled his mother's 'personal' patriotism: 'She believed in the monarchy, the church and the Empire because she saw herself as part of it'.[6] In 1924 J.H. Thomas, a former engine cleaner, railway fireman and union leader who became a Labour MP, claimed the British 'constitution, so broad, so wide, so democratic . . . and the Empire which provides it must be maintained'.[7]

National ceremonies, such as the 1935 silver jubilee of George V or the coronation of George VI, celebrated the monarchy, the nation and the empire with increasingly elaborate and often newly minted 'traditions'.[8] For the 1937 coronation a letter in the *Daily Telegraph* noted: 'In the East End practically every house is gaily decorated. Families with little to spare have saved up to express their feelings of loyalty in a burst of colour'.[9] A woman who grew up in inter-war Streatham recalled Empire Day celebrations: 'we would march around the playground (or the Hall, if wet) waving Union Jacks and singing "Land of our Birth" . . . it gave us a sense of belonging'. Her sister concurred: 'We were all very fervent and patriotic and waved little Union Jacks'.[10]

Radio provided immediate and detailed coverage of royal celebrations, and planners positioned microphones to broadcast the sound of carriages, horses and cheering crowds.[11] An observation of a working-class Bristol district noted: 'The fact that millions are listening into the same programme gives them the sensation of being part of a nation in a way that was experienced rarely and for shorter periods only in the past'.[12] Music hall songs during the war championed the typical British soldier: 'You are all true blue and we're proud of you./ Tommy Atkins you're all right'.[13] A less saccharine recruiting song sung by a female performer promised rewards to those who volunteered ('took the King's shilling'): 'But on Saturday, I'm willing, if you'll only take a shilling,/ To make a man of any one of you'.[14] By the 1930s, films celebrating the empire drew mass audiences. Even young Shirley Temple, the biggest box-office draw in Britain from 1935 to 1938, made imperial films such as *Wee Willie Winkie*, in which the star played the granddaughter of a British officer on the Indian North-West Frontier.[15]

Though media celebrations of empire, monarchy and patriotism sold newspapers and drew large audiences, it is difficult to judge their impact on workers' attitudes. Some working-class men and women remained sceptical of patriotism and empire and disinterested in the spectacle of royal celebrations. The daughter of a labourer in Bristol recalled reciting a poem celebrating British overseas trade 'going to fetch you your bread and butter': 'I thought, where's my bread, where's my butter?'[16] The Streatham girl who recalled Empire Day so fondly may have been moved more by the afternoon's half-holiday than by enthusiasm for empire: 'It was a tradition in our family to go "blue-belling" on Empire Day. We would take the open-top bus to Coulsdon, and pick bluebells there'.[17] On 12 May 1937, while thousands watched in person or listened over the wireless to the coronation of George VI, others took advantage of the day without work, as one observer found in a Leeds tea shop 'filled to the last table, mostly young couples of the working class dressed in their Sunday best and enjoying the day off'. Though a poster announced the day's historic broadcast, they ignored it: 'I heard nothing but orchestral music, which no doubt came from one of their gramophone records'.[18]

Even those who celebrated monarchy and empire and felt pride in their British identity maintained a critical perspective on government policies. During the First World War workers frustrated at employer actions and commodity shortages blamed the government. Investigators reported, 'working people have a vague and uneasy feeling that the authorities are not really working in their interest'. Another government study found that workers 'attribute their inability to obtain fuel and food not so much to the actual shortage as to the entire failure on the part of the Government to obtain control and to establish machinery for more equitable distribution'.[19] Unemployment and budget cuts undermined high expectations on the part of returning servicemen, who felt the governments' promises had been broken. A poem sold by unemployed veterans reflects this sense of betrayal: 'Where are those home-fires of welcome?/ Have they all burnt away?/ Have Tommy and Jack, now they've come back,/ In the unemployment ranks to stay?'[20]

Petty interference in working-class life by a range of officials bred resentment. One observer noted, 'Inspectors of every sort and kind harry the slum dwellers'.[21] Hoggart reported: 'there exists, with some reason, a feeling among working-class people that they are often at a disadvantage, that the law is in some things readier against them than against others, and that petty laws weigh more heavily against them than against some other groups'.[22] The most offensive interference came during the slump, when the means test required those receiving unemployment benefits to submit to invasive investigations. An unemployed millwright in Derby complained: 'After the monotony I hate most the visits of the Public Assistance Officer. He is very strict and gets to know everything about us. My wife is bad all day when he comes'.[23] Despite unfulfilled promises, petty harassment and offensive regulations, though, most workers accepted the general fairness of the British political system, and embraced monarchy and empire.[24]

This sense of Britishness, however, overlapped with local and regional identities. In established neighbourhoods outsiders met suspicion and often hostility. In a Bethnal Green cul-de-sac, 'there were often fights when our gang turned on those from neighbouring streets and told them to get back where they belonged . . . Even we small girls felt this bristling pride of belonging'.[25] The narrow sense of place developed in cohesive neighbourhoods, though, coexisted with broader regional identities. Carolyn Steedman recalls her mother's pride in her Lancashire heritage: 'if you were going to be working class, then you might as well be the best that's going, and for women, Lancashire and weaving provided that . . . distinction'.[26] Sport encouraged identification with towns, counties or regions, through support for local football clubs, county cricket, or the national sides of Wales or Scotland.[27] Lancashire dialect poetry reveals a complex mix of regional and national pride. A 1923 poem by Allen Clarke, 'In Praise o' Lancashire', advertises the superiority of the 'Lanky': 'There's not a foreign market, lads,/ But what its Lanky-made . . . An' there isn't a job that's wo'th owt/ But Lancashire gan it birth'. Londoners pale in comparison: 'It weren't yore chirpin' Cockneys/ That fit up th'world wi' gear'. Yet this Lancashire identity is tied to national pride as well, as Lanky lads 'Fowt weel at Waterloo;/ An' in th' Greit European War'.[28] Migrants often struggled to find acceptance. In 1950s' Banbury, migrants who came to the town in the 1930s were still viewed as 'foreign,' as 'Scots, Irish and Welsh', or 'Those northerners'.[29] Accent and dialect reinforced and reflected regional identities, but they also enforced class difference. As the BBC advocated 'received pronunciation', working-class speech patterns, celebrated by music hall and later film stars such as Gracie Fields, signified class as well as regional distinctions.[30]

Overlapping definitions of belonging and exclusion also applied to ethnic, religious and racial divisions within the working class. At times, these differences led to violent conflict. During the First World War hostility to Jews exploded in a pitched battle in Bethnal Green involving 2,000–3,000 Jews and gentiles. One eyewitness noted: 'All sorts of weapons were used – bars of irons, flat irons, logs of wood, and pistols'.[31] In 1919 a wave of race riots targeted black residents of port cities including London, Liverpool, Glasgow, Cardiff, South Shields and Newport. These riots reflected racist attitudes and competition for work. For example, in South Shields a union official refused to allow Arab sailors to sign up with the union and get places on a ship. His words, 'Don't let these Arabs sign on for the ship. Come on you black ————— you are not going to join the ship' incited the crowd, and the violence only subsided when soldiers and a navy squad intervened.[32]

Riotous violence remained exceptional, but many workers harboured persistent hostility to those defined as outsiders, particularly Catholics, Jews and immigrants from Asia or the Caribbean. A union publication complained of 'the gradual and stealthy advance of the Asiatic in his invasion of the British labour market'.[33] A St Helens woman recalled that, 'it couldn't be proved, but jobs seemed to go to Catholics, through the influence of Catholic councillors'.[34] The football rivalry between Celtic and Rangers fed Glasgow sectarian conflict, as in April 1930 when a group of Protestant Rangers' supporters sporting orange and blue flags and other symbols provoked an attack from a mostly Catholic gang. Both sides employed bricks, bottles and sticks in the ensuing street battle.[35] Ironically, those who experienced hostility were often no more tolerant. Emmanuel Shinwell, a Jewish leader of the British Seafarers' Union, complained of 'the employment of Chinese labour . . . some of the best ships were leaving with Chinese and other coloured labour'. In Salford a crowd of both black and white sailors gathered in the union office to challenge the recruitment of a group of Arab seamen. In this case an examination of the Arab workers' records revealed them to be 'local men' and they were allowed to accept employment on the ship.[36]

This example reveals the complexity of definitions and exclusions. At times enmity divided workers along religious or racial lines, but sometimes workers ignored these differences or overcame their prejudices. In this case workers across racial and ethnic lines agreed on a definition of 'local men' that included Arab, black and white sailors. Only a few months after the pitched street battle described above, East End Jews and gentiles cooperated in forming the Stepney Central Labour Party.[37] Though in some families, Catholic/Protestant intermarriage 'was talked about as an abhorrent thing', intermarriage rates rose in the inter-war period. The *London Catholic Herald* estimated intermarriage rates at 30 to 40 per cent in 1935. Residential segregation declined as well. In 1890 seven North Manchester parishes housed nearly 40 per cent of the city's Irish residents. By 1939 less than one quarter lived in these districts.[38] Children played together in mixed neighbourhoods, as a Preston woman who grew up in the 1920s recalled: 'Religion didn't come into it, because there were quite a few Catholics round us . . . They were your neighbours and they were your friends and that was all there was to it'.[39]

Despite differences, at the workplace and in neighbourhoods working-class people shared a sense of being similar to one another but different from those higher up the social scale. Richard Hoggart describes its origin in 'a knowledge, born of living close together, that one is inescapably part of a group . . . from the feeling that life is hard, and that "our sort" will usually get "the dirty end of the stick" '.[40] It is evident in the call, from the floor of a Labour Party conference in 1918, 'that it was about time that they were represented in Parliament by . . . one who had gone through the hoop, knew what it was to go short, and to have a bath in a wash-tub'.[41] At work, distinctions among manual workers grew less pronounced as semi-skilled work proliferated and wage differentials between skilled and unskilled narrowed (while the difference between skilled manual workers' wages and lower-middle-class salaries grew).[42] A government spokesman noted in 1920: ' "class consciousness" is obliterating the distinctions between those who follow different occupations in the same works'.[43] The organizational hierarchy in large workplaces reinforced the distinction between office staff or management and 'hands', or in the view of workers, 'them and us'.[44]

From the other direction, middle-class men and women perceived a chasm between themselves and the working class. According to C.F.G. Masterman in 1922, the suburban middle class, 'hates and despises the working classes . . . partly because it has contempt for them, and partly because it has fear of them . . . Just on its borders . . . are those great masses of humanity which accept none of its standards, and maintain life on a totally different plain'.[45] Many middle-class women who entered war work served in supervisory positions. They were often acutely conscious of the differences between themselves and working-class women. Monica Cosens 'did not like the look' of the working-class women with whom she worked. Apparently, the distaste was mutual, as she recalled that when a middle-class woman like her entered 'there is a defiance in the air. She is not gently treated'.[46] While some hostility between classes grew out of interactions in the workplace or elsewhere, social distance reinforced class differences. As an Irish worker recalled of his lack of contact with middle-class Irish people, 'There was simply no meaningful contact. We stuck to our circuit and they stuck to theirs'.[47]

Though some working-class children moved into the middle class, mobility across this divide remained rare throughout the inter-war period. Some working-class parents, particularly in light of the collapse of staple industries and the threat of prolonged unemployment, began to consider white-collar work more promising for their children. The widow of a victim in a Lancashire coal disaster sought assistance to gain her son training, claiming that she had been told he would 'make a good Accountant, or he would do well in Commercial Law, or as a shorthand Typist or Architect'.[48] While these attitudes spread and movement into the middle class probably grew somewhat more common, significant barriers continued to discourage mobility across the class divide. Working-class access to secondary education increased, but only 10 per cent of working-class boys born between 1910 and 1929 attended secondary schools (compared to 4 per cent of those born between 1899 and 1910).[49] This reflects social inequalities that closed off avenues for advance, but it also reveals working-class scepticism of upward mobility and advanced education. According to Hoggart, 'there is often a mistrust of "book-learning". What good does it do you? Are you any better off (i.e. happier) as a clerk? Or as a teacher?' This was closely linked to a deep suspicion of those who no longer belonged: 'Acting beyond the ideas of the group, "acting posh", "giving y'self airs" . . . all these are much disliked'.[50] Thus, in the 1930s half of the free places in grammar schools offered to working-class children were refused.[51] It was not easy to move out of the working class, and working-class consciousness and attitudes nurtured a reluctance to do so.

Formal and informal politics

Though the inter-war period saw a dramatic increase in support for the Labour Party, working-class consciousness still did not generate a unified position in national politics. Labour increased its share of the parliamentary vote from just above 7 per cent in 1910 to 23 per cent in 1918 and nearly 38 per cent in 1929 and again in 1935. However, the rise of Labour was not smooth or universal. Support for the party was stronger in some areas than in others, and even at its inter-war peak, Labour earned the support of fewer than half of working-class voters.[52] Nonetheless, Labour's grow-ing support, dependent primarily on working-class voters, reshaped the party system in inter-war Britain.

A number of different factors help account for Labour's rise. Even before the First World War, union growth and more intensive party organ-ization probably built a reservoir of potential Labour support.[53] The war created conditions that gave Labour a boost, most notably a further rise in union membership and the split in the Liberal Party.[54] The war also set the stage for franchise extension in 1918, including (for the first time) over 8 million women, and further reform in 1928 gave women equal access to the vote. Party leaders in Preston attributed success in 1929, in part, to the fact that 'a very considerable proportion of young married women of Preston – those of 21 upward who have been enfranchised – have thrown in their political lot with Labour'.[55] It is impossible, however, to know definitively to what extent the new franchise was responsible for the party's rise nationally.[56] Labour took advantage of these opportunities and others and developed positions that attracted significant working-class support.[57]

The particular factors accounting for Labour success varied from place to place. In some regions Labour took over parliamentary representation and domination of local councils from Liberals.[58] In Wales the Liberal Party controlled parliamentary politics before the war, including in 1906, when the Conservatives failed to win a single Welsh seat.[59] Disastrous results in the 1920s, though, left the Liberals on the defensive, and Labour won 25 of 36 Welsh constituencies in 1929.[60] In Tory strongholds Con-servatives enjoyed far more success holding on to working-class support, but Labour made some gains. In Birmingham Joseph Chamberlain built an impressive Conservative/Unionist bastion. By the 1920s, though, Labour had undermined the Tory monopoly, and in 1929 it won 6 of Birmingham's 12 seats. The government's response to the general strike of 1926 and its punitive Trades Disputes Act of 1927 pushed many Birmingham workers from the Tory embrace. Oswald Mosley, who became a Labour MP in Birmingham before embracing fascism, observed in 1927 that workers who had not voted for Labour previously 'understand how their rights are endangered when their trade unions are placed under the heel of powerful employers'.[61]

Despite these setbacks, working-class voters helped the Conservatives earn the largest share of the vote at each general election and remain in government alone or in coalitions for all but three years between 1915 and 1939.[62] Though many Conservative leaders feared the impact of franchise extension, some areas of prewar working-class Toryism such as Liverpool remained loyal to the party, and new Conservative appeals drew working-class voters in the 1920s and 1930s. Conservative rhetoric focused on revolutionary Russia and the dangers of socialism, as in a 1920 leaflet directed at women voters: 'the mother, instead of cooking for herself, her husband and children at home, may be ordered by the socialists to cook or wash up the dishes in some public restaurant where other families take their meals'. Another message to women demonized the unappreciative husband (often a union member). A play, distributed in leaflet form by the Conservatives, culminated with a working-class wife's stinging criticism of her husband's lack of appreciation: 'You, with your eight-hour day and your easy job, and no worry. Poor over-worked down-trodden slave you are, I don't think'.[63] More established links between some working-class voters and the Conservative Party, over issues such as patriotism and anti-Catholicism, continued to resonate with working-class voters in this period as well.[64]

Whether they voted Conservative or Labour, most workers had little interest in militancy, whether on the left or right. At various moments, however, militant working-class movements gained enough momentum to force the authorities to take note. Strikes on Clydeside during and immediately after the First World War won rent control and concessions at the workplace, and they left a legacy of a strong left-leaning Glasgow Labour leadership.[65] The militant movement on Clydeside provided the new Communist Party with a number of key leaders, but the communists, marginalized by the Labour Party, never succeeded in building a mass working-class membership.[66] They were important, however, in supporting two popular expressions of worker militancy, the National Unemployed Workers' Movement (NUWM) and the anti-fascist campaign. The NUWM leader, Wal Hannington, adopted a strategy of battling benefit cuts, 'by every day bringing steadily increasing masses of workers on to the streets in militant demonstrations'.[67] A participant in Manchester recalled a stand-off between thousands of hunger marchers and the assembled force of police and fire brigades. The police refused to let the marchers pass, and eventually a group of protesters began throwing bricks: 'The police went in with their batons. They were knocking people down. They turned on the hose pipes . . . There were women screaming and men fighting.

There was skin and hair flying'.[68] The established leaders of the Labour Party and union movement kept their distance from the NUWM because of its links to the communists, and it never became a large enough mass movement to threaten the existing order.

Another failed effort to build a mass movement against the established political and social order came from the right. Oswald Mosley, formerly a Labour MP, founded the British Union of Fascists (BUF). Modelled on movements in Italy and Germany, the BUF organized troops of 'Blackshirts' and staged provocative rallies. Though the national movement attracted primarily middle-class followers, in some areas workers joined the fascists. In Blackburn, according to one recollection, 'The district members were mainly millworkers and mechanics, most of whom were jobless'.[69] In 1936 the BUF began emphasizing anti-Semitism and focusing organizing efforts on London's East End. The fascists attracted over 2,000 members, including many workers, and in municipal elections won nearly a quarter of the vote in one East End district. On the other hand, anti-fascist organizations, sometimes led by communists, also grew in the East End, and by 1938 anti-fascist meetings in East London outnumbered those of the fascists themselves.[70]

Militant political organizations of the left or right engaged only a small minority of working-class men and women. As was the case before the First World War and franchise extension, the informal, everyday politics of households, neighbourhoods and workplaces pervaded working-class life far more than party politics or militant activism. Hierarchies of reputation and respect distinguished households and whole streets in working-class districts from one another. Inhabitants understood 'a fine range of distinctions in prestige from street to street. Inside the single streets there are elaborate differences of status'.[71] Within households, husbands enforced their authority, for example, when their homes 'weren't as things should be'. On the other hand, wives drew limits on that authority by manipulating their husbands or battling them directly.[72]

At work, conflict with employers proliferated outside the boundaries of union organization. A South Wales miner, frustrated at a humiliating routine of receiving reduced wages through a hole in a window from an abusive clerk: 'put his arm through the hole and grabbed this under-manager by his necktie, pulled him forward against the window breaking his nose with the force . . . It took four men to get him to let go'.[73] Workers who competed too hard or worked too fast earned the disdain of their peers, who preferred the ' "go slow – don't put the other man out of a job" attitude', while the ' "go getter" or the "livewire" . . . are mistrusted'.[74]

During the war and immediately after, resentment against high profits hardened these sentiments. A government report noted 'not merely an apathy in production but a deadweight of resistance to any suggestion that output should be increased'.[75]

Workers continued to regard the state with ambivalence. They needed government services, protection from police and support when in need, but they resented the condescension and interference that accompanied these benefits. Resistance to the police in working-class neighbourhoods persisted. Efforts to restrict street gambling created conflict, as in the recollection of 1930s' North London: 'I give him the bet and these blokes [undercover policemen] come down, they grabbed him . . . the women come out with these green apples . . . all these kids – they're throwing them at these two . . . who've got hold of the bookmaker. He got away!'[76] Unemployment relief, particularly after the imposition of the hated means test, led to conflict with authorities. Cheating the means test was seen as legitimate, especially if it included earning small amounts of cash on the side: 'the more widespread the subterfuges, the more they were accepted as a normal means of augmenting unemployment allowances'.[77] The barriers to gaining relief and the humiliations required sparked resistance. The NUWM leader recalled: 'Day after day bitter conflicts between the unemployed and the police took place'.[78] One unemployed man recalled, 'They treat you like a lump of dirt they do. I see a navvy reach across the counter and shake one of them [a clerk] by the collar the other day. The rest of us felt like cheering'.[79]

Conclusion

These conflicts over power and resources, both within working-class communities and with employers or other authorities, reflect working-class culture and identity more reliably than do party or militant politics. In their neighbourhoods, at work and in leisure, men, women and children experienced class distinctions and understood them through the lens of class identity, learned from parents and neighbours.[80] Experiences of inequality and difference as well as of similarity and community reinforced class feeling. This identity, however, was not exclusive. It overlapped with other forms of identity built around the region, the nation, ethnic differences, etc. Class identity did not lead to consistent support of a particular political movement or party, but this should not blind us to the continued salience of class in the lives of working men and women in Britain on the eve of the Second World War.

Notes

1 R. Hoggart, *The Uses of Literacy: Aspects of Working-Class Life with Special Reference to Publications and Entertainments* (Harmondsworth: Penguin, 1957), 85, 80, 87, 43.

2 Hoggart, *Uses of Literacy*, 10, 60, 53, 56, 79, 57.

3 B. Waites, *A Class Society at War: England 1914–1918* (Leamington Spa: Berg, 1987), 189.

4 G. Robb, *British Culture and the First World War* (Basingstoke: Palgrave, 2002), 9; P. Panayi, 'Anti-German riots in Britain during the First World War', in P. Panayi, ed., *Racial Violence in Britain in the Nineteenth and Twentieth Centuries*, rev. ed. (London: Leicester University Press, 1996), 74.

5 R. Roberts, *The Classic Slum: Salford Life in the First Quarter of the Century* (Harmondsworth: Penguin, 1973), 193.

6 J. Bourke, *Working-Class Cultures in Britain 1890–1960: Gender, Class and Ethnicity* (London: Routledge, 1994), 175, 171.

7 M. Pugh, 'The rise of Labour and the political culture of Conservatism, 1890–1945', *History* 87 (2002), 523–4.

8 D. Cannadine, 'The context, performance and meaning of ritual: the British monarchy and the "invention of tradition", c.1820–1977', in E. Hobsbawm and T. Ranger, eds, *The Invention of Tradition* (Cambridge: Cambridge University Press, 1983), 140, 151.

9 Bourke, *Working-Class Cultures*, 171–2.

10 D. Rockett, 'A Streatham childhood in the twenties', in D. Rockett and B. Hargreaves, eds, *Two Streatham Childhoods* (London: Streatham Society, 1980), 3; B. Hargreaves, 'A Streatham childhood in the thirties', in Rockett and Hargreaves, eds, *Two Streatham Childhoods*, 13.

11 Cannadine, 'Context, performance and meaning of ritual', 123, 142.

12 Bourke, *Working-Class Cultures*, 188.

13 P. Summerfield, 'Patriotism and empire: music-hall entertainment 1870–1914', in J.M. MacKenzie, ed., *Imperialism and Popular Culture* (Manchester: Manchester University Press, 1986), 38.

14 Robb, *British Culture*, 166.

15 J. Richards, 'Boy's Own empire: feature films and imperialism in the 1930s', in MacKenzie, ed., *Imperialism and Popular Culture*, 155.

16 S. Humphries, *Hooligans or Rebels? An Oral History of Working-Class Childhood and Youth 1889–1939* (Oxford: Blackwell, 1981), 43.

17 Rockett, 'Streatham childhood in the twenties', 3.

18 H. Jennings, and C. Madge, eds, *May the Twelfth: Mass-Observation Day-Surveys 1937 by over Two Hundred Observers* (London: Faber & Faber, 1937), 287–8.

19 Waites, *Class Society at War*, 201, 223.

20 Robb, *British Culture*, 93.

21 D. Vincent, *Poor Citizens: The State and the Poor in Twentieth-Century Britain* (London: Longman, 1991), 77.

22 Hoggart, *Uses of Literacy*, 54.

23 Bourke, *Working-Class Cultures*, 20.

24 R. McKibbin, 'Why was there no Marxism in Great Britain', in idem., *The Ideologies of Class: Social Relations in Britain 1880–1950* (Oxford: Clarendon Press, 1994), 18.

25 Bourke, *Working-Class Cultures*, 167.

26 C.K. Steedman, *Landscape for a Good Woman: A Story of Two Lives* (New Brunswick: Rutgers University Press, 1987), 23.

27 R. Holt, *Sport and the British: A Modern History* (Oxford: Clarendon Press, 1989), 172; J. Hill, *Sport, Leisure and Culture in Twentieth-Century Britain* (Basingstoke: Palgrave, 2002), 14–15; D. Russell, 'Sport and identity: the case of Yorkshire County Cricket Club, 1890–1939', *Twentieth Century British History* 7 (1996), 216, 225, 228.

28 P. Joyce, *Visions of the People: Industrial England and the Question of Class 1848–1914* (Cambridge: Cambridge University Press, 1991), 291ff.

29 P. Scott, 'The state, internal migration, and the growth of new industrial communities in inter-war Britain', *English Historical Review* 115 (2000), 347.

30 J.K. Walton, 'Britishness', in C. Wrigley, ed., *A Companion to Early Twentieth-Century Britain* (Oxford: Blackwell, 2003), 527.

31 J. Bush, 'East London Jews and the First World War', *London Journal* 6 (1980), 155.

32 J. Jenkinson, 'The 1919 race riots in Britain: a survey', in R.E. Lotz and I. Pegg, eds, *Under the Imperial Carpet: Essays in Black History, 1780–1950* (Crawley: Rabbit Press, 1986), 188–9, 182, 192.

33 L. Tabili, *'We Ask for British Justice': Workers and Racial Difference in Late Imperial Britain* (Ithaca: Cornell University Press, 1994), 91.

34 S. Fielding, *Class and Ethnicity: Irish Catholics in England, 1880–1939* (Buckingham: Open University Press, 1993), 36.

35 A. Davies, 'Football and sectarianism in Glasgow during the 1920s and 1930s', *Irish Historical Studies* 36 (forthcoming). I am grateful to the author for advance access to this article.

36 Jenkinson, 'The 1919 race riots', 185; Tabili, *We Ask for British Justice*, 1–2.

37 Bush, 'East London Jews', 158–9; Robb, *British Culture*, 29.

38 Fielding, *Class and Ethnicity*, 72, 29–30.

39 E. Roberts, *A Woman's Place: An Oral History of Working-Class Women 1890–1940* (Oxford: Basil Blackwell, 1984), 185.

40 Hoggart, *Uses of Literacy*, 61.

41 Waites, *Class Society at War*, 61.

42 M. Savage and A. Miles, *The Remaking of the British Working Class, 1840–1940* (London: Routledge, 1994), 26–8.

43 G.J. DeGroot, *Blighty: British Society in the Era of the Great War* (London: Longman, 1996), 295.

44 P. Pagnamenta and R. Overy, *All Our Working Lives* (London: BBC, 1984), 268–9; R. McKibbin, *Classes and Cultures: England 1918–1951* (Oxford: Oxford University Press, 1998), 138.

45 R. McKibbin, 'Class and conventional wisdom: the Conservative Party and the "public" in inter-war Britain', in idem., *Ideologies of Class*, 271–2.

46 DeGroot, *Blighty*, 129–30.

47 Bourke, *Working-Class Cultures*, 209.

48 T. Griffiths, *The Lancashire Working Classes c.1880–1930* (Oxford: Clarendon Press, 2001), 127.

49 Bourke, *Working-Class Cultures*, 118.

50 Hoggart, *The Uses of Literacy*, 63, 65.

51 McKibbin, *Classes and Cultures*, 263.

52 J. Yonwin, *UK Election Statistics: 1918–2004* (London: House of Commons Library, 2004), 11; M. Pugh, *The Making of Modern British Politics 1867–1939*, 2nd ed. (Oxford: Blackwell, 1993), 139, 194, 253, 259–60.

53 R. McKibbin, *The Evolution of the Labour Party 1910–1924* (Oxford: Clarendon Press, 1974), 72, 86–7; K. Laybourn, 'The rise of Labour and the decline of Liberalism: the state of the debate', *History* 80 (1995), 213.

54 T. Adams, 'Labour and the First World War: economy, politics and the erosion of local peculiarity?' *Journal of Regional and Local Studies* 10 (1990), 23, 28–30; Pugh, *Making of Modern British Politics*, 199.

55 M. Savage, *The Dynamics of Working-Class Politics: The Labour Movement in Preston, 1880–1940* (Cambridge: Cambridge University Press, 1987), 179.

56 D. Tanner, 'Class voting and radical politics: the Liberal and Labour Parties, 1910–1931', in J. Lawrence and M. Taylor, eds, *Party, State and Society:*

Electoral Behaviour in Britain since 1820 (Aldershot: Scolar, 1997), 115; Pugh, 'Rise of Labour', 515.

57 Savage, *Dynamics of Working-Class Politics*, 186–7; Tanner, 'Class voting and radical politics', 124; Griffiths, *Lancashire Working Classes*, 311.

58 K. Laybourn and J. Reynolds, *Liberalism and the Rise of Labour 1890–1918* (London: Croom Helm, 1984); C. Williams, *Democratic Rhondda: Politics and Society, 1885–1951* (Cardiff: University of Wales Press, 1996).

59 R.M. Jones, 'Beyond identity? The reconstruction of the Welsh', *Journal of British Studies* 31 (1992), 336.

60 J.P.D. Dunbabin, 'British elections in the nineteenth and twentieth centuries, a regional approach', *English Historical Review* 95 (1980), 245; D. Tanner, 'The pattern of Labour politics', in D. Tanner, C. Williams, and D. Hopkin, eds, *The Labour Party in Wales 1900–2000* (Cardiff: University of Wales Press, 2000), 16.

61 Pugh, 'Rise of Labour', 521.

62 Yonwin, *UK Election Statistics*, 11.

63 D. Jarvis, 'Mrs Maggs and Betty: the Conservative appeal to women voters in the 1920s', *Twentieth Century British History* 5 (1994), 139–40, 150.

64 Pugh, 'Rise of Labour', 517.

65 R.J. Morris, 'Skilled workers and the politics of the "Red" Clyde', *Journal of the Scottish Labour History Society* 18 (1983), 6, 11–12; J. Foster, 'Strike action and working-class politics on Clydeside 1914–1919', *International Review of Social History* 35 (1990), 42, 44.

66 J. Hinton, *The First Shop Stewards' Movement* (London: George Allen & Unwin, 1973), 14; J. Hinton, *Labour and Socialism: A History of the British Labour Movement 1867–1974* (Amherst: University of Massachusetts Press, 1983), 152.

67 J. Stevenson and C. Cook, *Britain in the Depression: Society and Politics, 1929–1939*, 2nd ed. (London: Longman, 1994), 170.

68 N. Gray, *The Worst of Times: An Oral History of the Great Depression in Britain* (Totowa, NJ: Barnes & Noble, 1985), 16–17.

69 S. Rawnsley, 'The membership of the British Union of Fascists', in K. Lunn and R.C. Thurlow, eds, *British Fascism: Essays on the Radical Right in Inter-War Britain* (New York: St Martin's Press, 1980), 160.

70 R.C. Thurlow, *Fascism in Britain: From Oswald Mosley's Blackshirts to the National Front*, rev. ed. (London: I.B. Tauris, 1998), 85, 95; Stevenson and Cook, *Britain in the Depression*, 232–3.

71 Hoggart, *Uses of Literacy*, 10.

72 Bourke, *Working-Class Cultures*, 72ff.

73 Gray, *The Worst of Times*, 32.

74 Hoggart, *Uses of Literacy*, 62.

75 Waites, *Class Society at War*, 220.

76 J. White, 'Police and people in London in the 1930s', *Oral History* 11 (1983), 38.

77 McKibbin, *Classes and Cultures*, 158 n. 180.

78 Vincent, *Poor Citizens*, 58.

79 McKibbin, *Classes and Cultures*, 158.

80 Steedman, *Landscape for a Good Woman*, 13–14.

Conclusion:
Change and continuity

Eric Hobsbawm, in an essay originally published in 1954, distinguished three periods in the history of the working class. The 1780s to the 1840s marked the 'classic age' of the 'Industrial Revolution'. From the 1840s to the 1890s capitalism ruled supreme, and, according to Hobsbawm, the labour aristocracy dominated working-class history. The 1890s to 1939 marked the era of imperialism and monopoly capitalism, as well as entry into 'the permanent crisis of the British economy'.[1] Others have chosen different dates or different emphases. Many historians focus on the middle of the nineteenth century as a key transition in working-class history, associated with the decline of Chartism and the abandonment of anti-capitalist opposition by most workers.[2] The First World War is often cited as a watershed, creating, in some scholars' views, a newly homogenous and conscious working class.[3] This study has carved up the period slightly differently, with sections starting and/or ending in 1832, 1870, 1914 and 1940. While this structure reflects discontinuities, this should not overshadow significant continuities in working-class life across the entire scope of this work.

Working-class families and neighbourhoods changed in significant ways. The unregulated construction and sanitary regimes of mid-century gave way to late-Victorian by-law housing and twentieth-century council estates. Rapid migration into central districts slowed in the last quarter of the nineteenth century, creating more stable neighbourhoods. After the First World War, however, many workers migrated from distressed regions and families moved into new estates. The large families characteristic of the Victorian working class gave way to more successful efforts to control fertility. Through these changes, though, the family remained the central institution in working-class life. Despite distinct gender roles and widespread marital conflict, most couples continued to view one another with affection. Mutual aid, the enforcement of standards, and conflicts generated by close quarters and shared public spaces characterized working-class neighbourhoods throughout the period. Though neighbourhoods were never entirely homogenous, the departure of most middle-class families from working-class districts early in the period created environments that helped separate workers from those higher on the social scale.

The economic context changed markedly across this period. Mid-Victorian Britain dominated the world economy, and its export industries helped fuel prosperity and high profits. By late-century, though, competition exerted pressure on British companies and declining profits fostered concern about a depression. After the First World War economic difficulties grew more severe, as once-dominant export industries fell into crisis and persistent unemployment drove many working-class families into dependence on the dole. Trade unions, enrolling a small group of privileged skilled workers in the mid-nineteenth century, grew in fits and starts to become mass organizations of workers across skill lines by the mid-twentieth century. Despite these changes, much remained constant in the experience of manual labour in Britain.

Whether skilled or unskilled, male or female, workers' experiences on the job shared many crucial characteristics. Economic insecurity, driven by workers' subordinate positions in labour markets, affected unskilled labourers and skilled craftsmen. The distinct interests of workers and bosses, sometimes manifested in strikes and militancy, sometimes mediated through cooperation and collective bargaining, nurtured working-class identity. Difficult and often dangerous working conditions left workers physically uncomfortable and vulnerable to declining productivity in middle age and to the potential for debilitating illness or injury. Most significantly, the fact of working with one's hands, of getting dirty, of not wearing a collar, marked manual labour as a distinctive way of life and nourished class consciousness.

Working-class men, and to a lesser extent women, gained progressively more access to leisure as working hours declined across the period. In the growing working-class districts of mid-century, a vibrant and raucous popular cultural grew from rural roots. Entrepreneurs soon took advantage of this market, and commercial leisure expanded with the urban population. Before the First World War cinema challenged music halls, and mass sport and the cheap press built great followings. In the twentieth century home-based pursuits such as reading and hobbies spread among workers. Amidst these changes, though, the crowded and often rowdy streets and markets in working-class districts remained crucial leisure sites. Middle-class authorities (and socialist activists) continued to disapprove of the prevalence of drink and gambling in working-class leisure. Though other classes drank and gambled, these pursuits remained remarkably segregated by class, and the distinctiveness of working-class leisure also reinforced class identity.

Chronologies such as Hobsbawm's emphasized changes in working-class politics. Chartist challenges to the political order collapsed, leaving the reformism and limited horizons of mid-Victorian labour leaders. In the twentieth century the growth of the Labour Party created a new mass working-class politics. These narratives tend to exaggerate discontinuity. Chartists sought improvement in workers' lives *within* the system. Such efforts continued, though often through different means, in the mid-Victorian period. While the rise of Labour in the twentieth century gave workers a place at the seat of power, most workers remained uninterested in formal politics, and many working-class voters continued to support the Tories. Formal politics, parties and mass movements could not rival the pervasiveness of informal politics in the lives of most working-class men and women. They struggled with employers, with state authorities and middle-class reformers, and often with one another, over authority, resources and respect. These battles often divided workers from one another, across gender, ethnic and geographical lines. But they also brought workers together against employers, the police and others who represented 'them'.

The language of 'us' and 'them' remained central to the way working people viewed their lives. Some of these definitions cut across class lines, for example Protestant against Catholic or English as opposed to Scot. Some divided workers on the basis of gender, skill or craft. On the other hand, throughout this period, working men and women identified with other workers, bound together by the experience of manual labour, by life in crowded working-class districts, by a public and often raucous leisure culture. The stories they heard and told, reinforced by their experiences at home, in their neighbourhoods, at work and play, made class an important, though never exclusive, part of their identities. Class consciousness did not grow directly from the structures of work under capitalism. It did, however, thrive in the experiences of working-class men and women in Britain between 1832 and 1940.

Notes

1   E.J. Hobsbawm, 'The labour aristocracy in nineteenth-century Britain', in *Labouring Men: Studies in the History of Labour* (New York: Basic Books, 1964), 272.

2   N. Kirk, *Change, Continuity and Class: Labour in British Society, 1850–1920* (Manchester: Manchester University Press, 1998), ch. 2.

3   B. Waites, *A Class Society at War: England 1914–1918* (Leamington Spa: Berg, 1987), 279.

Epilogue

In the decades since 1940 broad changes in British society have transformed the experiences of working men and women in significant ways. Some of these developments built on trends that originated before the Second World War, such as the growth of home-centred leisure and the Labour Party's ability to attract significant working-class support but never monopolize the working-class electorate. Other changes, such as the spread of consumerism across British society and the decline of manual labour, broke new ground. These transformations have chipped away at the distinctiveness of working-class life in Britain, leading one historian to suggest that 'the foundations, frontiers and points of reference of the class society have crumbled'.[1] Perhaps surprisingly, given these changes, class identity has proved resilient and remains central to how men and women understand themselves and society.

A number of factors, not least widespread destruction in German attacks, left a massive housing deficit when the Second World War ended. In the late 1940s and 1950s, millions of new homes rose to fill the breach, most of them built by local authorities. Working-class families who moved into these new homes echoed the sentiments of earlier estate pioneers. One woman recalled the advantages of her prefabricated post-war house: 'We thought that was lovely, houses having bathrooms . . . the prefab had a bathroom, and a fridge. So we were well off then'.[2] In 1938 council tenants represented only 10 per cent of the British housing market, but this increased to 32 per cent in 1981. By that point a new trend had begun, and between 1979 and 1986 a million council houses were sold to owner-occupiers, and nearly two-thirds of British homes were owner-occupied.[3] The vast majority of working-class men and women lived in rental housing throughout the period covered in this book. By the end of the twentieth century this was no longer the case.

A central aspect of working-class identity throughout this period involved the value of manual labour, often accompanied by a disdain for white-collar work. Though the war created a temporary boom in many traditional British industries, in the second half of the twentieth century jobs requiring manual work grew far less common. Well into the 1960s, though, full employment hid the trend away from manual work, allowing workers to demand better pay and conditions or move on to another job. A worker recalled the response to a disagreement with a supervisor: 'We sort of said, "Well stick your job. We're going". But I mean at that time you could leave a job on a Thursday and get another job on a Monday'.[4] However, beginning in the late 1960s, job opportunities in manual trades disappeared and unemployment again threatened workers. From 1966 to 1979 the British economy shed 2 million manufacturing jobs. The work-force, about two-thirds manual workers in 1951, became predominately non-manual by 1981. Growing service industries employed large numbers of women, and the proportion of women in the workforce grew from 37.3 per cent in 1961 to 47.4 per cent in 1977.[5] Though many of these new white-collar workers joined unions, manual labour, a pillar of working-class identity, employed fewer British men and women.

The post-Second World War period of full employment and economic health, combined with expanded government spending on social services, created unprecedented economic security and material abundance for workers. For two decades after the Second World War unemployment remained under 2 per cent. A survey carried out in York had found 31.1 per cent living in poverty in 1936 but only 2.8 per cent of York residents fell into that category in 1950. Average real earnings shot up by 150 per cent in the half-century beginning in 1945, and the benefits of the new consumer economy gradually spread into working-class homes. By 1975 three-quarters of British homes had refrigerators, two-thirds had washing machines and 90 per cent had televisions. In 1971 88 per cent of homes had a bath or shower, up from 62 per cent in 1951. From the 1970s, though, this expansion of consumption across the social spectrum slowed. Inequality increased, unemployment rose, and poverty began to spread again.[6]

Consumption and improvements in housing affected patterns of working-class leisure. Private, home-based activities, already growing more popular between the wars, came to dominate leisure for workers. One observer noted in 1959: 'For the first time in modern British history the working-class home has become a place that is warm and comfortable and able to provide its own fireside entertainment . . . [the husband] spends his evenings and his week-ends not with his workmates but at home with his family'. As television spread, it consumed free time. One working-class family that embraced television in the mid-1950s gathered around it, according to an observer, as if engaged in 'a strange ritual. The father said proudly; "The tellie keeps the family together. None of us ever have to go out now" '.[7] By 1969, according to one estimate, a quarter of all leisure time went to watching television.[8] Private leisure at home increasingly replaced the public, communal and class-specific leisure of the urban working class.

As the Second World War came to a close, the Labour Party won its first parliamentary majority, based on strong working-class support and more than a fifth of the middle-class vote.[9] In succeeding decades the party continued to win the allegiance of most working-class voters. However, as was the case earlier in the century, a significant minority of working-class electors supported the Conservatives. At the same time, some Labour Party leaders sought to de-emphasize the party's links to the working class. Anthony Crosland, a major figure in the party in the 1960s and 1970s, called for the creation of a society 'not bedevilled by the consciousness of class'. He also urged: 'we must now all learn to be middle-class'.[10] More recently, Prime Minister Tony Blair stressed the importance of 'Middle Britain' to Labour's fortunes, and complained: 'Britain is still, after all these years, a place where class counts'.[11] Labour was never able to count on the support of all workers, and it has downplayed its role as the political voice of the working class.

In many ways new social patterns have created a different way of life for the mass of British working men and women. Many own their own homes and fill them with the material signs of affluence. Fewer rely on the earnings of a male manual worker, as more women seek employment and white-collar jobs proliferate. Leisure is likely to be spent at home, rather than in the pub or out in the streets of working-class neighbourhoods. In all these ways, the distinctiveness of working-class life has faded. Yet British men and women continue to identify as working class. A 1993 study found that only 6 per cent of respondents failed to identify themselves as part of a particular social class.[12] In a 2002 MORI survey, two-thirds of respondents admitted to being 'working class and proud of it'.[13] In 1996 a Hull man responded to Labour MP John Prescott's claim to be middle class: 'If I think about the middle classes, I just picture them as earning a decent wage and buying their own house. But then, we do that too, some of us, don't we? So maybe we're not so different. But I know I'm working class'.[14] Despite changes in British life since 1940, class still matters in British society.

Notes

1 F. Bédarida, *A Social History of England 1851–1990*, 2nd ed. (London: Routledge, 1991), 322.

2 C. Langhamer, 'The meanings of home in postwar Britain', *Journal of Contemporary History* 40 (2005), 347–8.

3 Bédarida, *Social History*, 308.

4 J. Rule, 'Time, affluence and private leisure: the British working class in the 1950s and 1960s', *Labour History Review* 66 (2001), 227.

5 J. Cronin, *Labour and Society in Britain 1918–1979* (London: Batsford, 1984), 194–5; Bédarida, *Social History*, 304.

6 Bédarida, *Social History*, 212, 254–6, 316–17; P. Sinclair, C. Ryan and M. Walker, 'Continuity, change and consumption: British economic trends, 1945–1995', *Contemporary British History* 10 (1996), 41, 51.

7 Rule, 'Time, affluence and private leisure', 234–5.

8 Bédarida, *Social History*, 256.

9 S. Fielding, 'What did "the people" want?: The meaning of the 1945 general election', *Historical Journal* 35 (1992), 636.

10 Cronin, *Labour and Society*, 174; Bédarida, *Social History*, 286.

11 D. Cannadine, *The Rise and Fall of Class in Britain* (New York: Columbia University Press, 1999), 187, 189.

12 D.G. Lilleker, 'Whose Left? Working-class political allegiances in post-industrial Britain', *International Review of Social History* 47 (2002), 69.

13 *The Guardian*, 11 April 2006.

14 *The Independent*, 14 April 1996.

Bibliography

Ackers, P. 'West end chapel, back street Bethel: labour and capital in the Wigan Churches of Christ, c.1845–1945.' *Journal of Ecclesiastical History* 47 (1996): 298–329.

Acorn, G. *One of the Multitude*. London: William Heinemann, 1911.

Adams, T. 'Labour and the First World War: economy, politics and the erosion of local peculiarity.' *Journal of Regional and Local Studies* 10 (1990): 23–47.

Anderson, M. *Family Structure in Nineteenth Century Lancashire*. Cambridge: Cambridge University Press, 1971.

Anderson, M. 'Urban migration in Victorian Britain: problems of assimilation?' In *Immigration et Société en Europe Occidentale, XVIe–XXe Siècle*, edited by E. François. Paris: Editions Recherche sur le Civilisations, 1985.

Ashton, O.R. 'Chartism and popular culture, an introduction to the radical culture in Cheltenham Spa, 1830–1847.' *Journal of Popular Culture* 20 (1987): 61–81.

Attridge, S. *Nationalism, Imperialism and Identity in Late-Victorian Culture*. Basingstoke: Palgrave, 2003.

August, A. 'A culture of consolation? Rethinking politics in working-class London, 1870–1914.' *Historical Research* 74 (2001): 193–219.

August, A. *Poor Women's Lives: Gender, Work, and Poverty in Late-Victorian London*. London: Associated University Presses, 1999.

Bailey, P. *Leisure and Class in Victorian England: Rational Recreation and the Contest for Control, 1830–1885*. London: Methuen, 1987.

Bailey, P. *Music Hall: The Business of Pleasure*. Milton Keynes: Open University Press, 1986.

Bailey, P. 'The politics and poetics of modern British leisure.' *Rethinking History* 3:2 (1999): 131–75.

Bailey, P. 'Will the real Bill Banks stand up? Towards a role analysis of mid-Victorian working-class respectability.' *Journal of Social History* 12 (1979): 336–53.

Baker, W.J. 'The making of a working-class football culture in Victorian England.' *Journal of Social History* 13 (1979): 241–52.

Barker, T.C., and M. Drake, eds. *Population and Society in Britain 1850–1980*. New York: New York University Press, 1982.

Barret-Ducrocq, F. *Love in the Time of Victoria: Sexuality and Desire Among Working-Class Men and Women in Nineteenth-Century London*, trans. J. Howe. New York: Penguin, 1992.

Bédarida, F. *A Social History of England 1851–1990*, 2nd ed. London: Routledge, 1991.

Behlmer, G.K. *Friends of the Family: The English Home and Its Guardians, 1850–1940*. Stanford: Stanford University Press, 1998.

Belchem, J. *Industrialization and the Working Class: The English Experience, 1750–1990*. Portland: Areopagitica, 1990.

Belchem, J. *Popular Radicalism in Nineteenth-Century Britain*. New York: St Martin's Press, 1996.

Bell, T. *Pioneering Days*. London: Lawrence & Wishart, 1941.

Benson, J. *Rise of Consumer Society in Britain, 1880–1980*. London: Longman, 1994.

Benson, J., ed. *The Working Class in England 1875–1914*. London: Croom Helm, 1985.

Berg, M., and P. Hudson. 'Rehabilitating the Industrial Revolution.' *Economic History Review* 45 (1992): 24–50.

Bevir, M. 'The Labour church movement, 1891–1902.' *Journal of British Studies* 38 (1999): 217–45.

Biagini, E.F. 'British trade unions and popular political economy, 1860–1880.' *Historical Journal* 30:4 (1987): 811–40.

Biagini, E.F. *Liberty, Retrenchment and Reform: Popular Liberalism in the Age of Gladstone, 1860–1880*. Cambridge: Cambridge University Press, 1992.

Biagini, E.F., and A.J. Reid, eds. *Currents of Radicalism: Popular Radicalism, Organised Labour and Party Politics in Britain, 1850–1914.* Cambridge: Cambridge University Press, 1991.

Bienefeld, M. *Working Hours in British Industry: An Economic History.* London: Weidenfeld & Nicolson, 1972.

Blake, J. *Memories of Old Poplar.* London: Stepney Books, 1977.

Bourke, J. *Working-Class Cultures in Britain, 1890–1960: Gender, Class and Ethnicity.* London: Routledge, 1994.

Bourne, J. *Britain and the Great War.* London: Edward Arnold, 1989.

Branson, N. *Britain in the Nineteen Twenties.* Minneapolis: University of Minnesota Press, 1976.

Braybon, G., and P. Summerfield. *Out of the Cage: Women's Experiences in Two World Wars.* London: Pandora, 1987.

Briggs, A. *The History of Broadcasting in the United Kingdom.* Oxford: Oxford University Press, 1995.

Briggs, A. *Victorian Cities.* Harmonsdworth: Penguin, 1968.

Briggs, A. *Victorian People: A Reassessment of Persons and Themes 1851–1867,* rev. ed. Chicago: University of Chicago Press, 1972.

Broadberry, S.N., and N.F.R. Crafts. 'Britain's productivity gap in the 1930s: some neglected factors.' *Journal of Economic History* 52 (1992): 531–58.

Broadhurst, H. *Henry Broadhurst, M.P.* New York; London: Garland, 1984.

Brodie, M. *The Politics of the Poor: The East End of London 1885–1914.* Oxford: Clarendon Press, 2004.

Brooke, S. ' "A new world for women"? Abortion law reform in Britain during the 1930s.' *American Historical Review* 106 (2001): 431–59.

Brown, C.G. *The Death of Christian Britain: Understanding Secularisation, 1800–2000.* London: Routledge, 2001.

Brown, C.G. *Religion and Society in Scotland since 1707,* rev ed. Edinburgh: Edinburgh University Press, 1997.

Burgess, K. *The Challenge of Labour: Shaping British Society, 1850–1930.* London: Croom Helm, 1980.

Burgess, K. *The Origins of British Industrial Relations: The Nineteenth Century Experience.* London: Croom Helm, 1975.

Burnett, J. *Destiny Obscure: Autobiographies of Childhood Education and Family from the 1820s to the 1920s*. Harmondsworth: Penguin, 1982.

Burnett, J. *Plenty and Want: A Social History of Food in England from 1815 to the Present Day*, 3rd ed. London: Routledge, 1989.

Burnett, J. *A Social History of Housing, 1815–1985*, 2nd ed. London: Methuen, 1986.

Burnett, J., ed. *Useful Toil: Autobiographies of Working People from the 1820s to the 1920s*. Harmondsworth: Penguin, 1977.

Burton, A., ed. *After the Imperial Turn: Thinking With and Through the Nation*. Durham: Duke University Press, 2003.

Bush, J. 'East London Jews and the First World War.' *London Journal* 6 (1980): 147–61.

Buxton, N.K. 'Economic growth in Scotland between the wars: the role of production structure and rationalization.' *Economic History Review* 33 (1980): 538–55.

Bythell, D. 'The hand-loom weavers in the English cotton industry during the Industrial Revolution: some problems.' *Economic History Review* 17 (1964): 338–53.

Cadbury, E., M.C. Matheson, and G. Shann. *Women's Work and Wages: A Phase of Life in an Industrial City*. Chicago: University of Chicago Press, 1907.

Cannadine, D. *The Rise and Fall of Class in Britain*. New York: Columbia University Press, 1999.

Cannadine, D. 'Victorian cities: how different?' *Social History* (1977): 457–82.

Cecil, H., and P. Liddle, eds. *Facing Armageddon: The First World War Experienced*. London: Cooper, 1996.

Chandler, A.D. 'The growth of the transnational industrial firm in the United States and the United Kingdom: a comparative analysis.' *Economic History Review* 33 (1980): 396–410.

Childs, M. 'Labour grows up: the electoral system, political generations, and British politics 1890–1929.' *Twentieth Century British History* 6 (1995): 123–44.

Childs, M. *Labour's Apprentices: Working-Class Lads in Late Victorian and Edwardian England*. Montreal: McGill-Queen's University Press, 1992.

Chinn, C. *Better Betting with a Decent Feller: Bookmaking, Betting and the British Working Class, 1750–1990*. New York: Harvester Wheatsheaf, 1991.

Chinn, C. *Poverty Amidst Prosperity: The Urban Poor in England, 1834–1914*. Manchester: Manchester University Press, 1995.

Chinn, C. *They Worked All Their Lives: Women of the Urban Poor in England, 1880–1939*. Manchester: Manchester University Press, 1988.

Church, R.T. *Over the Bridge. An Essay in Autobiography*. London: William Heinemann, 1955.

Claeys, G. *Citizens and Saints: Politics and Anti-Politics in Early British Socialism*. Cambridge: Cambridge University Press, 1989.

Clapson, M. *A Bit of a Flutter: Popular Gambling and English Society, c.1823–1961*. Manchester: Manchester University Press, 1992.

Clark, A. *The Struggle for the Breeches: Gender and the Making of the British Working Class*. Berkeley: University of California Press, 1995.

Clarke, L. *Building Capitalism: Historical Change and the Labour Process in the Production of the Built Environment*. London: Routledge, 1992.

Clegg, H.A. *A History of British Trade Unions since 1889, vol. II: 1911–1933*. Oxford: Clarendon Press, 1985.

Clegg, H.A., A. Fox, and A.F. Thompson. *A History of British Trade Unions since 1889*. Oxford: Clarendon Press, 1964.

Coleman, D., and J. Salt. *The British Population: Patterns, Trends and Processes*. Oxford: Oxford University Press, 1992.

Colley, L. 'Britishness and otherness: an argument.' *Journal of British Studies* 31 (1992): 309–29.

Colley, L. *Britons: Forging the Nation, 1707–1837*. New Haven: Yale University Press, 1992.

Colley, L. 'Whose nation? Class and national consciousness in Britain 1750–1830.' *Past and Present* 113 (1986): 97–117.

Cook, C., and J. Stevenson. *The Longman Handbook of Modern British History 1714–2001*, 4th ed. London: Longman, 2001.

Copelman, D.M. *London's Women Teachers: Gender, Class and Feminism 1870–1930*. London: Routledge, 1996.

Cox, J. *The English Churches in a Secular Society: Lambeth 1870–1930.* Oxford: Oxford University Press, 1982.

Cronin, J. *Labour and Society in Britain 1918–1979.* London: Batsford, 1984.

Cross, G.S. *A Quest for Time: The Reduction of Work in Britain and France, 1840–1940.* Berkeley: University of California Press, 1989.

Crossick, G. *An Artisan Elite in Victorian Society: Kentish London, 1840–1880.* London: Croom Helm, 1978.

Cunningham, H. *The Challenge of Democracy: Britain 1832–1918.* London: Longman, 2001.

Cunningham, H. 'Jingoism in 1877–78.' *Victorian Studies* 14 (1971): 429–53.

Cunningham, H. *Leisure in the Industrial Revolution, c.1780–c.1880.* London: Croom Helm, 1980.

Cunningham, H. *The Volunteer Force: A Social and Political History 1859–1908.* Hamden, CT: Archon Books, 1975.

Damer, S. ' "Engineers of the human machine": the social practice of council housing management in Glasgow, 1895–1939.' *Urban Studies* 37 (2000): 2007–26.

Damer, S. *From Moorepark to 'Wine Alley': The Rise and Fall of a Glasgow Housing Scheme.* Edinburgh: Edinburgh University Press, 1989.

Daunton, M.J., ed. *The Cambridge Urban History of Britain, vol. III: 1840–1950.* Cambridge: Cambridge University Press, 2000.

Daunton, M.J. *Coal Metropolis, Cardiff 1870–1914.* Leicester: Leicester University Press, 1977.

Daunton, M.J., ed. *Councillors and Tenants: Local Authority Housing in English Cities, 1919–1939.* Leicester: Leicester University Press, 1984.

Daunton, M.J. *House and Home in the Victorian City: Working-Class Housing, 1850–1914.* London: Edward Arnold, 1983.

Davidoff, L., and C. Hall. *Family Fortunes: Men and Women of the English Middle Class, 1780–1850.* Chicago: University of Chicago Press, 1987.

Davidson, R. 'The Board of Trade and industrial relations, 1896–1914.' *Historical Journal* 21 (1978): 571–91.

Davies, A. 'Football and sectarianism in Glasgow during the 1920s and 1930s.' *Irish Historical Studies* 36 (forthcoming).

Davies, A. *Leisure, Gender, and Poverty: Working-Class Culture in Salford and Manchester, 1900–1939.* Buckingham: Open University Press, 1992.

Davies, A. 'The police and the people: gambling in Salford, 1900–1939.' *Historical Journal* 34 (1991): 87–115.

Davies, A., and S. Fielding, eds. *Workers' Worlds: Cultures and Communities in Manchester and Salford, 1880–1939.* Manchester: Manchester University Press, 1992.

Davies, M.L. *Maternity: Letters from Working Women: Collected by the Women's Co-operative Guild.* New York: Norton, 1978.

Davin, A. *Growing up Poor: Home, School and Street in London 1870–1914.* London: Rivers Oram Press, 1996.

Davis, J. 'A poor man's system of justice: the London police courts in the second half of the nineteenth century.' *Historical Journal* 27 (1984): 309–35.

Davis, M. *Comrade or Brother? A History of the British Labour Movement, 1789–1951.* London: Pluto Press, 1993.

DeGroot, G.J. *Blighty: British Society in the Era of the Great War.* London: Longman, 1996.

Dennis, R. *English Industrial Cities of the Nineteenth Century: A Social Geography.* Cambridge: Cambridge University Press, 1984.

Dewey, P.E. *War and Progress: Britain 1914–1945.* London: Longman, 1997.

Dickson, T., and J.H. Treble, eds. *People and Society in Scotland, vol. iii: 1914–1990.* Edinburgh: John Donald, 1992.

Dodd, W. *The Factory System Illustrated: In a Series of Letters to the Right Hon. Lord Ashley.* [1842]. London: Frank Cass, 1968.

Donajgrodzki, A.P., ed. *Social Control in Nineteenth Century Britain.* London: Croom Helm, 1977.

Doughty, M., ed. *Building the Industrial City.* Leicester: Leicester University Press, 1986.

Downs, L.L. 'Industrial decline, rationalization and equal pay: the Bedaux strike at Rover Automobile Company.' *Social History* 15 (1990): 45–73.

Downs, L.L. *Manufacturing Inequality: Gender Division in the French and British Metalworking Industries, 1914–1939*. Ithaca: Cornell University Press, 1995.

Dunbabin, J.P.D. 'British elections in the nineteenth and twentieth centuries: a regional approach.' *English Historical Review* 95 (1980): 241–67.

Dupree, M. *Family Structure in the Staffordshire Potteries, 1840–1880*. Oxford: Clarendon Press, 1995.

Durant, R. *Watling: A Survey of Social Life on a New Housing Estate*. London: P.S. King & Son, 1939.

Dutton, H.I., and J.E. King. *'Ten Per Cent and No Surrender': The Preston Strike, 1853–1854*. Cambridge: Cambridge University Press, 1981.

Eichengreen, B. 'Unemployment in interwar Britain: new evidence from London.' *Journal of Interdisciplinary History* 17 (1986): 335–58.

Eichengreen, B., and T.J. Hatton, eds. *Interwar Unemployment in International Perspective*. Dordrecht: Kluwer Academic, 1988.

Eley, G., and K. Nield. 'Farewell to the working class?' *International Labor and Working-Class History* 57 (2000): 1–30.

Eley, G., and K. Nield. *The Future of Class in History: What's Left of the Social*. Ann Arbor: University of Michigan Press, forthcoming 2007.

Eley, G., and K. Nield. 'Starting over: the present, the post-modern and the moment of social history.' *Social History* 20 (1995): 355–64.

Englander, D. and J. Osborne. 'Jack, Tommy, and Henry Dubb: the armed forces and the working class.' *Historical Journal* 21 (1978): 593–621.

Epstein, J. *In Practice: Studies in the Language and Culture of Popular Politics in Modern Britain*. Stanford: Stanford University Press, 2003.

Epstein, J. *The Lion of Freedom: Feargus O'Connor and the Chartist Movement, 1832–1842*. London: Croom Helm, 1982.

Epstein, J., and D. Thompson, eds. *The Chartist Experience: Studies in Working-Class Radicalism and Culture, 1830–60*. London: Macmillan, 1982.

Faley, J. *Up Oor Close: Memories of Domestic Life in Glasgow Tenements, 1910–1945*. Wendlebury: White Cockade, 1990.

Feldman, D. 'Immigrants in British History: a problem of integration?' Semi-Plenary Address, North American Conference on British Studies. Denver, CO, 2005.

Feldman, D., and G. Stedman Jones, eds. *Metropolis London: Histories and Representations since 1800, History Workshop Series*. London: Routledge, 1989.

Fielding, S. *Class and Ethnicity: Irish Catholics in England, 1880–1939*. Buckingham: Open University Press, 1993.

Fielding, S. 'What did "the people" want?: the meaning of the 1945 general election.' *Historical Journal* 35 (1992): 623–39.

Finn, M.C. *After Chartism: Class and Nation in English Radical Politics, 1848–1874*. Cambridge: Cambridge University Press, 1993.

Fishman, W.J. *East End 1888: Life in a London Borough among the Laboring Poor*. Philadelphia: Temple University Press, 1988.

Fletcher, I.C. ' "Prosecutions . . . are always risky business." Labour, Liberals, and the 1912 "don't-shoot" prosecutions.' *Albion* 28 (1996): 251–78.

Floud, R., and P. Johnson, eds. *The Cambridge Economic History of Modern Britain*. Cambridge: Cambridge University Press, 2004.

Floud, R., and D.N. McCloskey, eds. *The Economic History of Britain since 1700*, 2nd ed. Cambridge: Cambridge University Press, 1994.

Foakes, G. *Between High Walls: A London Childhood*. London: Shepheard-Walwyn, 1972.

Foakes, G. *My Part of the River*. London: Shepheard-Walwyn, 1974.

Foreman-Peck, J., S. Bowden, and A. McKinlay. *The British Motor Industry*. Manchester: Manchester University Press, 1995.

Foster, J. *Class Struggle and the Industrial Revolution: Early Industrial Capitalism in Three English Towns*. New York: St Martin's Press, 1975.

Foster, J. 'Strike action and working-class politics on Clydeside 1914–1919.' *International Review of Social History* 35 (1990): 33–70.

Fowler, D. *The First Teenagers: The Lifestyle of Young Wage-Earners in Interwar Britain*. London: Woburn Press, 1995.

Fox, E. 'Powers of life and death: aspects of maternal welfare in England and Wales between the wars.' *Medical History* 35 (1991): 328–52.

Frader, L., and S. Rose, eds. *Gender and Class in Modern Europe.* Ithaca: Cornell University Press, 1996.

Fraser, W.H. *A History of British Trade Unionism, 1700–1998.* New York: St Martin's Press, 1999.

Fraser, W.H., and R.J. Morris, eds. *People and Society in Scotland, vol. ii: 1830–1914.* Edinburgh: John Donald, 1990.

Freeman, A.J. *Boy Life and Labour: The Manufacture of Inefficiency.* [1914]. New York: Garland, 1980.

Freifeld, M. 'Technological change and the "self-acting" mule – a study of skill and the sexual division of labour.' *Social History* 11:3 (1986): 319–43.

Frost, T. *Forty Years' Recollections: Literary and Political.* London: Sampson Low, Marston, Searle & Rivington, 1880.

Gauldie, E. *Cruel Habitations: A History of Working-Class Housing 1780–1918.* New York: Harper and Row, 1974.

Gillis, J.R. *For Better, for Worse: British Marriages, 1600 to the Present.* Oxford: Oxford University Press, 1985.

Gittins, D. *Fair Sex: Family Size and Structure, 1900–39.* London: Hutchinson, 1982.

Glucksmann, M. *Women Assemble: Women Workers and the New Industries in Inter-War Britain.* London: Routledge, 1990.

Glynn, S., and J. Oxborrow. *Interwar Britain: A Social and Economic History.* London: George Allen & Unwin, 1976.

Golby, J.M., and A.W. Purdue. *The Civilisation of the Crowd: Popular Culture in England, 1750–1900.* New York: Schocken Books, 1985.

Gordon, E. *Women and the Labour Movement in Scotland, 1850–1914.* Oxford: Clarendon Press, 1991.

Gosden, P.H.J.H. *Self-Help; Voluntary Associations in the 19th Century.* London: B.T. Batsford, 1973.

Gospel, H.F. *Markets, Firms, and the Management of Labour in Modern Britain.* Cambridge: Cambridge University Press, 1992.

Gray, N., ed. *The Worst of Times: An Oral History of the Great Depression in Britain.* Totowa, NJ: Barnes & Noble, 1985.

Gray, R.Q. *The Aristocracy of Labour in Nineteenth-Century Britain, c.1850–1900*. London: Macmillan, 1981.

Gray, R.Q. *The Factory Question and Industrial England, 1830–1860*. Cambridge: Cambridge University Press, 1996.

Gray, R.Q. *The Labour Aristocracy in Victorian Edinburgh*. Oxford: Clarendon Press, 1976.

Green, S.J.D. *Religion in the Age of Decline: Organisation and Experience in Industrial Yorkshire, 1870–1920*. Cambridge: Cambridge University Press, 1996.

Gregg, R., and M. Kale. 'The Empire and Mr Thompson: making of Indian princes and English working class.' *Economic and Political Weekly* 32 (1997): 2273–88.

Griffiths, T. *The Lancashire Working Classes, c.1880–1930*. Oxford: Clarendon Press, 2001.

Gurney, P. *Cooperative Culture and the Politics of Consumption in England, 1870–1930*. Manchester: Manchester University Press, 1996.

Haines, M.R. 'Social-class differentials during fertility decline: England and Wales revisited.' *Population Studies* 43 (1989): 305–23.

Hammerton, A.J. *Cruelty and Companionship: Conflict in Nineteenth-Century Married Life*. London: Routledge, 1992.

Harling, P. 'Equipoise regained? Recent trends in British political history, 1790–1867.' *Journal of Modern History* 75 (2003): 890–918.

Harper, M. *Emigration from Scotland between the Wars: Opportunity or Exile?* Manchester: Manchester University Press, 1998.

Harrison, B.H. *Drink and the Victorians: The Temperance Question in England, 1815–1872*, 2nd ed. Keele: Keele University Press, 1994.

Harrison, M. *Crowds and History: Mass Phenomena in English Towns, 1790–1835*. Cambridge: Cambridge University Press, 1988.

Harrison, R., and J. Zeitlin, eds. *Divisions of Labour: Skilled Workers and Technological Change in Nineteenth Century England*. Urbana: University of Illinois Press, 1985.

Hartman, M.S., and L.W. Banner, eds. *Clio's Consciousness Raised: New Perspectives on the History of Women*. New York: Harper & Row, 1974.

Hatton, T.J., and R.E. Bailey. 'Natives and migrants in the London labour market, 1929–1931.' *Journal of Population Economics* 15 (2002): 59–81.

Heathorn, S. ' "Let us remember that we, too, are English": constructions of citizenship and national identity in English elementary school reading books, 1880–1914.' *Victorian Studies* 38 (1995): 395–427.

Heim, C.E. 'Structural transformation and the demand for new labour in advanced economies: interwar Britain.' *Journal of Economic History* 44 (1984): 585–95.

Hewitt, M. *The Emergence of Stability in the Industrial City: Manchester, 1832–67.* Aldershot: Scolar, 1996.

Hiley, N. ' "Let's go to the pictures": the British cinema audience in the 1920s and 1930s.' *Journal of Popular British Cinema* 2 (1999): 39–53.

Hill, J. *Sport, Leisure and Culture in Twentieth-Century Britain.* Basingstoke: Palgrave, 2002.

Hinton, J. *The First Shop Stewards' Movement.* London: George Allen & Unwin, 1973.

Hinton, J. *Labour and Socialism: A History of the British Labour Movement, 1867–1974.* Amherst: University of Massachusetts Press, 1983.

Hobsbawm, E.J. *Labouring Men: Studies in the History of Labour.* New York: Basic Books, 1964.

Hobsbawm, E.J. *Workers: Worlds of Labour.* New York: Pantheon Books, 1984.

Hobsbawm, E.J., and T.O. Ranger, eds. *The Invention of Tradition.* Cambridge: Cambridge University Press, 1983.

Hoggart, R. *The Uses of Literacy: Aspects of Working-Class Life, with Special Reference to Publications and Entertainments.* Harmondsworth: Penguin, 1957.

Holley, J.C. 'The two family economies of industrialism: factory workers in Victorian Scotland.' *Journal of Family History* 6 (1981): 57–69.

Holt, R. *Sport and the British: A Modern History.* Oxford: Clarendon Press, 1989.

Holt, R., ed. *Sport and the Working Class in Modern Britain.* Manchester: Manchester University Press, 1990.

Hopkins, E. *Working-Class Self-Help in Nineteenth Century England: Responses to Industrialization*. New York: St Martin's Press, 1995.

Hopkins, E. 'Working hours and conditions during the Industrial Revolution: a re-appraisal.' *Economic History Review* 35 (1982): 52–66.

Horn, P. *The Victorian and Edwardian Schoolchild*. Stroud: Sutton, 1989.

Horrell, S., and J. Humphries. 'The exploitation of little children: child labour and the family economy in the Industrial Revolution.' *Explorations in Economic History* 32 (1995): 485–516.

Hudson, P. *The Industrial Revolution*. London: Arnold, 1992.

Huggins, M. 'Horse-racing on Teesside in the nineteenth century – change and continuity.' *Northern History* 23 (1987): 98–118.

Humphries, S. *Hooligans or Rebels? An Oral History of Working-Class Childhood and Youth 1889–1939*. Oxford: Blackwell, 1981.

Hurt, J. *Elementary Schooling and the Working Classes, 1860–1918*. London: Routledge & Kegan Paul, 1979.

Itzkowitz, D.C. 'Victorian bookmakers and their customers.' *Victorian Studies* 32 (1988): 7–30.

Jarvis, D. 'Mrs Maggs and Betty: the Conservative appeal to women voters in the 1920s.' *Twentieth Century British History* 5 (1994): 129–52.

Jenkins, D.T. 'The cotton industry in Yorkshire, 1780–1900.' *Textile History* 10 (1979): 75–95.

Jennings, H., and C. Madge, eds. *May the Twelfth; Mass-Observation Day-Surveys 1937 by over Two Hundred Observers*. London: Faber & Faber, 1937.

John, A.V., ed. *Unequal Opportunities: Women's Employment in England 1800–1918*. Oxford: Basil Blackwell, 1986.

Johnson, J.H., and C.G. Pooley, eds. *The Structure of Nineteenth Century Cities*. London: Croom Helm, 1982.

Johnson, P. *Saving and Spending: The Working-Class Economy in Britain, 1870–1939*. Oxford: Clarendon Press, 1985.

Jones, D.J.V. *Crime, Protest, Community, and Police in Nineteenth-Century Britain*. London: Routledge & Kegan Paul, 1982.

Jones, R.M. 'Beyond identity – the reconstruction of the Welsh.' *Journal of British Studies* 31 (1992): 330–57.

Jones, S.G. *Sport, Politics and the Working Class: Organised Labour and Sport in Inter-War Britain*. Manchester: Manchester University Press, 1988.

Jones, S.G. *Workers at Play: A Social and Economic History of Leisure, 1918–1939*. London: Routledge & Kegan Paul, 1986.

Joyce, P. *Democratic Subjects: The Self and the Social in Nineteenth-Century England*. Cambridge: Cambridge University Press, 1994.

Joyce, P., ed. *The Historical Meanings of Work*. Cambridge: Cambridge University Press, 1987.

Joyce, P. *Visions of the People: Industrial England and the Question of Class, 1848–1914*. Cambridge: Cambridge University Press, 1991.

Joyce, P. *Work, Society, and Politics: The Culture of the Factory in Later Victorian England*. New Brunswick: Rutgers University Press, 1980.

Kearns, G., and C.W.J. Withers. *Urbanising Britain: Essays on Class and Community in the Nineteenth Century*. Cambridge: Cambridge University Press, 1991.

Kift, D. *The Victorian Music Hall: Culture, Class, and Conflict*, trans. R. Kift. Cambridge: Cambridge University Press, 1996.

Kirk, N. *Change, Continuity and Class: Labour in British Society, 1850–1920*. Manchester: Manchester University Press, 1998.

Kirk, N. 'The conditions of royal rule: Australian and British Socialist and Labour attitudes to the monarchy, 1901–1911.' *Social History* 30 (2005): 64–88.

Kirk, N. *The Growth of Working-Class Reformism in Mid-Victorian England*. Urbana: University of Illinois Press, 1985.

Kirk, N. 'In defence of class: a critique of recent revisionist writing upon the nineteenth-century English working class.' *International Review of Social History* 32 (1987): 1–47.

Kirk, N. *Labour and Society in Britain and the USA*, 2 vols. Aldershot: Scolar Press, 1994.

Knox, W.W. *Industrial Nation: Work, Culture and Society in Scotland, 1800–Present*. Edinburgh: Edinburgh University Press, 1999.

Koditschek, T. *Class Formation and Urban-Industrial Society: Bradford, 1750–1850*. Cambridge: Cambridge University Press, 1990.

Koditschek, T. 'The making of British nationality.' *Victorian Studies* 44 (2002): 389–98.

Lancaster, B. *Radicalism, Cooperation and Socialism: Leicester Working-Class Politics 1860–1906.* Leicester: Leicester University Press, 1987.

Langhamer, C. 'The meanings of home in postwar Britain.' *Journal of Contemporary History* 40 (2005): 341–62.

Langhamer, C. *Women's Leisure in England, 1920–60.* Manchester: Manchester University Press, 2000.

Laqueur, T.W. *Religion and Respectability: Sunday Schools and Working Class Culture, 1780–1850.* New Haven: Yale University Press, 1976.

Lavalette, M., ed. *A Thing of the Past?: Child Labour in Britain in the Nineteenth and Twentieth Centuries.* Liverpool: Liverpool University Press, 1999.

Law, C.M. 'The growth of urban population in England and Wales, 1801–1911.' *Transactions of the Institute of British Geographers* 41 (1967): 125–43.

Lawrence, J. 'Class and gender in the making of urban Toryism, 1880–1914.' *English Historical Review* 108 (1993): 629–52.

Lawrence, J. *Speaking for the People: Party, Language, and Popular Politics in England, 1867–1914.* Cambridge: Cambridge University Press, 1998.

Lawrence, J., and M. Taylor, eds. *Party, State, and Society: Electoral Behaviour in Britain since 1820.* Aldershot: Scolar, 1997.

Lawton, R. 'Mobility in nineteenth century British cities.' *Geographical Journal* 145 (1979): 206–24.

Laybourn, K. *Britain on the Breadline: A Social and Political History of Britain between the Wars.* Stroud: Sutton, 1990.

Laybourn, K. 'The rise of Labour and the decline of Liberalism: the state of the debate.' *History* 80 (1995): 207–26.

Laybourn, K., and J. Reynolds. *Liberalism and the Rise of Labour, 1890–1918.* London: Croom Helm, 1984.

Lazonick, W. 'Industrial relations and technical change: the case of the self-acting mule.' *Cambridge Journal of Economics* 3 (1979): 231–62.

Lazonick, W. 'Production relations, labour productivity, and choice of technique: British and U.S. cotton spinning.' *Journal of Economic History* 41 (1981): 491–516.

Lees, L.H. *Exiles of Erin: Irish Migrants in Victorian London*. Ithaca: Cornell University Press, 1979.

Lees, L.H. *The Solidarities of Strangers: The English Poor Laws and the People, 1700–1948*. Cambridge: Cambridge University Press, 1998.

Levine, D. *Reproducing Families: The Political Economy of English Population History*. Cambridge: Cambridge University Press, 1987.

Levine-Clark, M. *Beyond the Reproductive Body: The Politics of Women's Health and Work in Early Victorian England*. Columbus: Ohio State University Press, 2004.

Lewchuk, W. *American Technology and the British Vehicle Industry*. Cambridge: Cambridge University Press, 1987.

Lewis, J. *The Politics of Motherhood: Child and Maternal Welfare in England, 1900–1939*. London: Croom Helm, 1980.

Lilleker, D.G. 'Whose Left? Working-class political allegiances in post-industrial Britain.' *International Review of Social History* 47 (2002), 65–85.

Lindert, P.H., and J.G. Williamson. 'English workers' living standards during the Industrial Revolution: a new look.' *Economic History Review* 36:1 (1983): 1–25.

Lotz, R.E., and I. Pegg, eds. *Under the Imperial Carpet: Essays in Black History, 1780–1950*. Crawley: Rabbit Press, 1986.

Lovell, J. *British Trade Unions, 1875–1933*. London: Macmillan, 1977.

Lovell, J. 'Collective-bargaining and the emergence of national employer organization in the British shipbuilding industry.' *International Review of Social History* 36 (1991): 59–91.

Lovell, J. 'Sail, steam and emergent dockers unionism in Britain, 1850–1914.' *International Review of Social History* 32 (1987): 230–49.

Lown, J. *Women and Industrialization: Gender at Work in Nineteenth-Century England*. Minneapolis: University of Minnesota Press, 1990.

Lummis, T. *The Labour Aristocracy, 1851–1914*. Aldershot: Scolar Press, 1994.

Lunn, K., and R.C. Thurlow, eds. *British Fascism: Essays on the Radical Right in Inter-War Britain*. New York: St Martin's Press, 1980.

Lyons, J.S. 'Vertical integration in the British cotton industry, 1825–1850: a revision.' *Journal of Economic History* 45 (1985): 419–25.

MacKenzie, J.M. 'Another little patch of red.' *History Today* 55 (2005): 20–6.

MacKenzie, J.M., ed. *Imperialism and Popular Culture*. Manchester: Manchester University Press, 1986.

MacKenzie, J.M. *Propaganda and Empire: The Manipulation of British Public Opinion, 1880–1960*. Manchester: Manchester University Press, 1984.

MacRaild, D.M. *Irish Migrants in Modern Britain, 1750–1922*. New York: St Martin's Press, 1999.

MacRaild, D.M., and D.E. Martin. *Labour in British Society, 1830–1914*. New York: St Martin's Press, 2000.

Malcolmson, R.W. *Popular Recreations in English Society, 1700–1850*. Cambridge: Cambridge University Press, 1973.

Mandler, P., ed. *The Uses of Charity: The Poor on Relief in the Nineteenth-Century Metropolis*. Philadelphia: University of Pennsylvania Press, 1990.

Mangan, J.A., ed. *Making Imperial Mentalities: Socialisation and British Imperialism*. Manchester: Manchester University Press, 1990.

Mason, T. *Association Football and English Society, 1863–1915*. Brighton: Harvester Press, 1980.

Mass Observation. *The Pub and the People: A Worktown Study*. Welwyn: Seven Dials Press, 1970.

Mathias, P. *The First Industrial Nation: An Economic History of Britain, 1700–1914*, 2nd ed. London: Methuen, 1983.

Matthews, D. '1889 and all that – new views on the new unionism.' *International Review of Social History* 36 (1991): 24–58.

Mayfield, D., and S. Thorne. 'Reply to "The poverty of protest" and "The imaginary discontents".' *Social History* 18 (1993): 219–33.

Mayhew, H. *London Labour and the London Poor*. New York: Dover, 1968.

McAleer, J. *Popular Reading and Publishing in Britain, 1914–50*. Oxford: Clarendon Press, 1992.

McCann, P., ed. *Popular Education and Socialization in the Nineteenth Century*. London: Methuen, 1977.

McCarthy, K.D., ed. *Lady Bountiful Revisited: Women, Philanthropy, and Power*. New Brunswick: Rutgers University Press, 1990.

McCord, N., and D.J. Rowe. 'Industrialisation and urban growth in north-east England.' *International Review of Social History* 22 (1977): 30–64.

McIvor, A.J. *A History of Work in Britain, 1880–1950*. Basingstoke: Palgrave, 2001.

McIvor, A.J. 'Manual work, technology, and industrial health, 1918–39.' *Medical History* 31 (1987): 160–89.

McIvor, A.J. *Organised Capital: Employers' Associations and Industrial Relations in Northern England, 1880–1939*. Cambridge: Cambridge University Press, 1996.

McKenna, M. 'Municipal suburbia in Liverpool, 1919–1939.' *Town Planning Review* 60 (1989): 287–318.

McKenna, M. 'The suburbanization of the working-class population of Liverpool between the wars.' *Social History* 16 (1991): 173–89.

McKibbin, R. *Classes and Cultures: England 1918–1951*. Oxford: Oxford University Press, 1998.

McKibbin, R. *The Evolution of the Labour Party 1910–1924*. Oxford: Clarendon Press, 1974.

McKibbin, R. *The Ideologies of Class: Social Relations in Britain, 1880–1950*. Oxford: Clarendon Press, 1994.

McKinlay, A. 'From industrial serf to wage-labourer: the 1937 apprentice revolt in Britain.' *International Review of Social History* 31 (1986): 1–18.

McLeod, H. 'New perspectives on Victorian working class religion.' *Oral History* 14 (1986): 31–49.

McLeod, H. *Religion and Society in England: 1850–1914*. New York: St Martin's Press, 1996.

McWilliam, R. *Popular Politics in Nineteenth-Century England*. London: Routledge, 1998.

Meacham, S. *A Life Apart: The English Working Class, 1890–1914.* Cambridge, MA: Harvard University Press, 1977.

Melling, J. 'Non-commissioned officers: British employers and their supervisory workers, 1880–1920.' *Social History* 5 (1980): 183–221.

Merriman, J.M., ed. *Consciousness and Class Experience in Nineteenth-Century Europe.* New York: Holmes & Meier, 1979.

Messner, A. 'Land, leadership, culture, and emigration: some problems in Chartist historiography.' *Historical Journal* 42 (1999): 1093–109.

Miles, A. *Social Mobility in Nineteenth- and Early Twentieth-Century England.* New York: St Martin's Press, 1999.

Miller, S.M. 'In support of the "imperial mission"? Volunteering for the South African War, 1899–1902.' *Journal of Military History* 69 (2005): 691–711.

Mitchell, B.R. *Abstract of British Historical Statistics.* Cambridge: Cambridge University Press, 1962.

Mitchell, M. 'The effects of unemployment on the social condition of women and children in the 1930s.' *History Workshop Journal* 19 (1985): 105–27.

Mommsen, W.J., and H. Husung, eds. *The Development of Trade Unionism in Great Britain and Germany, 1880–1914.* London: George Allen & Unwin, 1985.

Morris, R.J. 'Skilled workers and the politics of the "Red" Clyde: a discussion paper.' *Journal of the Scottish Labour History Society* 18 (1983): 6–17.

Murphy, B. *A History of the British Economy, 1740–1970.* London: Longman, 1973.

Murray, W.J. *The Old Firm: Sectarianism, Sport, and Society in Scotland.* Edinburgh: John Donald, 1984.

Musson, A.E. *Trade Union and Social History.* London: Frank Cass, 1974.

Nauright, J.R., and T.J.L. Chandler, eds. *Making Men: Rugby and Masculine Identity.* London: Frank Cass, 1995.

Nicholas, K. *The Social Effects of Unemployment in Teesside.* Manchester: Manchester University Press, 1986.

O'Brien, M., and A. Eyles, eds. *Enter the Dream House: Memories of Cinemas in South London from the Twenties to the Sixties*. London: Museum of the Moving Image, 1993.

Olechnowicz, A. *Working-Class Housing in England between the Wars: The Becontree Estate*. Oxford: Clarendon Press, 1997.

Oliver, L. ' "No hard-brimmed hats or hat-pins please": Bolton women cotton-workers and the game of rounders, 1911–1939.' *Oral History* 25 (1997): 40–5.

Pagnamenta, P., and R. Overy. *All Our Working Lives*. London: BBC, 1984.

Panayi, P., ed. *Racial Violence in Britain in the Nineteenth and Twentieth Centuries*, rev. ed. London: Leicester University Press, 1996.

Parratt, C.M. *More Than Mere Amusement: Working-Class Women's Leisure in England, 1750–1914*. Boston: Northeastern University Press, 2001.

Pedersen, S. 'Gender, welfare, and citizenship in Britain during the Great War.' *American Historical Review* 95 (1990): 983–1006.

Pegg, M. *Broadcasting and Society 1918–1939*. London: Croom Helm, 1983.

Pelling, H. *A History of British Trade Unionism*. London: Macmillan, 1963.

Pember Reeves, M. *Round About a Pound a Week*. London: Virago, 1979.

Penn, R. *Skilled Workers in the Class Structure*. Cambridge: Cambridge University Press, 1984.

Perkin, H.J. 'The "social tone" of Victorian seaside resorts in the North-West.' *Northern History* 11 (1976): 180–94.

Philips, D. *Crime and Authority in Victorian England: The Black Country 1835–1860*. London: Croom Helm, 1977.

Pickering, P.A. *Chartism and the Chartists in Manchester and Salford*. Basingstoke: Macmillan, 1995.

Pickering, P.A. 'Class without words: symbolic communication in the Chartist movement.' *Past and Present* 112 (1986): 144–62.

Pilgrim Trust. *Men without Work: A Report Made to the Pilgrim Trust*. New York: Greenwood Press, 1968.

Pollard, S. *Britain's Prime and Britain's Decline: The British Economy 1870–1914*. London: Edward Arnold, 1989.

Pollard, S. *A History of Labour in Sheffield*. Liverpool: Liverpool University Press, 1959.

Pooley, C.G., and S. Irish. 'Access to housing on Merseyside, 1919–39.' *Transactions of the Institute of British Geographers* 12 (1987): 177–90.

Pooley, C.G., and J. Turnbull. *Migration and Mobility in Britain since the Eighteenth Century*. London: UCL Press, 1998.

Pooley, C.G., and I.D. Whyte, eds. *Migrants, Emigrants and Immigrants: A Social History of Migration*. London: Routledge, 1991.

Porter, B. *The Absent-Minded Imperialists: Empire, Society, and Culture in Britain*. Oxford: Oxford University Press, 2004.

Porter, J.H. 'Wage bargaining under conciliation agreements.' *Economic History Review* 23:3 (1970): 460–75.

Powell, D. 'The new Liberalism and the rise of Labour, 1886–1906.' *Historical Journal* 29 (1986): 369–93.

Price, R. *An Imperial War and the British Working Class: Working-Class Attitudes and Reactions to the Boer War 1899–1902*. London: Routledge & Kegan Paul, 1972.

Price, R. *Labour in British Society: An Interpretive History*. London: Routledge, 1986.

Price, R. *Masters, Unions and Men: Work Control in Building and the Rise of Labour, 1830–1914*. Cambridge: Cambridge University Press, 1980.

Proctor, T.M. '(Uni)Forming youth: Girl Guides and Boy Scouts in Britain, 1908–39.' *History Workshop Journal* 45 (1998): 103–34.

Pugh, M. *The Making of Modern British Politics 1867–1939*, 2nd ed. Oxford: Blackwell, 1993.

Pugh, M. 'The rise of Labour and the political culture of Conservatism, 1890–1945.' *History* 87 (2002): 514–37.

Pugh, M. *The Tories and the People 1880–1935*. Oxford: Blackwell, 1985.

Purvis, M. 'The development of cooperative retailing in England and Wales, 1851–1901: a geographical study.' *Journal of Historical Geography* 16:3 (1990): 314–31.

Quinault, R.E., and J. Stevenson. eds., *Popular Protest and Public Order. Six Studies in British History, 1790–1920*. New York: St Martin's Press, 1974.

Readman. P. 'The Conservative Party, patriotism, and British politics: the case of the general election of 1900.' *Journal of British Studies* 40 (2001): 107–45.

Reid, D.A. 'The decline of Saint Monday 1766–1876.' *Past and Present* 71 (1976): 76–101.

Reid, D.A. 'The "iron roads" and the "happiness of the working classes": the early development and social significance of the railway excursion.' *Journal of Transport History* 17 (1996): 57–73.

Reid, D.A. 'Weddings, weekdays, work and leisure in urban England 1791–1911: the decline of Saint Monday revisited.' *Past and Present* 153 (1996): 135–63.

Richards, J. *The Age of the Dream Palace: Cinema and Society in Britain, 1930–1939*. London: Routledge, 1984.

Robb, G. *British Culture and the First World War*. Basingstoke: Palgrave, 2002.

Robbins, K. *Great Britain: Identities, Institutions and the Idea of Britishness*. London: Longman, 1998.

Robbins, K. *Nineteenth-Century Britain: Integration and Diversity*. Oxford: Clarendon Press, 1988.

Roberts, E. *A Woman's Place: An Oral History of Working-Class Women, 1890–1940*. Oxford: Basil Blackwell, 1984.

Roberts, E. *Women's Work, 1840–1940*. Cambridge: Cambridge University Press, 1995.

Roberts, E. 'Working class standards of living in Barrow and Lancaster, 1890–1914.' *Economic History Review* 30 (1977): 306–21.

Roberts, R. *The Classic Slum; Salford Life in the First Quarter of the Century*. Harmondsworth: Penguin, 1973.

Rockett, D., and B. Hargreaves. *Two Streatham Childhoods*. London: Streatham Society, 1980.

Rodger, R. 'Concentration and fragmentation – capital, labour, and the structure of mid-Victorian Scottish industry.' *Journal of Urban History* 14:2 (1988): 178–213.

Rodger, R. *Housing in Urban Britain, 1780–1914*. Cambridge: Cambridge University Press, 1995.

Rodger, R. 'Political-economy, ideology and the persistence of working-class housing problems in Britain, 1850–1914.' *International Review of Social History* 32 (1987): 109–43.

Roper, M., and J. Tosh, eds. *Manful Assertions: Masculinities in Britain since 1800*. London: Routledge, 1991.

Rose, J. *The Intellectual Life of the British Working Classes*. New Haven: Yale University Press, 2001.

Rose, S. *Limited Livelihoods: Gender and Class in Nineteenth-Century England*. Berkeley: University of California Press, 1992.

Ross, E. 'Fierce questions and taunts: married life in working-class London, 1870–1914.' *Feminist Studies* 8 (1982): 575–602.

Ross, E. *Love and Toil: Motherhood in Outcast London, 1870–1918*. Oxford: Oxford University Press, 1993.

Ross, E. ' "Not the sort that would sit on the doorstep": respectability in pre-World War I London neighbourhoods.' *International Labor and Working-Class History* 27 (1985): 39–59.

Ross, E. 'Survival networks: women's neighbourhood sharing in London before World War One.' *History Workshop Journal* 15 (1983): 4–27.

Rowntree, B.S. *Poverty and Progress: A Second Social Survey of York*. London: Longmans, Green, 1941.

Rowntree, B.S. *Poverty; a Study of Town Life*. [1922]. New York: Howard Fertig, 1971.

Rowson, S. 'A statistical survey of the cinema industry in Great Britain in 1934.' *Journal of the Royal Statistical Society* 99 (1936): 67–129.

Royle, E. *Chartism*, 3rd ed. New York: Longman, 1996.

Royle, E., and J.A. Sharpe. *Modern Britain: A Social History, 1750–1997*, 2nd ed. London: Arnold, 1997.

Rubinstein, D. *School Attendance in London, 1870–1904: A Social History*. New York: A.M. Kelley, 1969.

Ruggles, S. *Prolonged Connections: The Rise of the Extended Family in Nineteenth-Century England and America*. Madison: University of Wisconsin Press, 1987.

Rule, J. 'Time, affluence and private leisure: the British working class in the 1950s and 1960s.' *Labour History Review* 66 (2001): 223–42.

Russell, D. 'Sport and identity: the case of Yorkshire County Cricket Club, 1890–1939.' *Twentieth Century British History* 7 (1996): 206–30.

Samuel, R. 'The workshop of the world: steam power and hand technology in mid-Victorian Britain.' *History Workshop Journal* 3 (1977): 6–72.

Samuel, R., E. MacColl, and S. Cosgrove, eds. *Theatres of the Left, 1880–1935: Workers' Theatre Movements in Britain and America.* London: Routledge & Kegan Paul, 1985.

Savage, M. *The Dynamics of Working-Class Politics: The Labour Movement in Preston 1880–1940.* Cambridge: Cambridge University Press, 1987.

Savage, M., and A. Miles. *The Remaking of the British Working Class, 1840–1940.* London: Routledge, 1994.

Scannell, P., and D. Cardiff. *A Social History of British Broadcasting, vol. 1: 1922–1939: Serving the Nation.* Oxford: Basil Blackwell, 1991.

Scott, J.W. 'The evidence of experience.' *Critical Inquiry* 17 (1991): 773–97.

Scott, P. 'The state, internal migration and the growth of new industrial communities in inter-war Britain.' *English Historical Review* 115 (2000): 329–53.

Seccombe, W. 'Patriarchy stabilized: the construction of the male breadwinner wage norm in nineteenth-century Britain.' *Social History* 11 (1986): 53–76.

Seccombe, W. 'Starting to stop: working-class fertility decline in Britain.' *Past and Present* (1990): 151–88.

Seccombe, W. *Weathering the Storm: Working-Class Families from the Industrial Revolution to the Fertility Decline.* London: Verso, 1995.

Sheppard, F. *London, 1808–1870: The Infernal Wen.* Berkeley: University of California Press, 1971.

Sinclair, P., C. Ryan and M. Walker. 'Continuity, change and consumption: British economic trends, 1945–1995.' *Contemporary British History* 10 (1996): 35–59.

Smith, D. *Conflict and Compromise: Class Formation in English Society, 1830–1914*. London: Routledge & Kegan Paul, 1982.

Smith, M. *Religion in Industrial Society: Oldham and Saddleworth 1740–1865*. Oxford: Clarendon Press, 1994.

Somers, M.R. 'Narrativity, narrative identity, and social action: rethinking English working-class formation.' *Social Science History* 16 (1992): 591–630.

Southgate, W. *That's the Way It Was: A Working Class Autobiography 1890–1950*. London: New Clarion Press, 1982.

Spiers, E.M. *The Late-Victorian Army 1868–1902*. Manchester: Manchester University Press, 1992.

Stedman Jones, G. *Languages of Class: Studies in English Working Class History, 1832–1982*. Cambridge: Cambridge University Press, 1983.

Stedman Jones, G. 'The mid-century crisis and the 1848 revolutions.' *Theory and Society* 12 (1983): 505–15.

Stedman Jones, G. *Outcast London: A Study in the Relationship between Classes in Victorian Society*. New York: Pantheon Books, 1984.

Steedman, C. *Landscape for a Good Woman: A Story of Two Lives*. New Brunswick: Rutgers University Press, 1987.

Steedman, C. *Policing the Victorian Community: The Formation of English Provincial Police Forces, 1856–80*. London: Routledge & Kegan Paul, 1984.

Stevenson, J. *British Society 1914–1945*. London: Allen Lane, 1984.

Stevenson, J., and C. Cook. *Britain in the Depression: Society and Politics, 1929–1939*, 2nd ed. London: Longman, 1994.

Storch, R.D. 'The plague of the blue locusts: police reform and popular resistance in northern England, 1840–1857.' *International Review of Social History* 20 (1975): 61–90.

Storch, R.D. 'The policeman as domestic missionary: urban discipline and popular culture in northern England, 1850–1880.' *Journal of Social History* 9 (1976): 481–509.

Storch, R.D., ed. *Popular Culture and Custom in Nineteenth-Century England*. London: Croom Helm, 1982.

Strange, J.M. *Death, Grief and Poverty in Britain, 1870–1914*. Cambridge: Cambridge University Press, 2005.

Swift, R. 'Urban policing in early Victorian England, 1835–86: a reappraisal.' *History* 73 (1988): 211–37.

Swift, R., and S. Gilley, eds. *The Irish in Britain: 1815–1939*. London: Pinter, 1989.

Swift, R., and S. Gilley, eds. *The Irish in Victorian Britain: The Local Dimension*. Dublin: Four Courts Press, 1999.

Swift, R., and S. Gilley, eds. *The Irish in the Victorian City*. London: Croom Helm, 1985.

Sykes, R. 'Physical-force Chartism: the cotton district and the Chartist crisis of 1839.' *International Review of Social History* 30:2 (1985): 207–36.

Tabili, L. *'We Ask for British Justice': Workers and Racial Difference in Late Imperial Britain*. Ithaca: Cornell University Press, 1994.

Tanner, D. *Political Change and the Labour Party 1900–1918*. Cambridge: Cambridge University Press, 1990.

Tanner, D., C. Williams, and D. Hopkin, eds. *The Labour Party in Wales 1900–2000*. Cardiff: University of Wales Press, 2000.

Taylor, A.J., ed. *The Standard of Living in Britain in the Industrial Revolution*. London: Methuen, 1975.

Taylor, B. *Eve and the New Jerusalem: Socialism and Feminism in the Nineteenth Century*. New York: Pantheon Books, 1983.

Taylor, D. *The New Police in Nineteenth-Century England: Crime, Conflict, and Control*. Manchester: Manchester University Press, 1997.

Taylor, M. *The Decline of British Radicalism, 1847–1860*. Oxford: Clarendon Press, 1995.

Tebbutt, M. *Women's Talk?: A Social History of Gossip in Working-Class Neighbourhoods, 1880–1960*. Aldershot: Scolar Press, 1995.

Thane, P., G. Crossick, and R. Floud, eds. *The Power of the Past: Essays for Eric Hobsbawm*. Cambridge: Cambridge University Press, 1984.

Thompson, D. *The Chartists: Popular Politics in the Industrial Revolution*. New York: Pantheon Books, 1984.

Thompson, D. *Queen Victoria: The Woman, The Monarchy, and the People*. New York: Pantheon Books, 1990.

Thompson, E.P. *The Making of the English Working Class*, 2nd ed. New York: Vintage, 1966.

Thompson, E.P. 'The Making of a Ruling Class.' *Dissent* 40 (1993): 377–82.

Thompson, E.P., and E. Yeo, eds. *The Unknown Mayhew. Selections from the Morning Chronicle, 1849–50*. New York: Schocken, 1971.

Thompson, F.M.L., ed. *The Cambridge Social History of Britain, 1750–1950*, 3 vols. Cambridge: Cambridge University Press, 1990.

Thompson, F.M.L. *The Rise of Respectable Society: A Social History of Victorian Britain 1830–1900*. Cambridge, MA: Harvard University Press, 1988.

Thompson, P. *The Edwardians*. Chicago: Academy Chicago, 1975.

Thompson, P. 'Playing at being skilled men: factory culture and pride in work skills among Coventry car workers.' *Social History* 13 (1988): 45–69.

Thompson, T., ed. *Edwardian Childhoods*. London: Routledge & Kegan Paul, 1981.

Thorne, S. *Congregational Missions and the Making of an Imperial Culture in Nineteenth-Century England*. Stanford: Stanford University Press, 1999.

Thorpe, A. *Britain in the 1930s: The Deceptive Decade*. Oxford: Blackwell, 1992.

Thurlow, R.C. *Fascism in Britain: From Oswald Mosley's Blackshirts to the National Front*, rev. ed. London: I.B. Tauris, 1998.

Tilly, C. *Stories, Identities, and Political Change*. Lanham: Rowman & Littlefield, 2002.

Tolliday, S. 'Militancy and organisation: women workers and trade unions in the motor trades in the 1930s.' *Oral History* 11 (1983): 42–55.

Tolliday, S., and J. Zeitlin, eds. *The Automobile Industry and Its Workers: Between Fordism and Flexibility*. New York: St Martin's Press, 1987.

Tolliday, S., and J. Zeitlin, eds. *The Power to Manage?: Employers and Industrial Relations in Comparative-Historical Perspective*. London: Routledge, 1991.

Tolliday, S., and J. Zeitlin, eds. *Shop Floor Bargaining and the State: Historical and Comparative Perspectives*. Cambridge: Cambridge University Press, 1985.

Tomes, N. 'A torrent of abuse: crimes of violence between working-class men and women in London 1840–1875.' *Journal of Social History* 11 (1978): 328–45.

Tranter, N. *British Population in the Twentieth Century*. New York: St Martin's Press, 1996.

Tyrrell, A. ' "God bless Her Little Majesty": the popularising of the monarchy in the 1840s.' *National Identities* 2 (2000): 109–26.

Vicinus, M. *Independent Women: Work and Community for Single Women, 1850–1920*. Chicago: University of Chicago Press, 1985.

Vincent, D. *Bread, Knowledge and Freedom: A Study of Nineteenth-Century Working Class Autobiography*. London: Europa Publications, 1981.

Vincent, D. *Poor Citizens: The State and the Poor in Twentieth-Century Britain*. London: Longman, 1991.

Waites, B. *A Class Society at War: England 1914–1918*. Leamington Spa: Berg, 1987.

Waller, P.J. *Democracy and Sectarianism: A Political and Social History of Liverpool 1868–1939*. Liverpool: Liverpool University Press, 1981.

Waller, P.J. *Town, City and Nation: England 1850–1914*. Oxford: Oxford University Press, 1983.

Walton, J.K. *The British Seaside: Holidays and Resorts in the Twentieth Century*. Manchester: Manchester University Press, 2000.

Walton, J.K. 'Co-operation in Lancashire 1844–1914.' *North-West Labour History* 19 (1994–5): 115–25.

Walton, J.K. 'The demand for working-class seaside holidays in Victorian England.' *Economic History Review* 34 (1981): 249–65.

Walton, J.K. 'The world's first working-class seaside resort? Blackpool revisited, 1840–1974.' *Transactions of the Lancashire and Cheshire Antiquarian Society* 88 (1992): 1–30.

Walton, J.K., and J. Walvin, eds. *Leisure in Britain 1780–1939*. Manchester: Manchester University Press, 1983.

Walvin, J. *Leisure and Society, 1830–1950*. London: Longman, 1978.

Ward, C., and D. Hardy. *Goodnight Campers!: The History of the British Holiday Camp*. London: Mansell, 1986.

Ward, J.T. *Popular Movements, c.1830–1850*. London: Macmillan, 1970.

Waters, C. *British Socialists and the Politics of Popular Culture, 1884–1914*. Manchester: Manchester University Press, 1990.

Webster, C. 'Health, welfare and unemployment during the Depression.' *Past and Present* (1985): 204–30.

Webster, C. 'Healthy or hungry thirties?' *History Workshop Journal* 13 (1982): 110–29.

Whipp, R. *Patterns of Labour: Work and Social Change in the Pottery Industry*. London: Routledge, 1990.

White, J. 'Police and people in London in the 1930s.' *Oral History* 11 (1983).

White, J. *The Worst Street in North London: Campbell Bunk, Islington, between the Wars*. London: Routledge & Kegan Paul, 1986.

Whiteside, N., and J. Gillespie. 'Deconstructing unemployment – developments in Britain in the interwar years.' *Economic History Review* 44 (1991): 665–82.

Whitston, K. 'The reception of scientific management by British engineers, 1890–1914.' *Business History Review* 71 (1997): 207–29.

Whitston, K. 'Scientific management and production management practice in Britain between the wars.' *Historical Studies in Industrial Relations* 1 (1996): 47–75.

Whitston, K. 'Worker resistance and Taylorism in Britain.' *International Review of Social History* 42 (1997): 1–24.

Williams, A. *Life in a Railway Factory*. New York: Garland, 1980.

Williams, C. *Democratic Rhondda: Politics and Society, 1885–1951*. Cardiff: University of Wales Press, 1996.

Williams, J. ' "A wild orgy of speed": responses to speedway in Britain before the Second World War.' *The Sports Historian* 19 (1999): 1–15.

Williamson, J.G. *Coping with City Growth during the British Industrial Revolution*. Cambridge: Cambridge University Press, 1990.

Williamson, J.G. 'Debating the British Industrial Revolution.' *Explorations in Economic History* 24 (1987): 269–92.

Williamson, J.G. 'Was the Industrial Revolution worth it? Disamenities and death in 19th century British towns.' *Explorations in Economic History* 19 (1982): 221–45.

Winter, J.M. 'Britain's "lost generation" of the First World War.' *Population Studies* 31 (1977): 449–66.

Winter, J.M. *The Great War and the British People*. Cambridge, MA: Harvard University Press, 1986.

Winter, J.M. 'The impact of the First World War on civilian health in Britain.' *Economic History Review* 30 (1977): 487–507.

Wohl, A.S. *Endangered Lives: Public Health in Victorian Britain*. London: J.M. Dent, 1983.

Wohl, A.S., ed. *The Victorian Family: Structure and Stresses*. New York: St Martin's Press, 1978.

Wright, D.G. *Popular Radicalism: The Working Class Experience, 1780–1880*. London: Longman, 1988.

Wright, T. 'Bill Banks's day out.' *The Savage Club Papers* 2 (1868): 214–30.

Wrigley, C., ed. *A Companion to Early Twentieth-Century Britain*. Oxford: Blackwell, 2003.

Wrigley, C., ed. *A History of British Industrial Relations 1875–1914*. Amherst: University of Massachusetts Press, 1982.

Wrigley, C., ed. *A History of British Industrial Relations, vol. II: 1914–1939*. Brighton: Harvester Press, 1987.

Wrigley, E.A., and R.S. Schofield. *The Population History of England 1541–1871*. London: Edward Arnold, 1981.

Yeo, E., and S. Yeo, eds. *Popular Culture and Class Conflict 1590–1914*. Brighton: Harvester Press, 1981.

Yonwin, J. *UK Election Statistics: 1918–2004*. London: House of Commons Library, 2004.

Zeitlin, J. 'From labour history to the history of industrial-relations.' *Economic History Review* 40 (1987): 159–84.

Index

abortion, 101, 175
anti-slavery movement, 73
apprenticeships, 35, 37, 39, 114, 115, 197, 198
assembly-line processes, 195, 196–7
authority, patterns of, 38–9

back-to-back housing, 18, 19, 97
birth control, 100–1, 175–6
blood sports, banning of, 52
Boer War, 151
books, 211
boxing, 215
Boy Scouts, 136, 219, 220
Boys' Brigade, 135
brawling, 52
British Union of Fascists (BUF), 236
Brooklands Agreement (1893), 118

Caroline, Queen, 11
Catholics
    anti-Catholicism, 71–2
    emancipation of, 10
    intermarriage, 149, 232
    see also Irish population
celebrations, 210, 228–9
change, pace of, 9, 10
Chartism, 59, 72, 74, 81
    aims of, 245
    insurrections, 76
    People's Charter, 75
    radicalism, 75
    strikes, 75–6
    suppression of, 77–8
    tactics of, 76
    as working-class movement, 76–7

child labour, 23, 30, 35–6, 101, 103, 114–15
cholera epidemics, 20
church attendance, 69–70, 136–8
cinema, 209, 212–14, 229
circuses, 55
class identity, 2–3, 68
    contemporary, 249
    us and them, 245
    working-class, 152, 227
    workplace, 232–3
Clyde conflict, 43
co-operative societies
    conviviality of, 60, 69
    growth of, 218–19
    rational improvement, 60–1
    repression and reform, 59–60
collective bargaining
    agreements, 118–19
    employer acceptance of, 117–18
    state support for, 198–9
    see also unions
commuters, 96
competitions, 52, 54–5, 59
Complete Suffrage Union, 76
conscription, 167–8
Conservatives
    union support for, 155
    working-class support for, 79, 93, 154–5, 234–5
cotton manufacture, 10
council houses
    amenities, 179–80
    high rents, 180, 181
    migration, 178
    post-First World War, 170
    provision of, 178–9

council houses (*continued*)
    sale of, 247
    sanitation, 97
    tenant cohorts, 180–1
    see also housing
courtship patterns, 22

dance halls, 135, 207, 209, 214
dilution system, 168–9, 199, 200
dock workers strike, 117
drinking, 51, 52, 58–9, 60, 61, 69
    see also pubs

economy
    context, changes in, 244
    expansion of, 31
    slowed growth from 1873, 92
education
    access to, 233
    compulsory, 101, 114–15, 157, 158,
        174
    self-education, 53
electoral system, 10, 68, 91
empire, 150–1, 155
    celebration of, 228–9
    racial difference, 73
employer workplace initiatives
    assembly-line processes, 195,
        196–7
    big companies, increase in, 111,
        194–5
    job segregation by sex, 197–8
    productivity, maximization of,
        112–13, 195
    rationalization, 194, 195
    restrictive practices, 196
    scientific management, 196
    semi-skilled workers, predominance
        of, 197–8
    skilled workers, undermining of, 113,
        197
    supervision, 110, 112
    wage cuts, 195
    women, as cheap labour, 197–8
    worker resistance, 115–16, 194
    youths, as cheap labour, 198
    see also machine technology
employment, full, 248
    see also unemployment

enfranchisement
    of women, 234
    of workers, 93, 153
ethnic differences, 148–9
    see also racism
evangelicalism, 57, 59
excursions, 55–6, 134, 217–18
exports, 92

Factory Act (1844), 78
fairs, 54, 55
families, 183
    budgeting, 103
    as central institution, 243–4
    children's contribution, 23, 101, 103,
        115
    elderly, support for, 23
    emotional and economic bonds,
        22–3
    extended family groups, 21–2
    family size, 100–1
    fertility control, 100–1
    gender roles, 101–2, 103–4
    inequality, 21, 23–4
    lodgers and kin, 22
    marital relationships, 22
    see also neighbourhood communities
fascism, 236
fertility
    control, 100–1
    decline in, 170, 173–4
festivals, calendar of, 51–2
First World War, 4
    conscription, 167–8
    dilution system, 168–9, 199, 200
    economy, 192
    living standards, 168
    patriotism, 167, 169, 170, 227, 229
    worker scepticism, 169–70
    working class, 243
football, 52, 92–3, 127, 133–4, 214–15
friendly societies
    conviviality of, 60–1, 69
    repression and reform, 59–60
    self-help, 138

gambling, 54–5, 59, 62, 92–3, 135–9,
    216–17, 221
games, 210

gender divisions
    church attendance, 69–70, 137–8
    job segregation by sex, 34, 36–8, 70,
        113–14, 152, 197–8
    leisure activities, 152
    marital responsibilities, 151
    neighbourhoods and homes, 151
    respectability, 70–1
    see also women
general strike 1926, 199, 200
George IV, King, 11
George V, King, 210, 228
George VI, King, 210, 228, 229
Girl Guides, 219, 220
great depression, 110–11
Great Exhibition (1851), 73
'great Whig betrayal', 73–74
greyhound racing, 215

health
    class and regional disparities, 183
    improved, 174–5
    infant mortality, 182
    inter-war improvement, 182
    life expectancy, increased, 182
    maternal mortality, 182
    nutritional gains, 182, 183
hobbies, 210–11
holidays, 55, 92–3, 134–5, 208, 217–18
Hornby v. Close 1866, 40
horse racing, 54–5, 59
housing
    around courts, 17, 18, 19
    back-to-backs, 18, 19, 97
    by-law housing, 97
    cellar dwellings, 18
    death rates, elevated, 20–1, 23
    development of, 17
    improved, from late 1870s, 97
    lodging houses, 17–18
    model dwellings, 97
    overcrowding, 19, 99–100
    poor conditions, 95, 181–2
    prefabs, 247
    regulation, lack of, 20–1
    rent controls, 181
    residential segregation, 100
    shared facilities, 17, 19
    shortage, 178–9

    tenements, 17, 18
    terraced houses, 18
    unregulated growth, 19–20
    see also council houses; sanitation

industrialization, 4, 10
intermarriage, 149, 232
Irish Home Rule, 155
Irish population
    anti-Irish sentiment, 71–2, 148, 155
    Irish migration, 14, 15–16

Jewish population, 148, 155, 231

labour, division of
    craftworkers, undermining of, 35
    job segregation by sex, 34, 36–8, 70,
        113–14, 152, 197–8
Labour Party
    First World War, 234
    franchise extension, 234
    politics of class, 249
    regional differences, 233–4
    working class support for, 155–6
Labour Representation Committee, 153,
    154
leaving certificate scheme, 168
leisure
    and class, 61–2
    commercialized, 51, 55–6, 92–3, 127,
        132–5, 139, 170, 212–18
    domestic, 131, 210–11, 248–9
    free, 209–10
    increased access to, 244–5
    informal, 129–31, 209–12
    money for, 56, 208–9
    philanthropic, and self-help, 135–9
    popular, 51–2, 219–20
    rational improvement, 57, 60–1, 135
    reduced working hours, 127–8
    repression and reform, 57–61
    socialist opposition, 138–9
    sponsorship of, 52, 219–20
    and women, 56, 128, 129, 208
Liberals
    cross-class alliances, 78
    union alliances, 42
    worker crackdowns, 154
    working-class support for, 93, 153

libraries, 58, 59
local identities, 73

machine technology
    assembly-line processes, 195, 196–7
    effects of, 30–1, 34–5, 110, 111, 112
    slow introduction of, 33–4
*Making of the English Working Class,
    The* (Thompson), 1, 4
manual labour
    enjoyment of, 202–3
    value of, 247–8
    working-class identity, 43–4
men, as primary breadwinners, 37–8,
    70–1
Methodists, 69
migration
    council estates, 178
    economic decline, 176
    expanding industries, 176–7
    housing shortages, 178
    impoverishment, 14
    of Irish, 14, 15–16
    migrant communities, 15–16, 177–8
    opportunity, call of, 14–15
    population growth, 178
    'push' and 'pull' factors, 14–15
    of Scottish, 177
    to towns, 13–14
    work shortages, 178
    of young people, 14
miners strikes, 117, 200
Mines Act (1842), 78
monarchy, 72–3, 150–1, 155, 227, 228–9
'monkey run', 207, 209, 220
motor industry, 176–7, 192, 196–7
Munitions Act (1915), 168
music halls, 53–4, 55, 56, 61, 92, 132–3,
    136, 229
mutualism, 218–19

narrative, and identities, 2–3
National Insurance Act (1911), 184
National Unemployed Workers'
    Movement (NUWM), 235–6
nationalism, 228
neighbourhood communities
    amenities, 96–7
    attachments, 97
    class divisions, 146

conflicts, 185–6
gender divisions, 151
hierarchies, 105, 156, 236
identity, 227, 230
male culture, violence of, 156–7
matriarchs, 156
midwives, 104
mutual aid, 104–5, 130
respectability, 147
sickness, 104
slum clearances, 173, 185
street activities, 129–30, 139
street fights, 131
support, 23, 104–5, 185
New Poor Law, 4
'new' social history, viii
Newport rising (1839), 72
nine hours movement, 127
nutrition, 182, 183

orphans, 23
outdoor relief, 74
Owenites, 59

Paisley, 23
party politics, 153–6
patriotism, 10–11, 150–1, 227, 229
pawnshops, 184
People's Charter, 75
    see also Chartism
police *see* street order, enforcement of
Poor Law (1834), 73–4, 80–1
population
    expansion, 9, 19, 31
    fertility, declining, 173–5
post-Second World War
Potteries, 15, 23, 34
power-looms, 4, 14, 30, 33–4
Preston lockout, 41, 72
processions, 210
Protestants, 72, 155
    intermarriage, 149, 232
    and Tories, 79
Public Health Act (1848), 21
pubs
    activities, 132
    self-education, 53
    singing saloons, 53
    women in, 56, 147, 217
    see also drinking

racism
    anti-Irish sentiment, 71–2, 148, 155
    anti-Jewish sentiment, 148, 155, 231
radicalism, 78–9
radio, 211–12, 228–9
rail excursions, 55–6, 134
railway construction, 99, 110
railway strike, 119
raucousness, 52
reading, 211
Reform Acts, 10, 68, 91
reform campaigns
    evangelicalism, 57, 59
    friendly societies, 59–60
    middle-class, 57, 59
    rational improvement, 57, 60–1, 135
    reform, limits of, 60–1
    self-improvement, 59
    street order, 57–8
    temperance, 57, 58, 59
    workers' opposition to, 58–9
    working-class, 57–8
regional identities, 149–50, 230–1
religion
    bribery, 158
    divisions, 231
    see also Catholics; church attendance;
        Protestants
respectability
    church/chapel, 69–70
    drinking, 147
    family reputations, 147
    gender roles, 70–1
    neighbourhood reputations, 147
    roughness, 68–9
    social hierarchy, 147–8
rowdiness, 61
Royal Commission on the Poor Laws
    (1909), 113

Saint Monday, 31–2, 51
Sanitary Act (1866), 21
sanitation
    housing conditions, 19, 20, 98–9
    lodging houses, 17–18
    water closets, 98
school see education
seaside holidays, 55, 134–5
Second World War, 4
sectarian conflicts, 3, 148–9, 231

self-acting mule, 34, 35
shipbuilding industry, 33, 35
slum clearances, 173, 185
social history
    class identities, 1, 2–3, 4
    cultural turn, 2, 4
    feminist theory, 2
    gender ideologies, 3
    histories of class formation, rarity of,
        4
    language and culture, focus on, 2
    linguistic theory, 2
    politics of everyday life, 3
    sectarian differences, 3
    social conditions, 1–2
    working-class politics, 3
social mobility, lack of, 233
social reform, and class, 78–9
    see also reform campaigns
speech, and class differences, 231
spending money, 56, 207, 208–9
sporting culture
    class boundaries, 216–17
    clubs and competitions, 215–17
    professional sport, 133–4
state
    ambivalence towards, 237
    health, 157
    interference from, 157–8, 230
    resistance to, 158–9
    and unions, 120–1
street activities, 52, 56–7, 129, 209
street order, enforcement of, 57–8, 80,
        81, 131, 157, 158, 220–1, 237
strikes
    anti-strike legislation, 201
    Chartism, 75–6
    dock workers, 117
    against employment of women, 37
    in factory age, 42–3
    general, 199, 200
    government attitudes, 120–1
    illegality of, 40
    intensification of, 116–17, 119–20
    miners, 117, 200
    post-First World War, 199–200
    railway, 119
    unofficial, 42–3, 200–1
    wage disagreements, 41
    workplace changes, 116

Sunday schools, 59, 69, 70
supervision, workplace, 110, 112
sweated system, 34, 38

Taylorism, 112
technology, new *see* machine technology
television, 248–9
temperance societies, 57, 58, 59, 60–1,
    135
Ten Hours Act (1847), 73, 78
textile factories, 33
Tolpuddle Martyrs, 74
Tories *see* Conservatives
Trade Disputes and Trade Unions Act
    (1927), 201
Trade Union Act (1871), 40

unemployment
    1929 slump, 192–3
    disparities, 193
    First World War, 192
    inter-war, 192–3
    long-term, 193–4
    new industries, growth of, 191, 192
    poverty, 184
    short-time working, 193
    wage cuts, 195
    women's employment, expansion of,
        192
unemployment relief, 184, 237
uniformed youth movements, 135, 136,
    219, 220
unions
    elitism, 41
    employer attitudes to, 40, 199
    employer organizations, 118–19
    legal restrictions, 40
    Liberal alliance with, 42
    manual work, enjoyment of, 202–3
    membership, 39–40, 116, 117,
        198–9
    middle-class hostility to, 40
    militancy, 119–20

organization of, 41–2
small-scale conflicts, 201
and state, 120–1
wage disagreements, 41
working conditions, 201–2
see also collective bargaining; strikes
urbanization
    late-Victorian period, 91–2
    residential patterns, shifts in, 16–17
    urban working class, formation of,
        13–24

values, working-class, 60–1
Victoria, Queen, 72, 150
Volunteer Force, 151

wages
    improvements in, 24
    and poverty, 183–4
wakes, 52, 54, 55
white-collar workers, 248
William IV, King, 72
women
    church attendance, 137
    denial and malnutrition, 184
    domestic responsibilities, 38, 70–1,
        128, 129, 184, 208
    in pubs, 217
    union membership, 120
    in workforce, 23, 34, 36–8, 37, 70,
        113–14, 116, 152, 197–8
    see also gender divisions
workhouses, 74–5
working conditions
    dangerous and unpleasant, 201–2
    improvement in, 92
    late Victorian period, 121–2
working hours
    48 hour week, 208
    excessively long days, 31
    and leisure, 127–8
    Saint Monday, 31–2
working men's clubs, 138, 218